Demographic Change in Southeast Asia

 Cornell University

Lindy Williams and Michael Philip Guest, editors

Demographic Change in Southeast Asia

Recent Histories and Future Directions

SOUTHEAST ASIA PROGRAM PUBLICATIONS
Southeast Asia Program
Cornell University
Ithaca, New York
2012

Cornell Southeast Asia Program Publications
640 Stewart Avenue, Ithaca, NY 14850-3857

Studies on Southeast Asia No. 57

Printed in the United States of America

ISBN: hc 978-0-87727-787-3
ISBN: pb 978-0-87727-757-6

Cover: designed by Mo Viele
Cover image: Photograph by Edmund Oh, reprinted with permission.

TABLE OF CONTENTS

ACKNOWLEDGEMENTS

The editors are extremely grateful to all those who have contributed to this volume. This has been a lengthy process, and the authors have been extremely patient and responsive throughout. Several anonymous reviewers provided excellent detailed advice that has strengthened the chapters considerably. We would also like to thank a number of people from Cornell's Southeast Asia Program (SEAP), without whom this volume would not have been possible. The book was the brainchild of Benedict Anderson, who first suggested SEAP take on a project of this kind. Without his initiation, we probably would not have begun the endeavor. Graduate students, Amanda Flaim and Edmund Oh, and author, Charles Hirschman, brainstormed in early stages and contributed substantially to the direction of the book. Deborah Homsher, the managing editor of SEAP Publications, has been supportive throughout the process and has guided us from start to finish. Paula Douglass and Fred Conner did a fantastic job of taking all of our prose, correcting it where needed, and polishing it for publication. Deborah and Fred have been abundantly patient with all of us as the chapters have undergone numerous iterations. Our sincere thanks also go to Daniel Ahlquist, Amanda Flaim, Tim Gorman, and Edmund Oh, who reviewed the penultimate draft of the book and caught a number of important editorial and substantive errors. Finally, we are grateful to Edmund Oh for sharing the photograph that has been selected for the cover of the book, and to Mo Viele for her work on the design of that cover. Thank you, one and all.

Lindy Williams
Michael Philip Guest

PREFACE

Lindy Williams and Michael Philip Guest

Eleven countries comprise modern Southeast Asia.[1] They have rich and diverse histories, and the pages that follow describe an important piece of those histories: the patterns of growth, changing compositions and distributions, and mobility among the human populations within the region. Southeast Asia has grown from a sparsely settled peripheral territory to a very densely settled one that now includes a number of powerful players in the global economy. At the time of this writing, ten of the eleven countries in the region are full members of the Association of Southeast Asian Nations (ASEAN), which is a significant political and economic alliance. Although population processes are often ignored or downplayed by social scientists interested in the engines of economic development and globalization, the chapters in this volume address a number of topics that are critical to the future social and economic well-being of people within the region.

This book is designed to provide an overview of the extensive regional demographic changes that have taken place in recent years. We focus on the last sixty years or so, in part because the quality of demographic data has been extremely uneven in Southeast Asia as a whole and reliable data have become available only comparatively recently. In addition, shifts in population size, density, and structure occurred comparatively slowly until the twentieth century but, then, changed dramatically, particularly from the 1950s onward. Largely for these reasons, most chapter authors begin their analyses in the years following World War II. The historical overview provided by Hirschman and Bonaparte is one exception, in that it places more recent trends in a broader temporal context. These authors trace settlement patterns and population dynamics back to the late nineteenth century, outlining some of the primary differences between island and mainland Southeast Asia, and identifying many of the cultural, political, geographical, and economic determinants, consequences, and correlates of population change.

Data collection has tended to be conducted by state entities that focus on populations within their national boundaries, and particularly on people who live in

---

[1] In order of current population size, from largest to smallest, the countries are Indonesia, the Philippines, Vietnam, Thailand, Myanmar, Malaysia, Cambodia, Lao People's Democratic Republic, Singapore, Timor-Leste, and Brunei Darussalam.

the most accessible regions. Members of highland communities and populations that shift across borders are, therefore, often underrepresented in or excluded from the data social scientists are able to analyze. The chapters in this volume are no exception. As Hugo indicates in his chapter on changing patterns of mobility among human populations, the tremendous increase in the scale of both internal and international migration that has occurred in recent decades has not been matched by improvements in the quality of the data that would be needed to thoroughly capture these processes and fully comprehend them. Increases in undocumented voluntary migration, seasonal patterns of mobility, and the movement of trafficked peoples all present particular problems for researchers hoping to understand the reasons people undertake migration in the first place and, then, stay where they are, continue on, or return home.

James Scott has argued that hill societies have long evaded state efforts at incorporation, and to a large extent they have also avoided (or been left out of) efforts by the state to gather accurate data about the people living within its borders.[2] Indeed, many of these societies remain invisible in part because of "their deliberate out-of-the-way locations, their mixed portfolio of linguistic and cultural identities, the variety of subsistence routines at their disposal, their capacity to fission and disperse like the 'jellyfish' tribes of the Middle East, and their capacity, thanks in part to valley cosmologies, to form new resistant identities at the drop of a hat."[3] The chapters in this volume do not render visible the demographic experiences of those who have evaded or been skipped over by censuses, large-scale surveys, and small-scale collection efforts.

Despite this unavoidable limitation, the chapters' authors make several important contributions to our understanding of the dramatic demographic changes that have been taking place in much of Southeast Asia. Of striking significance, for example, has been enhanced control over infectious diseases and its role in reducing mortality and increasing life expectancy. Advances in health and longevity have occurred throughout the region and have been consequential, not only for the individuals and families most immediately affected, but for nation-states as well. Clearly, these advances were tremendously welcome as a public health achievement. Until there was a commensurate decline in birth rates, however, this meant considerable population growth in the region. Indeed, Hirschman and Bonaparte note that Southeast Asia's population more than tripled, increasing from 176 million to 590 million between 1950 and 2010. This was cause for concern in some circles and alarm in a number of others. A host of policy initiatives aimed at fertility reduction were implemented with varying degrees of success. These included service provision, on the one hand, and policies aimed at attitudinal change, on the other. Government strategies to reduce fertility have varied in terms of government commitment, innovation, and level of forced compliance. Regionally, however, fertility eventually began to fall, at times dramatically, and by 2010, in several countries, it was below the level needed to replace the current population. As a consequence, some state governments have devised public policy initiatives to attempt to raise fertility at least to reach what is known as the replacement level.

---

[2] James C. Scott, *The Art of Not Being Governed: An Anarchist History of Upland Southeast Asia* (New Haven, CT: Yale University Press, 2009).
[3] Ibid., p. 327.

Also consequential, but perhaps less obviously so, are changing marriage patterns, including a rise in late marriage and an increase in the percentage of people who opt out of legal marriage entirely. These shifts have already played a major role in reducing fertility and may continue to do so. Growing tolerance for alternatives to marriage is of potential importance in many quarters in the region. Depending upon what form these alternatives eventually take, their adoption might have ongoing negative effects on fertility and may exert other influences on families and society as a whole. The chapters by Terence Hull on fertility, and Gavin Jones and Bina Gubhaju on marriage trends, provide detailed historical analyses of both topics. The information they offer also sets the stage for the chapter by Ghazy Mujahid on population aging.

For example, local norms about social support for older adults may have to be revised as a result of falling marriage and birth rates. At present, with fewer children born to parents who will live longer than did those in previous generations, population aging (i.e., increasing percentages of elderly people in national populations) is becoming a serious matter in a number of Southeast Asian countries. Among the many challenges arising from this process is concern over meeting the physical and emotional needs of seniors. In contexts in which care and support for the elderly have historically fallen to the family, the fact that parents are having fewer children warrants attention. Compounding the problem are both the very high toll taken by HIV/AIDS in parts of Southeast Asia and the heightened geographic mobility of people throughout the region. With respect to mobility, while the total number of potential caregivers may be shrinking in relation to the pool of surviving seniors, these potential caregivers are also increasingly living at a considerable distance from their parents. The separation may actually result in more than adequate financial support, for example, through remittance income, yet questions linger about the provision of other types of day-to-day assistance and emotional support.

More generally, the recent massive increases in human mobility in Southeast Asia, combined with the growing diversity of most migration streams, are having far-reaching impacts on those who move, the communities from which they originate, and the communities that receive them. Labor migration is vitally important as a means to secure livelihoods, and the mobility chapter in this volume, by Graeme Hugo, highlights recent patterns and trends, including the feminization of this form of migration. While much labor migration is often initially intended to be temporary, migrants may decide to make their moves permanent. In addition, increasingly, receiving states, often with aging populations, are promoting longer-term or permanent settlement. The advantages and disadvantages of encouraging "designer migrants" (i.e., those with specific skill sets or sought-after qualifications) to move are of potential interest to both sending and receiving nations.

All forms of migration, but especially migration that takes place over long distances or across international boundaries, can have important health consequences for those who move. The chapter on migration and health, by Mark J. VanLandingham and Hongyun Fu, considers the combination of structural factors and individual predispositions that may encourage migration in the first place and influence health outcomes in the second. These outcomes vary widely. For example, international migration may create emotional stress due to long-term separation from loved ones and due to substantial linguistic and cultural barriers. It may also result in an improved diet, access to quality health care, and life in a less-spoiled environment. Depending on whether social networks are present or absent in destination communities, the impacts of relocation may be mediated or intensified.

Internal migration, much of it rural to urban, has combined with international migration flows to large cities to contribute to the region's urbanization and to create what are now termed megacities. That so many of the large urban areas are located along the coast makes them potentially vulnerable to future disruption due to climate change. The chapter on population and environment, by Sara R. Curran and Noah Derman, considers the ways in which Southeast Asian environmental conditions initially facilitated population settlement and growth, and have subsequently been affected by population growth and changing economic conditions. Rich natural endowments combined with easily accessible ports and waterways encouraged early settlement as well as migration and trade. With the escalation of nation-building projects, both resources and people came under tightening government control. The authors contend that while agricultural intensification and expansion increased the region's carrying capacity, allowing for rapid population growth, this also set the stage for widespread environmental degradation. Overconsumption of resources in combination with poor land-use practices have contributed to pollution of the air, water, and soil, as well as to deforestation, soil erosion, over-fishing, and coastal-ecosystem collapses.

Migration plays a role in these processes that will require further research. In some cases, people enter fragile ecosystems because of population pressure in their places of origin. In other cases, deteriorating conditions in those at-risk areas may prompt out-migration, or at least factor into decisions to move elsewhere. Does the movement of people away from fragile ecosystems relieve stress on those areas, or might out-migrants' remittances actually contribute to heightened exploitation of the resources that remain? The authors contend that the environmental problems outlined in their chapter are compounded by patterns of economic growth, local and global market pressures, and the power of governments to exploit resources for socioeconomic development; further, they argue that increasing population density in cities has been occurring without adequate institutional capacity to contain the negative externalities associated with population growth and concentration. These will no doubt continue to be important local and regional concerns as we look to the future.

The topics considered by the chapters in this volume are clearly difficult to consider in isolation from one another. The demographic processes that provide the focus for each chapter are intimately interrelated. As a consequence, there is some overlapping content across chapters. We believe that this is largely unavoidable, and is not a liability. Indeed, the decision to allow for some overlapping content will enable a reader to peruse any individual chapter in any sequence. Each chapter is meant to be internally coherent. Together the chapters are designed to provide a comprehensive picture of the recent demographic history of the region of Southeast Asia and to offer some sense of what is likely to occur in the near future.

CHAPTER 1

POPULATION AND SOCIETY IN SOUTHEAST ASIA: A HISTORICAL PERSPECTIVE

Charles Hirschman and Sabrina Bonaparte

One of the characteristics of Southeast Asia before 1750, in contrast to adjacent India and China, was low population density. Most of the region was still covered by jungle as late as 1800, so that attacks by tigers were not uncommon even on the outskirts of substantial population centers.[1]

Prior to the twentieth century, there were a number of medium-size cities in Southeast Asia as well as some densely settled rice-growing regions, but much of Southeast Asia remained a sparsely settled region relative to East and South Asia.[2] The low population density of Southeast Asia reflected the character of a peripheral region with relatively weak states and large frontiers inhabited by populations of shifting cultivators. In 1900, the population of Southeast Asia was only about 80 million and almost one-third of this number was concentrated in Java alone.[3]

Southeast Asia is no longer at the periphery—demographically, economically, or politically. Characterized by sprawling megacities and a densely settled countryside, it is hard to imagine that tigers were once a major threat to those who lived on the outskirts of large Southeast Asian cities. With wild animals banished to zoos, and even the once ubiquitous trishaws and bicycles almost gone, the major features of Southeast Asia cities are shopping malls, congested roadways, and pervasive smog arising from urban industries and motorized transport. The subsistence economies of the Southeast Asian past have grown into dynamic economic engines producing

---

[1] Anthony Reid, "Economic and Social Change, c. 1400–1800," in *The Cambridge History of Southeast Asia, Volume Two: The Nineteenth and Twentieth Centuries*, ed. Nicholas Tarling (Cambridge: Cambridge University Press, 1992), pp. 460–461.

[2] Wilbur Zelinsky, "The Indochinese Peninsula: A Demographic Anomaly," *Far Eastern Quarterly* 9 (1950): 115–45.

[3] Colin McEvedy and Richard Jones, *Atlas of World Population History* (New York, NY: Penguin Books, 1978), pp. 190–203.

electronic goods, clothing and footwear, and household appliances for world markets. The economic, political, and strategic centrality of contemporary Southeast Asia is evident in the annual meetings of ASEAN (Association of Southeast Asian Nations, the influential, quasi-political association of the region), which draw representatives from all the major industrial blocs in the world.

These economic and political changes in Southeast Asia have been accompanied by extraordinary rates of population growth, especially during the second half of the twentieth century. At the end of the colonial era, circa 1950, the population of Southeast Asia was only one-third as large as that of Europe—the home of the primary colonial powers that ruled almost all of Southeast Asia for the first half of the twentieth century. Over the course of the last century, there was a dramatic reversal in the demographic balance between Southeast Asia and Europe. At the dawn of the twenty-first century, the population of Indonesia exceeded that of Russia—the largest European country—by almost 100 million. There are currently more Vietnamese and Filipinos than Germans. Thailand—a medium-size Southeast Asian country—has a larger population than either Italy or the United Kingdom. Even tiny Laos, with a population of 6 million in 2010, is home to more people than are many European countries, including Ireland, Finland, Denmark, and Norway. The combined population of the Southeast Asian countries of Brunei, Cambodia, Indonesia, Laos, Malaysia, Myanmar (Burma), Philippines, Singapore, Thailand, Timor-Leste and Vietnam was near 600 million at the end of the first decade of the twenty-first century. Southeast Asia is projected to be the home of more than 760 million by the middle of the century.[4]

The role of population in the development of Southeast Asia is generally neglected in both historical and contemporary studies. For example, the celebrated two-volume *Cambridge History of Southeast Asia*,[5] with the exception of essays by Anthony Reid and Norman Owen, largely ignores the role of population in Southeast Asian history. Yet, changes in population size, distribution, and structure are closely intertwined with the economic, social, and political transformations of the last one hundred years. In this chapter, we present a historical overview of contemporary demographic changes in Southeast Asia with primary attention to twentieth-century patterns of population growth, including factors driving fertility and mortality.

THE GEOGRAPHICAL CONTEXT

There is enormous diversity in all dimensions of Southeast Asian life. The demographic and geographic enormity of Indonesia stands in sharp relief to the tiny microstates of Brunei and Timor-Leste. Over the course of history, variations in topography have created ecological niches within Southeast Asia that have given rise to an incredible diversity of cultures. Rivers and calm seas led to the settlement of fishing villages and coastal trading centers. Lowland areas with natural irrigation or possibilities for flooded fields allowed for wet rice cultivation and the emergence of

---

[4] United Nations (Population Division of the Department of Economic and Social Affairs of the United Nations Secretariat), *World Population Prospects: The 2010 Revision* (New York, NY: United Nations, 2011), http://esa.un.org/unpd/wpp/Excel-Data/population.htm, accessed January 10, 2012.

[5] Tarling, ed., *The Cambridge History of Southeast Asia, Volume Two*.

peasant societies and despotic ruling classes. The uplands, which were more difficult for states to control and exploit, were generally inhabited by vibrant and diverse peoples free from the grip of civilization.

The sea, which sometimes serves to isolate Southeast Asia, also brought settlers and visitors from distant shores. For more than a millennium there have been frequent contact, trade, migration, and social exchange from other parts of Asia, and for the past five hundred years, European gunboats and merchants, along with adventurers and missionaries, have arrived as well. Outsiders have been drawn to Southeast Asia by the monsoons and by a desire for the natural and cultivated products of the region. Cultural influences from the outside have blended with local traditions in religion, economic organization, and statecraft.

The most significant geographical division has been between the regions, roughly defined as mainland and island Southeast Asia, but there is wide topographical diversity within both areas. Coastal plains, river valleys, highlands, and mountainous regions are found in every country, and often on the same island. Tropical forests have been pushed back for human settlement and cultivation over the centuries. Much of what was once frontier has been settled, to accommodate the major wave of population growth during the twentieth century, but there still remain large expanses of forested areas (although the lucrative timber industry has taken a significant toll on forests in recent decades).

Historically, settlement patterns in Southeast Asia were shaped by access to the sea and rivers. Fishing was a ubiquitous means of subsistence, and seaborne exchange and trade were central features of most societies throughout the region. Overland transportation of people and goods was made difficult by tortuous, primitive roadways until well into the twentieth century. Transportation and communication infrastructure were expanded during the colonial era, but priority was given to connecting major cities and selected rural areas where European-owned economic enterprises, such as mines and plantations, were located. Only with the development-minded policies following political independence did modern roads and transportation extend to most of the rural hinterland of Southeast Asia.

The primary agricultural crop of Southeast Asia is rice, which is grown in dry fields and in rain-fed or irrigated fields. Since wet rice (grown in irrigated fields) is a more productive crop than dry rice, there has been an evolutionary drift toward wet-rice cultivation accompanying population growth, although the historical trend has been interrupted from time to time. Over the last century, most frontier areas have been settled and irrigated rice fields dot the landscape.[6] The scale of human effort necessary to transform tropical forests or swampland into irrigated agricultural fields is possible only with a high population density and a centralized polity to coordinate the construction of irrigation systems.[7] The classical civilizations of Angkor, Majapahit, and the Red River Delta, based on large expanses of irrigated rice cultivation, were not determined by favorable geographical settings alone.

The differences between the mainland and island Southeast Asia also reflect the influences of culture, religion, and history. Buddhist beliefs, institutions, and traditions have shaped the historical evolution of social patterns and cultures in Burma, Thailand, Laos, Cambodia, and Vietnam. The primary cultural attribute of

---

[6] Lucien Hanks, *Rice and Man: Agricultural Ecology in Southeast Asia* (Chicago, IL: Aldine, 1972).

[7] Ester Boserup, *Population and Technological Change* (Chicago, IL: University of Chicago Press, 1981).

the Indonesian archipelago is adherence to Islam, although there are wide variations in practices and beliefs. Peninsular Malaysia is joined to mainland Southeast Asia by a narrow isthmus, but is generally considered part of island Southeast Asia because of shared religious, cultural, and linguistic traditions with the peoples of Indonesia. Island Southeast Asia also includes the Philippine archipelago, where Christianity has been the major religious tradition since the sixteenth century. These broad generalizations obscure considerable religious diversity within regions. There are significant Muslim populations in Singapore, southern Thailand, and the southern Philippines. There are also small Christian minorities throughout the region. Hinduism is the major religion in Bali and among the Indian minority populations of Malaysia and Singapore.

The predominant feature of the rural lowlands of both mainland and island Southeast Asia is wet (irrigated) rice and other agricultural fields interspersed with densely settled villages, which are in turn linked to small- and medium-size market towns. At the fringes of towns and cities, agricultural, manufacturing, and commercial enterprises blend together in a seamless fashion. At the core of each country are major metropolitan cities, including Jakarta, Bangkok, Singapore, Manila, Rangoon, Kuala Lumpur, and Ho Chi Minh City. Southeast Asian cities were founded as premodern trading entrepôts or as centers of colonial administration. But in recent decades, the physical landscape and economic structure of Southeast Asian metropolises increasingly resemble the modern cities of the West.

The spatial diversity of Southeast Asia is overlain with cultural and ethnic diversity. For most of history, small societies and local economies developed independently along the coastlines and in the innumerable ecological niches of difficult-to-navigate rivers and rugged terrain.[8] Eventually, many of these communities were absorbed into larger political and trading networks that created a sense of identity among people who shared a common language and culture. Some of these communities, such as the Thai and Vietnamese, have become the dominant groups of modern Southeast states, while others have become regional linguistic or ethnic communities.

Beyond the reach of modern cities and even of the rural lowlands are remote areas, often identified as highland and mountainous regions. These remote regions are generally populated by ethnic minorities that are rarely integrated into the national linguistic and social fabric. In addition to regional and indigenous minority groups, most Southeast Asian countries are also home to many "immigrant minorities," the largest of which is the population of Chinese descent. Chinese migration to Southeast Asia began well before the modern era, but major waves of migration from China occurred in the late nineteenth and early twentieth centuries, during the peak of European imperialism in the region.[9] Earlier waves of Chinese migrants generally blended into local populations, often adopting the local languages and culture. The process of assimilation slowed down during the colonial era, partially because of the much larger numbers of immigrants and also because of the segregation of immigrant workers in mining and plantation communities. Colonial policies also reinforced the sojourner status and marginality of Chinese

---

[8] O. W. Wolters, *History, Culture, and Region in Southeast Asian Perspectives* (Singapore: Institute of Southeast Asian Studies, 1982).

[9] Anthony Reid, *Sojourners and Settlers: Histories of Southeast Asia and the Chinese* (New Honolulu: University of Hawaii Press, 2001).

immigrants. Colonial rule was reinforced by maintaining economic and political divisions between local communities and the so-called immigrant populations.

THE HISTORICAL CONTEXT

In the years surrounding 1900, two Southeast Asian worlds were moving past each other. Moving to the backstage was the traditional world of Southeast Asian peasants and aristocratic elites. Moving forward, ascendant in all spheres of social, economic, and political life was European imperialism. Although Southeast Asian political and commercial development had been stunted by European naval dominance for more than two centuries,[10] the Southeast Asian countryside and the bulk of the population had been relatively unaffected by the direct hand of European colonialism. This changed dramatically in the last few decades of the nineteenth century as European imperialism reached beyond port cities to all corners of the region.

The new colonial world of large-scale plantations, mines, and administrative cities was constructed in every place that might conceivably yield a profit. If local powers could not be persuaded or bribed into acquiescence, military might was used to compel compliance. New political and social arrangements were institutionalized to ensure the profitable workings of the extractive economies of the colonial system.[11] In general, the colonial economy was based on monopolistic practices and the exploitation of cheap (and expendable) labor. Authoritarian colonial governments were legitimated by a belief in the racial superiority of the European governing class.[12]

Cities, Rural Economies, and Population Settlements

With the growth of the colonial economies of the late nineteenth and early twentieth centuries, urban centers, including traditional Southeast Asian ports and also new colonial cities, experienced rapid growth. In 1910, there were eleven Southeast Asian cities with populations of more than 100,000: Mandalay, Rangoon, Bangkok, Hanoi, Saigon-Cholon, Georgetown, Singapore, Batavia, Surakarta, Surabaya, and Manila.[13] By and large, these cities were administrative and commercial centers with only a minimal industrial base. Terry McGee notes that colonial cities functioned as economic intermediaries between the metropolitan powers and the colonial economy: they were cities "of clerks, retailers, administrators, hawkers, retailer merchants, and transport workers."[14] There was a secondary level of urban centers, including district headquarters, mining towns, and

---

[10] Anthony Reid, *Southeast Asia in the Age of Commerce, 1450–1680, Volume Two: Expansion and Crisis* (New Haven, CT: Yale University Press, 1993).

[11] Jan Bremen, *Labour Migration and Rural Transformation in Colonial Asia* (Amsterdam: Free University Press for Centre for Asian Studies Amsterdam, 1990).

[12] John Butcher, *The British in Malaya, 1880–1941: The History of a European Community in Colonial Southeast Asia* (Kuala Lumpur: Oxford University Press, 1979); Carl A. Irocki, "Political Structures in the Nineteenth and Early Twentieth Centuries," in *The Cambridge History of Southeast Asia, Volume Two*, pp. 79–130; Charles Hirschman, "The Making of Race in Colonial Malaya: Political Economy and Racial Ideology," *Sociological Forum* (1986): 330–61.

[13] T. G. McGee, *The Southeast Asian City* (London: G. Bell and Sons, 1967), p. 53.

[14] Ibid., p. 58.

railway stations that connected the major cities to the base of the extractive economy in the rural areas.

The colonial economy did little to stimulate economic development beyond the export sector. Profits from mines and plantations were returned to shareholders in the metropolitan countries or were used to expand the incomes of local managers and administrators, whose lifestyles were geared to extravagant consumption of imported goods. Economic investments were limited to the improvement of infrastructure (railroads, harbors, roads) to support the development of the extractive economy. Indigenous industrial development was a very low priority.

For the first half of the twentieth century, most of the Southeast Asian peasantry remained tied to subsistence rice production. The export sector found it more profitable to import cheap labor from China and India than to pay higher wages to attract domestic labor. The maintenance of an indigenous peasantry served the interests of local elites. The traditional obligations of peasants included corvée labor and "in-kind" payment (rice, livestock) to local rulers, landlords, and patrons. Yet, most peasants, especially in long-settled areas with a well-developed technology of rice production, probably considered themselves to be independent smallholders and not serfs in a feudal system.[15]

A somewhat smaller component of the rural sector consisted of commercialized peasants who participated in the growing market economy stimulated by the expanding colonial system. Many Southeast Asian regions had a long history of growing pepper and other spices for the world market, while other areas had produced rice to support the urban populations in the region. This sector expanded dramatically in the late nineteenth century with the demand for rice and other foodstuffs to feed the growing numbers of wage laborers in the enclave economies and colonial cities. The settlement and development of lower Burma, the Central Thai Plain, and the Mekong Delta were direct responses to the expanding world and regional market for rice.[16]

Alongside the traditional rural sector was the emerging economy of plantations and mines. Rural areas, often quite remote, were "opened up" with Western and Chinese capital and imported wage labor. These modern capitalist enterprises produced raw materials that fed the industrial development of Europe. Tin and gold had been mined for hundreds of years with local labor, and the products were shipped to China and other distant markets. But the scale of development, the massive importation of labor, and the potential profits to be made had all expanded to a much higher level than ever before. These dynamics were intertwined with the dramatic demographic changes of the twentieth century.

POPULATION GROWTH: A HISTORICAL OVERVIEW

The basic facts of population size and growth of early modern Southeast Asia are the subjects of considerable uncertainty and debate.[17] Early censuses, including most

---

[15] Francesca Bray, *The Rice Economies: Technology and Development in Asian Societies* (New York, NY: Basil Blackwell, 1986), pp. 176–77.

[16] Norman G. Owen, "The Rice Economy of the Mainland Southeast Asia, 1850–1914," *Journal of the Siam Society* 59, part 2 (1971): 78–143.

[17] Anthony Reid, "Low Population Growth and Its Causes in Pre-Colonial Southeast Asia," in *Death and Disease in Southeast Asia: Explorations in Social, Medical, and Demographic History*, ed. Norman G. Owen (Singapore: Oxford University Press, 1987), pp. 33–47; Norman G. Owen,

of those taken in the nineteenth century, were indirect—village leaders were asked to report the number of people living in their villages. Because population counts were used to assess taxes and to conscript labor, there was a strong incentive for communities to underreport their true population.[18] In addition, there were the usual problems of accurately enumerating populations in remote rural areas and in teeming city slums. Southeast Asian populations were often mobile, and most probably had a well-founded suspicion of government inquiries. For these reasons, we must treat historical (prior to modern census-taking) population figures with caution. Modest differences or changes in population figures can be easily confounded with measurement errors.

In general, the quality of demographic data from Southeast Asia improved dramatically over the course of the twentieth century. Some colonial authorities instituted modern population censuses, although the periodicity and quality varied widely. After political independence, each country in Southeast Asia set up an office of national statistics with census-taking as one of the major priorities. With assistance from the United Nations and other international organizations, national programs of population censuses and surveys were professionalized and the results were routinely published.

In Table 1, we provide a preliminary survey of the size and growth of the populations of Southeast Asian countries over the twentieth century, with projections to 2025 and 2050. For the first half the twentieth century, only two figures (at most) are provided—for (a census year during) the first decade of the century and for a year in the 1930s. These figures, based on colonial censuses and estimates of varying quality and completeness, are drawn from an earlier publication by the first author.[19] The population estimates from 1950 to 2010 and the projections to 2025 and 2050 are drawn from the online version of *World Population Prospects*, the authoritative compendium of international demographic data published by the Population Division of the United Nations.[20] The UN figures are based on the census results from each country, but have been adjusted using standard statistical and demographic methods to produce population estimates from 1950 to the present. Although not without error, the UN figures are probably the best (and certainly the most consistent and comparable) that are available for recent decades. The middle panel of Table 1 shows the average annual (percentage) growth rates for each interval between the population counts and projections. The lower panel shows the percentage share of each country of the total population of the region.

A demographic picture of Southeast Asia at the turn of the twentieth century shows two contrasting settlement patterns. At one extreme were areas of high population density and irrigated rice cultivation. The prototypical example was Java, which had a population of almost 30 million in 1901. Population density in Java, especially in east and central Java, was comparable to the very populous rural areas

"The Paradox of Nineteenth-Century Population Growth in Southeast Asia: Evidence from Java and the Philippines," *Journal of Southeast Asian Studies* 18 (March 1987): 45–57.

[18] Widjojo Nitisastro, *Population Trends in Indonesia* (Ithaca, NY: Cornell University Press, 1970); Bram Peper, "Population Growth in Java in the Nineteenth Century," *Population Studies* 24 (1970): 71–84; Ng Shui Meng, *The Population of Indochina: Some Preliminary Observations* (Singapore: Institute of Southeast Asian Studies, 1974), pp. 16–17.

[19] Charles Hirschman, "Population and Society in Twentieth-Century Southeast Asia," *Journal of Southeast Asian Studies* 25 (1994): 381–416.

[20] United Nations, *World Population Prospects*.

Table 1
Population Estimates (Millions) and Average Annual Growth Rates by Country:
1950 to 2010, with Projections to 2050 (continued on next page)

	Colonial Censuses		UN Population Estimates		
	c. 1900–11	1930–39	1950	1960	1970
World			2,532	3,038	3,696
Asia			1,403	1,708	2,135
SE Asia	~85	~130	173	219	285
% of World Pop			6.8%	7.2%	7.7%
% of Europe			31.6%	36.3%	43.5%
Brunei Darussalam			0.0	0.1	0.1
Cambodia	1.7		4.3	5.4	6.9
Indonesia	40.2	60.7	74.8	91.9	118.4
Laos	0.6		1.7	2.1	2.7
Malaysia	2.4	3.8	6.1	8.2	10.9
Myanmar/Burma	10.5	14.7	17.2	21.0	26.2
Philippines	7.6	16.0	18.4	26.0	35.5
Singapore	0.2	0.6	1.0	1.6	2.1
Thailand	8.3	11.5	20.6	27.3	36.9
Timor-Leste			0.4	0.5	0.6
Vietnam	14.9	17.6	28.3	35.2	44.9

	Colonial Censuses (percentage)	Estimated Average Annual Rate of Population Change (percentage)		
	c. 1900–11 to 1930–39	1950–55	1960–65	1970–75
World		1.8	1.9	2.0
Asia		2.0	2.0	2.3
SE Asia	1.7	2.2	2.6	2.5
Brunei Darussalam		5.5	4.4	4.5
Cambodia		2.2	2.5	0.5
Indonesia	1.6	1.8	2.5	2.5
Laos		2.4	2.3	2.5
Malaysia	1.8	2.8	3.2	2.4
Myanmar/Burma	1.3	1.9	2.1	2.4
Philippines	3.0	3.5	3.3	2.9
Singapore	4.4	4.9	2.8	1.7
Thailand	1.3	2.7	3.0	2.8
Timor-Leste		1.3	1.8	1.9
Vietnam	0.7	2.1	2.5	2.1

of China and India.[21] Other wet-rice cultivation areas in Southeast Asia, especially the Red River Delta (northern Vietnam) and parts of Luzon, had population densities that were similar to those of Java, but none covered such an extensive area or had such a large population.

---

[21] Widjojo, *Population Trends in Indonesia*, p. 75.

Table 1 (continued from previous page)
Population Estimates and Average Annual Growth Rates by Country:
1950 to 2010, with Projections to 2050

	UN Population Estimates (millions)				Projected	
	1980	1990	2000	2010	2025	2050
World	4,453	5,306	6,123	6,896	8,003	9,306
Asia	2,638	3,199	4,164	4,164	4,730	5,142
SE Asia	359	445	524	593	683	759
% of World Pop	8.1%	8.4%	8.6%	8.6%	8.5%	8.2%
% of Europe	51.8%	61.8%	72.1%	80.4%	91.8%	105.6%
Brunei Darussalam	0.2	0.3	0.3	0.4	0.5	0.6
Cambodia	6.5	9.5	12.4	14.1	16.7	19.0
Indonesia	150.8	184.3	213.4	239.9	271.9	293.5
Laos	3.2	4.2	5.3	6.2	7.4	8.4
Malaysia	13.8	18.2	23.4	28.4	35.2	43.5
Myanmar/Burma	32.9	39.3	45.0	48.0	53.2	55.3
Philippines	47.1	61.6	77.3	93.3	118.1	154.9
Singapore	2.4	3.0	3.9	5.1	5.8	6.1
Thailand	47.5	57.1	63.2	69.1	72.9	71.0
Timor-Leste	0.6	0.7	0.8	1.1	1.7	3.0
Vietnam	54.0	67.1	78.8	87.8	99.3	104.0

	Estimated Average Annual Rate of Population Change (percentage)				Projected	
	1980–85	1990–95	2000–05	2010–15	2025–30	2045–50
World	1.8	1.5	1.2	1.1	0.8	0.4
Asia	1.9	1.6	1.2	1.0	0.6	0.1
SE Asia	2.3	1.7	1.3	1.1	0.7	0.2
Brunei Darussalam	2.9	2.8	2.1	1.7	1.1	0.5
Cambodia	3.9	3.2	1.4	1.2	0.8	0.3
Indonesia	2.2	1.6	1.3	1.0	0.6	0.0
Laos	2.4	2.7	1.6	1.3	0.9	0.2
Malaysia	2.6	2.6	2.2	1.6	1.1	0.6
Myanmar/Burma	1.9	1.4	0.6	0.8	0.4	-0.1
Philippines	2.8	2.3	2.0	1.7	1.3	0.8
Singapore	2.3	2.9	1.7	1.1	0.6	-0.1
Thailand	1.9	0.9	1.1	0.5	0.1	-0.3
Timor-Leste	2.6	2.8	3.9	2.9	2.6	1.8
Vietnam	2.2	2.0	1.1	1.0	0.4	-0.1

At the other end of the continuum were vast areas of insular and mainland Southeast Asia that were sparsely settled, mostly by shifting cultivators.[22] The highlands of mainland Southeast Asia, most of the Malayan peninsula, and large parts of the Indonesian and Philippine archipelagoes had very low population densities until the modern era. Almost every country or territory encompassed high- and low-density areas.

---

[22] Zelinsky, "The Indochinese Peninsula: A Demographic Anomaly."

Table 1 (continued from previous page)
Population Estimates and Average Annual Growth Rates by Country:
1950 to 2010, with Projections to 2050

	Population Distribution			
	1950	1960	1970	1980
SE Asia Total	100%	100%	100%	100%
Brunei Darussalam	0.0%	0.0%	0.0%	0.1%
Cambodia	2.5%	2.5%	2.4%	1.8%
Indonesia	43.3%	41.9%	41.5%	42.0%
Laos	1.0%	1.0%	0.9%	0.9%
Malaysia	3.5%	3.7%	3.8%	3.9%
Myanmar/Burma	9.9%	9.6%	9.2%	9.2%
Philippines	10.6%	11.9%	12.4%	13.1%
Singapore	0.6%	0.7%	0.7%	0.7%
Thailand	11.9%	12.5%	12.9%	13.2%
Timor-Leste	0.3%	0.2%	0.2%	0.2%
Vietnam	16.3%	16.0%	15.8%	15.0%

Around 1900, many areas were in transition from low to high population densities. The expansion of irrigated fields for rice cultivation was spreading to the remaining frontiers of Java, lower Burma, central Siam, and the Mekong Delta. These demographic and agricultural changes were closely linked to massive political and economic forces (as will be addressed later), including the expansion of regional and long-distance markets, the development of export economies dependent on low-cost migrant labor, and improved transportation facilities.

During the first third of the century, the population of Southeast Asia, as a whole, grew from about 85 million to approximately 130 million, which implies an annual average growth rate of 1.7 percent. Compared to the rest of world during the early twentieth century, as well as Southeast Asian history, colonial Southeast Asia experienced very rapid population growth. But the population of Southeast Asia grew even faster during the early postcolonial era. From the 1960s to the 1980s, the average annual growth rate exceeded 2 percent before dropping below 2 percent in the 1990s. In the early decades of the twenty-first century, the United Nations estimates a growth rate of close to 1 percent per year and projects a continued decline in future decades, with a growth rate approaching zero by midcentury.

Growth rates of 2 percent (or higher) per year for a decade or so can lead to spectacular changes in population size. The 1950 Southeast Asia population of 173 million added 46 million in the 1950s, 66 million in the 1960s, 74 million in the 1970s, 86 million in the 1980s, and 79 million in the 1990s. Even assuming a continued decline (as noted above) in the population growth *rate*, the actual regional population continues to grow; it reached 593 million in 2010, and is expected to reach 683 million in 2025 and 759 million in 2050. To provide comparable benchmarks, UN population estimates and projections (and growth rates) are shown for the world and for all of Asia for the same periods between 1950 and 2050. The population growth of Southeast Asia has been slightly more rapid than the world as a whole. As a percentage of the world's population, Southeast Asia edged up only slightly, from

Table 1 (continued from previous page)
Population Estimates and Average Annual Growth Rates by Country:
1950 to 2010, with Projections to 2050[23]

	Population Distribution			Projected Distribution	
	1990	2000	2010	2025	2050
SE Asia Total	100%	100%	100%	100%	100%
Brunei Darussalam	0.1%	0.1%	0.1%	0.1%	0.1%
Cambodia	2.1%	2.4%	2.4%	2.4%	2.5%
Indonesia	41.4%	40.7%	40.4%	39.8%	38.7%
Laos	0.9%	1.0%	1.0%	1.1%	1.1%
Malaysia	4.1%	4.5%	4.8%	5.2%	5.7%
Myanmar/Burma	8.8%	8.6%	8.1%	7.8%	7.3%
Philippines	13.8%	14.8%	15.7%	17.3%	20.4%
Singapore	0.7%	0.7%	0.9%	0.8%	0.8%
Thailand	12.8%	12.1%	11.6%	10.7%	9.4%
Timor-Leste	0.2%	0.2%	0.2%	0.3%	0.4%
Vietnam	15.1%	15.0%	14.8%	14.6%	13.7%

7 percent in 1950 to 8.6 percent in 2000. The more dramatic comparison has been the shift in the demographic balance between Southeast Asia and Europe. This shift is entirely due to the timing of the demographic transitions—the historical process of declining mortality and fertility. Europe began its demographic transition in the

---

[23] Sources: **Burma:** M. Ismael K. Maung, "The Population of Burma: An Analysis of the 1973 Census," *Papers of the East-West Population Institute*, No. 97 (Honolulu: East-West Center Population Institute, 1986), p. 24. **Cambodia:** George S. Siampos, "The Population of Cambodia, 1945–1980," *Milbank Memorial Fund Quarterly* 48 (July 1970): 351. **Indonesia:** Graeme J. Hugo, Terence H. Hull, Valerie J. Hull, et al., *The Demographic Dimension in Indonesian Development* (Singapore: Oxford University Press, 1987), pp. 137, 153; Terence H. Hull and Gouranga Lal Dasvarma, "Fertility Trends in Indonesia, 1967–1985," *Bulletin of Indonesian Economic Studies* 24 (1988): 115–22. **Laos:** Ng Shui Meng, *The Population of Indochina: Some Preliminary Observations* (Singapore: Institute of Southeast Asian Studies, 1974), pp. 35–36; Arthur J. Dommen, "Laos in 1985: The Year of the Census," *Asian Survey* 26 (1986): 112–17. **Peninsular Malaysia:** Charles Hirschman, "Demographic Trends in Peninsular Malaysia, 1947–75," *Population and Development Review* 6 (1980): 114; Lim Lin Lean, Gavin Jones, and Charles Hirschman, "Continuing Fertility Transitions in Plural Society: Ethnic Trends and Differentials in Peninsular Malaysia," *Journal of Biosocial Science* 19 (1987): 413. **Philippines:** Mercedes B. Concepcion, "The Philippines: Population Trends and Dilemmas," *Philippine Population Journal* 1 (1985): 22–23. **Singapore:** Chang Cheng-Tung, *Fertility Transition in Singapore* (Singapore: Singapore University Press, 1974), pp. 18, 21. **Thailand:** Committee Population and Demography, National Research Council, *Fertility and Mortality Changes in Thailand, 1950-75* (Washington, DC: National Academy of Sciences, 1980), p. 10; John Knodel, Aphichat Chamratrithirong, and Nibhon Debavalya. *Thailand's Reproductive Revolution: Rapid Fertility Decline in a Third-World Setting* (Madison, WI: University of Wisconsin Press, 1987), pp. 55–56. **Vietnam:** Judith Banister, *The Population of Vietnam* (Washington, DC: U.S. Department of Commerce, Bureau of the Census, 1985), p. 22. **1985–89 and 1990–94 fertility rates:** John A. Ross, W. Parker Mauldin, and Vincent C. Miller, *Family Planning and Population: A Compendium of International Statistics* (New York, NY: The Population Council, 1993), pp. 16, 27. See also: United Nations, *World Population Prospects, the 2010 Revision*.

early 1900s, while Southeast Asia, on average, experienced rapid population growth for the better part of the twentieth century.

Fertility transitions—the decline from high to low fertility—began in several Southeast Asia countries in the 1970s and spread broadly in the last decades of the twentieth century. The lag in demographic transitions has led to a remarkable change in the relative demographic magnitudes of Europe and Southeast Asia. In 1950, Southeast Asia's population was only one-third that of Europe's, but within a century, there will be more Southeast Asians than Europeans (based on the UN projections noted earlier). In the paragraphs that follow, we offer a brief overview of the population trends in the major countries of Southeast Asia, beginning with the demographic giant, Indonesia.

Indonesia

Indonesia is the largest country in the region, both geographically and demographically. In spite of the controversy over nineteenth-century population estimates, most researchers agree that nearly half of the region's population lived in the then-Dutch East Indies at the dawn of the twentieth century, primarily in Java, which had a population of more than 30 million in 1900. The outer islands of Indonesia contained some pockets of high-density settlements, but, in general, most areas of Sumatra, Kalimantan, Sulawesi, and other islands were sparsely settled. At the time of independence in 1950, Indonesia had 75 million people, making it one of the most populated countries in the world.

There have been several distinct periods of population growth in Indonesia. For the first two decades of the twentieth century, growth was only about 1 percent per year; growth was slowed by cholera and influenza epidemics and by a series of poor harvests.[24] During the 1920s, growth expanded to more than 2 percent per year, with a widening gap in growth rates between Java and the outer islands. The growth rate of the outer islands was just below 3 percent per year and somewhat lower in Java. Population growth slowed during the middle decades of the twentieth century, most likely due to the erosion of the export sector during the Great Depression, the collapse of the entire economy during the Japanese occupation of World War II, and the turbulent years of the war for independence in the late 1940s.

Rapid population growth in Indonesia resumed after 1950 and was well over 2 percent per annum until the middle 1980s—perhaps as high as 3 percent in the outer islands. Current estimates show that there were almost 240 million Indonesians in 2010. Even with a much lower rate of growth in the coming decades, Indonesia will remain the regional demographic giant with a projected population of almost 300 million in 2050. With a somewhat slower growth rate than the region as a whole, Indonesia's share of Southeast Asia's overall population has declined from 43 percent in 1950 to 41 percent in 2000, and it will continue to decline, albeit only slightly in the coming decades.

Medium-Size Countries: Burma, Philippines, Thailand, and Vietnam

In 2010, the populations of the Philippines, Vietnam, Thailand, and Myanmar are 93 million, 88 million, 69 million, and 48 million, respectively. In terms of population,

---

[24] Graeme J. Hugo et al., *The Demographic Dimension in Indonesian Development*, p. 39.

these are some of the largest countries in the world. Even with falling growth rates, the populations of the Philippines and Vietnam are each projected to exceed 100 million, while Thailand and Burma will level off at just over 70 million and 55 million, respectively. All together, about one-half of the population of Southeast Asia lives in these four geographically medium-size countries.

The rapid growth of the Philippines is an anomaly. Even with some allowance for underenumeration, the Philippines was probably the smallest of the mid-size Southeast Asian countries in the early twentieth century. Rapid population growth during the twentieth century—perhaps as high as 3 percent in the 1950s and 1960s—put the Philippines on a course to become the second-largest country in the region, with a population of more than 93 million in 2010. With a sluggish demographic transition, the Philippine population is likely to exceed 150 million by 2050.

For the pre-World War II era, there was a series of administrative counts conducted by the various units of French Indochina.[25] If the territories that became Vietnam (Tonkin, Annam, and Cochinchina) are aggregated, the total population was about 14 million at the end of the first decade of the twentieth century. This figure was more than double that of the Philippines at the time. In spite of its initial large base, population growth in Vietnam appears to have been well below the regional average during the first half of the twentieth century. In 1936, the estimated population for all of Vietnam was 17.6 million. The UN data for the period after 1950 suggest that Vietnam appears to have grown around 2 percent per year from 1950 to 1990, roughly comparable to other countries in the region. This is somewhat surprising given that Vietnam experienced almost continuous warfare from World War II to the mid-1970s.[26] The first census of a unified Vietnam in 1979 counted almost 53 million persons. A rapid demographic transition in the 1980s and 1990s led to lower rates of projected growth for Vietnam for the twenty-first century. The population of 89 million in 2010 is projected to level off at around 104 million by 2050.

The 1911 Thai census showed a population of 8.3 million. With a rapid rate of growth approaching 3 percent at midcentury, Thailand reached a population of 47 million in 1980. In that year, Thailand was as populous as the Philippines and had just about 6 million fewer people than did Vietnam. The rapid pace of Thailand's demographic transition slowed subsequent population growth. Although Thailand remains one of the largest countries in the region, with a population of 69 million in 2010 (projected to grow to 71 million in 2050), it will be much less populous than the Philippines and Vietnam in the twenty-first century.

At the beginning of the twentieth century, Burma was larger, in demographic terms, than either Thailand or the Philippines. The first twentieth-century census (1901) of Burma covered four-fifths of the country, excluding only sparsely populated frontier areas, and enumerated 10.5 million people.[27] The population

[25] Meng Shui Ng, *The Population of Indochina: Some Preliminary Observations* (Singapore: Institute of Southeast Asian Studies, 1974).

[26] The references to the 1979 and 1989 censuses are Vietnam, General Statistical Office, *1979 Vietnam Census Report* (Hanoi: General Statistical Office, 1981); and *1989 Vietnam Population Census Reports* (four volumes), including an additional report entitled *Detailed Analysis of Sample Results* (Hanoi: General Statistical Office, 1991). See also Judith Banister, *Vietnam: Population Dynamics and Prospects*, Indochina Research Monograph, No. 6 (Berkeley, CA: Institute of East Asian Studies, University of California–Berkeley, 1993).

[27] M. Ismael K. Maung, "The Population of Burma," pp. 5–6.

growth of Burma during the early decades of the twentieth century appears to have been one of the lowest in the region. Yet, the UN estimates show that Burma grew rapidly during the second half of the century, from 17 million in 1950 to 45 million in 2000, and then to 48 million in 2010. The population of Burma grew at a rate of 2 percent per year from the 1950s through the 1980s but has slowed to 1 percent or less in the last two decades. The United Nations predicts a continued slowing of growth in the coming decades, with an expected population of 55 million in 2050.

Small-Size Countries: Malaysia/Singapore, Cambodia, and Laos

During the colonial era, Malaya (now Peninsular Malaysia) and Singapore were part of British Malaya. Singapore was the major administrative center for British colonial rule and also the major trading entrepôt. Historically, Malaya was a sparsely settled frontier region with a population of less than one million in the nineteenth century.[28] There were only a couple of densely settled areas of wet-rice production in Kedah (northwest) and Kelantan (northeast). The population of Malaya was transformed in the late nineteenth and early twentieth centuries by large-scale migration from China, India, and the Indonesian archipelago. Immigrant workers were recruited to work as "cheap labor" in tin mines, rubber plantations, and other sectors of the colonial export economy.

Singapore was retained as a British colony when Malaya became independent in 1957. Then, in 1963, Malaysia was formed as the federation of Malaya, Singapore, and two British colonies—Sabah and Sarawak—on the island of Borneo. Singapore left the federation in 1965 following a political crisis and became an independent city-state. Singapore's population will level off at around 5 to 6 million in the coming decades. The first census of Malaysia in 1970 counted a population of 11 million. With rapid growth in recent decades, the population of Malaysia had grown to 28 million by 2010 and is projected to level off at around 43 million by 2050. Malaysian national population trends are a composite of different demographic trajectories of the major ethnic communities of Malays, Chinese, and Indians. Major streams of immigrant labor from China and India in the late nineteenth and early twentieth centuries meant that about 50 percent of the population of Malaya consisted of non-Malays at the time of independence in 1957. With faster demographic transitions among Chinese and Indians, their share of national population has declined. In the early twenty-first century, about two-thirds of the Malaysian population consists of Malays and other indigenous peoples.

Present-day Cambodia was the home of the great Khmer Empire from the ninth to the thirteenth centuries, where there may have been as many as 4 million people.[29] This large population was dependent on a well-developed irrigation system and a strong polity to coordinate labor for planting, harvesting, and maintaining the flow of water to crops. Under pressures from ascendant rivals as well as from internal struggles, the Khmer civilization eventually collapsed. The chronology of events remains unknown, but the factors that led to a demographic collapse are clear. Without a strong and centralized polity, it was impossible to organize labor to

---

[28] Nicholas N. Dodge, "Population Estimates for the Malay Peninsula, with Special Reference to the East Coast States," *Population Studies* 34 (1980): 437–75.

[29] Irene Taeuber, "Population Growth in Southeast Asia," in *Demographic Analysis: Selected Readings*, ed. Joseph J. Spengler and Otis Dudley Duncan (Glencoe, IL: Free Press, 1956), p. 69.

maintain the complex irrigation system that supported the large population. In the 1860s, French administrators working with tax rolls estimated the population of Cambodia to be less than 1 million.[30] Census counts of the early 1900s range from 1.7 to 2.4 million. These estimates are inexact, but suggest that the population of nineteenth and early twentieth century Cambodia was only a fraction of the historic population of the Khmer empire.

Based on projections from the 1963 census, the United Nations estimates that the population of Cambodia was almost 7 million in 1970.[31] Then catastrophe struck. Following a civil war and carpet bombing of rural areas by the United States (as an extension of the US–Vietnam War), the Khmer Rouge took power and ruled Cambodia from 1975 to 1978. During this era, Cambodia has been characterized as a *killing field*. Although the loss of life cannot be precisely known, Patrick Heuveline[32] estimated that between 1 and 3 million Cambodians lost their lives to executions, forced marches, and starvation during the relatively brief Khmer Rouge era.[33] Even though fertility added to the population, the UN figures in Table 1 show absolute population decline in Cambodia between 1970 and 1980.

Following the mass mortality of the Khmer Rouge era, the population of Cambodia rebounded with a growth rate of over 3 percent per year in the 1980s, followed by a lower but still high rate of just below 2 percent per annum in the last two decades. The United Nations estimates that the 1980 population of Cambodia, 6.5 million, grew to 14 million in 2010 and is expected to reach 19 million in 2050.

During the French colonial era in the early twentieth century, Laos was a peripheral region with a population of less than 1 million. The first modern census of Laos in 1985 enumerated a population of 3.6 million.[34] The United Nations estimates that the population of Laos grew from less than 2 million in 1950 to a little more than 6 million in 2010. The United Nations projects that by midcentury, the population of Laos will be around 8 million.

Micro States: Brunei and Timor-Leste

Prior to the colonial era, Brunei was a powerful kingdom whose influence extended far beyond its Borneo land base. Shrunken to a small principality during the nineteenth century, it would most likely have been absorbed as part of Malaysia in the 1960s had it not been for its colossal wealth based on oil and natural gas deposits. Contemporary Brunei resembles a Middle Eastern sheikdom, with cradle-to-grave welfare benefits for its few hundred thousand citizens.

Timor-Leste is the eastern half of the remote island of Timor in the eastern Indonesian archipelago. Timor-Leste was a Portuguese colony until the Portuguese

---

[30] David P. Chandler, *A History of Cambodia*, second edition (Boulder, CO: Westview Press, 1982), p. 100.

[31] See also Ibid.; Siampos, "The Population of Cambodia, 1945–1980," pp. 317–60; and Ea Meng-Try, "Kampuchea: A Country Adrift," *Population and Development Review* 1 (June 1981): 209–228.

[32] Patrick Heuveline, "Between One and Three Million in Cambodia: Toward the Demographic Reconstruction of a Decade of Cambodian History (1970–1980)," *Population Studies* 52 (1998): 49–65.

[33] Ea Meng-Try, "Kampuchea: A Country Adrift," pp. 209–28.

[34] Arthur J. Dommen, "Laos in 1985: The Year of the Census," *Asian Survey* 26 (January 1986): 112–17.

empire collapsed in 1975. After a brief moment of independence, Timor-Leste (formerly known as East Timor) was forcibly absorbed into Indonesia in 1976. After decades of struggle, and the support of external powers, Timor-Leste became an independent country in 2002. In 2010, Timor-Leste had a population of 1 million. Assuming that its rapid rate of growth continues, Timor-Leste's population could reach 3 million by 2050.

INTERPRETING TWENTIETH-CENTURY POPULATION GROWTH

Modest differences in demographic rates over a few generations can lead to extraordinary changes in population size. Southeast Asian population growth rates of 1 percent to 2 percent during the first half the twentieth century and even higher rates during the 1950s and 1960s are the primary reason for the stark reversal of the relative demographic balance between Europe and Southeast Asia.

These patterns of population growth reflect, in large part, the broader social, economic, and political trends that shaped twentieth-century Southeast Asia. Our interpretation begins with a general outline of twentieth-century Southeast Asian history. While such an exercise is fraught with oversimplification, given the diversity of the region, it provides a useful template with which to read population dynamics.

The first three decades of the twentieth century saw a continuation of the process of "opening up" the region to export industries (mining, plantations, and smallholdings) and growing political and economic integration of the colonies with the imperial powers of Great Britain, Holland, France, and the United States. In many ways, imperialism created the conditions for improved economic welfare. Roads were built, domestic markets were expanded, modern cities developed with schools and hospitals, and extraordinary amounts of goods and money flowed into the economy. These developments bypassed the bulk of the population in the rural subsistence sector, and there is some evidence that living standards may have deteriorated in Java and perhaps in other areas.[35] On the other hand, for many Southeast Asian peasants who grew rice for the market or became rubber smallholders, and for the small, but expanding, commercial and government employee classes, there were probably rising living standards, especially in the 1920s.

Whatever signs of growth and the fragile prosperity were evident in the early twentieth century (and this growth was limited to some sectors and regions) disappeared with the onset of a depression in the 1930s. As the export sector stagnated, colonial governments suffered losses of revenues and tried to squeeze more taxes from the already overburdened peasantry. Migration flows of labor within the region and from other areas slowed down and may have even reversed. The Depression of the 1930s was followed by even worse times during World War II, when the Japanese military occupied most of the region. International trade dried up and much employment in the urban economy and the export sectors disappeared, forcing substantial numbers of workers to return to rural areas and the subsistence economy.

The collapse of Japanese military rule in 1945 created a political vacuum that the returning colonial powers and indigenous nationalist movements struggled to fill by

---

[35] Clifford Geertz, *Agricultural Involution: The Processes of Ecological Change in Indonesia* (Berkeley, CA: University of California Press, 1963).

whatever means available. In some countries, the transition to independence was relatively peaceful and the general trend was toward economic recovery and reconstruction, though not to the prewar colonial model. In other countries (Indonesia and Vietnam), the imperial powers fought to keep their colonies and delayed the postwar recovery for another decade or two. In a rather perverse way, Cold War conflicts in Asia (first, in Korea, then, in Indochina) brought considerable economic gains to several countries in Southeast Asia. The price of rubber, a primary export crop of the region, rose to record levels in the 1950s.[36] The American military presence in the late 1960s and early 1970s stimulated international investment in infrastructure in several countries as well as increased consumer spending.

In general, the post-independence era in Southeast Asia has been marked by rapid economic growth and significant improvements in population welfare and consumption. Development-oriented governments in Thailand, Malaysia, Singapore, and Indonesia have invested heavily in education and promoted the export of electronics and other goods to expanding international markets.[37] Economic progress, however, has been uneven across the region. The Philippines and Burma, which had relatively well-educated populations in the 1950s, seemed poised for rapid development. Yet both countries have been floundering for decades with problems of slow economic growth and political strife. For other former colonies, the transition from colonial rule to political independence varied widely from peaceful accommodations to protracted revolutions across Southeast Asia. The initial wars of independence in Indochina in the 1940s and 1950s became intertwined with Cold War struggles in the 1960s and 1970s. American political and military intervention in Vietnam led to a series of civil and regional wars with catastrophic consequences.

It is difficult to discern clear demographic trends for Southeast Asia during the first half of the twentieth century. The data are sparse and subject to serious problems of unreliable measurement. The very low rates of population growth in some regions may well be due to depressed living conditions.[38] The impact of the influenza epidemic of 1917–18 may be partially responsible for some of the low growth rates in Indonesia and elsewhere.[39] In several countries, the relative prosperity of the 1920s was reflected in higher rates of population growth. International migration from China and India was a major factor in the rapid growth of the population of Peninsular Malaysia during the first three decades of the century.

Throughout Southeast Asia, in general, there was a slowdown in population growth during the years surrounding World War II and a very rapid rise in population growth in the decades after the war. The hard years of depression and World War II ended the significant influx of labor migration from outside the region. Although there is no direct evidence, there was probably little progress in longevity during this period.

---

[36] Norman Owen, ed., *The Emergence of Modern Southeast Asia: A New History.* (Honolulu: University of Hawaii Press, 2005), p. 380.

[37] World Bank, *The East Asian Miracle: Economic Growth and Public Policy* (New York, NY: Oxford University Press, 1993).

[38] Pierre Gourou, *The Peasants of the Tokin Delta: A Study of Human Geography*, two volumes, trans. Richard R. Miller (New Haven, CT: Human Relations Area Files, 1955 [1936]).

[39] Colin Brown, "The Influenza Pandemic of 1918 in Indonesia," in *Death and Disease in Southeast Asia*, pp. 235–56.

The post-World War II era stands out as a unique period of extraordinarily rapid population growth. From 1950 to 2010, the population of Southeast Asia more than tripled, increasing from 176 million to 590 million. Rapid population growth was primarily a result of record declines in mortality rates, which were pervasive across the region. Population growth slackened in several countries during the 1970s and 1980s, as fertility declines took hold.[40] The relatively high proportion of younger to older people in Southeast Asian populations slowed the impact of declining fertility on population growth rates. Even with slowing growth rates (around 1 percent or less), the population of the region is projected to increase to 766 million by 2050, about 50 percent higher than the population in 2000.

THE DEBATE OVER POPULATION GROWTH IN SOUTHEAST ASIAN HISTORY

One of the most debated issues among demographers and historians is the reported high rates of population growth in nineteenth-century Southeast Asia. Some researchers expressed doubt that the reported high population growth rates during the colonial era were accurate.[41] The conventional explanation for rising population figures is declining mortality, and there was considerable skepticism that mortality had fallen significantly during the colonial era. Factors that might have reduced mortality such as poverty alleviation or improvements in health care were not high priorities of colonial regimes. An alternative explanation was expressed by some analysts, namely, that the reported high rates of growth in colonial Southeast Asia were an artifact of poor population data. If the size of pre-colonial populations had been underestimated, it would appear that rapid population growth followed from colonial rule. Thus, the argument was that the reported high rates of population growth during the nineteenth century were simply an artifact of improved demographic measurement.

After a careful review of the debate and of potential measurement problems, Owen[42] and Reid[43] concluded that nineteenth-century population growth rates in Southeast Asia were credible and most likely above 2 percent per annum. This level of growth, which exceeded that of Europe for the same period, represented a clear break from the very low levels of population growth in Southeast Asia in earlier centuries.[44]

Owen and Reid conclude that the major reason for the rapid increase in nineteenth-century population growth rates was the sharp reduction in warfare under colonial rule. Although traditional warfare in premodern Southeast Asia did not lead to large numbers of military causalities, it did affect agricultural systems that sustained civilian populations. Frequent periods of warfare almost certainly

---

[40] Gavin Jones, "The Population of Southeast Asia," working paper no. 81, Demography Program, Research School of Social Sciences, Canberra, 1999.

[41] Widjojo, *Population Trends in Indonesia*, pp. 71–84.

[42] Norman G. Owen, "The Paradox of Nineteenth-Century Population Growth in Southeast Asia: Evidence from Java and the Philippines," *Journal of Southeast Asian Studies* 18 (March 1987): 45–57.

[43] Reid, "Low Population Growth and Its Causes," pp. 33–47.

[44] Anthony Reid, *Southeast Asia in the Age of Commerce, Volume One: The Lands Below the Winds* (New Haven, CT: Yale University Press, 1988); Anthony Reid, "Economic and Social Change," pp. 460–507.

disrupted food production systems, especially irrigated rice cultivation.[45] Traditional patterns of warfare may also have discouraged the expansion of agriculture and regional trade.[46] Fisher[47] reports that the Burmese attack on Arakan lowered the population of the province from 500,000 in 1785 to 100,000 in 1824 and that the Siamese invasion of Kedah in the late eighteenth century reduced the population of the state to half.

Reid[48] argues that some of the rise in population growth in nineteenth-century Southeast Asia may be attributed to rising fertility. The spread of Islam and Christianity led to more permanent settlements that increased the value of child labor. Formal religions may also have discouraged premarital sexual activity and, thereby, reduced the incidence of gonorrhea and other sexually transmitted diseases that contributed to high levels of sterility in the region.[49]

Another important factor in the second half of the nineteenth and the early decades of the twentieth centuries may have been the settlement of frontier regions.[50] Migrants to frontier areas, in general, tend to marry earlier and have more children than farmers in long-settled rural communities. This interpretation is reinforced with the long-standing observation of lower rates of population growth in densely settled Java and higher population growth in frontier settlements in the outer islands of Indonesia.[51]

The higher rate of population growth (and fertility) in frontier regions can best be explained by a model of population dynamics in traditional rice-growing communities. Shifting cultivation of "dry padi" was the predominant mode of agriculture in most parts of Southeast Asia until the nineteenth century. Population pressure, often in the context of strong polities, gradually led to construction of irrigation systems and the cultivation of wet rice, which yielded much larger harvests per unit of land than did shifting cultivation. In spite of the demand for more food, the transition from shifting cultivation to irrigated cultivation was not an automatic development or even the most likely social response to population pressure. The endless frontier in most regions offered an easier option—migration.[52] The large harvests from wet rice led to permanent settlements and a transformation of the social and economic fabric of community life. According to Clifford Geertz,[53] wet-rice cultivation has the unique capacity to support more labor and sustain a

---

[45] Reid, "Economic and Social Change," pp. 460–507.

[46] Warren S. Thompson, *Population and Progress in the Far East* (Chicago, IL: University of Chicago Press 1959), p. 349.

[47] See Charles A. Fisher, "Some Comments on Population Growth in South-East Asia, with Special Reference to the Period Since 1830," in *The Economic Development of South-East Asia*, ed. C. D. Cowan (London: Allen and Unwin, 1964), pp. 48–71. It is unclear to what extent these war-related population declines were due to mortality or to out-migration.

[48] Reid, "Economic and Social Change," pp. 460–507.

[49] Ibid.

[50] Mark VanLandingham and Charles Hirschman, "Population Pressure and Fertility in Pre-Transition Thailand," *Population Studies* 55 (2001): 233–48.

[51] Hugo et al., *The Demographic Dimension*, p. 35.

[52] Peter Xenos, "The Ilocos Coast Since 1800: Population Pressure and the Ilocano Diaspora, and Multiphasic Response," in *Population and History: The Demographic Origins of the Modern Philippines*, ed. Daniel F. Doeppers and Peter Xenos, Monograph Number 16 (Madison, WI: Center for Southeast Asian Studies, University of Wisconsin, 1998), pp. 39–70.

[53] Geertz, *Agricultural Involution*.

growing population. Although there are limits to the demographic absorptive capacity of rice growing communities, it is far greater than most other crops.

The construction and maintenance of irrigation facilities represented an enormous investment by a large number of farmers over many years. The scale of labor necessary for such an investment was far greater than would be available from a group of households or an extended kinship alliance.[54] In most cases, the construction of irrigation facilities was coordinated (compelled) by a centralized political authority that had effective power to mobilize and control labor from many villages in an area. The power of strong states that led to improved agricultural productivity did not necessarily raise the living standards of the peasantry. Political power could also be used to abuse the peasant population by greater taxation and labor conscription. The need for labor on a large scale to maintain irrigation systems also limited peasants' scope of geographic mobility thus and may have discouraged innovation.

The delicate balance in civil engineering needed to direct water flows over large expanses of landscape meant that irrigated agricultural systems were highly vulnerable to disruption. War, natural calamities, or the decline of peasant populations for whatever reason (disease, flight) could result in the collapse of centralized political systems. Irrigated rice cultivation probably waxed and waned with the rise and fall of strong political institutions. In a provocative hypothesis, Wilbur Zelinsky[55] suggests that the low population density of much of Southeast Asia was due the region's political instability relative to East or South Asia.

The spread of wet-rice agriculture to frontier areas in Southeast Asia during the late nineteenth century and early twentieth century, however, seems to have been a decisive development in Southeast Asian history and a primary reason for the accelerated rapid population growth in modern times. The growing demand for rice and an increasingly sophisticated commercial and transportation system gave tremendous impetus to Southeast Asian agricultural development in the late nineteenth century. Although there is considerable debate over the timing and scope of Southeast Asia's participation in the worldwide rice market in the late nineteenth century, there is no doubt that expanded production of rice transformed the Southeast Asian socioeconomic and physical landscape.[56] There had always been regional and long-distance trade in rice and other commodities in Southeast Asia. Indeed, Southeast Asia's commercial revolution of the sixteenth century was largely based on the trade of agricultural products produced for a world market.[57]

The enormous demand for rice stimulated production for the market among the traditional community of subsistence farmers and, more importantly, led to a massive wave of migration to frontier areas. There was a corresponding increase in

---

[54] Bray, *The Rice Economies*, ch. 2.

[55] Zelinsky, "The Indochinese Peninsula: A Demographic Anomaly."

[56] Norman G. Owen, "The Rice Economy of the Mainland Southeast Asia 1850-1914," *Journal of the Siam Society* 59 (Part 2): 78–143; Cheng Siok-Hwa, *The Rice Industry of Burma, 1852–1940* (Kuala Lumpur: University of Malaya Coop Bookshop, 1968); Michael Adas, *The Burma Delta: Economic Development and Social Change on an Asian Rice Frontier, 1852–1941* (Madison, WI: University of Wisconsin Press, 1974); James C. Ingram, *Economic Change in Thailand, 1850–1970* (Palo Alto, CA: Stanford University Press, 1971); Peter A. Coclanis, "Southeast Asia's Incorporation into the World Rice Market: A Revisionist View," *Journal of Southeast Asian Studies* 24,2 (September 1993): 251–67.

[57] Reid, *Southeast Asia in Age of Commerce*, ch. 1.

the demand for foodstuffs, rice in particular, from the expanding export sector of mines and plantations, which employed hundreds of thousands of laborers. The growth of colonial cities further increased the demand for rice and other agricultural goods at the same time demand for Southeast Asian rice was on the rise in distant markets, especially Europe.[58]

The primary rice exporting areas were developed in lower Burma, central Siam, and Cochinchina.[59] In the Burma Delta, the area under rice cultivation expanded tenfold from the 1850s to the 1930s.[60] While the expansion of rice cultivation was most dramatic in these areas, settlement of frontier areas throughout Southeast Asia was ongoing during this period.

Rice production, especially in newly settled frontier areas, was accompanied by accelerating population growth, including an increase in the peasant population. Permanent settlements, relative to a shifting-cultivation way of life, were more conducive to higher fertility. New settled villages in frontier regions created conditions that encouraged fertility. For example, the increased availability of land probably led to a relaxation of constraints on early marriage, which would have contributed to a higher rate of population growth. Although there are few measures of health and well-being, a low population-to-land ratio on the frontier might have ensured a stable and relatively abundant food supply. The growth of urban populations (and immigrant populations in the export sector) created the demand for rice exports that stimulated the expansion into frontier areas and the creation of additional zones of wet-rice cultivation during the nineteenth and early twentieth centuries.

THE DECLINE OF MORTALITY IN SOUTHEAST ASIA

The greatest human achievement of the twentieth century is the increase in longevity. In the early twenty-first century, life expectancy is greater than 60 years (or nearly so) in every Southeast Asian country and well over 70 in several. The numbers alone, however, do not convey the human meaning of this accomplishment. In much of Southeast Asia, it is now common for both husbands and wives to survive until the end of their reproductive period. Most parents can reasonably expect to live to see their grandchildren. Neither of these outcomes was experienced by the majority of the population in any country in the world at the turn of the twentieth century. Around 1900, life expectancy was in the range of 45 to 50 years in most Western countries.[61] Life expectancy was probably lower in Southeast Asia, although historical data on mortality in the region are too poor to document this point.[62] The gap in longevity between developed and developing countries probably widened during the first half of the century (with improvements in health and life expectancy occurring sooner in the West than in Asia). However, there is no doubt

---

[58] Coclanis, "Southeast Asia's Incorporation into the World Rice Market."

[59] Bray, *The Rice Economies*, pp. 43, 95.

[60] Adas, *The Burma Delta*, p. 22.

[61] Judah Matras, *Introduction to Population: A Sociological Approach* (Englewood Cliffs, NJ: Prentice Hall, 1977), p. 133.

[62] An excellent survey of the state of knowledge on historical patterns of mortality in Southeast Asia is presented in Norman G. Owen, "Toward a History of Health in Southeast Asia," in *Death and Disease in Southeast Asia*, pp. 3–30.

that international differences in life expectancy narrowed dramatically in the second half of the century.

For the decades prior to 1950, there are very few sources for the systematic study of mortality trends in Southeast Asia. Registration of births and deaths by civil authorities, the backbone of mortality measurement in developed countries, remains incomplete in most Southeast Asian countries, with the exceptions of Singapore and Malaysia, although innovative methods of indirect demographic estimation based on survey and census data have yielded a substantial body of estimates of Southeast Asian mortality for recent decades. Historians and demographers are beginning to sift through parish records and other archival sources to study historical patterns of Southeast Asian mortality.[63] Fine-grained historical studies of health and mortality should continue to provide a new vista for understanding the impact of colonial rule.

There are few clear generalizations about levels and trends in morbidity (illness or population health) and mortality for the early decades of the twentieth century. Population growth seems to have been exceptionally high—around 1 percent to 2 percent per year—in most of Southeast Asia for the last half of the nineteenth century.[64] This would seem to imply a moderate level of mortality or at least that episodes of very high mortality were relatively rare. However, several accounts point in the opposite direction. In a compelling argument, Bram Peper[65] finds little evidence to support the thesis that either living standards or health services had improved enough to substantially reduce mortality. Peter Smith[66] observed a rising frequency of episodes of crisis mortality (when mortality rates spike) in the late nineteenth century in the Philippines and concluded that the diffusion of disease from increased trade and a general deterioration of peasant livelihoods were the primary reasons for the outbreaks of higher mortality. The commercialization of peasant agriculture may well have led to higher incomes and better health at some times and in some places, while the opposite trend was evident at other times.

Health conditions remained very poor in much of Southeast Asia well into the twentieth century. Colonial visitors to the east coast state of Kelantan on the Malayan Peninsula reported extremely unsanitary areas around village houses and generally unhealthy conditions.[67] Common afflictions included pneumonia, dysentery, malaria, hookworm, yaws, and venereal disease, but the major killers were smallpox and cholera. Both diseases swept through areas on a periodic basis, causing many deaths in a relatively brief span of time.[68] Also, the influenza pandemic of 1918 had a major impact on mortality in Indonesia[69] and probably in other areas as well.

---

[63] Peter C. Smith, "Crisis Mortality in the Nineteenth Century Philippines: Data from Parish Records," *Journal of Asian Studies* 38 (1978): 51–76; Peter C. Smith and Ng Shui-Meng, "The Components of Population Change in Nineteenth Century Southeast Asia: Village Data from the Philippines," *Population Studies* 36 (1982): 237–55; Owen, ed., *Death and Disease in Southeast Asia*; Owen, "The Paradox of Nineteenth-Century Population Growth in Southeast Asia"; Doeppers and Xenos, ed., *Population and History: The Demographic Origins of the Modern Philippines*.

[64] Owen, "The Paradox of Nineteenth-Century Population Growth in Southeast Asia."

[65] Peper, "Population Growth in Java"; a similar interpretation is given in Widjojo, *Population Trends in Indonesia*.

[66] Smith, "Crisis Mortality in the Nineteenth Century Philippines."

[67] Dodge, "Population Estimates for the Malay Peninsula," p. 441.

[68] Ibid., p. 442.

[69] Hugo et al., *The Demographic Dimension*, p. 108.

Nonetheless, a reasonable case can be made that mortality stabilized at moderately high levels in the late nineteenth and early twentieth centuries. A crude birth rate (births per thousand population) of 40 to 45 (moderately high) combined with a crude death rate (deaths per thousand population) of 20 to 25 would still yield a very high annual growth rate of about 2 percent per year. This interpretation does not require an assumption of declining mortality, only that periods of exceptionally high mortality ("crisis mortality") were relatively rare. Frequent periods of crisis mortality would have reduced the overall population growth rate below the 1 percent to 2 percent level. The validity of this thesis depends on the argument that the colonial era fostered conditions that stabilized mortality.

As noted earlier, colonial domination probably reduced levels of indigenous warfare that disrupted agricultural systems and trade. A second argument is that the colonial era saw an expansion of transportation networks and thus access to a secure supply of food for cities even during crises. The demand created by the growing proletarian workforce on plantations, at mines, and in the cities stimulated an enormous expansion of the production of rice and other foodstuffs for the market. The increase in commercial production meant there was a greater potential for market forces to respond to changes in demand caused by poor harvests in local areas, thus, easing potential cases of crisis mortality. More efficient markets should also have stimulated production that led to high levels of consumption and improved levels of nutrition. Achieving population growth did not depend on lowering mortality as much as on stabilizing mortality at moderate levels and limiting periods of crisis mortality. The modern health/medical sector (i.e., hospitals, doctors, and nurses) gradually developed in most Southeast Asian countries over the first four decades of the twentieth century. Although this was primarily an urban phenomenon, some public health initiatives did reach out to rural populations and reduced the spread of endemic diseases.[70]

In every country of Southeast Asia, the years of World War II were ones of extreme economic hardship. Following the difficult years of the Great Depression, when the export sector declined, the 1940s saw the complete collapse of the mining and plantation sectors. Laborers from the export enclaves and cities migrated to rural areas to become subsistence farmers. Cash crops, the production of which employed a major fraction of the workforce in many countries, lost their international markets. Local incomes plummeted and imported goods, including medicines, were unavailable. All accounts suggest that mortality rose to record levels during the Japanese occupation of Southeast Asia from 1942 to 1945.[71]

The general pattern for postwar Southeast Asia is one of dramatically declining mortality. This was a global trend fueled by political changes (decolonialization), expanded world trade, and new developments in public health and medical knowledge. Until the 1930s, when sulfa drugs were introduced, the ability of medicine to cure disease was limited to first aid and nursing care. On the heels of sulfa drugs came penicillin and other antibiotics in the late 1940s and 1950s. For the first time in history, relatively simple interventions, such as injections, led to dramatic reductions in mortality, especially for infants and children.

---

[70] Peper, "Population Growth in Java," pp. 108–9.

[71] A. J. Stockwell, "Southeast Asia in War and Peace: The End of European Colonial Empires," in *The Cambridge History of Southeast Asia, Volume Two*, p. 336.

Table 2
Life Expectancy and Fertility Rate by Country,
Estimates from 1950 to 2010 and Projections to 2050 (continued on next page)

	Life Expectancy at Birth			
	1950–55	1960–65	1970–75	1980–85
World	47.7	51.2	58.5	62.1
Asia	42.9	46.4	57.0	61.6
SE Asia	**42.4**	**49.2**	**54.1**	**60.1**
Brunei Darussalam	57.7	63.6	68.0	71.3
Cambodia	39.4	43.4	40.3	48.4
Indonesia	38.8	46.9	53.4	58.8
Laos	42.4	44.5	46.6	49.8
Malaysia	55.4	60.6	64.9	68.1
Myanmar/Burma	36.0	44.1	51.6	55.3
Philippines	55.4	58.6	61.4	63.7
Singapore	60.2	66.4	69.1	72.2
Thailand	50.7	56.6	61.0	67.6
Timor-Leste	30.0	35.0	39.9	39.9
Vietnam	40.4	45.4	47.8	59.0

	Total Fertility Rate			
	1950–55	1960–65	1970–75	1980–85
World	4.95	4.91	4.45	3.59
Asia	5.82	5.59	5.00	3.69
SE Asia	**6.05**	**6.25**	**5.62**	**4.22**
Brunei Darussalam	7.00	6.56	5.87	3.92
Cambodia	6.29	6.29	5.54	7.00
Indonesia	5.49	5.62	5.30	4.11
Laos	5.94	5.97	5.99	6.36
Malaysia	6.23	6.23	4.58	3.73
Myanmar/Burma	6.00	6.10	5.90	4.30
Philippines	7.42	6.98	5.98	4.92
Singapore	6.61	5.12	2.82	1.59
Thailand	6.14	6.13	5.05	2.95
Timor-Leste	6.44	6.37	5.54	5.39
Vietnam	6.20	7.33	7.15	4.93

The other postwar development that affected patterns of mortality was the spread of massive public health campaigns. DDT spraying in the late 1940s and 1950s helped reduce the incidence of malaria. There were also large-scale programs to inoculate school children against most of the major childhood endemic diseases. These innovations were often first sponsored by international agencies, but soon became part of national health programs throughout Southeast Asia. The rapid decline of mortality in the second half of the twentieth century is evident in the

Table 2 (continued from previous page)
Life Expectancy and Fertility Rate by Country,
Estimates from 1950 to 2010 and Projections to 2050[72]

| | Life Expectancy at Birth (cont.) | | | Projected | |
	1990–95	2000–05	2010–15	2025–30	2045–50
World	64.4	66.4	69.3	72.4	75.6
Asia	64.9	67.6	70.4	72.7	76.7
SE Asia	**64.9**	**68.0**	**71.1**	**74.8**	**78.0**
Brunei Darussalam	74.2	76.7	78.2	79.9	81.7
Cambodia	55.8	58.8	63.7	69.5	73.3
Indonesia	63.1	66.4	70.1	74.3	76.8
Laos	56.3	62.8	67.9	72.4	75.5
Malaysia	70.6	72.5	74.6	77.1	79.1
Myanmar/Burma	58.8	62.4	66.0	71.1	74.6
Philippines	65.8	67.1	69.2	72.5	75.5
Singapore	76.8	79.4	81.3	83.0	84.7
Thailand	72.3	72.9	74.4	76.9	78.9
Timor-Leste	48.6	58.2	63.2	69.1	73.1
Vietnam	67.9	73.1	75.5	78.0	79.9

| | Total Fertility Rate (cont.) | | | Projected | |
	1990–95	2000–05	2010–15	2025–30	2045–50
World	3.04	2.62	2.45	2.29	2.17
Asia	2.97	2.41	2.18	1.99	1.88
SE Asia	**3.11**	**2.45**	**2.13**	**1.90**	**1.83**
Brunei Darussalam	3.28	2.28	1.98	1.73	1.66
Cambodia	5.44	3.41	2.42	1.86	1.62
Indonesia	2.90	2.38	2.06	1.79	1.71
Laos	5.88	3.70	2.54	1.88	1.60
Malaysia	3.42	2.96	2.57	2.24	1.97
Myanmar/Burma	3.10	2.25	1.94	1.68	1.65
Philippines	4.14	3.70	3.05	2.56	2.14
Singapore	1.84	1.33	1.37	1.63	1.84
Thailand	1.99	1.68	1.53	1.47	1.70
Timor-Leste	5.69	6.96	5.92	4.20	2.77
Vietnam	3.23	1.93	1.75	1.56	1.71

United Nations estimates of life expectancy at birth, presented in the top panel of Table 2. The figures for the twenty-first century are projections, assuming that current trends continue.

---

[72] United Nations, *World Population Prospects, the 2010 Revision.*

The decline in mortality over the post–World War II era has been remarkable, even breathtaking. In the early 1950s, life expectancy for Southeast Asia as a whole was a little over 40 years—well below Western standards, and even below the world average.[73] The achievements in preventative health care and curative medicine in Southeast Asia in subsequent decades were phenomenal. By the turn of the twenty-first century, life expectancy in Southeast Asia was just short of 70 years—a gain of more than 5 years of life per decade from 1950 to 2000. In the early twentieth century, mortality in the region was lower (better) than for the world as whole. These trends are projected to continue, with a life expectancy of 78 years by the middle of the twenty-first century expected.

The exceptional cases of Singapore, a modern city-state, and Brunei, a tiny oil-rich welfare state, had first-world levels of longevity for the entire period—60 in the early 1950s and over 80 in the early twenty-first century. The rest of Southeast Asia can be roughly divided into two groups of countries—those with relatively well-developed public health programs and hospitals and those with a minimal health infrastructure beyond the largest cities. The first group of countries—Malaysia, Thailand, and the Philippines—had moderate levels of mortality in the 1950s with life expectancies in the high 40s or low 50s. All three countries experienced continued gains and currently have life expectancies from 69 in the Philippines to 74 in Malaysia.

Thailand's mortality transition—the decline from high to low mortality—is an anomaly. With a life expectancy of about 52 in the early 1950s, Thailand made remarkable progress in reducing mortality over the next three decades and achieved a life expectancy of about 68 in the 1980s. In spite of rapid socioeconomic progress and a very good health infrastructure, life expectancy in Thailand appears to have stalled since the mid-1980s. A recent study suggests that the slow progress in reducing mortality in Thailand may be primarily due to a rise in the number of deaths among young men in the 1990s both on account of HIV-AIDS and motorcycle accidents.[74]

The second group of countries, including Cambodia, Laos, Indonesia, Myanmar, and Vietnam, had much higher mortality immediately following World War II than did the more developed countries in the region. This second group had life expectancies in the low 40s in the 1950s—about 10 years lower than the first group of countries. In addition to much lower levels of economic development, some of these countries were devastated during World War II and experienced protracted wars of independence in the late 1940s and early 1950s, which may account for the lower life expectancy.

Two of the largest of these very poor countries, however, have since experienced dramatic gains in longevity. In Indonesia, life expectancy rose about 30 years, from around 39 in the early 1950s to 70 in the early twenty-first century. Corresponding figures for Vietnam were 40 and 75. Gains in longevity of 6 to 7 years per decade are a remarkable achievement. During the twenty-year period from the early 1970s to the early 1990s, life expectancy increased by 8.75 years per decade—almost a one-year

---

[73] Life expectancy was forty years or less in most of Southeast Asia—except for the Philippines, Malaysia, and Thailand, where life expectancy was in the high 40s or low 50s, and Singapore, where life expectancy was 60.

[74] Kenneth Hill, Patama Vapattanawong, Pramote Prasartkul, et al., "Epidemiologic Transition Interrupted: A Reassessment of Mortality Trends in Thailand, 1980–2000," *International Journal of Epidemiology* 36 (2007): 374–84.

gain in average longevity in each calendar year. Over this period, Vietnam has gone from a country with one of the highest mortality figures in the region to longevity levels comparable to those of developed countries. Investments in health care and socioeconomic progress can make a huge contribution to the decline in mortality.

The poorest countries in the region—Cambodia, Laos, Myanmar, and Timor-Leste—have the highest mortality in Southeast Asia. They have made progress, albeit uneven, over the last half of the twentieth century, but still have life expectancies in the mid-60s. There are periods of improvement and stagnation in each country. Life expectancy was only 40 in Cambodia in the mid-1970s, three years lower than in the 1960s. The killing fields of the murderous Khmer Rouge regime left their mark. There was no progress with respect to mortality (and perhaps an increase in the death rate) in Timor-Leste from the mid-1970s to the mid-1980s. This period coincides with the conquest and occupation of Timor-Leste by Indonesia following Portuguese decolonization.

Data on sex differentials with regard to life expectancy (data reported in the UN volume, but not shown here), show that females have lower mortality than do men at all ages in every country in the region. While some fraction of the female advantage in longevity is certainly biological, it is true for every society that gender differences in behavior and environmental influences account for much of this phenomenon. The single most important behavioral factor for male-female differences in mortality in most societies is smoking, but accidents (e.g., on motorcycles) and other risky behaviors may also be contributing factors.[75]

THE FERTILITY TRANSITION IN SOUTHEAST ASIA

High fertility was a functional necessity in most traditional societies, including Southeast Asia. Under conditions of high mortality, high fertility is required to maintain a population. Demographic theory suggests that most preindustrial populations were conditioned to maintain a loose, homeostatic balance of demographic size within the productive capacity of the environment, social organization, and prevailing technology of food production.[76] In most cases, mortality is thought to have been the equilibrating mechanism, but practices that limited fertility may also have been important. For example, many preindustrial populations limited fertility through a variety of social mechanisms that were culturally sanctioned. Cultural norms about age at marriage, divorce, remarriage after widowhood or divorce, duration of breastfeeding, periods of sexual abstinence, and spousal separation are all part of the cultural repertoire of keeping fertility at moderate levels in societies where resources are limited.

In preindustrial Europe, delayed marriage and celibacy emerged as social mechanisms to constrain the potential growth of populations. In Southeast Asia, youthful marriage seems to have been universal (or almost so). Women did not necessarily marry at puberty, but the typical range was probably between 15 and 21

[75] Ibid.; Alan Lopez and Lado Ruzicka, eds., *Sex Differentials in Mortality: Trends, Determinants, and Consequences* (Canberra: Department of Demography, Australian National University, 1983).

[76] E. A. Wrigley, *Population and History* (New York, NY: McGraw Hill, 1969); Ronald D. Lee, "Population Dynamics of Humans and Other Animals," *Demography* 24 (1987): 443–65; Charles Hirschman, "Why Fertility Changes?" *Annual Review of Sociology* 20 (1994): 203–33.

years.[77] Other cultural patterns, including frequent divorce (in the Malay world and Java) and a long duration of breastfeeding may have reduced fertility to moderate levels.[78] Mark VanLandingham and Charles Hirschman[79] found a systematic relationship between population density and fertility in pretransition Thailand (prior to the decline of fertility in the 1970s). Although fertility was high everywhere, it was considerably higher in frontier (low density) regions. They argue that cultural patterns that reduced fertility, such as delayed marriage, periods of sexual abstinence, and spousal absence in long-settled regions, may have been relaxed among migrants to frontier regions.

Systematic data on fertility were not collected in Southeast Asia until questions about the actual number of children born (regardless of their survival) first appeared in censuses and surveys in the 1940s and 1950s. Data for the oldest women in these censuses offer some information about traditional fertility levels. Older women, however, are somewhat prone to understate their total number of live births— children who died early in infancy or were given up for adoption are not always reported. Another problem is that the 1930s and 1940s may well have been a period of below-average fertility because of the Great Depression and World War II. Nonetheless, the available figures offer some evidence of traditional high-fertility levels for Southeast Asia.

In a 1952 survey of four towns in Burma (Myanmar), women aged 49 and older had borne, on average, 6.1 children.[80] The earliest fertility surveys in Thailand reported a cumulative fertility measure of almost 7 births per woman.[81] A much lower range of 4.3 to 4.5 births per woman was reported by older Malay women in the 1947 census of colonial Malaya.[82] Peter Smith[83] estimates a crude birth rate in the high 40s to low 50s for the Philippines around the turn of the century.

These measures of completed fertility (total number of births per woman) are consistent with total fertility rates (TFR) measured worldwide for the 1950s, estimated by the United Nations (see the lower panel of Table 2). The TFR represents the total number of children the average woman would give birth to, assuming her lifetime fertility follows the age-specific fertility rates observed in a single calendar year (or group of years). The TFR indexes in Southeast Asia countries in the 1950s were very high—around 6 births per woman, ranging from a high of 7.3 in the

---

[77] Reid, *Southeast Asia in an Age of Commerce*, p. 160.

[78] Masri Singarimbun and Chris Manning, "Marriage and Divorce in Mojolama," *Indonesia* 17 (April 1974): 67–85; Gavin Jones, "Malay Marriage and Divorce in Peninsular Malaysia: Three Decades of Change," *Population and Development Review* 1 (1981): 255–79; Knodel et al., *Thailand's Reproductive Revolution: Rapid Fertility Decline in a Third-World Setting*.

[79] VanLandingham and Hirschman, "Population Pressure and Fertility in Pre-Transition Thailand."

[80] Philip M. Hauser and Evelyn M. Kitagawa, "Demographic Glimpses into Burma, 1952," in *Demographic Analysis: Selected Readings*, ed. Joseph J. Spengler and Otis Dudley Duncan (Glencoe, IL: Free Press, 1956), pp. 760–83.

[81] Knodel et al., *Thailand's Reproductive Revolution*, p. 58.

[82] Charles Hirschman and Dorothy Fernandez, "The Decline of Fertility in Peninsular Malaysia," *Genus* 36 (1980): 118.

[83] Peter C. Smith, "The Turn of the Century Birth Rate: Estimates from Birth Registration and Age Structure," in *A Demographic Path to Modernity: Patterns of Early Transition in the Philippines*, ed. Wilhelm Flieger and Peter C. Smith (Quezon City: University of the Philippines Press, 1975), pp. 82–90.

Philippines to a low of 5.5 in Indonesia. With the exception of Singapore, there was no sign of declining fertility in Southeast Asia in the 1950s and 1960s.

During the 1970s and 1980s, there were unmistakable signs of fertility transitions in most countries.[84] For the region as a whole, the TFR declined from 6.2 in the 1960s to 4.2 in the 1980s. By the mid-1980s, fertility was below replacement level (less than 2) in Singapore.[85] Within Singapore, the three main ethnic groups, Malays, Chinese, and Indians, had below-replacement-level fertility in the 1980s.[86] Although Singapore, as a large city–state, is a special case, there were remarkable declines (1.5 to 2 births) in many Southeast Asian countries as well. Fertility declined by 3 births in Thailand. Compared with industrial countries, fertility was still moderately high in Southeast Asia in the 1980s, with about 4 births per woman (3 in Thailand), but these levels were dramatically lower than those of a couple of decades earlier.

From the 1990s to the early twenty-first century, fertility continued to decline throughout Southeast Asia, though the pace of decline varied considerably. Thailand was the pacesetter, joining the ranks of countries with below-replacement fertility in the years 2000–05 (TFR of 1.7).[87] Several other countries in Southeast Asia were only a step or two behind Thailand.[88] Singapore has an almost unbelievable TFR of 1.3 births per woman. Other major countries in the region, including Vietnam, Indonesia, Myanmar, and Malaysia, had TFRs below or just above replacement level. The rapid declines in Vietnam and Myanmar are particularly impressive, given the slower pace of development in these countries.[89] The trend toward declining fertility has been slower to come about in the Philippines than in the rest of Southeast Asia. The Philippines TFR remains at 3.1 in the early twenty-first century.

At the beginning of the second decade of the twenty-first century, the United Nations estimates overall fertility (the TFR) in Southeast Asia to be between 2.1 and 2.2. A fertility rate of just above two births per woman is considered to be the replacement level. The overall regional estimate rests on assumptions that fertility in Indonesia and Vietnam continue to decline. The United Nations projects that fertility in other Southeast Asian countries, including the Philippines and Cambodia, will reach replacement level in the next few decades.

---

[84] Also see the chapter by Hull in this volume.

[85] "Replacement level" refers to sufficient progeny for the replacement of the mother and father in the next generation.

[86] Gavin W. Jones, "Fertility Transitions among Malay Populations of Southeast Asia: Puzzles of Interpretation," *Population and Development Review* 16 (September 1990): 513.

[87] Charles Hirschman, JooEan Tan, Aphichat Chamratrithirong, et al., "The Path to Below-Replacement Fertility in Thailand," *International Family Planning Perspectives*, 20,3 (September 1994).

[88] Charles Hirschman and Philip Guest, "The Emerging Demographic Transitions of Southeast Asia," *Population and Development Review* 16 (1990): 121–52; John C. Caldwell, "The Asian Fertility Revolution: Its Implications for Transition Theories," in *The Revolution in Asian Fertility: Dimensions, Causes, and Implications*, ed. Richard Leete and Iqbal Alam (Oxford: Clarendon Press, 1993), pp. 299–316.

[89] Nyan Myint, "Recent Levels and Trends of Fertility and Mortality in Myanmar," *Asia-Pacific Population Journal* 6 (1991): 3–20; Daniel Goodkind, "Vietnam's One- or Two-Child Policy in Action," *Population and Development Review* 21 (1995): 85–111.

Interpretations of the Fertility Decline in Southeast Asia

If the current pace of fertility decline continues, replacement-level fertility (just over two children per woman) should be reached early in the twenty-first century in most countries and regions of Southeast Asia. Indeed, if the recent history of East Asia and Singapore is any guide, modern fertility levels may not stop at the replacement level, but continue to decline to a level below that which is needed to replace the parental generation. The explanation for these rapid fertility declines, although hotly debated, is likely to be the complex interplay of rapid socioeconomic change (including access to modern healthcare), organized family planning programs, and spatial and social diffusion processes that vary in significance and intensity over time.

A generation ago, the conventional wisdom was that the postponement of marriage had only contributed modestly to the temporal decline in fertility in Southeast Asia.[90] However, the record high levels of marital postponement (and even non-marriage) suggest that changing patterns of marriage have contributed greatly to low and to ultra-low fertility in several Southeast Asian countries.[91] The most celebrated case is Singapore, where "the flight from marriage" and declining fertility among the highly educated population prompted the government to organize social activities to encourage unmarried persons in their twenties and thirties to marry and have babies.[92]

Young and universal marriage was the historical norm in Southeast Asia, although the Philippines and Myanmar (Burma) may have been exceptions. The trend toward marital postponement throughout the region has prevailed for several decades, but the trend accelerated in the 1980s and 1990s in many countries with predominately rural populations, including the Philippines, Thailand, Malaysia, Vietnam, and Myanmar.[93] In all of these countries, the proportion of women in their early thirties who had not married was in the double digits. The figures for marital postponement are even higher in cities and among those with higher levels of

---

[90] Robert Retherford and Lee-Jay Cho, "Comparative Analysis of Recent Fertility Trends in East Asia," in *International Population Conference*, Volume 2 (Liege: International Union for the Scientific Study of Population, 1973), pp. 163–81; Hirschman and Guest, "The Emerging Demographic Transitions of Southeast Asia," pp. 121–52.

[91] Gavin Jones, "Not 'When to Marry' but 'Whether to Marry': The Changing Context of Marriage Decisions in East and Southeast Asia," in *(Un)tying the Knot: Ideal and Reality in Asian Marriage*, ed. Gavin W. Jones and Kamali Ramdas (Singapore: Asian Research Institute, National University of Singapore, 2004); Gavin Jones, "The 'Flight From Marriage' in Southeast and East Asia," *Journal of Comparative Family Studies* 36 (2005): 93–119. See also the chapter by Jones and Gubhaju in this volume.

[92] Richard Leete, "The Continuing Flight from Marriage and Parenthood among the Overseas Chinese in East and Southeast Asia: Dimensions and Implications," *Population and Development Review* 20 (1994): 815; Mui-Teng Yap, "Singapore's 'Three or More' Policy: The First Five Years," *Asia-Pacific Population Journal* 10 (1995): 39–52.

[93] Gavin W Jones, "Population and Family in Southeast Asia," *Journal of Southeast Asian Studies* 26 (1994): 184–95; Gavin W. Jones, "The Demise of Universal Marriage in East and South-East Asia," in *The Continuing Demographic Transition*, ed. G. W. Jones, R. M. Douglas, J. C. Caldwell, et al., (Oxford: Clarendon Press, 1997), pp. 51–79; Jones, "Not 'When to Marry' but 'Whether to Marry"; Jones, "The 'Flight From Marriage.'"

education. In several countries of Southeast Asia, the average age at marriage of both women and men is above age 25, which is higher than in some Western countries.

The changes in marriage systems are remarkable given that universal marriage and marriage at a young age were the historical norm. It appears that access to and expansion of secondary (and tertiary) education has been the primary factor leading to later marriage (especially for women, but men are also affected). With the postponement of marriage, there also appears to have been a disruption in traditional matchmaking customs. Another hypothesis is that some highly educated men in Southeast Asia may prefer to marry women with lower educational attainment because they are considered to be more likely to follow traditional gender norms than are highly educated women. Although there is likely to be an adjustment in marriage patterns before high levels of celibacy are reached, the current pattern of marital postponement is likely to accelerate the downward trend in fertility in most Southeast Asian countries

The initial declines in fertility in the 1970s and 1980s were driven by lower marital fertility because of a widespread adoption of modern contraception. In the absence of increased contraception, other social changes, including declines in spousal mortality and reduced duration of breastfeeding, would probably have led to an increase in marital fertility.

There are two interpretations of the widespread adoption of contraception and rapid fertility declines in Southeast Asia—the efficacy of family planning programs and the rapid pace of socioeconomic change. These explanations are not alternative paradigms, but complementary emphases. In their classic study of Thailand's reproductive revolution, John Knodel and colleagues conclude that the rapid pace of fertility decline in Thailand was due to a combination of four factors: rapid social and economic development, a favorable cultural setting (female autonomy and weak intergenerational influences in reproductive decisions), a desire for fewer children, and an effective national family planning program.[94] The challenge for the field has been to test the relative significance of these explanatory factors in different times and places. At present, the research record points to a broad mosaic of patterns and causes and no simple overarching interpretation.

The fundamental prerequisite for declining fertility is declining mortality, especially declines in infant and child mortality.[95] In Southeast Asia, mortality declines began in the decade after World War II, as antibiotics, other aspects of modern medicine, and preventive health programs were introduced and spread in many Southeast Asian countries. According to demographic transition theory, declines in mortality and other aspects of socioeconomic change are predicted to increase pressures on families and married couples to lower their desired number of children and to increase their "demand" for family planning.

Impressionistic evidence would suggest that governmentally sponsored family-planning programs have been the major reason for rising contraceptive use in Thailand, Indonesia, and other Southeast Asian countries with declining fertility. Family-planning programs were instituted in many Southeast Asian countries in the 1970s, at about the same time that fertility began to edge downward in the region. Several authors have attributed the decline of fertility in Indonesia to a successful

---

[94] Knodel et al., *Thailand's Reproductive Revolution*.

[95] Hirschman and Guest, "Emerging Demographic Transitions of Southeast Asia," pp. 121–52.

family-planning program there,[96] and some observers attribute the slower declines in fertility in Malaysia and the Philippines to relatively less-energetic family-planning programs in those countries. These conjectures, however, are very difficult to evaluate empirically because the emergence and characteristics of family-planning programs are correlated with other determinants of fertility decline, most notably socioeconomic development.

Perhaps the single most important cultural characteristic of Southeast Asia is the relatively high status of women, especially when compared to East Asia and South Asia.[97] While women still face many socioeconomic obstacles in Southeast Asia, the situation there is quite different from the patriarchal societies of East and South Asia. Southeast Asian kinship systems are typically bilateral, with equal importance attached to the husband's and wife's families. With the possible exception of Vietnam, there is no strong sex preference for children in Southeast Asia,[98] nor are there strong prescriptions on residence with the groom's family after marriage. Cultural variables are difficult to quantify, especially at the micro level, which makes it a challenge to estimate their relative roles in shaping fertility levels and change. But it seems likely that greater freedom for women to pursue nonfamilial roles and to influence household decision-making have been important factors in the region's rapid fertility decline.

Using econometric techniques to control for the endogenous role of family-planning inputs, Paul Gertler and John Molyneaux find that almost all of the decline in fertility in Indonesia between 1982 and 1987 was due to rising incomes and levels of education and that very little of the fertility decline could be attributed directly to family-planning efforts.[99] These findings do not rule out the interpretation that the Indonesian family-planning programs played an important role through the provision of readily available means of fertility control (and at a modest cost) for women who were already motivated to limit the number of children they would have, which is what Warren Robinson and Jawalaksana Rachapaetayakom[100] argue was the major role of the Thai family-planning program. Family-planning programs may play a more influential role in the origins of a fertility transition than on its continuation.

---

[96] Ronald Freedman, Siew-Ean Khoo, and Bondan Supraptilah, "Use of Modern Contraceptives in Indonesia: A Challenge to the Conventional Wisdom," *International Family Planning Perspectives* 7,1 (March 1981): 3–15; Terence H. Hull, Valerie J. Hull, and Masri Singarimbun, "Indonesia's Family Planning Story: Success and Challenge," *Population Bulletin* 32 (1977), Washington, DC, Population Reference Bureau; John Ross and S. Poedjastoerti, "Contraceptive Use and Program Development: New Information from Indonesia," *International Family Planning Perspectives* 9 (1983): 68–77.

[97] Reid, *Southeast Asia in the Age of Commerce*; Penny Van Esterik, *Women of Southeast Asia* (Dekalb, IL: Center for Southeast Asian Studies, Northern Illinois University, 1982).

[98] Kua Wongboonsin and Vipan Prachuabmoh Ruffolo, "Sex Preference for Children in Thailand and Other Southeast Asian Countries," *Asia-Pacific Population Journal* 10 (1995): 43–62.

[99] Paul J.Gertler and John W. Molyneaux, "How Economic Development and Family Planning Programs Combined to Reduce Indonesian Fertility," *Demography* 31 (1994): 33–63.

[100] Warren C. Robinson and Jawalaksana Rachapaetayakom, "The Role of Government Planning in Thailand's Fertility Decline," in *The Revolution in Asian Fertility: Dimensions, Causes, and Implications*, ed. Richard Leete and Iqbal Alam (Oxford: Clarendon Press, 1993), pp. 54–66.

Pavalavalli Govindasamy and Julie DaVanzo[101] conclude that public policies, other than family-planning programs, have been more influential in promoting more rapid fertility declines among the Chinese and Indian populations than among the Malay population of Malaysia during the 1970s and 1980s. The Malaysian government provided educational and economic subsidies (as part of an affirmative-action program) for Malays that reduced the costs of having and rearing children in a rapidly modernizing society. Richard Leete[102] adds the additional interpretation that Malay fertility has remained high because of the resurgence of Islam and pronatalist cultural values. There are, however, quite wide variations in levels and trends of Malay fertility between Singapore and Malaysia and across states in Malaysia, which raise questions about a simple cultural or religious preference for high fertility.[103]

In an innovative study, John Bryant[104] compares the trend in the actual levels of fertility in individual countries from 1950 to 2000 (based on the United Nations estimates) with the fertility levels predicted by development indicators (GDP, life expectancy, and educational enrollments). He finds that the sharp downward trend in fertility in many Southeast Asian countries parallels the rapid socioeconomic development of the region.[105] However, the actual downward trend was even sharper than that predicted by development indicators in Singapore, Thailand, Indonesia, and Vietnam. In Malaysia, the downward trend in fertility was very similar to that predicted by development, while in the Philippines, the fertility transition lagged behind the pace of development. These findings suggest that the impact of family-planning programs or other external factors may explain variations in the pace of fertility declines in the region.

POPULATION AND SOCIAL CHANGE IN SOUTHEAST ASIA

Demographic patterns and trends are important indicators for at least two reasons. First, they reveal the basic "facts" about central aspects of human societies. The sizes of families, cities, and countries, as well as their composition and geographical distribution, are critical aspects of the environment for individuals and for international relations. Demography does not determine destiny, but population size and structure do influence opportunities, pressures, and constraints. The rapid growth of Southeast Asian populations in the second half of the twentieth century created exceptional demand for education and health services and also put pressures on labor and housing markets. It appears that most Southeast Asian countries have been able to weather these demographic pressures and even raise per capita levels of well-being during the era of exceptionally rapid growth.

---

[101] Pavalavalli Govindasamy and Julie DaVanzo, "Ethnicity and Fertility Differentials in Peninsular Malaysia: Do Policies Matter?" *Population and Development Review* 18 (1992): 243–67.

[102] Richard Leete, "The Continuing Flight from Marriage and Parenthood among the Overseas Chinese in East and Southeast Asia: Dimensions and Implications," *Population and Development Review* 20 (1994): 811–29.

[103] Charles Hirschman, "The Recent Rise in Malay Fertility: A New Trend or a Temporary Lull in a Fertility Transition?" *Demography* 23 (1986): 161–84; Gavin W. Jones, "Fertility Transitions Among Malay Populations of Southeast Asia: Puzzles of Interpretation," *Population and Development Review* 16 (1990): 507–37.

[104] John Bryant, "Theories of Fertility Decline and the Evidence from Development Indicators," *Population and Development Review* 31 (2007): 101–27.

[105] Ibid., figure 1a.

Although population growth in Southeast Asia has slowed and is likely to approach zero sometime in the mid- to late twenty-first century, the legacy of the twentieth-century's growth eras has created huge national populations in many countries in the region. This is particularly important in the international context when the earlier modernization of Europe (and the West, more generally) sparked demographic transitions in the early twentieth century and much slower population growth in economically advanced regions. Large populations, especially poor ones with little human capital, are not considered to be an economic or even a military resource in the modern world. However, more pervasive and low-cost transportation and communications systems mean that even distant populations can be considered as potential workers and customers for international businesses. The increasing international prominence of Southeast Asia is partially due to its growing demographic weight.

Second, demographic indicators provide a window to social change. The study of twentieth-century demographic change in Southeast Asia, and how the population of the region grew from 80 million in 1900 to nearly 600 million in little more than a century, reflects the impact of political, economic, and social forces on the everyday lives of people in the region via mortality and fertility rates. Since fertility rates in Southeast Asia remained relatively high and stable until the 1970s and 1980s, the key reason for population growth rates of 1 percent (or higher) was likely due to lowered mortality.

There are two components of high mortality. First, there is "normal" high mortality, which is caused by chronic conditions, including endemic disease, poor sanitation, and an undernourished population. The other aspect of high mortality is periodic bouts of crisis mortality caused by epidemics, famines, and wars. During periods of "normal" high mortality, populations can and do continue to grow, if fertility levels are also high. In fact, many preindustrial agrarian societies had rates of population growth of 1 percent or greater for long periods. The accumulated demographic growth from these normal times is often wiped out during periods of crisis mortality, when deaths exceed births for a sustained period of time. Periods of population decline are generally shorter than eras of growth, but a severe plague, a lost harvest, or a war can reverse decades, or even centuries, of slow population growth.

In the nineteenth and twentieth centuries, mortality levels in Europe and Southeast Asia were undergoing change. In both Europe and Southeast Asia, there was a reduction in the frequency of crisis mortality episodes (the 1944–1945 famine in Vietnam was an exception). In Europe, economic growth and modernization began to produce lower levels of "normal" mortality as well through improved levels of nutrition, urban sanitation, and some aspects of better health care. Even without a reduction in "normal" mortality in Southeast Asia (and the available evidence suggests little reduction), the decline in the frequency of crisis mortality episodes seems to have sparked an era of fairly rapid population growth beginning in the nineteenth century and continuing through the twentieth.

The reason that rapid population growth continued (even with crude death rates of 20 to 25) was that fertility remained high throughout Southeast Asia until the 1970s. Here is where the contrast with Europe becomes instructive. In mid-nineteenth-century Europe, before fertility levels began to decline, European fertility was only moderately high, with total fertility rates of 4 or 5 births per woman, which was well below Southeast Asia's high fertility of 6 or more births per woman. As mortality was declining in Europe in the late nineteenth and early twentieth centuries, fertility also began to decline, reaching replacement levels in many countries by the 1930s.[106] Even though European population growth continued, it did so at moderate levels; witness the moderate expansion of only 60 percent for the century.

In Southeast Asia, fertility levels remained high for another 50 to 70 years. Southeast Asian fertility transitions may have been delayed by the policies of European imperialism. The noted demographer Irene Taeuber[107] observed that "the natural dynamics of colonialism lowered mortality (but) perpetuated high fertility. Colonial policy did not favor the industrialization, urbanization, and advancing education that were associated historically with declining fertility among Western peoples. Insofar as the partial diffusion of the Western economy and society influenced fertility of the East it tended toward increase rather than decrease."[108]

The colonial order tended to reinforce traditional society as the ideal for the rural peasantry. It was not just colonial ideology but colonial policies that slowed socioeconomic change and modernization. Only a small minority of the population in colonial Southeast Asia was able to obtain more than primary level schooling and to participate in the modern urban economy. The net result was that modern incentives for lowered fertility did not reach the bulk of the population. The opportunities for innovation in the rural-sector movement to the frontier or in planting cash crops were labor intensive activities that reinforced the family economy. More children meant more family labor and potentially more income. In spite of 50 to 100 years of continued population growth, high fertility was a rational response to the circumstances prevailing until the end of colonialism in the post–World War II era.

The rapidity of the decline of fertility from the 1970s to the 1990s is due to a number of factors, including the population pressure created by reduced infant and child mortality from the 1950s onward. Even within the context of the rural family economy, there might well have been a slow demographic response of lower fertility as the limits of land and production were strained by families of four to six surviving children. But the fertility declines were accelerated by the forces of modernization: mass education, growing consumer aspirations, and prospects for modern sector employment also contributed to a weakening of incentives for large families. The costs of having and raising children were felt and had to be weighed against alternatives. The availability of family-planning programs was another factor that combined with these structural incentives to bring fertility down more rapidly than expected.[109]

The consequences of population growth on society are more difficult to assess. The Malthusian perspective of a race between population, on the one hand, and food, resources, and living space, on the other, is always incomplete and often a misleading interpretation of the relationship between population numbers and social change. The impact of population growth on society must be understood within a

---

[106] Ansley Coale and Susan Cotts Watkins, eds., *The Decline of Fertility in Europe* (Princeton, NJ: Princeton University Press, 1986).

[107] Irene Taeuber, "Population Growth in Southeast Asia," p. 756.

[108] Daniel Chirot, *Social Change in the Modern Era* (San Diego, CA: Harcourt Brace Jovanivich, 1986), p. 175.

[109] Knodel et al., *Thailand's Reproductive Revolution*.

broad perspective that includes conflicts between resources, obligations, and aspirations within households, communities, and the society at large. Throughout most of Southeast Asian history, the primary population problem has been one of a labor shortage. The high levels of "normal" mortality meant that many households and small settlements were perpetually at risk of losing the minimum supply of labor necessary to maintain their subsistence economy. Traditional local elites always needed more manpower to wage war or produce an economic surplus. Moreover, the demand for cheap labor for export-sector industries accelerated during the colonial era.

Rapid population growth in the late nineteenth and early twentieth centuries certainly created demographic pressures in some areas with limited agricultural land and productivity. Rapid population growth has the potential to double populations in local areas in 35 to 70 years (the first figure is based on annual growth rates of 2 percent and the second figure assumes a 1 percent annual growth rate). In many areas, migration was a more likely response than lowered fertility. Given the large expanse of uncultivated areas, movement to frontier areas became a widespread pattern in late nineteenth and early twentieth-century Southeast Asia. The creation of new zones of wet-rice production in lower Burma, central Siam, and Cochinchina was a response to the growing demand for rice. The settlement of these areas would not have been possible without the availability of "surplus" labor from already densely settled areas that were strained by continued population growth.

While migration was one response, it was not an option that was available or attractive to many peasants. The relatively elastic productive limits of wet-rice agriculture meant that additional labor could be used to prepare the fields, maintain the irrigation system, weed the fields, and harvest each rice stalk.[110] In such an environment, infinite subdivision of plots of land and multiple job holding in the off-season are common strategies to maintain a minimal standard of survival. Densely settled communities also seem to have lower fertility than sparsely settled areas or transitional frontier areas. Central and east Java, and the rice bowl of Kedah and Perils, have historically had low fertility. It may not be conscious family planning but, rather, patterns of high divorce, long breastfeeding, or sexual abstinence that are the social mechanisms that restrain population growth in such circumstances. More detailed research is needed to explain how these processes evolved and were reinforced by cultural traditions.

The consequences of population growth should be strongest for the post–World War II era. During the last 30 to 40 years, growth rates have regularly exceeded 2 percent and sometimes 3 percent per year. Yet it is difficult to point to specific outcomes that are unambiguously a response to population pressure at the household or community level. Pressures on the absorptive capacity of schools and labor markets have surely been strained. The increase in the number of the "underemployed" (those without productive economic roles or in marginal employment) is due, at least to some degree, to the increasing number of youth reaching adulthood over the last 15 to 25 years.[111]

---

[110] Geertz, *Agricultural Involution*; Anne Booth, "Accommodating a Growing Population in Javanese Agriculture," *Bulletin of Indonesian Economic Studies* 21 (1985): 115–45.

[111] Hugo et al., *The Demographic Dimension*, ch. 8.

Perhaps the most visible demographic response over the last two decades has been the sharp decline in fertility throughout the region. In societies where there are no cultural barriers to family planning, and contraceptives are widely available (e.g., Thailand), fertility has dropped from high (6 to 7 births per woman) to low (fewer than 2 children per woman) levels in a single generation. With similar demographic and economic pressures in other societies, it seems that low fertility spread throughout the region in the late twentieth century. An important explanation for lowered fertility has been the postponement of marriage. High levels of educational attainment and labor-force participation by women have caused a dramatic rise in women's average age at marriage in many Southeast Asian countries.

The rapid demographic transitions in Southeast Asia over the last few decades have probably accelerated because of favorable socioeconomic trends, including rising educational levels and above-average rates of economic growth. There are reciprocal influences, with small families easing pressures on family budgets and allowing more investment in human capital and savings. This "demographic dividend" (a virtuous circle) is neither inevitable nor permanent. Periodic economic downturns and the growth of an elderly population with few adult children may well squeeze family budgets and savings in the coming decades.

Another major question is the future of traditional marriage. With signs that 10 to 15 percent of women may never marry, and even higher percentages among highly educated women in urban areas, the traditional norm of universal marriage is likely to weaken in Southeast Asia. Western societies have adapted to the decline in marriages by tolerating unmarried couples' cohabitation arrangements and childless relationships. Historically, Western societies have also experienced moderately high levels of celibacy. Continued research on demographic patterns and trends will provide a leading indicator of cultural change in Southeast Asia.

CHAPTER 2

FERTILITY IN SOUTHEAST ASIA

Terence H. Hull

The group of eleven countries under the heading of "South-Eastern Asia" in United Nations data and documents is a modern construction. In many ways it is more a statistical convenience than political, economic, or social reality. Academic reference to the region most often refers to Southeast Asia, and the political unit formed in 1967 encompassing most countries in the region is called ASEAN, or the Association of Southeast Asian Nations. Timor-Leste is the only regional nation not yet a full member of ASEAN, but it does have observer status. In short, while Southeast Asia is better known for its internal variety than cohesive similarities, it does have a strong identity both within and outside its boundaries. The distinctiveness of Southeast Asian history and culture is central to an understanding of the levels and trends of fertility in the last half century and the prospects for fertility change in the future.

"Before the Second World War, all but one of the eleven countries that today make up Southeast Asia were ruled by colonial powers."[1] Burma (Myanmar), Malaysia (and Singapore), and Brunei were under British rule. Cambodia, Laos, and Vietnam were grouped as Indochina and under French control. The Philippines was ruled from Spain for centuries, only to be taken over by the United States before finally gaining independence in 1945. The whole of Indonesia was administered by Holland as the Netherlands East Indies, home to hundreds of distinct ethnic groups settled across thousands of islands. Sharing one of those islands was Portuguese-controlled East Timor, which was to gain independence only at the dawn of the twenty-first century. Thailand alone was relatively free of European colonial control and was autonomous throughout the twentieth century.

As a region, the eleven nations are notable for disparities in religion, gender roles, education, and governance—all key sociocultural determinants of fertility and demographic structure. Colonialism served to create and consolidate nations. In the process, the new nations institutionalized differences reflecting their dominant religions, ideologies, and worldviews. Each nation is characterized by notions of majoritarianism used to define its state or culture. Indonesia claims to be the largest

---

[1] Milton Osborne, *Exploring Southeast Asia: A Traveller's History of the Region* (Sydney: Allen and Unwin, 2002), p. 6.

national population of Muslims, Thailand's monarchy and national identity is linked to Buddhism, Vietnam and Laos are Communist uniparty states, while Catholicism guides much of the political debate of the Philippines and Timor-Leste.

Southeast Asia is essentially a region with a rich history of coastal trading relationships that tie together societies and precolonial cultural traditions, thus setting Southeast Asians off from the Sinic and Indic cultural groups to the north and west. Prior to the coming of the patriarchal legal structures and traditions introduced by Christianity, Islam, and colonial rulers, nuclear family forms and strong status and roles of women were central to the social structures and indigenous belief systems of the region. Family structures and gender roles differentiated Southeast Asia from the countries of South Asia and East Asia, but these cultural characteristics also formed points of connection and modification when traders, emissaries, and warriors made contact with local rulers and markets dotted along the ports and estuaries of the region. Across hundreds of years, the movements of peoples and flow of ideas change. The protonations of Southeast Asia absorbed practices and beliefs that were at times in conflict. The roles of Southeast Asian women, especially in Indonesia, Malaysia, and the Philippines, reflected a mixture of strength and subservience that remains to the present day.[2] For instance, Javanese tradition invests women with great control over family and often business affairs, but Islamic teachings are interpreted to define their husbands as the head of the household and prime decision maker. This syncretic contradiction provides openings for women to take charge over their reproductive decisions at the same time it formalizes the control of men over the types and timing of contraceptive behavior.

Between 1950 and 2000, the demographic profile of Southeast Asia was steadily shaped by social forces arising out of evolving social and cultural institutions, and out of extreme contrasts of fate as political conflicts rocked the region. Most importantly, formal schooling was promoted by governments who saw the education of the citizenry as the key to economic development. In most countries, girls participated in this innovation almost as much as boys. Initially, primary education, then secondary and tertiary education, had a major impact on the life course of children, reducing the rates of early marriage and in the process delaying and eventually reducing the number of births that women would have.

Waves of armed conflict struck many nations, often with catastrophic results, as in Cambodia, Vietnam, and Timor-Leste. Sometimes persistent local disruption, like the rebellions in Mindanao, Aceh, Papua, Southern Thailand, and Myanmar, distracted central governments from development activities. Inevitably, such conflicts interrupted government social-welfare programs, including family-planning services, at least in the enclaves but sometimes throughout the nation.

As Table 1 shows, the populations of each of the countries rose precipitously between 1950 and 2009. Indonesia was, and still is, the regional giant, accounting for almost 40 percent of the population, while the Philippines, Vietnam, and Thailand each had more than 10 percent, with Myanmar coming up quickly with its fifty million people representing 9 percent of the total. The population projections to the

---

[2] Hildred Geertz, *The Javanese Family—A Study of Kinship and Socialization* (New York, NY: Free Press of Glencoe, 1961); Julia Suryakusuma, "State Ibuism: Appropriating and Distorting Womanhood in New Order Indonesia," in *Sex, Power, and Nation: An Anthology of Writings, 1979–2003*, ed. Julia Suryakusuma (Jakarta: Metaphor Publishing, 2004), pp. 161–88; Julia Suryakusuma, "The State and Sexuality in New Order Indonesia," in *Fantasising the Feminine in Indonesia*, ed. Laurie J. Sears (Durham, NC: Duke University Press, 1996), pp. 92–119.

year 2050 imply that the region as a whole could add another two hundred million in the coming four decades, with much of that growth expected to occur in the island nations of the Philippines and Indonesia.[3] The engines to that growth are the region's different fertility trends and rates, exacerbated by demographic momentum inherited from earlier high fertility.

Table 1
Southeast Asia Population, 1950–2100

	Population (in thousands)						
	1950	2010	2010 (%)	2015	2025	2050	2100
Brunei Darussalam	48	399	0	433	495	602	667
Cambodia	4346	14138	2	15015	16687	18965	16661
Indonesia	74837	239871	40	251880	271851	293456	254178
Laos	1683	6201	1	6628	7429	8384	6956
Malaysia	6110	28401	5	30714	35186	43455	46946
Myanmar	17158	47963	8	49902	53194	55296	46941
Philippines	18397	93261	16	101421	118088	154939	177803
Singapore	1022	5086	1	5375	5801	6106	5659
Thailand	20607	69122	12	70876	72884	71037	58166
Timor-Leste	433	1124	0	1301	1744	3006	4742
Vietnam	28264	87848	15	92443	99335	103962	82604
Southeast Asia	**172905**	**593414**	**100**	**625988**	**682694**	**759208**	**701323**

Source: UNDESA, *World Population Prospects: The 2010 Revision* (New York, NY: United Nations Department of Economic and Social Affairs, 2011), available at http://esa.un.org/unpd/wpp/Excel-Data/population.htm (accessed March 14, 2012).

FERTILITY LEVELS AND TRENDS

Similar to that of the rest of the world, Southeast Asia's history of fertility change over millennia was mainly a story of large family sizes oscillating around an average of 5 to 7 live births per woman, with a small number of children surviving into adulthood. The forces determining short-term increases or declines in population growth tended to reflect periodic changes in weather affecting crop yields or outbreaks of social conflicts disrupting the stability of social institutions. These disrupted both mortality and fertility rates.[4]

The nineteenth century brought major changes to the political and technological environments. Colonialism, irrigation and commercialization of agriculture, improved communications, expansion of central-government powers, and the

---

[3] United Nations (Population Division of the Department of Economic and Social Affairs of the United Nations Secretariat), *World Population Prospects: The 2010 Revision* (New York, NY: United Nations, 2011), http://esa.un.org/unpd/wpp/Excel-Data/population.htm, accessed January 10, 2012.

[4] Peter Boomgaard, *Children of the Colonial State: Population Growth and Economic Development in Java, 1795–1880* (Amsterdam: Free University Press, 1989); David Henley, "Forced Labour and Rising Fertility in Colonial Indonesia," *Asian Population Studies*, 7,1 (2011): 3–13.

ideologies of modernism promoted social efforts to control mortality. Eradicating infectious disease and famine became priority objectives of governments and between 1800 and 1950 national mortality rates fell while extreme mortality events, such as famines and plagues, were tempered. The result was an increase in survivorship and, with fertility rates remaining high, a consequent increase in the numbers of people.

By the mid-twentieth century, governments that had welcomed population growth as a sign of modernity started to see the larger populations as a threat to social welfare and a challenge to any attempt to expand educational and developmental agendas. The population growth was characterized as an explosion, and governments were encouraged to diffuse it through the promotion of contraceptive services. By the late 1960s, most married couples in Southeast Asia were being encouraged by their governments to have small families, and both national and international agencies were investing large sums in the promotion of population control through euphemistically named family-planning programs.

According to the 2010 assessment of fertility trends published by the UN Population Division,[5] all countries in Southeast Asia experienced major fertility declines between 1970 and 2005, but some had large and steady transitions (Singapore, Indonesia, Thailand, Malaysia), others had lethargic declines (Philippines, Malaysia), and a few experienced transitory reversals due to social disruptions (Cambodia, Timor-Leste, Laos). The distinct patterns are pictured in Figure 1. The timing of the decline also varied, from the very early fertility falls of Singapore and Thailand to the much later initiation of decline in Laos and Timor-Leste.

To some degree, the patterns can be related to the structures of governance and the maintenance or otherwise of social tranquility. Nations that had a commitment to democratic development in the second half of the twentieth century tended to build programs promoting both family planning and schooling for girls. In contrast, countries in the midst of armed struggles were forced to divert their resources and attention away from the needs of individual citizens, instead calling on people to sacrifice for the sake of the nation. So we see the patterns of fertility decline following the periods of social peace and development. For all countries, though, the direction of fertility is downward over the long run.

While the dominant paradigm governing fertility in Southeast Asia is the trend toward smaller family sizes in successive generations, there are exceptions related to either transient regimes or religious struggles. The Philippines stands out as a nation caught in a continuous struggle over family-building norms. Often this is characterized as a product of the influence of Roman Catholicism and, particularly, the influence that church leaders wield in shaping the public agenda. Religious references are certainly common in parliamentary and executive-government conflicts, which have crippled family-planning programs.[6] But the experiences of European countries show that a population's majority Roman Catholic belief is not necessarily a barrier to contraceptive use or even to the practice of abortion.

---

[5] United Nations, *World Population Prospects*.

[6] Alejandro N. Herrin, "Development of the Philippines' Family Planning Program: The Early Years, 1967–80," in *The Global Family Planning Revolution: Three Decades of Population Policies and Programs*, ed. Warren C. Robinson and John A. Ross. (Washington, DC: World Bank, 2007).

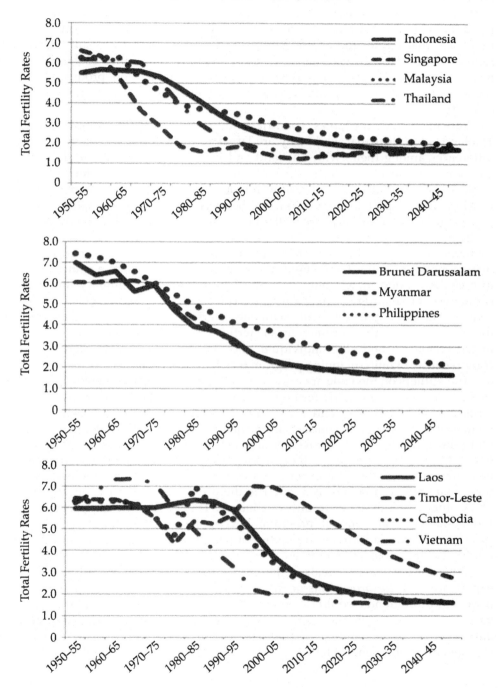

Figure 1
Fertility Transitions in Southeast Asia

Source: UNDESA, *World Population Prospects: The 2010 Revision* (New York, NY:
United Nations Department of Economic and Social Affairs, 2011).

There must be some other factors that intrude on the Philippine experience to hold back family-planning programs and make it difficult for women to access contraception and abortion. Macho cultures, huge disparities in income, and the politics of elite conflict have probably all contributed. It is the convergence of these influences that creates the unique Philippine character, with the result that fertility rates have not declined there as much as in other large countries of the region. For many Filipinos, the idea of a large and growing population producing a huge diaspora is a matter of pride, irrespective of the persistence of poverty in the country.[7]

Looking at the four largest countries—Indonesia, the Philippines, Vietnam, and Thailand—it is clear that while they are largely bunched together, there are distinct differences among them, with Thailand and Indonesia leading the fertility decline, and Vietnam and particularly the Philippines lagging behind. Referring again to Table 1, we see that these apparently minor differences led to a rearrangement of ranking with respect to population size between 1950 and 2009. While Vietnam's population was a third larger than the Philippines' in 1950, today the population of Vietnam is almost 10 percent smaller than that of the Philippines, all because Vietnam's fertility decline was much steeper (though it started at roughly the same time). Observers in the 1960s could never imagine that Vietnam, a country engaged in a civil war, and increasingly hammered by international military interventions, could recover to promote a unitary government with a strong policy of fertility control. Yet this is precisely what happened starting in 1975. The leaders who won the war realized that promotion of fertility control was crucial to economic improvement at both the individual and national levels and embarked on a comprehensive family-planning program to achieve this goal.[8]

The outliers on the table are also the smaller nations, including Singapore, which experienced a dramatic early fertility decline, and Timor-Leste, where a reduction in fertility is just beginning and the result of which remains to be seen. The small nations also display great contrasts in the quantity and quality of demographic data, with Singapore having full coverage and Brunei and Timor-Leste suffering many gaps in fertility data and other demographic indices. Scale is important in government programs. The experiences of small nations in promoting health and family planning can be best compared to the provinces or districts of large nations. Thus, Singapore's dramatic fertility decline was faster and more comprehensive than Indonesia's overall national program, but in the small, culturally homogenous provinces of Bali and Yogyakarta, efficient health services produced similar falls in fertility to that found in Singapore.

What Figure 1 also reveals is the clear contrast between the estimates of past experience and the projections of future trends—the past is irregular while it was assumed future trends would be smooth. It is important to understand the sources of variation in the past before trying to set out assumptions to project the future. To gain a better understanding of past and future trends we need to consider the component determinants of fertility, the so-called "intermediate variables" of Kingsley

---

[7] Herrin, "Development of the Philippines' Family Planning Program."

[8] Terence H. Hull and Valerie J. Hull, "Health Systems in Indonesia and Vietnam: Transitions to Uncertain Futures," *Health and Development in South East Asia*, ed. Paul Cohen and John Purcal (Canberra: Australian Development Studies Network, 1995), pp. 120–48.

Figure 2
Recent and Projected Trends in Fertility of Women Ages 15 to 19

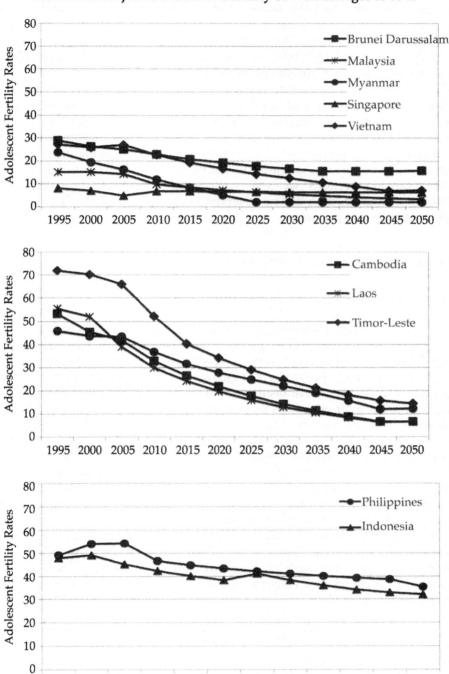

Source: UNDESA, *World Population Prospects: The 2010 Revision* (New York, NY: United Nations Department of Economic and Social Affairs, 2011)

Davis and Judith Blake[9] that have come to be referred to as "proximate" determinants.[10] These are the behaviors related to the initiation and regular conduct of sexual intercourse and the factors that can prevent or prematurely terminate pregnancy. Essentially, they are behaviors shaping the biology of reproduction. Social and cultural variables, like religion, income, and gender roles, can only have an impact on fertility if they influence the proximate behaviors. For example, while people might refer to Catholicism as a determinant of Philippine fertility, the underlying behavior they need to reference is the impact of Church teaching on the practice of contraception and abortion. Similarly, low levels of education are associated with high fertility, but only because, relative to their more-educated counterparts, less-educated women are likely to marry earlier and may not seek out and adopt contraceptive methods. The fertility trends shown in Figure 2 (on previous page) are really vectors of changing patterns of proximate behaviors. For this reason, in the following sections we will consider the major changes in marriage, contraception, and abortion that have served to change fertility to date and that will determine trends into the future.

PRINCIPAL COMPONENTS OF FERTILITY CHANGE

Singlehood, Marriage, and Marital Disruption

Across the Southeast Asian region, cultural and social changes have transformed family formation patterns. The spread of educational systems during the past century have led to an increase in the average age of marriage of both women and men.[11] In the past, large proportions of girls would have been married in their teens, but in recent years they have been more likely to be either enrolled in schools or engaged in using their education in modern service or manufacturing occupations. Increasingly, educated young adults take the initiative to find their own partners, eschewing the practice of arranged marriages (particularly of adolescent girls to older men) that was common among their parents' generation. This tends to mean that girls marry substantially later, while for boys the delay may be more modest, resulting in a narrower-than-before gap between the ages of the partners. The freedom to find one's own partner makes for a much more companionate form of marriage—sometimes based on romance, certainly based on friendship—and the resulting relationships are less likely to produce the early divorces seen in many societies in the early twentieth century. Focusing on fertility, it is important to consider the impact that such changes have on the amount of the reproductive lifespan women spend in a conjugal union—be that while legally married[12] or, at least, in a relationship likely to result in the bearing and raising of children.

---

[9] Kingsley Davis and Judith Blake, "Social Structure and Fertility: An Analytical Framework," *Economic Development and Cultural Change*, 4,3 (1956): 211–35.

[10] John Bongaarts and Robert G. Potter, *Fertility, Biology, and Behavior* (New York, NY: Academic Press, 1983).

[11] Gavin W. Jones, Terence H. Hull, and Maznah Mohamad, eds., *Changing Marriage Patterns in Southeast Asia: Economic and Socio-Cultural Dimensions* (London: Routledge, 2011).

[12] Across Asia the formalization of marriage in government laws has not always been reflected in the definitions used in censuses and surveys. For example, in Indonesia the census definition of marriage includes cohabitation that is accepted by the community. Thus, while a

Table 2
Decadal Trends of Singulate Mean Age at Marriage (SMAM)
among Females in Southeast Asia

	1960	1970	1980	1990	2000	2010
Brunei Darussalam	19.5	22.4	23.6	25.1		
Cambodia	21.3			22.5	23.0	
Indonesia	18.7	19.3	20.0	21.7	23.4	22.3
Laos			21.2		20.5	
Malaysia	19.4	22.1	23.5	24.6	24.9	
Myanmar	21.3	21.3	22.4		25.8	..
Philippines	22.2	22.8	22.4	23.8	23.3	
Singapore	20.3	24.2	26.2	27.0	26.5	
Thailand	24.0	22.0	22.8	23.5	24.1	
Timor-Leste					22.8	
Vietnam			23.0	22.7	23.3	

Source: Terence H. Hull, "Statistical Indices of Marriage Patterns in Insular Southeast Asia," in *Changing Marriage Patterns in Southeast Asia: Economic and Socio-Cultural Dimensions*, ed. Gavin W. Jones, Terence H. Hull, and Maznah Mohamad (London: Routledge, 2011).

Table 2 provides data showing the rising age at first marriage, calculated as the singulate mean age at marriage (SMAM), an indirect measure of marriage age. The SMAM is used when there are not comprehensive and readily available data from marriage certificates that might allow the calculation of the average ages of the wives and husbands at the time of union. If all members of the population are asked about their marital status, it is possible to use the percentages of men and women who are *single* in each age group to work out the average age at which people shift from being single to being married. While not the same as the average ages of brides in each year, it does provide a very useful and comparable statistic to monitor changes in marriage patterns between successive surveys or between countries. From the experiences of women in Southeast Asia shown in Table 2, it is clear that, almost without exception, the late twentieth century has seen a shift away from teenage marriage to nuptials after age twenty and, in some cases, well after age twenty-five. Put another way, whereas, formerly, many girls were married within a few years of menarche, today women, on average, spend up to a decade or more in a state of sexual maturity before they enter into a socially acceptable sexual union. Also, the nature of an "acceptable" union has changed under the influence of religious and government regulations that have increasingly formalized the definitions of marriage, and attacked the customary acceptance of cohabitation as an informal definition of marriage. Moreover, as political leaders strove to specify cultural practices acceptable as part of national identity, terms such as "free sex" and "living together" came to be used as symbols of Western decadence, to be condemned and rejected by "Eastern Morality."

---

large proportion of couples in Eastern Indonesian provinces are not legally married due to difficulties agreeing on a bride price, they are listed as married in the census, and appear as married in the calculation of the SMAM.

The rise in the age-at-time-of-marriage does not mean that there are no young newlyweds, but, rather, that the proportion of women who delay marriage beyond age twenty has grown. At the same time, the age at menarche across Asia has fallen as nutrition has improved. Today, women are fully mature, from a physical standpoint, and increasingly educated and experienced with regard to working by the time they are deemed, or feel themselves to be, ready for marriage.

Another way of expressing this transformation of the amount of potential reproductive life spent outside a union from which offspring might be expected is shown in the calculation of Hutterite-weighted marital status indices.[13] These calculations provide an overview of the differing impacts on fertility potential as the proportions of women in different marital-status categories change. They are technical measures used to derive insights about marriage dynamics when registration data on marriage, divorce, and death are limited and the main sources of information on matrimony are the questions about current marital status routinely asked on censuses and large sample surveys. Most countries record the proportions of people that are single, married, divorced, and widowed, but some nations also note if people are cohabiting (sometimes called a common law union) or if they have separated but remain legally married. By standardizing (or weighting) the resulting tables according to the fertility patterns of the highest recorded human fertility (the Hutterite religious groups of North America), the resulting indices reflect the amount of time women spend in different marital-status categories while in a state of potential reproduction. The indices thus magnify the experiences of women at peak fecundity between the ages of twenty and thirty-four and discount the marital status of women over forty, when they are likely to be menopausal. In most countries of the region, three dynamics are evident. First, the proportion of women in a state of singlehood rises fairly steadily over time as shown in Table 3. Second, though not shown in this chapter, the proportion of women who are in a state of widowhood tends to fall as men's life expectancy rises over time. Third, there are confusing and contradictory trends in the proportion of women who are in a "divorced" state at any given time. The indices for widowed and divorced generally have very small values in all the countries of Southeast Asia because young women (who are at the potential peak of their childbearing period) tend to remarry quickly if their first union is disrupted by divorce or the death of their spouse.[14]

Divorce, like marriage, is a social institution constructed on foundations of religious and civil law, subject to a wide range of economic and cultural influences. The trends shown in the "Divorced" indices in Table 3 are reflections of the socioreligious diversity of the region. Indonesia and Malaysia have falling indices of divorce, while Vietnam and the Philippines have gradually rising indices. In the case of the first two, both predominantly Muslim societies, the patterns reflect the changing dynamic of marriage under Islamic law. Over the centuries, very young ages at marriage were matched with high rates of divorce. Both men and women who found themselves in unhappy marriages could enlist the support of their families or communities to arrange a divorce. For men, the solution was relatively simple—the formal recitation of rejection of the wife, usually in front of a local religious official. Even for women of most cultural groups across Indonesia and

---

[13] Terence H. Hull, "Statistical Indices of Marriage Patterns in Insular Southeast Asia," in *Changing Marriage Patterns in Southeast Asia*, pp. 20–24.

[14] Ibid., p. 24.

Malaysia, a clear rejection of the husband, backed up by the support or at least the acquiescence of her father or other male relatives, could force the husband to accede to the termination of the relationship. Outsiders often depict such divorces as "easy," but for the families the process is often fraught, even though relatively free of stigma.

Table 3
Trends of Hutterite Marital Status Indices for Proportions Single (Is) and Divorced (Id)

	Proportion Single (Is)					
	1960	1970	1980	1990	2000	2010
Brunei Darussalam	0.208	0.356	0.389	0.407	—	—
Cambodia	0.248	—	—	0.315	0.346	—
Indonesia	0.121	0.157	0.205	0.276	0.308	0.304
Malaysia	0.184	0.313	0.374	0.376	0.391	—
Myanmar	0.249	0.295	0.346	—	—	—
Philippines	0.353	0.387	0.362	0.401	0.390	—
Singapore	0.256	0.432	0.479	0.432	0.407	0.434
Thailand	0.383	0.303	0.351	0.345	0.346	—
Timor-Leste	—	—	—	—	0.338	—
Vietnam	—	—	0.319	0.333	0.334	0.328
	Proportion Divorced (Is)					
	1960	1970	1980	1990	2000	2010
Brunei Darussalam	0.014	0.000	0.010	0.015	—	—
Cambodia	0.042	—	—	0.038	0.037	—
Indonesia	0.042	0.045	0.038	0.025	0.019	0.020
Malaysia	0.030	0.010	0.012	0.010	0.009	—
Myanmar	0.017	0.023	0.022	—	—	—
Philippines	0.007	0.007	0.008	0.009	0.012	—
Singapore	0.005	0.006	0.010	0.015	0.022	0.022
Thailand	0.037	0.013	0.026	0.009	0.011	—
Timor-Leste	—	—	—	—	0.006	—
Vietnam	—	—	0.009	0.012	0.014	0.019

Note: There are no data for Laos.

Source: Terence H. Hull, "Statistical Indices of Marriage Patterns in Insular Southeast Asia," in *Changing Marriage Patterns in Southeast Asia: Economic and Socio-Cultural Dimensions*, ed. Gavin W. Jones, Terence H. Hull, and Maznah Mohamad (London: Routledge, 2011).

In fact, one reason the proportion of women in a current state of divorce is low stems from the relative ease of speedy remarriage. The trends we see reflect the rapid rise of age at marriage, which produces more mature decision making and often more emotionally secure unions. Divorce in Muslim Southeast Asia has thus been falling quite steadily.

The interpretation of regional patterns of divorce poses two problems. First, there has been a failure of many censuses to distinguish and record states of formal divorce versus informal or alternative forms of separation. This is particularly important in the Philippines, where the Catholic Church has opposed secular legal divorce, instead offering annulments to couples who could prove incompatibility and who could find a compliant church official to issue the necessary papers. Those who could not get an annulment could opt for a separation, with legally married persons then forming de facto unions with other partners. The term "marital status" on censuses is, thus, a notoriously difficult question to answer for rich and poor alike, since some respondents may be focusing on legal, religious, or community norms in framing their answers.

Second, even when accurately recorded, the social institution of divorce presents an analytical conundrum. In many contexts, divorce is directly related to failure to reproduce. Women abandoned by their partners because they have not or cannot become pregnant are thus not prevented from childbearing because they are divorced—rather, they are divorced because they are unable (or unwilling) to bear children. For this reason, if we are interested in assessing the impact of marital status on fertility, the rather small quantitative impact of being in a state of divorce may be working in either direction (that is, divorced or not, the women in question are not likely to bear children).

Overall, the biggest impact on fertility is reflected in the indices of singlehood and marriage. In Table 3, all ten countries display patterns of rising rates of singlehood, which indicates a falling proportion of persons in the "married" state. This implies that fertility decline is in part a matter of marriage delay, at least as it works to delay the timing of first birth. Of course, the same drivers that delay marriage—education and occupation of young women—are also likely to be transforming the motivations for childbearing and supporting innovative norms for smaller families.[15]

One caveat is needed in the interpretation of data in tables 2 and 3. That comes from the occasional inconsistencies among censuses, social surveys, and demographic and health surveys (DHS) due to differences in the ways questions are asked or samples are drawn. For instance, in Indonesia and the Philippines, censuses or sample surveys conducted immediately prior to or following a DHS tend to produce lower proportions of single people (and thus higher proportions of married people) relative to the DHS results. Investigation of this inconsistency in Indonesia indicates that the DHS samples tended to miss single women in the household listings that were supposed to count all women.[16] The result is that total fertility rates might have been overstated by the DHS data. The factors that result in this problem with the samples are the same factors as those that delay marriage. Women living in university dormitories or factory barracks are not visited by DHS interviewers. Until statistical agencies deal with the challenges of rapid social change that undermine efforts to draw a representative sample of all women, any calculations of fertility levels and trends will be subject to error.

Of course there is another debate across the region that has great relevance to fertility trends—the changing likelihood of pregnancy occurring before marriage. Older generations insist that single women should be assumed to be abstinent, and unmarried young people tend to hide information about their sexual behavior from

---

[15] Across Southeast Asia today, educated women who are asked about their "ideal family size" are more likely to say two children, in contrast to women from previous generations who gave responses of four or five children, or, in a reflection of the fatalism they brought to the issue, answer with "[it's] up to God."

[16] Terence H. Hull and Wendy Hartanto, "Resolving Contradictions of Indonesian Fertility Estimates," *Bulletin of Indonesian Economic Studies*, 45,1 (2009): 61–71.

survey interviewers. Nonetheless, recent surveys indicate that Southeast Asian women are increasingly likely to be sexually active before their nuptials, as indicated both through careful, direct questioning and by comparing date of marriage and date of first birth. In Thailand, initiation of sex occurs premaritally in a majority of women; among less-educated women, this is often before the age of eighteen. Premarital sex is also common in the Philippines, particularly among the more-educated urbanites. Premarital sex is less common and happens later among Vietnamese women.[17] Most countries of the region have few surveys that record reliable information on nonmarital sexual behavior, both because respondents prefer to reject such questions and because officials do not want to ask what they regard as sensitive questions for fear of being accused of condoning such behavior.

Contraception

Contraceptives in Southeast Asia have been available for free or at a reduced price for decades. The governments of Singapore, Thailand, Vietnam, and Indonesia have long maintained strong family-planning programs designed to reduce high rates of population growth. While hamstrung by religious and political criticisms condemning family planning as immoral, the government of the Philippines tried, under various administrations and with the assistance of international aid agencies, to provide contraceptives to the population.

Ideally, women's contraceptive options would be geared to the reproductive stage of their lives. Young, unmarried, sexually active women need access to methods that are reliable and easily accessible. Safe-sex messages also stress the need for methods that have the dual purpose of preventing disease as well as pregnancy, which generally means the use of male or female condoms. Young married women in monogamous relationships may prefer to have methods that do not intrude on their sexual pleasure, and they may be tolerant of a higher chance of pregnancy. Later, as they fulfill their family-size desires, they may want methods that provide the lowest risk of pregnancy. At the same time, they may want to avoid methods that involve long-term exposure to artificial hormones, opting instead for the security and relative permanence of sterilization. Across a population, this translates into use of a wide range of methods, with choice being strongly related to the age of users and to preferences regarding permanence, reversibility, cost, convenience, and impact on sexual relations and pleasure. These characteristics are not apparent in the contraceptive mixes show in the available data in Table 4 for each of the countries of Southeast Asia.

Comparisons across the region are difficult, given the lack of good systems for assessing current use of contraceptives. Brunei, for example, lacks any reliable reports on contraceptive use. Data from Singapore and Malaysia are over a decade out-of-date, and even countries that conduct regular large-sample surveys sometimes use widely divergent questions and sampling procedures. Despite

---

[17] Chai Podhisita and Peter Xenos, "Survey Comparisons of the Sexual Risk Behavior of Young Adults in Thailand, Vietnam, and the Philippines," Bangkok, Institute for Population and Social Research, Mahidol University, undated (see: www.ipsr.mahidol.ac.th/IPSR/Contents/Books/FullText/2009/356_Survey-Comparision-Sexual-Risk.pdf, accessed September 28, 2011).

evidence of high rates of premarital sex in many countries, surveys are often limited to the experience of currently or ever-married women.[18]

Table 4 (continued on next page)
Contraceptive Use: Percentage Using Contraception among Women
Ages 15 to 49 Who Are Married or in Union

	Year(s)	Any Method	Total Modern	Tubectomy	Vasectomy	Pill	Injectable
Brunei Darussalam	NA	NA	NA	NA	NA	NA	NA
Cambodia	2005	40.0	27.1	1.7	0.1	12.6	7.9
Indonesia	2007	61.4	57.4	3.0	0.2	13.2	31.8
Laos	2005	38.0	35.0	4.7	0.0	15.9	10.6
Malaysia	1994	54.5	29.8	NA	NA	13.4	NA
Myanmar	2007	41.0	38.4	4.4	1.0	10.8	19.7
Philippines	2008	50.7	33.6	9.2	0.0	15.7	2.6
Singapore*	1997	62.0	55.0	NA	NA	10.0	NA
Thailand	2006	81.1	79.8	26.6	0.9	36.7	12.4
Timor-Leste	2009/10	22.3	20.8	0.8	0.0	1.7	15.9
Vietnam	2007	79.0	68.2	4.4	0.3	10.4	0.9
Southeast Asia	**2009**	**62.2**	**54.7**	**7.2**	**0.3**	**15.6**	**17.7**

* Ages 15 to 44 for Singapore

Perhaps the most distinctive aspect of birth control behaviors in the region is the varied pattern, from one nation to another, of women's choice of contraceptive methods. The use of the term "choice" may be inappropriate in this context, because women in many settings do not have many options, and in some places they may face heavy pressure from providers to conform to a limited range of methods promoted by the government.

The very rapid decline of fertility in Thailand, famously called a "revolution" by analysts,[19] was importantly regarded as evidence of the success of voluntary family planning and the application of novel forms of contraception. In the 1970s, Thailand was famous as a highly successful demonstration of the injectable forms of contraception, but, as Table 4 shows, Thai women in the twenty-first century choose from among the full range of methods, and, in doing so, they reach the highest recorded rates of contraceptive use in the region.

In Vietnam, with perhaps the most rigid family-planning program in the region, the most common method used is the IUD, followed by tubectomy. The government program pushes strongly a policy of limiting family size to two children, preferably spaced some years apart. This is particularly enforced among Communist Party members and government bureaucrats. Elsewhere in the society, women are

---

[18] "Ever-married" refers to those who are currently married, divorced, or widowed. This means that they have been married at least once, though currently they may be unmarried.

[19] John Knodel, Aphichat Chamratrithirong, and Nibon Debavalya, *Thailand's Reproductive Revolution: Rapid Fertility Decline in a Third-World Setting* (Madison, WI: University of Wisconsin Press, 1987).

voluntarily choosing to delay marriage and limit family size so as to be free to work in the newly industrializing economy. Whether from government pressure or economic pressure, though, the clear result is that contraceptive use is high and fertility, therefore, is low.

Table 4 (continued from previous page)
Contraceptive Use: Percentage Using Contraception among Women Ages
15 to 49 Who Are Married or in Union

	Implant	IUD	Condom	Other Modern Methods**	Rhythm	Withdrawal	Other Traditional Methods
Brunei Darussalam	NA	NA	NA	NA	NA	NA	NA
Cambodia	0.2	1.8	2.9	0.0	4.5	8.3	0.2
Indonesia	2.8	4.9	1.3	0.0	1.5	2.1	0.4
Laos	0.0	2.9	0.8	0.0	2.0	0.9	0.6
Malaysia	NA	3.9	5.3	7.2	8.8	6.9	8.9
Myanmar	NA	1.8	0.7	0.0	1.2	0.7	0.6
Philippines	0.0	3.7	2.3	0.0	6.4	9.8	0.8
Singapore*	NA	5.0	22.0	18.0	<----- 7.0 ----->		
Thailand	0.8	1.2	1.2	0.0	0.9	NA	0.4
Timor-Leste	0.8	1.3	0.2	0.0	0.9	0.4	0.3
Vietnam	0.1	43.7	8.3	0.0	7.2	3.3	0.3
Southeast Asia	**1.3**	**9.9**	**2.8**	**0.1**	**3.3**	**3.3**	**0.8**

* Ages 15 to 44 for Singapore
** Male and female sterilization, as well as some other nontraditional methods, are grouped in the "Other Modern Method" category.

Sources: UNDESA, *World Population Prospects: The 2010 Revision* (New York, NY: United Nations Department of Economic and Social Affairs, 2011), available at http://esa.un.org/unpd/wpp/Excel-Data/population.htm, accessed March 14, 2012. Also published as Department of Economic and Social Affairs, *World Contraceptive Use 2011*, Wallchart, ST/ESA/SER.A/301, Sales Number E.11.XIII.2.

Laos figures updated from the *Lao Reproductive Health Survey 2005*, available at http://countryoffice.unfpa.org/lao/drive/laoreproductivehealthsurvey.pdf, p. 59, accessed March 14, 2012.

In recent years, women in Indonesia have increasingly had to rely on private providers for contraceptives. The government began promoting the private sector in the late 1980s because they foresaw the coming economic burdens of public funding for all contraceptives as the numbers of users exceeded more than half of married women.[20] The government continued to play a major role in promoting contraceptive

---

[20] Terence H. Hull, "Formative Years of Family Planning in Indonesia," in *The Global Family Planning Revolution: Three Decades of Population Policies and Programs*, ed. Warren C. Robinson and John A. Ross (Washington, DC: World Bank, 2007); Terence H. Hull, "Caught in Transit: Questions about the Future of Indonesian Fertility," in *Completing the Fertility Transition, Population Bulletin of the United Nations, Special Issue Nos. 48/49*, United Nations publication, Sales No. E.02.XIII.15. 2002 (actual appearance 2009), pp. 375–88.

use, but pulled back from actually providing or subsidizing contraceptives. Instead, private clinics and, particularly, the services of private midwives, replaced the government as the major providers. Such midwives find it much more profitable to promote the use of injectables, rather than the wide variety of methods that existed under the government-run program in the 1980s.

In the Philippines, nongovernmental organizations and low-key government clinics provide cheap or free pills, but women also take advantage of tubectomy services, which offer a reliable and definitive birth control option. In the Congress and in the president's office, birth control is regarded as controversial due to the influence of local Catholic bishops who prefer to promote forms of abstinence. This helps to explain why nearly 15 percent of women are said to be using the so-called natural methods of rhythm and withdrawal. These methods involve the careful monitoring of a woman's menstrual periods or vaginal secretions, and the timing of intercourse to coincide with times of very low risk of conception. The methods require detailed knowledge, disciplined modification of sexual behavior, and a high degree of couple collaboration—three things that are not easy to maintain in many social and cultural settings in Asia.[21]

Laos and Cambodia[22] have very low contraceptive-use rates, with women relying mainly on pills; Timor-Leste, with the lowest rate of contraceptive use in the region, depends primarily on injectables. In all three countries, government involvement in family planning has been half-hearted at best, and oppositional at worst. Nonetheless, the fact of continuing fertility decline in the face of government indifference shows both the motivation of women to control their fertility and their ability to do so with some form of technology that they must work hard to obtain.

Singapore has the lowest fertility in Southeast Asia, but it also has the highest reported use of condoms,[23] which is sometimes regarded as an ineffective method of contraception. Singapore's published contraceptive prevalence rate (CPR) is nearly fifteen years old. It is lower than the more recent CPRs for Indonesia, Thailand, and Vietnam, but in the absence of recent, publicly available survey results, we cannot be sure about the contraceptive behavior of today's Singaporeans. The 1994 data for Malaysia is even older than Singapore's and likely to be less accurate.

Poor though the data appear to be, the major implication appears to be twofold. First, as is true elsewhere in the world, the role of governments in Southeast Asia is crucial in promoting effective forms of contraception. When governments fail, contraceptive supplies can be difficult to maintain. Nonetheless, individual women often find ways to control their fertility. Second, if contraceptive choice is a positive element of reproductive rights, many women in Southeast Asia fall short of having their rights recognized and served. This latter point is perhaps more complex than might first appear. It implies that a lack of variety in the contraceptive technologies adopted by populations is an indicator of program failure. It also implies that governments that fail regularly to monitor contraceptive use through reliable medical records or routine representative surveys are seriously falling short of their duties of care. Both definitions of failure seem to be relevant to most countries of

---

[21] Alejandro N. Herrin, "Development of the Philippines' Family Planning Program."

[22] Jacqueline Desbarats, *Prolific Survivors: Population Change in Cambodia: 1975–1993* (Tempe, AZ: Arizona State University Program for Southeast Asian Studies, 1995).

[23] Yap Mui Teng, "Singapore: Population Policies and Programs," in *The Global Family Planning Revolution.*

Southeast Asia. The lack of government monitoring also makes it difficult to project future contraceptive use and, consequently, future fertility. Without a better understanding of women's desires and behaviors today, the situation tomorrow is uncertain.

Abortion

Information on abortion is remarkably untrustworthy across Southeast Asia, even in countries where abortion is legal and supported by the government.[24] In part this is because abortion is complex; the characteristics of the women who seek to terminate pregnancy, the variety of practitioners who offer services, and the differences in methods used all combine to make measurement difficult. Many

Table 5
Abortion-Related Laws in Southeast Asia (circa 2009)

	Gestation limits (weeks since last menses started)	Grounds on which induced abortion was permitted						
		To save woman's life	To preserve physical health	To preserve mental health	Rape or incest	Fetal impairment	Economic or social reasons	Upon request
Brunei Darussalam	NA	NA	NA	NA	NA	NA	NA	NA
Cambodia	14	X	X	X	X	X	X	X
Indonesia	6	X	—	—	X	X	—	—
Laos	NA	X	X	—	—	—	—	—
Malaysia	NA	X	X	X	—	—	—	—
Myanmar	NA	X	NA	NA	NA	NA	NA	NA
Philippines	NA	[X]	NA	NA	NA	NA	NA	NA
Singapore	24	X	X	X	X	X	X	X
Thailand	none	X	X	X	X	X	—	—
Timor-Leste	NA	X	[X]	NA	NA	NA	NA	NA
Vietnam	none	X	X	X	X	X	X	X

Note: Bracketed [X] indicates that the ground is not explicit in the law but effectively allowed in practice. NA indicates that there is no information published on the national laws while a dash indicates no mention of the issue in the law.

Sources: Adapted from United Nations, *World Abortion Policies 2011*, http://www.un.org/esa/population/publications/2011abortion/2011wallchart.pdf, accessed March 14, 2012. Singapore data: IFPP 108; Thailand data: Andrea Whittaker, "The Struggle for Abortion Law Reform in Thailand," *Reproductive Health Matters* 10,19 (May 2002): 45–53, available at http://ssrn.com/abstract=960430, accessed March 14, 2012.

---

[24] Andrea Whittaker, ed., *Abortion in Asia: Local Dilemmas, Global Politics* (New York, NY: Berghahn Books, 2010).

things women do to attempt a termination, such as the use of folk or herbal practices, are likely to fail, but the attempt alone reflects powerful motivation and may indicate that there will be subsequent attempts to terminate the pregnancy. The provision of effective abortion methods by both traditional and modern practitioners is not necessarily associated with institutions that can be relied upon to record or report procedures.

In most Southeast Asian cultures, strong distinctions are made between the married and the unmarried, with the result that many young women seeking an abortion do so in secret, even if the state places no legal barrier to their choice. As Table 5 shows (see previous page), the legal profiles across the nations varies, while in Table 6 we see that many countries lack any national data on abortion rates or ratios. It can be said, therefore, that the numbers used in policy discussions tend to be unreliable.

Table 6
Abortion Rates and Ratios in Southeast Asia

	Year	Rate[a]	Ratio[b]	Notes
Brunei Darussalam	NA	NA	NA	
Cambodia[c]	2005	20.2	21.6	
Indonesia[d]	2000	37	43	Abortion (spontaneous and induced)
Laos	NA	NA	NA	
Malaysia	NA	NA	NA	
Myanmar	NA	NA	NA	
Philippines[e]	2000	27.0	18	
Singapore[f]	2008	12.6	NA	
Thailand[g]	1978	27.7	NA	
Timor-Leste	NA	NA	NA	
Vietnam[f]	2007	18.4	NA	
Southeast Asia[h]	2003	39.0	45	Induced abortion (safe and unsafe)

[a] National abortion rate is terminations per 1,000 women of childbearing age

[b] National abortion ratio is terminations per 100 births each year

[c] Tamara Fetters and Ghazaleh Samandari, "An Estimate of Induced Abortion in Cambodia," paper presented at 2009 IUSSP meetings in Marrakech.

[d] Budi Utomo et al., "Incidence and Social-Psychological Aspects of Abortion in Indonesia: A Community-Based Survey in 10 Major Cities and 6 Districts, Year 2000," Center for Health Research, University of Indonesia (Jakarta) and UN Population Fund, 2001.

[e] Fatima Juarez, Josefina Cabigon, Susheela Singh, and Rubina Hussain, "The Incidence of Induced Abortion in the Philippines: Current Level and Recent Trends," *International Family Planning Perspectives* 31,3 (September 2005): 140–49.

[f] United Nations (Population Division of the Department of Economic and Social Affairs of the United Nations Secretariat), World Population Prospects: The 2010 Revision (New York, NY: United Nations, 2011), http://esa.un.org/unpd/wpp/Excel-Data/population.htm, accessed January 10, 2012.

[g] John Knodel, Aphichat Chamratrithirong, and Nibon Debavalya, *Thailand's Reproductive Revolution: Rapid Fertility Decline in a Third-World Setting* (Madison, WI: University of Wisconsin Press, 1987).

[h] Gilda Sedgh et al., "Legal Abortion Worldwide: Incidence and Recent Trends," *International Family Planning Perspectives* 33,3 (2007): 106-116.

To some degree, these shortcomings are unlikely to affect assessments of future fertility declines. At the present time, total fertility is below 3 children per woman on average in all countries except Timor-Leste and Laos. Total fertility is at or below replacement in Indonesia, Brunei, Vietnam, Thailand, and Singapore. In such situations, any temporary change to make abortions illegal is not likely to have a major impact on fertility overall, although such a change may have a negative impact on the welfare of large numbers of vulnerable women. Low-fertility societies tend to have a variety of institutions that help women achieve their fertility desires in the face of barriers that criminalize abortion. It is for this reason that women in the Philippines continue to have access to abortion despite the constitutional prohibition and widespread religious opposition to the practice. There are many private physicians and nongovernmental organizations that defy the law to provide safe abortion, although sometimes this is available only at a price that is beyond the reach of the poor.[25]

The legality and mainstream acceptance of abortion in societies is important for many reasons that have indirect influences on the structure of fertility. Moral and legal restrictions on provision of reproductive health services to unmarried women create the circumstances in which unwanted pregnancies force women to use unsafe abortion practitioners. Lack of appropriate contraceptive options for married women likewise forces women to challenge restrictive laws, with the unfortunate consequence that they find themselves taking risks when they should be giving priority to protecting their reproductive and sexual health. Faced with limited options, and motivated by desires to have loving and pleasurable relationships, women too often find themselves literally "in trouble," but it is a trouble that is caused by restrictive social conventions. For this reason, one of the most active wings of feminist advocacy in Southeast Asia is directed to the reform of laws related to abortion and contraception. In Indonesia, Thailand, and the Philippines, these struggles have achieved limited success, but the groups are not dissuaded from the goal of greater choice for women. The question is whether their persistence will eventually overcome the resistance or if conservative political and religious groups will continue to deny women access to safe abortion.

FERTILITY FUTURES

In considering the future trends in fertility across the Southeast Asian region, it is important to distinguish between the concepts of errors and uncertainties. From our review of marriage rates, contraceptive use, and abortion access, it is clear that the information on which we base our analyses is flawed and, sometimes, nonexistent. These are examples of errors in data. At the same time, even when we do have reasonable estimates of current or past behavior, there are often reasons to be uncertain about where those trends might lead in future.

Predicting future fertility requires prediction of components. We need to assess what will happen to institutions shaping behaviors related to marriage, contraception, and pregnancy termination. While much behavior reflects economic

---

[25] Corazon M. Raymundo, Zelda Zablan, Josefina V. Cabigon, et al., *Unsafe Abortion in the Philippines: A Threat to Public Health* (Manila: Demographic Research and Development Foundation, 2001).

and cultural conditions, the attention of policymakers is most often focused on political considerations directed to the management of laws and on budgeting for projects and programs. In most countries, these are matters of active debate and the outcomes will depend on many domestic and international forces.

Trends toward women waiting to marry until they are older, or opting not to marry at all, or opting for childless partnerships, are related to women's education and occupation. These dimensions of human capital appear to be steadily expanding across the region, but there remain substantial differences both within and between countries. If women in Timor-Leste and Laos gain higher education and better jobs than their mothers and grandmothers had, they are likely to have fewer children, but the experiences of some countries indicate that efficient and supportive family-planning programs can reduce fertility even among less-educated women engaged in family-based work, as attested to by the success of the Thai and Indonesian family-planning program over the last forty years of promotion.[26]

Religious mobilization in some settings appears to be encouraging reaction against secular trends. The 2010 census of Indonesia showed a widespread decline in the age of marriage for the first time in a century, at least part of which appears to be due to the influence of religious leaders who exhort their young followers to marry within the group rather than risking romantic alliances with nonmembers. These results have puzzled analysts and policy makers. It may take some years before the real reasons for marital-behavior changes are understood and definitive studies published. In the meantime, it is clear that the changes are pressing fertility upward, at least temporarily.

Additionally, in Malaysia and Indonesia, the first decade of the twenty-first century has produced heated social debates over polygamy. While still a rare practice, critiques of polygamy have expanded to include strong feminist arguments condemning the practice as a threat to the position of women in society. In general, Southeast Asian Muslims are required to have the agreement of the first wife before taking a second wife in legal marriage, but some men avoid this by resorting to informal unions or secret cohabitation. In Indonesia, a series of regulations have been promulgated to force government employees to obtain the approval of their work supervisor before taking a second (or third or even fourth) spouse. Again, such controls are often avoided by men who attempt to circumvent the law in their attempts to set up multiple households for reasons of personal fulfillment or based on the idea that polygamy enhances their status among their peers. For many feminist advocates, social acceptance of polygamy undermines respect and security of all women and not just those in multiple-marriage situations.

Trends show divorce rising in some countries while falling in others, but these trends are unlikely to produce big enough changes in marital disruption or stability that they would have a major impact on fertility. To a large extent, divorce patterns can be ignored until they are found to be followed by a decline in remarriage rates, but this has not occurred among most cultures of the region. Similarly, the increased longevity of women's male partners will not mean that women will have more children, since most widowhood occurs after the woman herself is beyond the childbearing years.

---

[26] T. H. Hull and H. Mosley, *Revitalization of Family Planning in Indonesia* (Jakarta: Government of Indonesia and United Nations Population Fund, 2009).

Contraception is the major determinant of fertility behavior, and it is also the factor that is theoretically most responsive to government policy. It is generally promoted in international agreements as an acknowledged element of women's reproductive rights. It is also technologically feasible and proven to be effective. Its sheer effectiveness also opens the potential for variability over time if government programs improve or fail. Being tractable to policies surrounding services and motivations makes this the variable most likely to determine long-term fertility levels. We already see policies being put in place to reduce fertility from high to low levels in Laos and Timor-Leste. By contrast, Singapore's government is implementing policies to increase fertility to replacement level (See Gavin Jones and Bina Gubhaju in this volume). The Indonesian government remains concerned that it might not be able to maintain fertility at current levels if contraceptive service programs fail under the management of local governments, and there is frequent talk of a population explosion or baby boom, at least in part to validate the established role of the family-planning program.

It appears that individual demands for abortion will remain high irrespective of legal constraints. The continuing rise of the age at marriage, and the signs of inadequacy in the range of effective contraceptive methods available to women at different life stages, mean that unwanted pregnancies will continue to occur in large numbers. One of the concerns in the near future is that institutional battles over abortion in many countries will spill over into ongoing challenges to the legitimacy of providing *any* contraceptives to sexually active women. Should that happen, many of the justifications for small families may come under attack and increasing numbers of women will be required to bear unwanted progeny, irrespective of their personal feelings and situations.

In short, the behaviors surrounding the immediate determinants of fertility are all subject to uncertainty. Most uncertain are the trends in contraceptive efficiency, effectiveness, and accessibility, because the current patterns of services are far from ideal. Also uncertain, but of less importance to fertility, are the changes in the institution of divorce and legality of abortion services.

Some of the attempts to predict behavior use statistical-regression methods, which spread from economics to other areas of social research. Paul Schultz[27] offers a warning about the application of some of these methods. Regression focuses on individual behavior, linking individual social variables with individual biological behaviors. In one example, Schultz shows that the data used by analysts consisted only of currently married women, who were thus self-selected for behavior that shaped the outcome of tests to link the independent and dependent variables. This focus on individual behavior in designing models for prediction depends heavily on how the people of interest are defined or selected in the research design.

Another problem is that individual's options are a function of a legal framework that can be determined by small minorities, even in democratic societies. If individual values and preferences alone determined the use of abortion to resolve unwanted pregnancies, the United States would not have such large state and county variations in the prevalence of abortion. That would mean more abortions, less geographic differences with respect to the provision of abortion services, and a totally different approach to social policy. Similarly, in Southeast Asia, the high

---

[27] T. Paul Schultz, "Testing the Neoclassical Model of Family Labor Supply and Fertility," *The Journal of Human Resources* 25,4 (1990): 599–634.

estimates of abortions that are carried out secretly imply that many women approve of (or at least see the vital need for) pregnancy termination and resort to desperate measures to attain services. Politics at multiple levels of government are heavily shaped by the influence of lobbying, money, and manipulation of political institutions, and, as many feminists argue, are products of predominantly male politicians. When abortion issues are argued about and the debate focuses on abstract values rather than individual rights, it can be difficult to predict the direction, much less the distance, the abortion issue will go. This is one of the problems of predicting the future of both abortion and contraception in many Southeast Asian countries and results in a degree of uncertainty that grows bigger the further we peer into the future.

The reproductive and sexual-health regulations likely to prevail in the middle of the twenty-first century are uncertain. This may hamper our ability to create reasonable predictions for fertility over the medium term. To a large degree, the path that marriage patterns, contraceptive trends, and abortion incidence will take is shaped by institutional inertia built into the factors shaping individual decision making. The situation on the day after tomorrow will depend to some degree on what happens tomorrow, but the construction of a path of behavior into the future will be subject to crucial direction-changing events that may be speculated upon but not predicted.

Social change is always possible, but it is seldom random. Thus, if we were to look to the future of Southeast Asian fertility to and beyond the year 2020, we could be confident that the disparate economies and cultures will not all converge to the same point as has often been assumed in population projections. The complex behaviors may have some tendency to point in the same direction—rising age at marriage, falling fertility, rising life expectancy—but the context of different populations will produce different forces for change that will make fertility an irregular, but partially predictable, vector. What we should be identifying and attempting to predict are some of the key social institutional changes that, once taken, will carry individuals into an entirely new decision framework. We do this to some extent by focusing on the education of women. But we can go further in identifying the legal framework surrounding all elements of reproductive health and the government's role in the promotion of equitable access to services. Scenarios of likely change might include speculations about investment in family planning, reform of abortion laws, and commitment to women's education.

Finally, in all the considerations about the elements of social change likely to shape future fertility, it is important to constantly remind governments that the elimination of errors in data on reproductive health is a major step in addressing the uncertainties surrounding behaviors. We need more and better data on fertility, marriage, contraception, and abortion if we are to understand the true nature of the problems women face and develop the sorts of programs that can contribute to improvements in individual and family welfare. At a time when many government officials regard calls for better data as "academic," it is a challenge to convince them of the importance of data.

CHAPTER 3

MARRIAGE TRENDS IN SOUTHEAST ASIA

Gavin Jones and Bina Gubhaju

THE SETTING OF SOUTHEAST ASIA

The family plays a central role in the cultures represented in Southeast Asia. Not only this, but the rhetoric of national development in many countries of the region (certainly in Indonesia, Malaysia, and the Philippines) envisages the family as the cornerstone of national development. The family in this official rhetoric is very much the traditional family, consisting of a couple in a heterosexual relationship and their children. Indeed, in terms of adherence to tradition, the ideology goes well beyond this in Indonesia, where, under the official ideology of the New Order government, women are seen as existing to serve their husbands, their families, and the state.[1] In contrast to this traditional family-focused ideology, the socialist family model in Vietnam in the 1950s attempted to break away from the traditional family and matrimonial system, "key features of which were arranged marriage, early marriage, polygamy, gender inequality, and protection of patriarchal rights."[2]

Families in the region are formed through marriage, and although the prevalence of cohabiting relationships is almost certainly increasing (and has always been considerable in the case of the Philippines), such relationships are still not officially acceptable. Marriage, then, is central to the formation of the families on which national development is seen to depend. One could therefore expect that the civil registration of marriage would be important in Southeast Asian countries, and this is indeed the case, though there is still contestation about what constitutes a marriage. For example, in Indonesia, some traditionalist Muslims argue that all that is required is that a union between a woman and man be conducted in accordance with Islamic teachings, irrespective of whether the union meets civil law requirements for

---

[1] Julia Suryakusuma, "State Ibuism: The Social Construction of Womanhood in the Indonesian New Order" (master's thesis, Institute of Social Studies, The Hague, 1987); Susan Blackburn, *Women and the State in Modern Indonesia* (Cambridge: Cambridge University Press, 2004).

[2] Catherine Scornet, "State and the Family: Reproductive Policies and Practices," in *Reconfiguring Families in Contemporary Vietnam*, ed. Magali Barbieri and Daniele Belanger (Palo Alto, CA: Stanford University Press, 2009), p. 49.

registration. In some predominantly Christian parts of Eastern Indonesia, many couples raise a family without ever having gone through an official ceremony or registration that makes their union legal, partly because they cannot meet the full cost of *belis* (bridewealth payment).[3]

Marriage trends reflect trends in gender and intergenerational relations. Traditional arranged marriage placed considerable power in the hands of parents, in particular the father. The weakening of the system of arranged marriage throughout the region reflects at a deep level the abdication of this power by the older generation, in particular by males of that generation. It can be seen as a largely voluntary abdication, rather than one brought on by revolutionary means. It can best be seen as a recognition of changing times (in Indonesia, *perobahan zaman*) and parallels remarkable developments in education, increasing urbanization, and involvement of women in economic activities outside the household.

In Southeast Asia, childbearing outside of marriage is not accepted (provided that we broaden the concept of marriage a little to include those who are not legally married but are recognized by the community to be married), and this means that marriage can be seen as the gateway to the possibility of childbearing. As such, marriage trends have important implications for fertility trends. Any increase in the average marrying age of women into and beyond their mid-twenties not only limits their potential fertility by shortening the length of time they are exposed to the risk of childbearing during their fertile period, but also lowers population growth rates by extending the mean length of generation.

Southeast Asia is characterized by a rich mosaic of cultures and religions, as well as by differences in political and economic systems and wide differences in levels of economic development. For these reasons, considerable differences in marriage patterns are to be expected and are, indeed, found.

DATA ISSUES

Marriage statistics can be obtained from several different sources:

(1) *Administrative records.* Registrations of marriages are recorded in the vital statistics database of every country. Unfortunately, these data are often not readily accessible to researchers. If available, these data can be used to calculate age-specific marriage rates to observe trends.

(2) *Cross-sectional marital status data.* Information on the marital status of individuals is collected in many censuses and surveys. These data are useful for tracking the singulate mean age at marriage (SMAM) and percentages never married in particular five-year age groups over time. Unlike vital statistics data, marital status—normally categorized as never married, currently married, widowed, or divorced (sometimes including separated)—as recorded in censuses and surveys is a self-defined state.

(3) *Data on age at first marriage.* A few censuses and surveys, including the World Fertility Surveys (WFS), the Demographic and Health Surveys

---

[3] Peter Hagul, "Dowry System and Extended Family Network: A Case Study in Manggarai and Nagakeo, Flores, Indonesia," in *Changing Marriage Patterns in Southeast Asia: Economic and Socio-Cultural Dimensions*, ed. Gavin Jones, Terence Hull, and Maznah Mohamad (London: Routledge, 2011).

(DHS), and other household surveys, in addition to collecting data on marital status of respondents, ask respondents to retrospectively recall their date of marriage and may include information on the exact day, month, and year of marriage. This information is useful for studying trends in age at marriage for different birth cohorts and can be used to examine issues of timing and duration of marriage.

(4) *Marriage data obtained from longitudinal surveys.* Cross-sectional surveys only provide static figures, except for those surveys that have retrospective questions on marital history, thus enabling the researcher to know whether someone currently married had previously been widowed or divorced. A few longitudinal surveys that are available in Southeast Asia (e.g., Indonesian and Malaysian Family Life Surveys) that collect detailed marital histories and prospective marital status data enable further analysis of transitions into and out of various states of marriage.

While each one of these sources provides invaluable data on marriage, such data need to be interpreted cautiously. The definition and meaning of what constitutes marriage is complex, thus, the way statistics capture these events may not accurately reflect what is happening in reality. Registration data only record legal marriages in the conventional sense. Thus they may not include religious marriages that have not been officially registered. Moreover, in some countries vital statistics data may be incomplete. In Southeast Asia, only Singapore has complete enough data to show detailed trends using marriage registration figures. While data from the censuses and surveys capture marriages that are not officially registered, the categories of marital status included in these surveys are often problematic as well. De facto cohabiting relationships are typically not recorded as a separate category. The one exception is the Philippines, where a cohabitation category has been included in its census (and the DHS) since the 1990s. Elsewhere, cohabitation, if growing, may not be accurately reflected in the figures currently available on marital status. In Indonesia, cohabiting couples are likely to designate themselves as "married" for the marital status question or the interviewer may record the couple as "married."

In recent Southeast Asian DHS surveys (e.g., Vietnam, 2005; and Cambodia, 2005) a separate category of cohabitation is included in the marital status question. However, the percentage reporting cohabitation is less than 1 percent in both countries. Due to the sensitive nature of the issue it is difficult to gauge the extent to which cohabitation is growing, as survey data may not provide reliable estimates. Qualitative studies in Hanoi (and surrounding areas) suggest that many single women are engaging in noncohabiting sexually intimate long-term relationships.[4]

A further data concern with household surveys, particularly the DHS, is that these surveys may be underestimating the single population due to their sampling strategy that is limited to the household population and their focus on behavior that is only pertinent to married women (with regard to Indonesian DHSes, see Terence

---

[4] Daniele Belanger and Khuat Thu Hong, "Single Women's Experiences of Sexual Relationships and Abortion in Hanoi, Vietnam," *Reproductive Health Matters* 7,14 (1999); Daniele Belanger, "Single and Childless Women of Vietnam: Contesting and Negotiating Female Identity?" in *Gender in Practice in Vietnam*, ed. Rydstrom Helle and Lisa Drummand (Singapore: National University of Singapore Press, 2004).

Hull and Henry Mosley, 2009[5]). The sample does not include people residing in institutions, which may include military housing, boarding schools, university dormitories, factory dormitories, and shared living arrangements. This is of concern in Southeast Asia where there has been a growing number of women migrating to urban areas to study or to work. Many of these individuals may not be counted in the surveys.

While each one of the above data sources has its own limitations, they are nonetheless invaluable for marriage research. In the next sections, changes in marriage patterns that have occurred in Southeast Asia in the past four decades are examined using data obtained from censuses and demographic and health surveys.

TRENDS IN AGE AT MARRIAGE

Trends toward later and less marriage for both males and females are quite marked in this previously "universal marriage" region (see Tables 1 and 2). The trends can be summarized overall by focusing on the SMAM, which has risen universally in these Southeast Asian countries since 1960, though the extent of the increase in age at marriage has differed considerably.

Table 1
Percentage of Never Married Females by Age Group in
Various Southeast Asian Countries, 1960–2005

Country, age group	1960	1970	1980	1990	2000	2005
Cambodia	1962 census				1998 census	2004 CIPS
15-19	85.1	n.a	n.a	n.a	87.6	89.3
20-24	31.6	n.a	n.a	n.a	39.4	43.4
25-29	9.4	n.a	n.a	n.a	16.8	18.8
30-34	4.2	n.a	n.a	n.a	10.0	9.5
35-39	2.9	n.a	n.a	n.a	6.8	7.5
40-44	2.2	n.a	n.a	n.a	5.4	5.9
45-49	2.1	n.a	n.a	n.a	4.2	5.1
SMAM	21.3	n.a	n.a	n.a	22.5	22.8
Indonesia						
15-19	n.a	62.6	69.9	81.8	89.3	90.8
20-24	n.a	18.5	22.3	35.7	43.1	51.4
25-29	n.a	5.0	7.4	11.2	16.7	19.7
30-34	n.a	2.2	3.4	4.5	6.9	8.1
35-39	n.a	1.4	1.9	2.7	3.5	4.3
40-44	n.a	1.2	1.4	2.0	2.4	2.6
45-49	n.a	1.0	1.2	1.5	2.0	2.0
SMAM	n.a	19.3	20.0	21.6	22.7	23.4

---

[5] Terence Hull and Henry Mosley, *Revitalization of Family Planning in Indonesia* (Jakarta: Government of Indonesia and United Nations Population Fund, 2009).

Country, age group	1960	1970	1980	1990	2000	2005
Malaysia	1957 census			1991 census		
15-19	71.1	82.5	89.7	92.1	95.2	n.a
20-24	28.3	41.4	51.3	60.1	66.6	n.a
25-29	7.6	13.4	20.9	25.8	29.0	n.a
30-34	2.6	5.7	9.9	12.1	12.1	n.a
35-39	1.4	3.5	5.3	8.0	7.8	n.a
40-44	1.3	2.2	3.7	6.0	5.8	n.a
45-49	1.3	1.6	3.0	4.1	5.1	n.a
SMAM	20.3	22.1	23.5	24.6	24.9	n.a
Myanmar		1973 census	1983 census	1991 PCFS	2001 FRHS	
15-19	n.a	78.0	83.2	89.3	91.6	n.a
20-24	n.a	35.5	42.1	56.0	64.9	n.a
25-29	n.a	16.6	21.5	32.4	40.8	n.a
30-34	n.a	9.3	12.8	19.6	25.9	n.a
35-39	n.a	7.0	8.9	13.8	18.6	n.a
40-44	n.a	6.2	6.7	10.4	14.8	n.a
45-49	n.a	5.9	5.9	9.1	11.8	n.a
SMAM	n.a	21.3	22.4	24.5	25.8	n.a
Philippines						
15-19	87.3	89.2	85.9	89.7	89.8	n.a
20-24	44.3	50.3	45.5	55.9	56.8	n.a
25-29	19.5	21.5	21.1	27.4	27.4	n.a
30-34	11.6	11.7	11.9	13.4	13.8	n.a
35-39	8.1	8.0	8.0	8.7	8.6	n.a
40-44	7.6	7.3	7.0	7.2	6.5	n.a
45-49	7.1	6.7	6.7	6.2	5.7	n.a
SMAM	22.2	22.8	22.4	23.8	23.9	n.a
Singapore						2005 GHS
15-19	n.a	95.2	97.7	98.6	99.0	99.4
20-24	n.a	64.6	73.8	78.5	83.8	86.5
25-29	n.a	22.6	34.0	39.3	40.2	46.3
30-34	n.a	9.6	16.7	20.9	19.5	22.1
35-39	n.a	5.1	8.5	14.8	15.1	15.0
40-44	n.a	3.3	6.0	11.5	13.6	14.3
45-49	n.a	1.1	4.2	7.3	12.5	13.3
SMAM	n.a	24.2	26.2	27.0	26.5	26.9

Country, age group	1960	1970	1980	1990	2000	2005
Thailand						
15-19	86.1	80.8	83.3	85.3	88.8	n.a
20-24	38.6	37.9	43.5	48.4	56.0	n.a
25-29	14.1	15.6	20.9	25.5	29.0	n.a
30-34	6.7	8.1	11.8	14.1	16.1	n.a
35-39	4.1	5.2	7.3	9.6	11.6	n.a
40-44	3.1	3.9	5.3	7.0	9.3	n.a
45-49	2.6	3.0	4.1	5.2	8.0	n.a
SMAM	22.4	22.0	22.8	23.5	24.1	n.a
Vietnam				1989 census	1999 census	2005 VDHS
15-19	n.a	n.a	n.a	87.6	90.7	93.1
20-24	n.a	n.a	n.a	42.0	45.7	51.5
25-29	n.a	n.a	n.a	17.5	17.8	17.2
30-34	n.a	n.a	n.a	10.9	9.8	9.4
35-39	n.a	n.a	n.a	8.4	7.5	5.5
40-44	n.a	n.a	n.a	5.8	6.6	4.3
45-49	n.a	n.a	n.a	3.3	5.8	4.9
SMAM	n.a	n.a	n.a	23.0	22.8	23.1

CIPS = Cambodia Inter-Censal Population Survey, 2004
FRHS = Myanmar Fertility and Reproductive Health Survey, 2001
GHS = Singapore General Household Survey, 2005
PCFS = Myanmar Population Change and Fertility Survey, 2001
VDHS = Vietnam Demographic and Health Survey

Sources: Census Reports, various countries and years.
Note: Data from a census year that is different from the years at the head of the columns, or a data source other than Census Reports, are noted as such. All other figures are from censuses of the respective years.

Table 2
Percentage of Never Married Males by Age Group in
Various Southeast Asian Countries, 1960–2005

Country, age group	1960	1970	1980	1990	2000	2005
Cambodia	1962 census				1998 census	2004 CIPS
15-19	98.0	n.a	n.a	n.a	97.0	98.4
20-24	65.8	n.a	n.a	n.a	58.5	62.5
25-29	20.5	n.a	n.a	n.a	21.5	21.6
30-34	5.4	n.a	n.a	n.a	7.0	7.1
35-39	2.8	n.a	n.a	n.a	2.6	2.7
40-44	2.0	n.a	n.a	n.a	1.5	0.9
45-49	1.8	n.a	n.a	n.a	1.0	0.4
SMAM	24.4	**n.a**	**n.a**	**n.a**	24.2	24.6

Country, age group	1960	1970	1980	1990	2000	2005
Indonesia						
15-19	n.a	94.9	96.4	97.6	96.9	98.5
20-24	n.a	58.6	59.4	71.7	74.2	81.8
25-29	n.a	18.5	19.5	29.0	34.4	41.5
30-34	n.a	6.1	6.0	9.4	11.8	14.5
35-39	n.a	3.0	2.5	4.6	4.6	5.7
40-44	n.a	2.1	1.6	3.4	2.2	2.6
45-49	n.a	1.8	1.1	2.9	1.5	1.4
SMAM	**n.a**	**23.8**	**24.1**	**25.2**	**25.9**	**27.0**
Malaysia	1957 census			1991 census		
15-19	97.0	96.8	98.7	98.7	98.9	n.a
20-24	68.7	73.4	80.4	85.4	87.6	n.a
25-29	28.5	31.6	39.9	49.1	54.0	n.a
30-34	12.0	12.2	14.5	20.2	24.4	n.a
35-39	8.0	6.4	7.2	10.4	11.7	n.a
40-44	6.5	4.2	4.9	6.0	7.3	n.a
45-49	7.1	3.4	4.0	3.9	5.1	n.a
SMAM	**24.6**	**25.6**	**26.6**	**27.9**	**28.5**	**n.a**
Myanmar		1973 census	1983 census	1991 PCFS	2001 FRHS	
15-19	n.a	92.2	93.3	96.7	97.4	n.a
20-24	n.a	55.2	60.1	69.9	75.4	n.a
25-29	n.a	23.7	28.1	37.6	46.4	n.a
30-34	n.a	10.3	12.7	19.6	25.4	n.a
35-39	n.a	6.1	7.2	11.4	15.3	n.a
40-44	n.a	4.4	4.8	6.2	9.1	n.a
45-49	n.a	3.5	3.8	4.3	5.7	n.a
SMAM	**n.a**	**23.9**	**24.6**	**26.3**	**27.6**	**n.a**
Philippines						
15-19	97.0	97.6	96.3	97.2	95.3	n.a
20-24	65.5	69.3	63.3	73.4	72.2	n.a
25-29	27.1	30.1	27.3	38.3	39.9	n.a
30-34	11.4	13.1	12.6	16.9	20.7	n.a
35-39	6.1	7.1	7.6	8.9	12.1	n.a
40-44	4.1	4.8	5.4	5.9	7.8	n.a
45-49	3.2	3.7	4.2	4.5	6.1	n.a
SMAM	**24.9**	**25.4**	**24.8**	**26.3**	**26.4**	**n.a**

Country, age group	1960	1970	1980	1990	2000	2005
Singapore						2005 GHS
15-19	n.a	99.5	99.6	99.8	99.9	99.9
20-24	n.a	88.5	91.9	94.2	95.2	96.3
25-29	n.a	48.0	54.9	64.1	64.2	70.6
30-34	n.a	21.5	21.5	34.0	30.7	33.9
35-39	n.a	10.8	10.6	18.1	19.7	19.6
40-44	n.a	7.2	8.2	10.9	14.8	15.2
45-49	n.a	5.9	6.4	8.5	10.5	12.8
SMAM	**n.a**	**27.8**	**28.4**	**29.9**	**30.0**	**30.1**
Thailand						
15-19	92.9	93.1	95.8	96.1	96.6	n.a
20-24	64.2	61.3	66.4	70.8	77.9	n.a
25-29	25.2	23.7	27.0	35.8	45.4	n.a
30-34	8.8	9.8	11.5	17.0	23.1	n.a
35-39	4.5	5.1	6.1	8.9	13.4	n.a
40-44	2.9	3.1	4.3	5.2	8.5	n.a
45-49	2.3	2.3	3.5	3.8	5.8	n.a
SMAM	**24.7**	**24.7**	**24.9**	**26.0**	**27.4**	**n.a**
Vietnam				1989 census	1999 census	2005 VDHS
15-19	n.a	n.a	n.a	95.7	97.5	98.2
20-24	n.a	n.a	n.a	58.3	69.6	75.0
25-29	n.a	n.a	n.a	21.7	29.2	34.4
30-34	n.a	n.a	n.a	6.8	9.8	11.4
35-39	n.a	n.a	n.a	3.2	4.4	3.7
40-44	n.a	n.a	n.a	2.0	2.6	2.5
45-49	n.a	n.a	n.a	1.5	1.5	2.2
SMAM	**n.a**	**n.a**	**n.a**	**24.1**	**25.4**	**26.0**

CIPS = Cambodia Inter-Censal Population Survey, 2004
FRHS = Myanmar Fertility and Reproductive Health Survey, 2001
GHS = Singapore General Household Survey, 2005
PCFS = Myanmar Population Change and Fertility Survey, 2001
VDHS = Vietnam Demographic and Health Survey

Sources: Census Reports, various countries and years.
Note: Data from a census year that is different from the years at the head of the columns, or a data source other than Census Reports, are noted as such. All other figures are from censuses of the respective years.

Female Age at Marriage

Indonesia, Malaysia, Myanmar, and Singapore show the most marked delays in marriage. In the past four decades, female SMAM increased from 19 to 23 in Indonesia; 20 to 26 in Malaysia, 22 to 26 in Myanmar, and 24 to 27 in Singapore. The Philippines already had a relatively late-marriage pattern in 1960 (24.9) and has not shown much increase since then (to 26.4 in 2000).

The SMAM is not a perfect measure, particularly in cases where the age at marriage has been steadily rising. This is why other measures—including the percentages never married in individual five-year age groups—are also included in the tables. The levels and trends of nonmarriage differ substantially between countries, though the trend is toward increasing nonmarriage. The proportion never married in the 15 to 19 age group is useful in tracking trends in teenage marriage, though it must be stressed that the proportion never married in this age group substantially understates the proportion who marry as teenagers, because some (in some cases, many) of those who are still single in this age group at the time of the census will marry before they reach age 20. In any event, the proportions never married in the 15 to 19 age group show a considerable decline in teenage marriage in all countries of Southeast Asia. There has been a particularly sharp drop in Indonesia, where, in 1970, 38 percent of teenage girls were married compared to 10 percent in 2005.

Increases in the proportions never married among women in the twenties and thirties are quite marked in some countries. Figure 1 illustrates the increases in some countries and particularly the differences between countries in historical trajectories as well as current levels of nonmarriage among women aged 30 to 34. These rising trends continue among women in their late forties. The most recent data available for various countries indicate that in the 45 to 49 age group, more than 5 percent of women in Cambodia, Malaysia, Vietnam, the Philippines, and Thailand, and just over 10 percent of women in Myanmar and Singapore, remain never married. This reflects a situation very different from the universal-marriage pattern of earlier times.

In the period since 1990, two countries in the region—Vietnam and Singapore—have been exceptions to the trends toward rising proportions of never-married (single) in particular age groups. In Vietnam, a slight decline in singlehood has occurred at ages 25 to 34, and a more pronounced decline at ages 35 to 39. Marriage in Vietnam has been affected by excess mortality of males during the American war. Thus, women aged 30 to 44 in the 1989 census (aged 15 to 29 in 1974) would have been most affected by the marriage squeeze (which we describe in more detail later).[6] With the squeeze ending by 2005, there is evidence of slight declines in proportions never married in these age groups. It should be noted, however, that the 2005 data for Vietnam are from the DHS and no comparable census data are yet available for recent years.[7]

---

[6] Daniel Goodkind, "The Vietnamese Double Marriage Squeeze," *International Migration Review* 31,1 (1997).

[7] Since the DHS is a sample survey that is subject to nonresponse error, results from the census may be slightly different.

Figure 1
Percentage of Never Married Females and Males,
Aged 30–34, 1960–2005

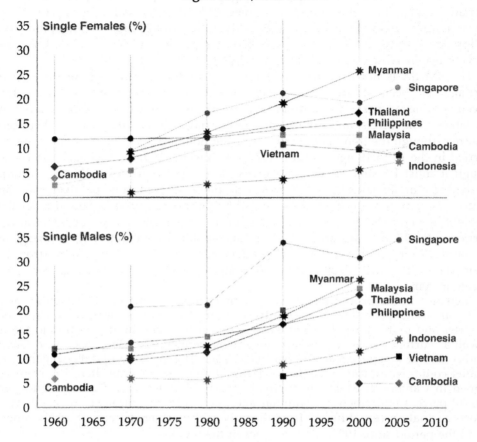

In Singapore, where the rise in proportions of females never married in their late twenties and thirties had already stalled in the 1990s (see Table 1), further increases in singlehood are observed in the 25 to 34 age groups, but there has been little change at ages 35 to 49. For Singaporean men, as for women, there seem to have been further increases in singlehood in the 25 to 34 age groups, but a stall in proportions single in the 35 to 44 age groups. Singapore is the only country in the region where good data are available on annual trends in marriage rates. Based on these data, between 1997 and 2007, the median age at marriage of resident males and females increased by about one and a half years in each case, reaching 29.8 for males and 27.2 for females in 2007. Figure 2 shows trends in the age-sex-specific marriage rates. Marriage rates for males and females display very different patterns, with high rates for females more concentrated at younger ages (20 to 24 and 25 to 29) and high rates for males spread over a wider age range. Trends between 1997 and 2007 show a sharp decline at ages 25 to 29 for both sexes. In the case of males, this has resulted in an upward shift in the peak marriage rate from ages 25 to 29 to ages 30 to 34. Rates from 30 to 34 and up have remained roughly unchanged for females and have risen somewhat for males. It should be kept in mind that these rates apply to the residual numbers of unmarried males and females, which have been rising over time as a result of falling marriage rates at the younger ages. For this expanding pool of singles in their thirties and forties, marriage rates have maintained (or in the case of males, slightly surpassed) their former levels, but this will not be enough to prevent the proportions who reach age 45 to 49 without marrying from increasing.

Figure 2
Marriage Rates—Singapore, 1997–2007

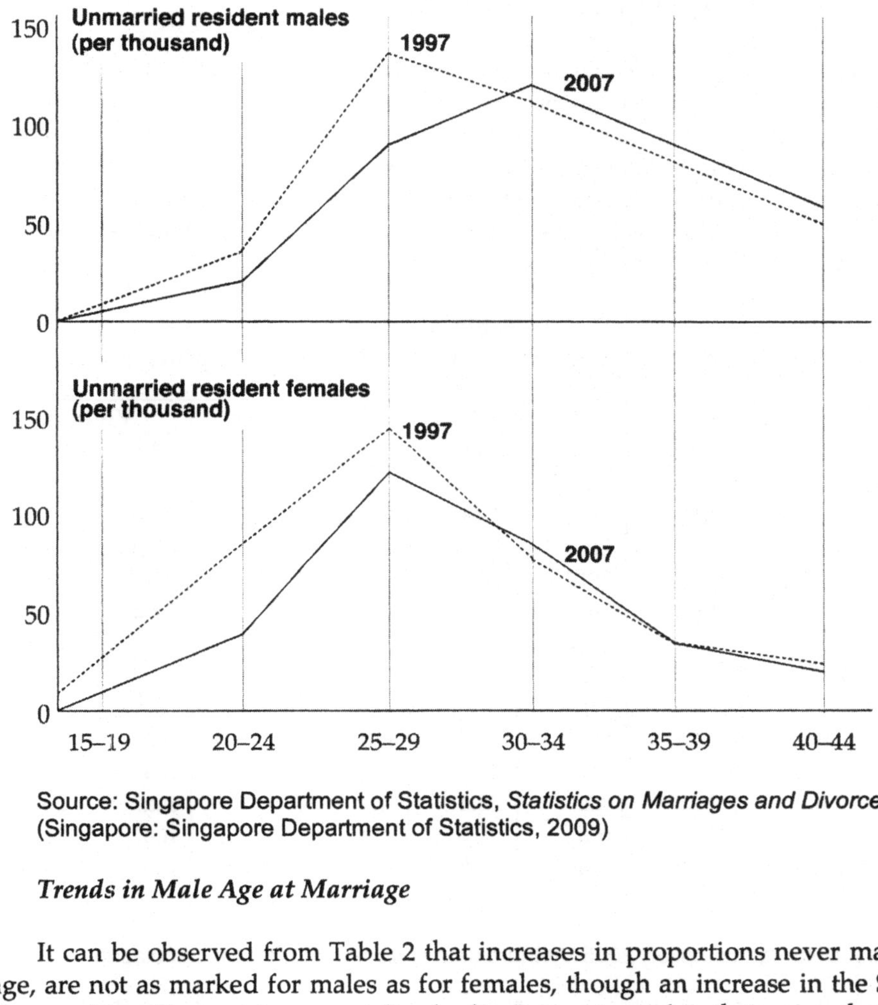

Source: Singapore Department of Statistics, *Statistics on Marriages and Divorces 2008* (Singapore: Singapore Department of Statistics, 2009)

Trends in Male Age at Marriage

It can be observed from Table 2 that increases in proportions never married, by age, are not as marked for males as for females, though an increase in the SMAM is observed for all countries except Cambodia. It is universal in the region that a higher proportion of males than females remain single in their twenties, reflecting both norms of males marrying someone younger than themselves and the perceived expectation for a man to be capable of providing for a family before marrying. In their thirties, in most countries of the region more males continue to be single than females (see Figure 1), though in some cases this trend no longer holds by ages 35 to 39. By ages 40 to 49, a higher proportion of females than males remain single. This is not universally the case, however. For example, in the Philippines and Singapore, the proportions remaining single at this age are essentially the same for males and females, while in Malaysia a slightly higher proportion of males remain single at these ages.

In general, the evidence points to a greater difficulty in finding a spouse for those females remaining unmarried in their thirties and forties than for unmarried males at these ages. However, the extent to which the lower rate of entering marriage at these ages by females stems from their weaker position in the marriage market and the extent to which it is volitional is not clear.

Age at First Marriage: Evidence from the DHS

Data on exact age at first marriage is available from the DHS, thus changes in marital timing by age groups can be assessed using data from these surveys. It is important to note here that age at first marriage in the DHS is the age at which a respondent began actually *living with* his or her partner. This increases the recorded age at marriage of some early marriages, where the respondent only begins to live with the husband/wife several years after the marriage ceremony has taken place. It also means that the DHS considers those in informal unions married.

Table 3
Median Age at First Marriage: Indonesia, Cambodia, Philippines, Vietnam

	Indonesia		Cambodia		Philippines		Vietnam	
	1991	2003	2000	2005	1993	2003	1997	2005
Females								
25-29	18.6	20.2	19.9	20.1	22.0	22.2	21.0	21.9
30-34	17.8	19.9	20.4	19.9	21.7	22.3	21.3	21.2
35-39	17.4	18.9	19.7	20.5	21.4	22.0	21.3	21.3
40-44	16.8	18.3	20.4	19.8	21.5	21.6	21.4	21.6
45-49	16.9	17.9	19.1	20.4	21.3	21.9	21.7	21.8
Males								
25-29	n.a.	23.5	n.a.	22.6	n.a.	n.a	n.a.	25.1
30-34	n.a.	24.5	n.a.	21.8	n.a.	25.2	n.a.	24.5
35-39	n.a.	24.3	n.a.	22.4	n.a.	24.5	n.a.	23.6
40-44	n.a.	23.6	n.a.	21.6	n.a.	24.7	n.a.	24.3
45-49	n.a.	23.6	n.a.	21.8	n.a.	24.2	n.a.	24.3

Source: DHS stat compiler; 2005 Vietnam data is from author's own calculation

Table 3 shows the median age at first marriage, by age group, for the countries where a DHS survey has been conducted in Southeast Asia—Indonesia, Cambodia, Philippines, and Vietnam. Median age at first marriage refers to the exact age by which 50 percent of the entire cohort has married. Data are shown for females and males from the earliest and latest round of surveys for each country.[8] Comparatively,

---

[8] For Indonesia and the Philippines, the earliest round of surveys is from the early 1990s and the most recent one is ten years later. Vietnam's earliest survey is in 1997 and the most recent one, in 2005. Cambodia is the only country where the earliest and latest surveys are five years apart and where the earlier survey is from 2000.

Indonesia has the earliest age at marriage for the earlier cohorts. Though the earlier Indonesian data are from a 1991 survey (much earlier than the surveys in the other countries), the 2002–03 survey also shows a median age at marriage of just under 18 years for the 45 to 49 age groups. This is one to two years lower than the median age at marriage in Cambodia for the 45 to 49 age groups in both the 2000 and 2005 surveys and more than two years lower than for the other countries. However, the median age at marriage for the 25 to 29 age group in the year 2002–03 in Indonesia increased considerably, reaching roughly the Cambodian level. Median age at marriage in Indonesia increased substantially from 16.9 among the 45 to 49 age group in 1991 (birth cohort of 1942–1946) to 20.2 among the 25 to 29 age group in 2002–03 (birth cohort of 1973–1977). Median age at marriage for men remained stable at about 24 years in each successive birth cohort in the 2002/03 survey, indicating a closing of the average age gap between spouses from 5.7 years to 3.3 years between the earliest and latest birth cohorts.

None of the other countries covered by DHS surveys shows very much change in median age at marriage. For Cambodian females, this remained unchanged at about twenty years, and among males it increased slightly for the youngest cohort. In both the Philippines and Vietnam, median age at marriage for females is about twenty-one to twenty-two years. For males, median age at marriage increased from 24 to 25 in both countries. As the DHS considers age at first cohabitation as age at first marriage, the increasing trend in reported levels of cohabiting unions in the Philippines means that the DHS figures may be disguising an actual increase in the age at formal marriage.

DIFFERENTIALS IN AGE AT MARRIAGE

The previous section discussed differentials in marriage trends among countries. There is, however, considerable variation in age at marriage within countries. Figures 3 and 4 show trends and differentials in age at first marriage by urban-versus-rural status and education for various birth cohorts[9] in Indonesia, Philippines, Cambodia, and Vietnam from DHS data. Figure 3 shows that median age at marriage for women is higher in urban areas than in rural areas. In Indonesia, the difference is quite large, but age at marriage increased in both urban and rural areas over time. In the Philippines, there is about a two-year difference in age at marriage between urban and rural areas, but age at marriage has been increasing in urban areas while it remains unchanged in rural areas.

In Cambodia, age at marriage was only slightly higher in urban than in rural areas, though the increase was greater among urban women. In Vietnam, there is a substantial difference in age at marriage between urban and rural areas. There has been an increase in urban areas while slight declines were observed in rural areas.

With regard to differences in median age at marriage by education levels (Figure 4), though in all countries median age at marriage is youngest for women with no education and oldest for women with a secondary or higher level of education, the magnitude of the difference between education levels and over time varies by

---

[9] Data from the 25–29 age group and the 45–49 age group of the earliest and latest rounds of surveys for each respective country are combined to present results as changes over birth cohorts. Male data are not shown because an earlier survey is not available to determine trends.

country. In Indonesia, substantial differences in median age at marriage with respect to education level as well as over time are observed. This suggests that age at marriage has increased not only among women with a secondary or higher level of education but also among women with no education.

Figure 3
Median Age of Females at First Marriage,
by Urban vs. Rural and Birth Cohort

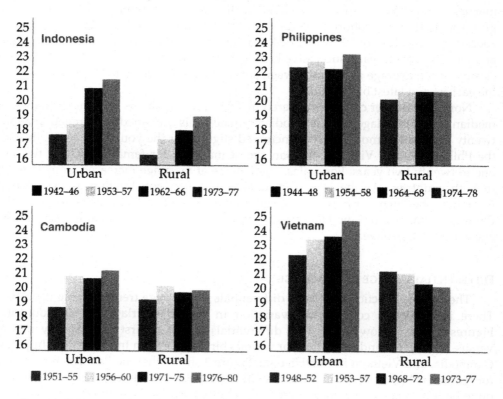

Source: Demographic and Health Surveys

In the Philippines, large differences in median age at marriage between education groups is evident—median age at marriage is about four to five years higher for women with secondary and higher-level education compared with women with no education. However, age at marriage did not increase over time. In Cambodia, the difference between education levels and time period is only slight, but there was an almost two-year increment in the median age at marriage, from 19.6 to 21.3, between the earliest and latest birth cohort among women with a secondary and higher-level education. No large difference in age at marriage between education levels is evident in Vietnam, but age at marriage across cohorts fluctuated or declined slightly for education levels over time.

The available evidence from Southeast Asia from the 1980, 1990, and 2000 population censuses also shows a marked gradation in proportions of women never married, by educational level, controlling for age. Those with tertiary education had by far the highest proportions of "never married" individuals. This was the case, for example, for Peninsular Malaysia, Thailand, Myanmar, and the Philippines, and for the major metropolises of Bangkok, Singapore, and Jakarta.[10] Data for two smaller cities in Indonesia (Medan and Yogyakarta) confirm the relationship.[11]

Figure 4
Median Age of Females at First Marriage,
by Education and Birth Cohort

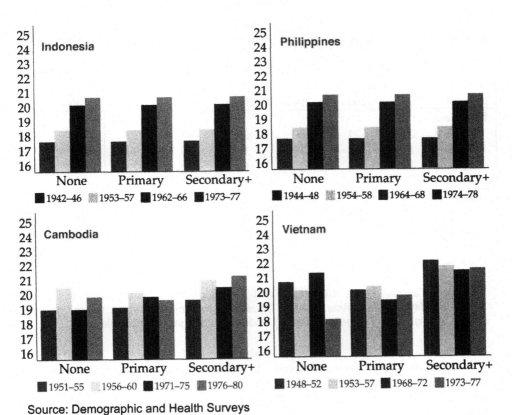

Source: Demographic and Health Surveys

---

[10] Stella R. Quah, "The Social Significance of Marriage and Parenthood in Singapore: Policy and Trends," in *The Family as an Asset: An International Perspective on Marriage, Parenthood and Social Policy*, ed. Stella R. Quah (Singapore: Times Academic Press, 1990); Stella R. Quah, *Family in Singapore: Sociological Perspectives*, second edition (Singapore: Times Academic Press, 1998); Peter Xenos and Socorro A. Gultiano, "Trends in Female and Male Age at Marriage and Celibacy in Asia," Papers of the Program on Population No. 120 (Honolulu, HI: East-West Center, 1992), p. 22; Philip Guest and JooEan Tan, *Transformation of Marriage Patterns in Thailand* (Salaya: Institute for Population and Social Research, Mahidol University, 1994); Gavin W. Jones, "The Demise of Universal Marriage in East and South-East Asia," in *The Continuing Demographic Transition*, ed. Gavin W. Jones, Robert M. Douglas, John C. Caldwell, et al. (Oxford: Clarendon Press, 1997), pp. 58–60; Gavin W. Jones, "Not 'When to Marry' but 'Whether to Marry': The Changing Context of Marriage Decisions in East and Southeast Asia," in *(Un)tying the Knot: Ideal and Reality in Asian Marriage*, ed. Gavin W. Jones and Kamalini Ramdas (Singapore: Asia Research Institute, National University of Singapore, 2004), pp. 10–14.

[11] Augustina Situmorang, "Staying Single in a Married World: Never-Married Women in Yogyakarta and Medan," *Asian Population Studies* 3,3 (2007): Table 5.

Tables 4 to 7 present census-based information for females in Singapore, Malaysia, and Thailand showing further evidence of a link between more education and higher proportions never married. The relationship is not as clear-cut with respect to males, except in Singapore and Malaysia where, at ages above thirty, there is a sharply inverse pattern for males, relative to females: the highest levels of nonmarriage are found among men with the lowest level of education. Thailand, where better-educated men were least likely to marry, is an exception to this trend.

Table 4
Percentage Never Married by Age, Sex, and Education, Singapore, 2000 and 2005

Age groups	Below secondary		Secondary		Post-secondary		University	
	2000	2005	2000	2005	2000	2005	2000	2005
Female								
25-29	21	21	30	34	43	47	54	56
30-34	13	13	17	17	23	24	27	28
35-39	10	10	14	14	20	17	23	20
40-44	9	10	15	14	20	18	22	21
Male								
25-29	62	67	58	63	70	69	69	73
30-34	40	42	29	35	28	33	28	32
35-39	28	29	18	22	15	18	13	14
40-44	21	23	14	14	9	12	7	8

Source: Yap Mui Teng, "Ultra-Low Fertility in Singapore: Some Observations," in *Ultra-Low Fertility in Pacific Asia: Trends, Causes and Policy Issues*, ed. Gavin Jones, Paulin Tay-Straughan and Angelique Chan (London: Routledge, 2009), Table 8.3.

Table 5
Percentage of Never Married Chinese, by Age, Sex, and Education, Peninsular Malaysia, 1991 and 2000

Age groups	Primary		Secondary		Tertiary	
	1991	2000	1991	2000	1991	2000
Female						
25-29	20.0	28.5	38.8	38.0	61.3	64.5
30-34	10.1	10.8	21.1	15.9	28.7	30.3
35-39	6.7	7.0	15.2	10.2	22.1	16.7
40-44	5.5	5.2	12.4	8.8	19.8	17.4
45-49	3.3	4.3	12.4	10.0	16.4	11.5
Male						
25-29	59.9	73.7	63.4	68.0	70.3	73.8
30-34	32.6	44.3	31.4	35.9	26.9	30.1
35-39	19.3	23.8	15.6	18.8	12.2	15.8
40-44	10.1	15.0	8.6	11.8	5.9	7.9
45-49	6.8	9.9	4.7	7.0	3.6	6.7

Source: Tey Nai Peng, "Trends in Delayed and Non-Marriage in Peninsular Malaysia," *Asian Population Studies*, 3,3 (2007), Table 6.

Table 6
Percentage of Never-Married Malays, by Age, Sex, and Education,
Peninsular Malaysia, 1991 and 2000

Age	Primary		Secondary		Tertiary	
groups	1991	2000	1991	2000	1991	2000
Female						
25-29	16.0	18.2	23.6	18.6	37.7	33.1
30-34	8.6	11.8	10.6	8.2	13.4	12.6
35-39	5.4	5.4	6.8	6.4	8.3	7.1
40-44	4.1	4.3	8.1	4.7	14.5	3.4
45-49	2.4	3.2	4.3	4.0	12.1	6.3
Male						
25-29	45.3	54.4	45.0	45.2	42.5	47.1
30-34	15.5	27.5	13.6	17.2	9.3	10.1
35-39	8.2	13.1	6.1	6.7	2.1	3.9
40-44	3.6	7.6	3.1	4.0	1.3	2.5
45-49	2.6	4.4	2.2	2.6	0.0	1.6

Source: Tey Nai Peng, "Trends in Delayed and Non-Marriage in Peninsular Malaysia,"
Asian Population Studies 3,3 (2007), Table 6.

Table 7
Percentage never married, by age and education, Thailand, 2000

Age groups	Completed primary school or less	Completed lower secondary	Completed upper secondary	Attended tertiary	All levels
Female					
20-24	31.9	43.9	65.9	86.9	57.2
25-29	14.8	25.5	36.7	62.9	29.1
30-34	9.3	16.4	23.8	35.1	15.6
35-39	7.0	14.3	17.0	22.7	10.7
40-44	6.3	11.9	8.7	18.9	8.5
45-49	5.9	12.2	11.8	17.5	7.4
50-54	4.6	11.5	8.8	16.9	5.8
Male					
20-24	67.9	72.7	81.0	91.1	77.0
25-29	36.7	42.0	48.0	67.1	45.0
30-34	17.2	21.1	22.7	34.4	21.3
35-39	9.4	13.2	14.3	18.7	11.8
40-44	6.1	6.8	9.4	9.2	6.8
45-49	3.9	6.2	5.8	7.3	4.6
50-54	3.0	2.8	4.4	5.7	3.3

Source: unpublished data from the 2000 population census

In summary, the trend toward later marriage was most pronounced in urban areas, particularly in the large cities of the region, and was intimately related to trends in female education and in the life-course trajectories of young women resulting from these trends in education.[12] Increasing education and emerging patterns of labor-force participation for young women are crucial to understanding trends in marriage in the region. Although in some cultures raising education levels for young women can be seen as a stratagem for securing for them a more desirable husband, in Southeast Asia quite generally the main motivation for educating females seems to be an increasing acceptance that boys and girls should be given more or less equal treatment and that, having been educated through senior high school or tertiary level, it is reasonable for young women to enter the workforce. The correlation between more education and time spent in the workforce, on the one hand, and later marriage, on the other, is quite marked in Southeast Asia. This, of course, does not prove the direction of causation or even direct cause and effect. Although it is plausible to argue that extended education and workforce participation lead to delayed marriage, in many cases, continuing in education and entering the workforce may be a result, rather than a cause, of not marrying, and sometimes other factors are causally related to both the extended education and the delayed marriage.

REASONS AND MOTIVATION FOR DELAYED MARRIAGE

As recently as four or five decades ago, in much of Southeast Asia, to raise the question of why marriages were being delayed would have been tantamount to asking what motivations parents had for delaying the marriages of their daughters because most marriages were arranged. This was certainly the case in the Malay-Muslim world, among Chinese and Indian populations in the region,[13] and, perhaps to a slightly lesser extent, in Vietnam.[14] In Thailand,[15] the Philippines, and Cambodia, as well as Vietnam from the war period onward,[16] there was more scope for the exercise of agency by the young, but the choice of a marriage partner was usually subject to parents' approval and would not normally take place without it. This is no longer the case, and, as noted earlier, to a quite remarkable extent parents have abdicated their former role in this regard. The key question needing to be answered nowadays if we wish to understand marriage decisions is, what are the factors motivating individuals to marry soon, later, or never?

The effect of education and changing patterns of labor-force participation are central to the marriage changes already summarized. In Indonesia, the proportion of young women aged 15 to 19 and 20 to 24 who are either in school or working in the

---

[12] Gavin W. Jones, "The Flight From Marriage in East and Southeast Asia," *Journal of Comparative Family Studies* 36,1 (2005).

[13] Gavin W. Jones, *Marriage and Divorce in Islamic Southeast Asia* (Singapore: Oxford University Press, 1994), pp. 131–44.

[14] Rukmalie Jayakody and Vu Tuan Huy, "Family Change in Vietnam's Red River Delta: From War, to Reunification, to Renovation," in *Reconfiguring Families in Contemporary Vietnam*, ed. Magali Barbieri and Daniele Belanger (Palo Alto, CA: Stanford University Press, 2009), p. 206.

[15] Bhassorn Limanonda, *Mate Selection and Post-Nuptial Residence in Thailand* (Institute of Population Studies, Chulalongkorn University, 1979).

[16] Daniele Belanger and Khuat Thu Hong, "Parents' Involvement in Children's Marriage: Intergenerational Relations in the Choice of a Spouse in Hanoi, Vietnam," *Vietnamese Society in Transition: The Daily Politics of Reform and Change*, ed. John Kleinen (Amsterdam: Het Spinhuis, 2001).

formal sector has risen steadily over the last three decades.[17] This reflects a changing life-course trajectory for young women, along which marriage is postponed and young women do not simply follow their parents' choice in the matter. Traditionally, in Southeast Asia, women needed a husband for the economic security he afforded and to fulfill traditional expectations, which made marriage mandatory for any woman who was not physically or mentally handicapped. But with changing education and work patterns, a large cohort was created of women who not only had an independent income but for whom marriage and its expected outcome— childbearing—would cause tangible disadvantages, for example, in disruption to their career and loss of independence.

The factors contributing to delayed marriage in the region are complex, but can perhaps be divided into three categories.

1. Perceived desirability of marriage
Among the most important factors in this category are:
- Expansion of education. In the poorer countries in the group, notably Indonesia, this means that girls remain in school beyond the traditional age of marriage, but, more importantly, educational expansion and trends in labor markets have opened up employment possibilities for women, widened their aspirations, and freed many from financial dependence on men. "Later and less" marriage has particularly characterized the growing group of women with tertiary education.
- Increasing uncertainty in the labor market (felt in varying degrees throughout the region). Men and couples in serious relationships are reluctant to marry until they can build up some capital, and women are increasingly cautious about marrying a man with poor earning prospects.
- Rising divorce rates. The incidence of failed marriages and informal unions in many countries of the region is probably leading to increasing caution in choosing a marriage partner.
- Time constraints due to work. The growing urban populations in countries such as Singapore, Malaysia, Thailand, Indonesia, and the Philippines face issues of work pressures, including very long hours of work (especially when travel to and from work is included).
- Increasingly sexually permissive societies. Access to sex outside of marriage is easier to come by.[18] The recent passage of the pornography

---

[17] Terence Hull, "Demographic Perspectives on the Future of the Indonesian Family," *Journal of Population Research* 20,1 (2003): Table 3.

[18] Increasing sexual permissiveness has been documented for some countries in the region. In Vietnam, surveys showed that 31 percent of men who married in 1992–2000 reported having had premarital sex, though the proportion was lower among women (8 percent in the south, 12 percent in the north). These percentages were higher than for earlier cohorts (Sharon Ghuman, Vu Manh Loi, Vu Tuan Huy, et al., "Continuity and Change in Premarital Sex in Vietnam," *International Family Planning Perspectives* 32,4 [2006]). In Thailand, a study in Chiangmai found that among adolescents ages 17 to 20 from a range of backgrounds, almost two-thirds of the males and more than one-third of the females had experienced sexual intercourse (Arunrat Tangmunkongvorakul, "Sexual Health in Transition: Adolescent Lifestyles and Relationships in Contemporary Chiang Mai, Thailand," [PhD dissertation, Australian National University, 2008], Table 6.1). Considerably lower proportions than these have been measured in many surveys in the region, but the studies using peers as interviewers

law in Indonesia may seem to contradict this, but passage of this law can be seen to reflect the belief of many, particularly traditionalist Muslims, that permissiveness is getting out of hand.

2. Disincentives to have children

Marriage can rarely be separated from its expected outcome in Southeast Asia, that is, the bearing and raising of children. An important issue is the extent to which trends in nonmarriage are behaviorally and motivationally linked to trends in fertility. To what extent do people avoid marriage because they want to avoid having children? While perhaps there is less pressure placed on those who marry to have a child quickly than there is in East Asian Confucianist-influenced societies, it is still the case that the most straightforward way to avoid having children is not to marry.[19] Therefore, factors relating to reluctance to begin raising a family also work against marriage:

- The costs of childrearing are increasing, both the direct financial costs and the opportunity costs of women's interrupted career development.
- There is increasing pressure, especially in the cities, to engage in "intensive parenting," that is, bringing children the benefits of coaching, music lessons, and so on, and ensuring that the child is "successful." Women bear the brunt of fulfilling societal expectations about intensive parenting.
- While survey evidence in Southeast Asia bearing on men's attitudes toward their role in household management and childcare is very hard to find, there is reason to believe that the very slow changes in men's contributions to these activities in Japanese and Korean households in which both spouses work also characterize most Southeast Asian populations.[20] Women who can expect to be economically independent are aware of the difficulty of finding a mate who shares their values and expectations and may be increasingly uncertain about what value and priority to place on marriage and family formation.

3. Marriage squeeze

The decline in arranged marriage has cast the onus of finding a spouse onto the individuals concerned, but a well-developed marriage market has not emerged (though there are interesting developments in commercial and Internet matchmaking).[21] The trends in education and employment already discussed provide an entirely new context for marriage markets. Whereas the traditional emphasis on hypergamy —women "marrying up"—made sense when educated women were an aberration and were greatly outnumbered by educated men, it becomes impossible

---

and those using more-private methods such as self-administered questionnaires tend to measure much higher levels of sexual experience (Tangmunkongvorakul, "Sexual Health in Transition," pp. 240–41 and the studies cited therein).

[19] Jones, "Not 'When to Marry' but 'Whether to Marry,'" p. 17.

[20] Noriko Tsuya and Larry L. Bumpass, eds., *Marriage, Work, and Family Life in Comparative Perspective: Japan, Korea, and the United States* (Honolulu, HI: University of Hawaii Press, 2004).

[21] Gavin W. Jones and Bina Gubhaju, "Factors Influencing Changes in Mean Age at First Marriage and Proportions Never Marrying in the Low-Fertility Countries of East and Southeast Asia," *Asian Population Studies* 5,3 (2009), pp. 259–60.

to sustain when women become the majority of educated persons in the marriageable ages.

A brief description of the issue of "marriage squeeze" for educated women in Southeast Asian cities is perhaps needed. The first point is that the almost universal decline in fertility throughout the region has until recently not altered the overall triangular shape of the population pyramid at the marriageable ages, in which successively larger cohorts have been moving up the pyramid. Given the traditional gap in marriage ages for males and females, this makes for an excess of marriageable females in their 20s and 30s, ages at which marriage is most common. This is particularly so in some metropolitan cities of the region, where sex ratios are lowered by female-dominated migration patterns: The sex ratio among recent migrants aged 15 to 24 in 2000 was 60 males per 100 females in Metro Manila, 62 in Jakarta, and 84 in Bangkok; at ages 25 to 34, the number of males per 100 females was 91 in Metro Manila, 95 in Bangkok, and 123 in Jakarta.[22] Equally important, in recent decades, the great improvements in educational opportunities in Southeast Asian countries have been even more marked for females than for males, as already discussed. This has lowered the ratio of well-educated men to well-educated women in marriageable age cohorts. Further, educated women have been delaying marriage to establish themselves in their careers. Given the persistence of traditional norms about suitable marriage partners, by which men favor brides who are younger and less-educated than the men themselves, once the educated women reach the point of looking seriously for a spouse, they are likely to find slim pickings in the field of potential mates. The problem is exacerbated by a "values gap" between educated women and many of their potential spouses. Feminist values have been increasingly adopted by educated women in the region, but male attitudes toward gender roles, including the sharing of housework and raising of children, have been slower to change.[23] Thus, many educated women in the region would share the perception, and experience, that the problem of the marriage market is not so much the lack of available males as the shortage of men who share modern women's values and expectations.[24]

Take the example of Malaysia. Assume that the average age gap between husbands and wives is five years—as, indeed, it used to be in Malaysia. Then we can compare the numbers of men ages 20 to 49 with the number of women ages 15 to 45 with secondary education or more. In 1970, the ratio of these numbers was 1.17. In 1980 it was .99; in 1990, 1.01; and by 2000, 0.82. In other words, the 1990s saw a change from a situation in which the numbers of males and females in these age-education groups were approximately equal at the beginning of the decade to a situation in which there were 22 percent more females than males at the end of the decade. In light of these figures, increasing nonmarriage for educated women is not hard to understand.

Peter Stein argued that the state of being single can be categorized based on an element of choice (voluntary versus involuntary) and permanence (temporary and stable) and that membership in these categories changes over time and with

---

[22] Mike Douglass and Gavin Jones, "Mega-Urban Region Dynamics in Comparative Perspective," in *Mega-Urban Regions in Pacific Asia: Urban Dynamics in a Global Era*, ed. Gavin W. Jones and Mike Douglass (Singapore: NUS Press, 2008), ch. 11.

[23] Quah, *Family in Singapore*, ch. 5.

[24] Hull, "Demographic Perspectives on the Future of the Indonesian Family," p. 8.

changing situations.[25] Survey information in Singapore showing a general desire to marry[26] suggests that there is a good deal of involuntary singlehood around, and this is probably the case more widely in Southeast Asia. Few studies have been conducted, however, to probe the background of singles in their thirties and forties in the region, notable exceptions (all studying single women, not men) being Augustina Situmorang,[27] Rozita Ibrahim and Zaharah Hassan,[28] and JooEan Tan[29].

4. Summary

Ever-increasing levels of education for women place more women in the tertiary-educated category long characterized by later and less marriage and marriage-squeeze issues related to hypergamy. Besides this, urbanization and changing aspirations and lifestyles have affected both men and women across the board throughout Southeast Asia, irrespective of their levels of education. In general, rising age at marriage has been less dramatic in Southeast Asia than in the highly developed economies of Japan, Korea, Taiwan, and Hong Kong. Nevertheless, Singapore has matched these countries in rising age at marriage, until the trend leveled off some fifteen years ago, and Myanmar has shown a remarkable rise in age at marriage, perhaps reflecting both the factors prevalent elsewhere and the effect of economic stagnation and repression of political expression in a population entering the period under review with high expectations.[30]

AGE DIFFERENCES BETWEEN SPOUSES

Throughout the world to varying degrees, and certainly in Southeast Asia, there is a tendency for men to marry women younger than themselves. There also appears to be a tendency for the average age gap between spouses at the time of marriage to narrow as societies modernize and education levels increase. Southeast Asia has always been differentiated from South Asia and the Middle East by the fact of its smaller age gap between husband and wife and a higher proportion of women

---

[25] Peter J. Stein, *Single Life: Unmarried Adults in Social Context* (New York, NY: St. Martin's Press, 1981).

[26] Quah, *Family in Singapore;* Quah, "The Social Significance of Marriage and Parenthood in Singapore"; David Chan, *Attitudes on Family: Survey on Social Attitudes of Singaporeans 2001* (Singapore: Ministry of Community Development, Youth, and Sports, 2002).

[27] Situmorang, "Staying Single in a Married World"; Augustina Situmorang, "Delayed Marriage Among Lower Socio-Economic Groups in an Indonesian Industrial City," in *Marriage Trends in Southeast Asia.*

[28] Rozita Ibrahim and Zaharah Hassan, "Understanding Singlehood from the Experiences of Never-Married Malay Muslim Women in Malaysia: Some Preliminary Findings," *European Journal of Social Sciences* 8,3 (2009).

[29] JooEan Tan, "Social Relationships in the Modern Age: Never-Married Women in Bangkok, Jakarta, and Manila," *Journal of Comparative Family Studies* 41,5 (2010).

[30] Special factors that appear to operate in the Myanmar case include the reluctance of both men and women to marry and establish a family in uncertain economic and political circumstances, the general unacceptability of divorce as a way of escaping an unsatisfactory marriage, and the fact that singlehood is socially acceptable, particularly when the motive is to look after aged parents. (Based on the first author's detailed discussions with a group of about twenty-five female government officials in Yangon in 2005.)

marrying younger men.[31] Spouses' age differences in the region have tended to be greater for women who married very young, who were uneducated, and whose marriages were arranged. In general, however, age differences between spouses in the region are tending to narrow over time. Male ages at marriage in Southeast Asia have generally been rising less rapidly than female ages at marriage, resulting in a gradual convergence in male and female ages at marriage.[32] There are, of course, differences between countries and cultural groups with respect to average age-difference between spouses, yet in Malaysia, where the major ethnic groups of Asia are represented, there is little difference between the groups in the proportion of women who marry men at least five years older than themselves: 44 percent among Malays, 39 percent among Chinese, and 45 percent among Indians. For the Malays and Chinese, though, the proportion of tertiary-educated women with such a wide age gap is substantially less than for those with lower levels of education.[33]

TRENDS IN DISSOLUTION OF MARRIAGE

In the Philippines, divorce is impossible, though annulment of some marriages (a figure which rose from 4,520 cases in 201 to 8,282 cases in 2010) does occur.[34] Therefore, the Philippines will be excluded from this discussion. Throughout the remainder of the region, there has been considerable variation in levels of divorce across societies. In the period before 1970, the Muslim populations of Indonesia, Malaysia, and Thailand had by far the highest rates of divorce, the Thai Buddhist population had a moderate divorce rate, and the Balinese, Malaysian Chinese and Indians, and Thai Chinese had the lowest divorce rate.[35] Cultural differences are important in explaining these differences. In Chinese societies, divorce was strongly frowned on, and couples were likely to remain in unhappy marriages for the sake of "family honor." Among Indian couples, divorce was not really an option for the women, because at marriage they were essentially lost to their natal family. By contrast, in Malay-Muslim society, where the key elements of family honor to be preserved were avoidance of premarital pregnancy and ensuring marriage of all daughters, divorce was an accepted way out if arranged marriages at very young ages did not work out satisfactorily.[36]

The conventional wisdom in Western social science that modernization leads to increases in divorce rates is frequently incorrect when applied to Southeast Asia.[37]

---

[31] John B. Casterline, Lindy Williams, and Peter McDonald, "The Age Difference Between Spouses: Variations Among Developing Countries," *Population Studies* 40,3 (1986).

[32] Xenos and Gultiano, "Trends in Female and Male Age at Marriage and Celibacy in Asia," pp. 14–20; Jones, *Marriage and Divorce in Islamic Southeast Asia*, pp. 102–9.

[33] Tey Nai Peng, "Trends in Delayed and Non-Marriage in Peninsular Malaysia," *Asian Population Studies* 3,3 (2007): Table 8.

[34] "Filipino Marriage Annulments Increase by 40 Percent," *The China Post*, March 28, 2011.

[35] Charles Hirschman and Bussarawan Teerawichitchainan, "Cultural and Socioeconomic Influences on Divorce During Modernization: Southeast Asia, 1940s to 1960s," *Population and Development Review* 29,2 (2003).

[36] Jones, *Marriage and Divorce in Islamic Southeast Asia*, pp. 218–23.

[37] Gavin W. Jones, "Modernization and Divorce: Contrasting Trends in Islamic South-East Asia and the West," *Population and Development Review* 23,1 (1997a); Tim B. Heaton., Mark Cammack, and Larry Young, "Why is the Divorce Rate Declining in Indonesia?" *Journal of*

Among the Muslim population of Malaysia and Indonesia, earlier trends were for divorce rates to fall from among the highest in the world in the 1950s and 1960s[38] to levels considerably lower than those in most Western countries by the 1990s.[39] This decline in divorce rates was related to the changing ways marriages were entered into, as girls remained longer in school and their parents forsook the tradition of arranged marriage. Self-arranged marriages at older ages faced much less risk of an early collapse. Legal changes also played a role in making divorce more difficult to obtain, but these changes followed rather than led the decline in divorce rates. Up to 1993, at least, divorce rates among Muslims in the major cities of Indonesia and Malaysia were continuing to trend downward, despite rapid economic and social development, though among Muslims in Singapore the divorce rate was slowly increasing.[40]

Almost universally throughout the region, the popular press takes for granted that divorce rates are now rising, frequently based on impressionistic evidence because data on divorces are sparse in many cases. However, there *is* clear evidence of rising divorce rates in Singapore and Thailand, where the general divorce rate (divorces per 1,000 population aged 15+) rose from 1.0 and 0.8 in 1980 to 1.5 and 1.3 in 1995, respectively, and, in the case of Singapore, to 1.9 in 2005.[41] There is also clear evidence of rising divorce rates in Malaysia since 2002, for both non-Muslims and Muslims.[42] It is likely that these trends reflect "modern divorce," that is, divorce rates reflecting the same kinds of causes that are leading to rising divorce rates in Western countries. As for Indonesia, the divorce rate seems to have begun increasing since reaching a low in 2003.[43]

POLYGAMY

Monogamy has been the dominant marriage pattern in Southeast Asia for many centuries.[44] In areas affected by the spread of Islam, polygyny (men having more

---

Marriage and Family 63,2 (2001); Hirschman and Teerawichitchainan, "Cultural and Socioeconomic Influences on Divorce."

[38] Indeed, the states of Kelantan and Trengganu in Malaysia and the province of West Java in Indonesia appear to have had the highest rates in the world in the 1950s among substantial populations with recorded divorce data (Gavin W. Jones, "Malay Marriage and Divorce in Peninsular Malaysia: Three Decades of Change," *Population and Development Review* 7,2 [1981]).

[39] Jones, *Marriage and Divorce in Islamic Southeast Asia*, pp. 165–202.

[40] Jones, "Modernization and Divorce," Figure 5; Heaton et al., "Why is the Divorce Rate Declining in Indonesia?"

[41] Singapore divorce statistics are detailed and accurate. Indeed, there is information on trends in a more refined measure of divorce, namely divorces per 1,000 married resident males and females. The figure rose from 3.7 males and 3.8 females in 1980 to 6.5 males and 6.5 females in 2000 and to 7.7 males and 7.3 females in 2009 (Singapore Department of Statistics, *Population Trends 2010* [Singapore: Singapore Department of Statistics, 2010]).

[42] Tey Nai Peng, "Understanding Marriage and Divorce Trends in Peninsular Malaysia," in *Marriage Trends in Southeast Asia*.

[43] Mark Cammak and Tim Heaton, "The Recent Upturn in Divorce in Indonesia" (paper presented at Workshop on Marital Dissolution in Asia, Asia Research Institute, National University of Singapore, May 6–7, 2010).

[44] Anthony Reid, "Female Roles in Pre-Colonial Southeast Asia," *Modern Asian Studies* 22,3 (1988), p. 151.

than one wife) was considered permissible, but this did not mean it was common.[45] In 1930, in the Netherlands Indies as a whole, only 2.6 percent of husbands were in polygamous marriages and in Java, only 1.9 percent. Among Islamic populations, polygamy was most common in West Sumatra and Lampung.[46] In the 1970s, about 4 percent of women in Java were married to a polygynous husband. The corresponding figure was almost 9 percent in Sulawesi and, in general, polygyny remained more common in areas outside Java. The great majority of polygamous husbands had only two wives; having two wives was between three and five times more common than having three or more wives, depending on the province. In Malaysia, polygamous marriages were almost 3 percent of all Muslim marriages entered into between 1984 and 1991. The highest rates were in Kelantan and Terengganu.[47] More recent data for 2004 recorded 1.3 percent of Malay husbands having more than one wife.[48]

Polygamy was therefore not very common in the Muslim areas of Southeast Asia. Nor was it common in a legally accepted sense in other areas, though in countries such as Thailand and the Philippines, in both of which the practice of polygamy is illegal under civil law, keeping a mistress (or minor wife, *mia noi* in Thailand) was certainly not rare. Throughout Southeast Asia, polygamy or the keeping of mistresses appeared to be more common among the nobility, high government officials, and wealthy men.[49] Though there are some indications that the incidence of polygamy may have declined of late, the evidence is not clear-cut.[50] More recently, the advocacy of polygamy on grounds that it is condoned by Islam has become more common in Indonesia and Malaysia, though this advocacy has been strongly opposed by women's groups in particular.[51]

Many wives were unwilling to tolerate their husband's taking a second wife and chose divorce instead. As divorce was much more frequent than polygamy throughout the Malay world, the occurrence of polygamy itself could not have been a major cause of divorce in more than a small percentage of cases. "The overt threat of [polygamy], however, may have been a factor disrupting marriages in many more cases, and the implied threat of it based simply on its acceptance by religion and culture may have been a factor making for suspicion and distance in the husband-wife relationship in many instances, thus providing a fertile breeding ground for divorce."[52]

---

[45] Actually, in Indonesia, in 1930, polygyny was most common in parts of East Nusatenggara—in Sumba and Flores—where traditional beliefs had not been fully superseded by Islam (Sumba) or Catholicism (Flores).

[46] Jones, *Marriage and Divorce in Islamic Southeast Asia* , pp. 269–70.

[47] Ibid., Table 7.3.

[48] Tey, "Understanding Marriage and Divorce Trends in Peninsular Malaysia."

[49] Malaysian data for 2004, however, show polygamy being more common among lesser educated and rural men (Tey, "Understanding Marriage and Divorce Trends in Peninsular Malaysia").

[50] Jones, *Marriage and Divorce in Islamic Southeast Asia*, ch. 7.

[51] Greg Fealy and Virginia M. Hooker, eds., *Voices of Islam in Southeast Asia: A Contemporary Sourcebook* (Singapore: Institute of Southeast Asian Studies, 2006), pp. 339–52.

[52] Jones, *Marriage and Divorce in Islamic Southeast Asia*, p. 277.

INTERNATIONALIZATION OF MARRIAGE

A key feature of marriage trends in the wealthy countries of East Asia (Japan, South Korea, Taiwan, Singapore) has been an upsurge in recent years in the proportion of international marriages, mostly involving foreign brides rather than foreign husbands, with many of the brides originating from Southeast Asia. The men concerned tend to be those facing difficulties in local marriage markets, whether because of low education, poor job prospects, rural residence, having been divorced, and, in some cases, because they are looking for qualities in a wife that they feel local women have lost.[53] The Southeast Asian countries that feature most strongly as sources of brides in such marriages are Vietnam and the Philippines. Filipina marriage-migration streams used to be directed primarily to Western countries, especially the United States, but the streams have branched off in recent years, with Japan the dominant Asian destination, followed by South Korea and Taiwan.[54]

In the case of South Korea, Vietnamese brides, although fewer than those from China, have since 2006 made up one quarter to one third of all foreign brides, greatly surpassing those from the Philippines, which until 2002 had been more numerous than those from Vietnam.[55] Vietnamese brides are considerably younger and less educated at the time of marriage than Filipino brides[56] and have the widest age gap with their spouses relative to brides from any other country.

It is important to note that, with the exception of Singapore (where, in 2005, 27 percent of men married foreigners but only 7 percent of women did so[57]), international marriages involving Southeast Asian partners are predominantly Southeast Asian women marrying foreign men, not the other way round. For example, in 2000, among the resident population in Thailand in 2000, the number of foreign men married to Thai women was twice as high as that of foreign women married to Thai men. If figures had been available on Thais married to foreigners but living outside Thailand, the ratio may well have been even greater. Of the foreign husbands, the majority were Chinese (41 percent) and other East Asians (14 percent), Westerners (21 percent), and Burmese and Laotians (17 percent).[58]

Internet dating services play an important, and probably increasing, role in promoting such marriages, as do commercial marriage brokerage agencies.[59] Given these trends, as well as increasing population mobility, student flows, and marriage-

---

[53] Gavin W. Jones and Hsiu-Hua Shen, "International Marriage in East and Southeast Asia: Trends and Research Emphases," *Citizenship Studies* 12,1 (2008).

[54] Nimfa B. Ogena, Minda Cabilao Valencia, and Golda Myra R. Roma, "Filipina Marriage Migration Streams to Japan, Taiwan, and South Korea," in *Cross-Border Marriage: Process and Dynamics*, ed. Doo-Sub Kim (Seoul: Institute of Population and Aging Research, Hanyang University, 2008), pp. 169–70.

[55] Cheong-Seok Kim, "Features of International Marriage of Korean Men to Women From Four Asian Countries," in *Cross-Border Marriage: Process and Dynamics*, ed. Doo-Sub Kim (Seoul: Institute of Population and Aging Research, Hanyang University, 2008), Table 1.

[56] Ibid., Table 2.

[57] Jones and Shen, "International Marriage in East and Southeast Asia," Table 3.

[58] Bhassorn Limanonda, "Motivation and Process of Marriage Migration: A Case Study of Thailand," in *Cross-Border Marriage*, p. 223.

[59] Nicole Constable, *Romance on a Global Stage: Pen Pals, Virtual Ethnography, and "Mail Order" Brides* (Berkeley, CA: University of California Press, 2003); Nicole Constable, ed., *Cross-Border Marriages: Gender and Mobility in Transnational Asia* (Philadelphia, PA: University of Pennsylvania Press, 2004).

market problems for men in some of the countries to which brides from Southeast Asia are increasingly going, it is likely that cross-border marriages will play an increasing role in Southeast Asian marriage patterns.

CONCLUSIONS

Marriage trends in Southeast Asia are as diverse as the cultures represented in the region. Although the trend toward later and less marriage is fairly general, it is far more marked in some countries (e.g., Myanmar, Thailand) than in others (e.g., Vietnam, Philippines). In general, though, economic and social developments seem to be contributing to later marriage. The pool of potential partners is widening, with greater population mobility and communications through the Internet and mobile phones, not to mention marriage brokerages, and this is resulting in increasing international marriage. Evidence on cohabitation is scarce, but it appears to remain fairly rare, except in the Philippines. Divorce rates appear to be on the rise generally throughout the region, reflecting increasing strains on marriages in rapidly changing societies and, perhaps, increasing individualism and unwillingness to remain in an unsatisfactory marriage to protect the family reputation.

CHAPTER 4

POPULATION AGING
IN SOUTHEAST ASIA

Ghazy Mujahid

Demographic realities may take more time to unravel, but are no less visible, than economic realities, and, in fact, can be more strikingly apparent. Four to five decades ago, a visitor to Southeast Asia[1] could hardly fail to notice the large numbers of children and expectant mothers in the population. High fertility was drawing the attention of governments and donors alike and was considered a significant constraint on development.[2] With vigorous family-planning campaigns, most countries succeeded in bringing down fertility levels, some by as much as 30 to 40 percent within 20 to 25 years.[3] The resulting demographic realities are now strikingly visible.[4] With dwindling increments to the child population, coupled with improved

The author thanks Ms. Nyda Mukhtar, Washington University (St. Louis, MO), for comments on an earlier draft.

[1] Southeast Asia comprises eleven countries: Brunei Darussalam, Cambodia, Indonesia, Lao People's Democratic Republic (Laos), Malaysia, Myanmar (Burma), Philippines, Singapore, Thailand, Timor-Leste, and Vietnam. All except Timor-Leste are members of the Association of Southeast Asian Nations (ASEAN), founded in 1967.

[2] For a discussion and references on this concern during the 1950s and 1960s, see Robert Weintraub, "The Birth Rate and Economic Development: An Empirical Study," *Econometrica* 30,4 (1962): 812–17.

[3] The fertility transition and its causal factors have continued to be a widely discussed issue since the onset of the fertility decline. See, among others, T. Dyson and M. Murphy, "The Onset of Fertility Transition," *Population and Development Review* 11,3 (1985): 399–440; Lant H. Pritchett, "Desired Fertility and the Impact of Population Policies," *Population and Development Review* 20,1 (1994): 1–55; and A. Rammohan, "Fertility Transition in South and Southeast Asia," *ASEAN Economic Bulletin* 21,2 (August 2004): 183–97.

[4] The issue has drawn increasing attention and the area has become one of the most researched in Southeast Asian demography. Limitations of space preclude citing the major research on this topic. However, the works of University of Michigan Emeritus Professor John E. Knodel, one of the most prolific writers on the subject, provide valuable insight into various aspects of population aging, focusing particularly on Cambodia, Thailand, and Vietnam. See the website for the Population Studies Center for information about his major work on this topic: www.psc.isr.umich.edu/pubs/select.html?ID=54, accessed January 30, 2012.

health and increasing life expectancy, one cannot now fail to notice the presence of a large number of older persons, defined as those aged 60 years and older.[5] In most Southeast Asian countries[6] one now sees older persons on the roads, in shops, in buses, in trains, in parks, that is, virtually everywhere. There are more older people and they are healthier—able to go around on their own.[7] This chapter reviews trends in this dominant feature of Southeast Asia's emerging demographic scenario, comparing changes since 1950 with changes that can be realistically projected through 2050. It discusses the challenges and opportunities that foreseeable increases in the proportion of the older population—commonly referred to as "population aging"—present and what governments are doing and what more they need to do to cope with this inevitable demographic change.

This chapter first describes the changes in fertility and mortality that have taken place in Southeast Asia. It then reviews the changing age structure of the population, which in every country is shifting, albeit at different rates, toward an increasing proportion of older persons in the population. Following is a discussion of the various social, cultural, and economic issues resulting from the projected demographic changes. It concludes with a brief survey of policy measures that governments have put in place to address aging-related issues. As there are considerable differences between the eleven countries, the region offers varied country experiences that serve as a basis for policy recommendations, which are summarized at the end.

FERTILITY AND MORTALITY TRENDS

Regional Perspective

At the beginning of the 1950s, fertility was high in Southeast Asia, with an average TFR (total fertility rate) of 6.05 (Table 1). The rate had declined to 4.81 by 1975–1980. The drop in fertility was modest compared to the average for less developed countries[8] and Asia.

During the next three decades, Southeast Asia experienced a more rapid decline in fertility and the TFR fell by more than half, to its 2005–2010 level of 2.26. The decline has been much greater than the average for Asia and less developed regions.

---

[5] This definition of *older person* was endorsed by countries participating in the Second World Assembly on Aging, held in Madrid in April 2002.

[6] There are exceptions, like Cambodia and Timor-Leste, for which the change, though foreseeable, has not as yet become evident.

[7] "Population aging" has been receiving attention in the literatures since the mid-1980s: S. Gunasekaran, "Demographic Problems of Southeast Asia," *Southeast Asian Affairs* (1987): 45–62; Linda G. Martin, "The Aging of Asia," *Journal of Gerontology* 43,4 (1988): 99–113; Charles Hirschman and Philip Guest, "The Emerging Demographic Transitions of Southeast Asia," *Population and Development Review* 16,1, (1990): 121–52; and Tengku Aizan Hamid, "Demography of Population Ageing in South East Asia: Past, Present, and Future Trends" (paper presented at the South East Asian Conference on Aging, Kuala Lumpur, 2010).

[8] Includes all countries except Europe, United States, Canada, Australia, New Zealand, and Japan.

It is projected that the rate will stabilize after declining further to below-replacement level after 2025.[9]

Table 1
Fertility Trends, 1950–2050

	1950–55	1975–80	2005–10	2025–30	2045–50
World	4.95	3.84	2.52	2.29	2.17
Less developed countries	6.07	4.54	2.67	2.35	2.19
Asia	5.82	4.05	2.28	1.99	1.88
Southeast Asia	6.05	4.81	2.26	1.90	1.83

Source: UNDESA, *World Population Prospects: The 2010 Revision* (New York, NY: United Nations Department of Economic and Social Affairs, 2011)

As fertility rates declined, there was an increase in life expectancy at birth. Substantial declines in mortality, reflected in improving life expectancy rates, characterized Southeast Asia during the period 1950–1975 as a result of improved availability of quality health care services to an increasing proportion of the population. As shown in Table 2, the resulting gains in life expectancy at birth were substantial.

Table 2
Life Expectancy at Birth (in years), 1950–2050

	1950–55	1975–80	2005–10	2025–30	2045–50
World	47.7	60.7	67.9	72.4	75.6
More developed countries	65.9	72.1	76.9	80.3	82.7
Less developed countries	42.3	57.8	65.9	70.8	74.4
Asia	42.9	59.8	69.0	73.6	76.7
Southeast Asia	42.4	56.7	69.3	74.7	78.0

Source: UNDESA, *World Population Prospects: The 2010 Revision* (New York, NY: United Nations Department of Economic and Social Affairs, 2011)

Life expectancy at birth in Southeast Asia during the early 1950s was only 42 years, marginally below the average for Asia and 24 years below the average for the countries classified as "more developed."[10] The region witnessed substantial declines in mortality during the second half of the twentieth century, and life expectancy at birth is now estimated at nearly 70 years, that is, up by 27 years, and exceeding that for the less developed countries as well as for Asia. Though still below the average for more developed countries, the gap has narrowed to 7.6 years. Further gains in life expectancy, though smaller given the larger base, are projected during the period 2000–2050. By 2050, life expectancy is expected to reach 78 years, higher than the average for Asia and above the average for the less developed regions and the world as a whole. If these projections are correct, life expectancy in the region will be only 4.7 years less than the average for the more developed countries.

---

[9] For a detailed discussion of fertility trends, see Chapter Two, *"Fertility in Southeast Asia."*

[10] Includes Europe, United States, Canada, Australia, New Zealand, and Japan.

As a region, Southeast Asia was thus characterized by high fertility/high mortality during the early 1950s. There was a decline in both fertility and mortality during the twenty years from 1955 to 1975. However, after 1975 the region witnessed a far more rapid decline in fertility, while life expectancy continued to improve.

Country Experiences[11]

The extent of fertility decline and improvements in life expectancy varied widely across the region. As shown in Table 3, fertility was high in all Southeast Asian countries, with the lowest TFR being 5.50 in Indonesia.[12]

Table 3
Fertility Trends in Southeast Asia, 1950–2050

	1950–55	1975–80	2005–10	2025–30	2045–50
Cambodia	6.30	4.70	2.80	1.90	1.60
Indonesia	5.50	4.70	2.20	1.80	1.70
Laos	5.90	6.20	3.00	1.90	1.60
Malaysia	6.20	3.90	2.70	2.20	2.00
Myanmar	6.00	4.90	2.10	1.70	1.60
Philippines	7.42	5.46	3.27	2.56	2.14
Singapore	6.61	1.84	1.25	1.63	1.84
Thailand	6.14	3.92	1.63	1.47	1.70
Timor-Leste	6.44	4.31	6.53	4.2	2.77
Vietnam	6.20	5.89	1.89	1.56	1.71

Source: UNDESA, *World Population Prospects: The 2010 Revision* (New York, NY: United Nations Department of Economic and Social Affairs, 2011)

In all countries except Vietnam, fertility had declined considerably by the mid-1970s. Laos was the only country where fertility increased. The most striking drop in fertility took place in Singapore, where the TFR fell by 70 percent, from a high of 6.61 to a below-replacement level of 1.84. Fertility rates continued to fall except in Timor-Leste, where the TFR is reported to have increased to its present level of 6.53. Fertility is projected to decline, and by 2050 it is expected that most countries will have below-replacement fertility.[13] In Philippines, fertility will be near replacement level and in Timor-Leste, fertility is projected to be 2.77. Intercountry variations in fertility declines can be explained by the pace of economic development and improvements in the provision of quality reproductive health care services, as well

---

[11] Figures for Brunei Darussalam are included in the totals for Southeast Asia. However, since country-level data for Brunei Darussalam are not comparable due to the small size of its population (less than 0.4 million), it is not included in intercountry comparisons.

[12] All figures used are from United Nations sources to allow intercountry comparability, therefore, data may differ from those available from the corresponding national sources.

[13] UNDESA makes three projections for changes in fertility: high, medium, and low variants. These are based respectively on an assumption of slow, moderate, and rapid changes in fertility in past trends and expected future changes in health policies and services. All projections used in this chapter are the medium variant.

as cultural and historic factors. For example, in Philippines and Timor-Leste, fertility declines have been more sluggish because of a predominantly Catholic population.

At the beginning of the 1950s, life expectancy at birth in most Southeast Asian countries was below 50 years, with less than 40 years in four nations (Table 4). Malaysia, Singapore, and Thailand were the only exceptions, with life expectancy being slightly more than 60 years in Singapore. Life expectancy improved during the period 1950–1980 in all countries except Cambodia, where life expectancy fell by 8 years due to the conflict situation during the Pol Pot era. Life expectancy then picked up, and between 1980 and 2005 the country witnessed an improvement of 30 years in life expectancy, the largest increase in the region. Life expectancy has continued to improve in all countries and it is estimated that at present it exceeds 60 years in every country, is greater than 70 years in three countries (Malaysia, Thailand, and Vietnam), and greater than 80 years in Singapore. Two factors have influenced the variations in the extent of intercountry improvements in life expectancy. One is the lower life expectancy in the base year (as in the case of Cambodia), and the other is the rate of improvement in the coverage of access to health services. Further increases in life expectancy are projected for each country, and by 2050 life expectancy will likely be greater than 70 years in all countries, exceed 75 years in six countries, and exceed 80 years in Singapore and Vietnam.

Table 4
Life Expectancy at Birth (in years) in Southeast Asia, 1950–2050

	1950–55	1975–80	2005–10	2025–30	2045–50
Cambodia	39.4	31.2	61.5	69.5	74.3
Indonesia	38.8	56.3	67.9	74.3	77.6
Laos	42.4	48.0	66.1	72.4	76.3
Malaysia	55.4	66.6	73.4	77.1	79.7
Myanmar	36.0	54.5	63.5	71.1	75.5
Philippines	55.4	62.6	67.8	72.5	76.3
Singapore	60.2	71.0	80.6	83.0	85.2
Thailand	50.7	63.6	73.6	76.8	79.5
Timor-Leste	30.0	31.2	60.8	69.1	74.2
Vietnam	40.4	52.4	74.3	78.0	80.4

Source: UNDESA, *World Population Prospects: The 2010 Revision* (New York, NY: United Nations Department of Economic and Social Affairs, 2011)

CHANGES IN AGE STRUCTURE

Regional Perspective

Declining fertility and increasing life expectancy, described above, result in a shift in the age distribution of a population toward the older age groups. Falling fertility reduces the number of births, thereby, reducing the "inflow" of individuals into the younger age cohorts. Improvements in life expectancy result in an increasing number of persons reaching the age of 60 years and also surviving longer than 60 years, resulting in a slowdown of the "outflow" from the older cohorts. The combined effect of falling fertility rates and improving life expectancy is, therefore, a decrease in the additions to the population of younger ages and an increase in the number of those 60 years and older.

Figure 1 depicts past and projected trends in the annual number of births in Southeast Asia. During the 1950s, the average annual number of births in the sub-region was 8 to 9 million. The number of births increased gradually and peaked at 12 million during the 1980s. This was despite the decline in the fertility, as the past higher levels of fertility contributed to a continuing increase in the number of women of reproductive age (15 to 49 years), which more than offset the impact of declining fertility on the number of births. As a result of the combined effect of the decline in TFR and the slowing down of the increase in the population of women of reproductive ages,[14] the average annual number of births started declining during the closing years of the last century and is estimated to have fallen to 11.1 million per year. It is projected to decline to 10 million in 2025 and further to 9 million by 2050.

Figure 1
Annual Births in Southeast Asia, 1950–2050

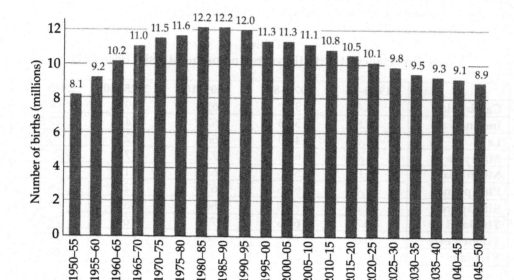

Source: UNDESA, *World Population Prospects: The 2010 Revision* (New York, NY: United Nations Department of Economic and Social Affairs, 2011)

Increasing life expectancy results in an increasing proportion of the population able to reach age 60 years, that is, to enter old age. Hence, while the number of births will decrease during the period 2010–2050, an increasing proportion of the population will be able to reach the age of 60. It is estimated that 80 percent of the children born today can be expected to reach age 60 years. By 2050, this survival rate

---

[14] It should be noted that the absolute number of women within the reproductive-age range (15–49 years) will not decline. However, the size of the increment (that is, the addition to the number of women of reproductive age) in each subsequent year will start declining after 2025.

is projected to have increased to 91 percent. A larger proportion of the population will therefore reach old age. Moreover, life expectancy of older persons, that is, the average number of years a person is expected to live after reaching 60 years of age, has also been increasing, and will continue to do so. Life expectancy at age 60, which is now 18.2 years, is projected to increase gradually to 21.9 years by 2050. Life expectancy and survival rates are expected to improve in all countries, as there are still opportunities to increase the coverage and scope of quality health services, particularly geriatric services, in all countries of the region. With an increasing percentage of the population reaching age 60 years and surviving longer, older persons will account for an increasing proportion of the total population.[15] The impact of declining fertility and improvements in life expectancy on the age structure of the population is highlighted in Figure 2.

Figure 2
Southeast Asia's Changing Age Structure, 1950–2050

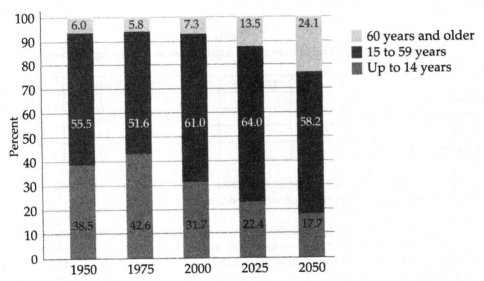

Source: UNDESA, *World Population Prospects: The 2010 Revision* (New York, NY: United Nations Department of Economic and Social Affairs, 2011)

In 1950, older persons accounted for 6.0 percent of the region's population, while children (0 to 14 years) constituted 38.5 percent. During the period 1950–1975, the proportion of older people declined marginally to 5.8 percent and that of the child population increased to 42.6 percent. The proportion of the working-age population (15 to 59 years) declined from 55.5 percent to 51.6 percent. Southeast Asia's population was thus becoming younger.[16] This could be explained by a relatively

---

[15] All figures for survival rates and life expectancy at 60 years and older are from UNDESA, *World Population Ageing 2009* (New York, NY: United Nations Department of Economic and Social Affairs, 2010).

[16] This was similar to the trend in the less developed countries (where the older population declined from 6.3 percent to 6.1 percent) and in Asia (where it declined from 6.7 percent to 6.6 percent). UNDESA, *World Population Prospects: The 2010 Revision* (New York, NY: United Nations Department of Economic and Social Affairs, 2011).

rapid decline in improvements in life expectancy at earlier ages as a result of a marked fall in the high infant and child mortality rates during the earlier periods. The next quarter (1975–2000) saw a significant change in trends reflecting the past declines in fertility and improvements in life expectancy. By the turn of the century, the share of the child population had fallen to 31.7 percent and that of working-age and older populations had increased to 61.0 percent and 7.3 percent, respectively.

The projected changes in the age structure show that by 2025, the older population will constitute 13.5 percent of the total population and the share of the child population will have declined to 22.4 percent. During the following twenty-five years, the trends are expected to continue, and it is estimated that in 2050 the share of the child population will have declined to 17.7 percent and older persons will constitute 24.1 percent of the total population. According to estimates, nearly one in four persons (compared to the current one in thirteen persons) will be above the age of 60 years in 2050. The proportion of the older population in Southeast Asia's total population will exceed the average for less developed regions, but will fall slightly short of the average for Asia.

Table 5
Percentage of Population Increase Attributed to Those Age 60 and Older

	1950–75	1975–2000	2000–25	2025–50
World	9.3	12.8	31.3	63.9
Less developed regions	5.9	10.0	26.4	59.8
Asia	6.7	6.5	14.8	24.4
Southeast Asia	5.5	9.6	34.3	118.6

Source: UNDESA, *World Population Prospects: The 2010 Revision* (New York, NY: United Nations Department of Economic and Social Affairs, 2011)

Table 5 shows that since 1975 the progress of population aging in Southeast Asia has been more rapid than it has been on average in the rest of the world, the developing countries, and Asia, and is projected to continue to grow relatively older than the rest of the world.[17] The indicator used to measure relative aging during a given period is the proportion of the older population in the increase in total population during that period.

During the period 1950–1975, older persons accounted for 5.5 percent of the total increase in population of Southeast Asia and 9.3 percent and 6.7 percent for the World and Asia, respectively. Of the total increase in population in Southeast Asia during the period 2000–2025, older persons will account for 34 percent, that is, more than the average increases for the World, less developed regions and Asia (Table 5). During the period 2025–2050, the older population will continue to increase in

---

[17] It should be pointed out that this means the progress of population aging in the region has been more rapid than in the rest of the world as an aggregate, not more rapid than in every other region in the world. For example, in both Europe and East Asia (Japan, People's Republic of China, Mongolia, the Republic of Korea, and the People's Democratic Republic of Korea) progress of population aging has been faster than that found in Southeast Asia.

Southeast Asia while there will be an absolute decline in the population under age 60.[18]

Table 6 highlights the overall impact of changing demographic trends in terms of the growing size of the older population. The older population increased at a lower rate than total population during the period 1950–1975, but outpaced it between 1975 and 2000. During the period 2000–2050, the differential in the rates of increase is projected to further increase.

Table 6
Increase in Older Population in Southeast Asia, 1950–2050

	1950–75	1975–2000	2000–25	2025–50
Average annual rate of increase in total population	2.5%	2.0%	1.1%	0.4%
Average annual rate of increase in older population	2.3%	2.9%	3.6%	2.8%
Increase in number of older persons (000)	8,161	19,400	54,497	90,755

Source: UNDESA, *World Population Prospects: The 2010 Revision* (New York, NY: United Nations Department of Economic and Social Affairs, 2011)

While population growth is expected to slow down to an average annual rate of 0.5 percent during the period 2025–2050, the older population will continue to increase, on average, five times faster, at an annual rate of 2.6 percent. As the data in Table 5 show, older persons will constitute a growing proportion of the increase in total population. Such growth has implications for policy makers and providers of services for older persons. The increase in the years 2000 to 2025 is expected to be 54 million—nearly double the increase between 1975 and 2000. The older population will likely increase further to 85 million between 2025 and 2050. The first half of this century will see an increase of 139 million in the older population in Southeast Asia (five times the increase of the second half of the last century, which was 28 million).

Intercountry Variations

Evidence presented in the previous section supports the finding that population aging follows, with a time lag, decreases in fertility and mortality. Table 7 summarizes evidence on past and projected trends in population aging in individual countries.

In 1950, the proportion of older persons in the total population varied from a low of 3.7 percent in Singapore to a high of 7.3 percent in Malaysia. By the turn of the century, the differentials had increased from a low of 4.1 percent in Timor-Leste to a high of 10.7 percent in Singapore. The region's decrease in fertility played a role in creating an aging population, with Singapore and Thailand experiencing the most significant drop in fertility (see Table 3). By 2000, Thailand ranked second highest in terms of proportion of older population. In Timor-Leste, where fertility levels had

---

[18] The child population (0 to 14 years) will decline by 16.8 million and the working-age population (15 to 59 years) will increase by only 11.8 million, resulting in an absolute decline of 5 million in the under-60 population.

increased, the proportion of older persons declined. In Cambodia, fertility declined significantly, but the share of the population represented by older persons remained unchanged. This can be explained by the ongoing warfare during the 1970s, as a result of which a large number of young adults, who would have formed part of the older population at the turn of the century, were killed.

Table 7
Population Aging in Southeast Asia

	Older persons as percentage of total population				
	1950	1975	2000	2025	2050
Cambodia	4.5	4.6	4.7	9.5	19.0
Indonesia	6.2	5.6	7.3	13.2	25.5
Laos	3.8	5.3	5.6	8.4	18.8
Malaysia	7.3	5.4	6.2	13.1	20.4
Myanmar	5.7	6.2	7.2	13.0	24.5
Philippines	5.5	5.0	5.0	8.9	15.3
Singapore	3.7	6.8	10.7	27.1	37.8
Thailand	5.1	5.3	10.3	21.3	31.8
Timor-Leste	5.5	4.5	4.1	5.2	7.0
Vietnam	7.0	7.3	7.8	15.3	30.8

Source: UNDESA, *World Population Prospects: The 2010 Revision* (New York, NY: United Nations Department of Economic and Social Affairs, 2011)

Projections for 2050 show significant increases in the proportion of older persons in almost all countries, with wide intercountry variations. By 2050, while older persons are expected to account for almost 40 percent of Singapore's population, the proportion of older persons in Timor-Leste's population will likely be less than 8 percent. Older persons are expected to constitute more than a quarter of the population in Thailand and Vietnam in 2050, while in another three countries (Indonesia, Malaysia, Myanmar) the proportion will likely exceed 20 percent and in the remaining three (Cambodia, Laos, Philippines), between 10 and 20 percent. Though countries with large aging populations are faced with serious policy decisions, countries with small aging populations should not be complacent. In fact, for the future, Singapore may not need to be as concerned as Timor-Leste and Cambodia, where the proportion of older persons is less than half that of Singapore. Put another way, countries that have experienced rapid growth of their aging population for some years are more likely to have policy frameworks and service delivery systems already in place, and on which they can build, whereas countries where aging is an emerging phenomenon will need to focus on efforts to establish aging-related policy and infrastructure, despite having "late starter" advantages, such as learning from the experience of those countries that started aging much earlier. The data in Table 8 show the changing importance of the older cohort in each country. Note that in Singapore and Thailand, the increase in the older population between 2025 and 2050 may be less than during the period 2000–2025. In all other countries the number of older persons will continue to increase.

Table 8

Increase in Older Population in Southeast Asia

	Percentage of older persons in increase in total population			Increase in older population (000)		
	1950–2000	2000–25	2025–50	1950–2000	2000–25	2025–50
Cambodia	4.9	23.5	88.9	394	997	2,024
Indonesia	7.8	34.7	180.2*	10,812	20,299	38,930
Laos	6.4	15.4	100.3*	232	326	958
Malaysia	5.8	27.0	51.1	995	3,179	4,227
Myanmar	8.1	44.6	317.3*	2,245	3,674	6,669
Philippines	4.8	16.3	35.6	2,854	6,658	13,105
Singapore	13.2	61.3	242.4*	383	1,154	732
Thailand	12.8	92.9	-384.0**	5,447	9,040	7,093
Timor-Leste	2.5	6.1	9.5	10	56	120
Vietnam	8.3	44.1	363.3*	4,177	9,068	16,819

* *Increase in older population while population under age 60 declines*
** *Increase in older population while total population declines*

Source: UNDESA, *World Population Prospects: The 2010 Revision* (New York, NY: United Nations Department of Economic and Social Affairs, 2011)

Age-Sex Structure of the Older Population

The age-sex structure of the older population has a profound effect in terms of the implications of population aging and should be taken into account in formulating policies and programs for addressing aging-related issues. Population aging is usually marked by an aging of the older population itself. That is, as the proportion of older persons in population increases, there is also a shift in the distribution of older persons toward the older age cohorts. Moreover, despite a higher male to female ratio at birth, older women outnumber older men as a result of the higher female life expectancy.

Table 9 summarizes the aging and "feminization"[19] of older populations as projected for the countries of Southeast Asia. At the turn of the century, the "oldest old," that is, those persons 80 years old and older, accounted for 8.9 percent of Southeast Asia's older population. It is projected that this proportion will increase to 10.2 percent in 2025 and further to 18.0 percent in 2050. In most countries, the share of the oldest old in the population is projected to increase during the period 2000–2025 and in all by even more between 2025 and 2050. In Singapore, if current projections are correct, more than a third of the older population will be 80 years and older by 2050. In terms of the sex distribution of the older population, older women constituted 54.0 percent of Southeast Asia's older population in 2000. The proportion is expected to increase to 54.4 by 2025 and remain unchanged until 2050.

---

[19] It should be noted that while the term "feminization" implies a process (that is, an increasing share of the population being women), it has come to be used widely in the literature on aging to mean "a more than 50 percent proportion being women."

Table 9
Aging and "Feminization" of Older Population in Southeast Asia

	Oldest old as percentage of older population			Percentage of females in ...					
				Older population			Oldest old		
	2000	2025	2050	2000	2025	2050	2000	2025	2050
Southeast Asia	*8.9*	*10.2*	*18.0*	*54.0*	*54.4*	*54.4*	*60.2*	*62.1*	*60.7*
Cambodia	6.9	7.1	10.7	64.3	57.9	55.3	61.0	66.4	64.5
Indonesia	7.3	10.4	17.7	54.2	53.3	54.0	60.1	61.9	59.2
Laos	7.4	7.9	10.9	54.7	54.3	54.2	63.6	61.2	63.6
Malaysia	7.8	7.9	16.5	50.9	51.8	53.1	54.0	54.3	57.5
Myanmar	8.4	6.9	13.0	54.6	54.6	55.7	59.6	60.3	64.0
Philippines	8.3	8.1	14.3	56.1	56.0	55.0	63.1	63.1	61.1
Singapore	12.1	13.0	33.6	53.7	53.0	53.5	62.7	58.5	58.7
Thailand	10.9	12.7	23.7	54.6	55.7	56.2	60.2	62.6	65.0
Timor-Leste	2.9	7.8	8.6	50.0	54.4	51.4	100.0	57.1	61.1
Vietnam	11.7	11.1	20.2	56.7	55.1	53.4	59.8	64.0	59.7

Source: UNDESA, *World Population Prospects: The 2010 Revision* (New York, NY: United Nations Department of Economic and Social Affairs, 2011)

The proportion of women is even higher in the oldest old population than it is in the older population. Women accounted for more than 60 percent of Southeast Asia's oldest old population in 2000. This proportion is expected to increase to 62.1 percent in 2025 and then decline to 60.7 percent in 2050. In all countries of Southeast Asia, the proportion of females in the oldest old population is higher than in the total older population. In Thailand, women will likely constitute 65 percent of the oldest old population in 2050, that is, there will be nearly two women age 80 years and older for every man in the oldest old cohort. It should be noted that in Cambodia the proportion of women in the older population was much higher than in any other country of Southeast Asia at the turn of the century (see Table 9). This is explained by the larger number of adult males who, as mentioned previously, lost their lives as a result of conflicts and warfare during the mid-1970s.

The higher proportion of women in the older population adds a gender dimension to population aging, as women are more vulnerable than men in old age. They are usually less educated and as such more financially dependent. Also, a much higher proportion of women spend their later years without a spouse. This is explained by (a) the husband usually being older; (b) the greater longevity of women; and (c) a much higher incidence of remarriage among men on losing a spouse. Being "single" in old age adds to older women's vulnerability.[20]

---

[20]For a discussion of the greater vulnerability of older women, see Ghazy Mujahid, *Population Ageing in East and Southeast Asia: Current Situation and Emerging Challenges* (Bangkok: UNFPA Papers in Population Ageing, No. 1, 2006), pp. 16–18.

Spatial Distribution of Older Persons

The older population is not distributed evenly across a country. The proportion of older persons is lower in urban areas despite the lower fertility and mortality rates in an urban population.[21] This is explained by the high rate of out-migration of young family members from rural areas. Table 10 summarizes information for countries for which data are available. In all countries, the proportion of older persons is higher in the rural population relative to urban areas.

Table 10
Rural–Urban Differences in Population Aging
in Selected Southeast Asian Countries

	Year	Percentage of persons over age 60 in total population		Percentage of females age 60 and over in population	
		Urban	Rural	Urban	Rural
Cambodia	1998	4.5	6.0	60.9	57.7
Indonesia	2000	6.2	7.9	53.1	51.8
Malaysia	2000	5.4	7.5	52.7	51.8
Philippines	1990	5.0	5.5	54.9	51.3
Thailand	2000	9.0	9.6	55.5	53.8
Timor-Leste	2004	3.5	6.5	49.7	48.4
Vietnam	1999	7.5	8.1	58.3	58.7

Source: Ghazy Mujahid, *Population Ageing in East and Southeast Asia: Current Situation and Emerging Challenges* (Bangkok: UNFPA Papers in Population Ageing, No. 1, 2006), p. 28.

Another feature, common to all countries except Vietnam, is a lower proportion of females in the rural older population. This can be attributed to the high incidence of return to rural areas of male urban retirees and the likelihood of rural elderly widows moving to urban areas to join the families of urban-based offspring, particularly sons who have a tendency to migrate to urban areas as young adults.[22] The exceptional situation in Vietnam could be the result of regulations affecting migration. However, since migratory movements of adults of working age from rural to urban areas are usually underrecorded to bypass regulations, it is plausible that aging of rural-area populations may be more pronounced than the data suggest.[23]

---

[21] United Nations, *Fertility Behaviour in the Context of Development*, (New York, NY: Department of International Economic and Social Affairs, Population Studies No. 100, 1987).

[22] See Ronald Skeldon, "Ageing of Rural Populations in South-East and East Asia," in *World Ageing Situation* (New York, NY: United Nations Department of Economic and Social Affairs, 2001), pp. 38–54.

[23] Ibid.

KEY AGING-RELATED ISSUES

Old age is usually associated with high morbidity and an increasing risk of disability and poverty. Moreover, with increasing age, older persons may have a growing feeling of being unwanted and an economic and social burden.[24] Hence, the increasing proportion and number of older persons give rise to a number of social, economic, and cultural issues that need to be addressed. The overarching concern is to ensure that older persons are able to lead healthy and active lives in which their dignity and economic and social freedoms are guaranteed. This calls for governments to ensure that the needs and concerns of older persons are met. Of primary importance is to provide the older population with access to (a) health care services, (b) long-term care services, (c) appropriate living arrangements, and (d) means of income security.

Health Care Services

The incidence of morbidity and hence the frequency of accessing health services—outpatient consultations, inpatient admissions, and clinical tests—are known to increase with age.[25] Evidence available from Singapore shows that, while people age 65 and over constituted 7 percent of the population, they accounted for 17 percent of all hospital admissions and 19 percent of outpatient polyclinic visits.[26] In addition to a higher incidence of morbidity among older persons, an important contributory factor to increasing health expenditures is the shift in the pattern of morbidity commonly referred to as the "epidemiological transition."[27] As the age distribution shifts more and more toward older cohorts, infectious and nutritional disorders yield place to chronic, degenerative, and mental illnesses as the leading causes of morbidity. Many disabling, chronic, and terminal diseases affecting older persons require prolonged management. The higher incidence of morbidity and the epidemiological transition together call for increasing and restructuring health services to cater to the changing morbidity pattern.

Per capita health expenditures of older persons are estimated to be higher than those of the not old; while within the older population, the more aged incur even higher expenses than the less aged.[28] While evidence from a number of developed countries is available to show the linkages between population aging and health

---

[24] For a detailed discussion of various aspects of aging, see M. L. Johnson, V. L. Bengtson, P. G. Coleman, et al., *The Cambridge Handbook of Age and Aging* (Cambridge: Cambridge University Press, 2005).

[25] The impact of increasing life expectancy on the onset of morbidity and its duration is being widely discussed in the developed countries. See B. M. Hellner, *Care At Home* (Washington, DC: AARP, 2005).

[26] Phai Kai Hong, "Financing Health and Long-Term Care for Aging Populations in the Asia Pacific Region," in *Ageing in the Asia Pacific Region: Issues, Policies, and Future Trends*, ed. David R. Phillips (London: Routledge, 2000).

[27] David R. Phillips, "Problems and Potential of Researching Epidemiological Transition: Examples From Southeast Asia," *Social Science and Medicine* 33,4 (1991); H. P. Kai Hong Phua, "Health and Healthcare Systems in Southeast Asia: Diversity and Transitions," *Lancet* 377,9673, (2011): 429–37.

[28] A. Mahal and P. Berman, *Health Expenditures and the Elderly: A Survey of Issues in Forecasting, Methods Used, and Relevance for Developing Countries* (Cambridge, MA: Harvard Burden of Disease Unit, Center for Population and Development Studies, 2001).

expenditures, such evidence is hard to come by for developing countries. Per capita health expenditure of older persons has been estimated to be three to five times higher than of the not old; while within the older population, that of the oldest old is two to three times higher than of the "younger elderly."[29]

The requirements of meeting the health care demand of the rapidly growing older and oldest populations call for increased budgetary allocations. Policy makers may be faced with making hard choices in the allocation of health care resources. Unless other expenditures can be scaled down, officials would have to increase taxes or shift part of the burden to the older persons by either raising insurance premiums or recovering at least part of the costs through service charges.[30]

Long-term Care Services

The incidence of disability is known to increase with old age. A significant outcome of many disabilities is impaired mobility, which increases dependence on care givers. In a number of cases the disability may be permanent, which makes the elderly person dependent until death. With age, the chances of moving from active to disabled status increase, while the chances of recovery to active status decrease. Evidence available from surveys (Table 11) indicates the progression of disability with age and its higher incidence among older women.

Table 11
Incidence of Disability by Age and Sex

Age (years)	China 1992		Cambodia 2004	Thailand 1999	
	Percentage reporting at least one functional limitation				
	Male	Female	All	Male	Female
60–69	4.8	8.6	16.2	14.6	14.9
70–79	14.5	25.8	30.4	19.4	23.4
80+	37.4	58.7	44.2	27.6	36.0

Source: Ghazy Mujahid, *Population Ageing in East and Southeast Asia: Current Situation and Emerging Challenges* (Bangkok: UNFPA Papers in Population Ageing, No. 1, 2006), p. 32.

---

[29] Ibid.; Y. Iwamoto, *Issues in Japanese Health Expenditures*, (Tokyo: Second International Forum of the Collaboration Project, March 2001); and T. Fukawa and N. Izumida, "Japanese Health Expenditures in a Comparative Context," *Japanese Journal of Social Security Policy* 3,2 (1984): 51–61.

[30] In view of rapid population aging, the Japanese government has, over a period of time, been introducing reforms to its Universal Health Insurance System for older persons. Measures to safeguard the financial viability of the system have included increasing the minimum age of coverage, increasing premiums, and reintroducing partial payments for treatment costs depending on income criteria. For a comprehensive review, see R. S. Jones, "Health-Care Reform in Japan: Controlling Costs, Improving Quality, and Ensuring Equity," OECD Economics Department Working Papers, No. 739, OECD Publishing, 2009.

Moreover, a higher incidence of disability among older women implies that feminization of the older population adds to the burden of disability. A number of studies have also shown that women have a lower probability of recovering from disability than men. Aging and feminization of the older population—with feminization being more pronounced among the oldest old—would therefore further increase the demand for long-term care facilities.[31] Policy makers in Southeast Asia should thus pay increasing attention to the growing needs of long-term care facilities.[32]

Appropriate Living Arrangements

In all countries of Southeast Asia, older persons normally reside with and are taken care of by their family members. Traditionally, in most cases it is the offspring who take responsibility for care of parents in their old-age. Co-residing with younger siblings or their families as well as with nephews, nieces, and other relatives is also not uncommon. The tacit traditional intergenerational agreement is that parents raise children and when the children attain adulthood they are expected to "repay" the parents by providing care and support to the parents in their old age.[33] However, despite its continuing strength, this traditional guarantee of family support for the elderly has been coming under increasing stress due to population aging. Table 12 summarizes data for two demographic indicators—the *potential-support ratio* and the *parent-support ratio*—which can be used to indicate the impact of aging on the support and care base available to older persons.

The "potential-support ratio" is the ratio of population age 15 to 64 years to the population age 65 years and older, a calculation that is based on the assumption that the former are economically active and the latter are dependent. It is used to indicate the support that the older population might rely on for physical care and financial assistance. The "parent-support ratio" is defined as the population aged 85 years and older per 100 persons age 50 to 64 years. This ratio relates population 85 years old and older to their presumed offspring assumed to have been born when the parents were in their twenties and thirties. This ratio reflects the potential burden of parental care on the population age 50 to 64 years. Like the potential-support ratio, it serves to indicate the trend over time in the resource base of family support available to the oldest population.

---

[31] In a study of the impact of aging on health and elderly care, Leslie Mayhew concludes: "Large increases in disability due to aging are predicted, regardless of the methodology used. The association between aging and disability will lead to potentially large increases in the numbers of people requiring personal care in both MDCs (more developed countries) and LDCs (less developed countries) … The number of individuals with disabilities in LDCs will continue to grow." Leslie Mayhew, *Health and Elderly Care Expenditure in an Aging World*, (Laxenburg: International Institute for Applied Systems Analysis, 2000), p. 36.

[32] For a discussion of the issue as emerging in various countries, see David Phillips and Alfred Chan, eds., *Aging and Long-Term Care National Policies in the Asia-Pacific* (Singapore: ISEAS/IDRC, 2002).

[33] E. J. Croll, "The Intergenerational Contract in the Changing Asian Family," *Oxford Development Studies* 34,4 (2006): 473–91; and R. J. Chou, "Filial Piety by Contract? The Emergence, Implementation, and Implications of the 'Family Support Agreement' in China," *Gerontologist* 51,1, (2011): 3–16.

Table 12
Shrinking Support Base for the Elderly in Southeast Asia, 1950–2050

	Potential-Support Ratio (population ages 15 to 64/ population ages 65+)				Parent-Support Ratio (population ages 85+/ population ages 50 to 64)			
	1950	2000	2025	2050	1950	2000	2025	2050
Southeast Asia	*15.2*	*13.3*	*7.6*	*3.6*	*1.2*	*2.5*	*3.5*	*10.2*
Cambodia	20.5	18.3	11.3	5.4	0.6	1.2	1.5	3.5
Indonesia	14.4	14.0	8.2	3.3	1.1	1.9	3.1	10.2
Laos	27.6	14.7	12.7	5.6	0.0	1.7	1.9	3.4
Malaysia	10.7	16.5	7.7	4.3	2.8	1.5	2.2	7.7
Myanmar	18.5	13.1	8.4	3.8	0.8	2.0	1.7	5.3
Philippines	14.7	18.3	11.0	6.1	1.5	1.8	2.1	5.8
Singapore	24.4	9.7	3.4	1.7	1.6	3.9	7.2	35.4
Thailand	16.8	10.0	4.6	2.4	2.0	4.0	5.9	17.6
Timor-Leste	17.5	21.2	15.9	14.6	0.0	0.0	1.8	1.8
Vietnam	15.3	11.1	6.9	2.7	0.9	4.4	4.6	13.8

Source: UNDESA, *World Population Prospects: The 2010 Revision* (New York, NY: United Nations Department of Economic and Social Affairs, 2011)

For Southeast Asia as a region, the potential-support ratio declined from 15.2 to 13.3 during the period 1950–2000. It is projected to decline to 7.6 by 2025 and to 3.6 by 2050. While at the turn of the century there were 13 persons of working age to support one older person, according to projections there will be fewer than 4 in 2050. A similar trend is projected for all countries of the region, with the most significant decline of potential support in Singapore, where the number of working-age persons per older population will fall from 9.7 at the turn of the century to a likely 1.7 in 2050. At the same time, the parent-support ratio will increase, indicating an increasing average number of old parents that people aged 50-64 years will, per tradition, be expected to support. While in 2000 in Southeast Asia, only 2.5 percent of persons in the age group 50–64 had older parents to support, that number may reach 10.2 by 2050. In all countries the parent-support ratio is projected to increase, with the most significant increase expected in Singapore where, according to projections, the ratio will almost double during the period 2000–2025 and then increase another fivefold between 2025 and 2050.

A decline in aged parents living with their offspring, which has already been noticeable in a number of countries, is projected to intensify due to, among other factors, the changing age structure.[34] In addition to shrinking family size, the availability of family support in general, and co-residence arrangements in particular, are being adversely affected by the increasing trend toward nuclear

---

[34] The issue has drawn increasing attention since the 1980s. See A. Chamratrithirong, P. Morgan, and R. Rinduss, "Living Arrangements and Family Formation," *Social Forces* (June 1988): 926–50; UN-ESCAP, *Aging in Asia and the Pacific: Emerging Issues and Successful Practices* (Bangkok, United Nations Economic and Social Commission for Asia and the Pacific, Social Policy Paper No. 10, 2002); and UNDESA, *Living Arrangements of Older Persons Around the World* (New York, NY: United Nations Department of Economic and Social Affairs, 2005).

families, as well as both internal and external migration.[35] Increasing economic activity among women adds to the logistics that discourage co-residence. Traditionally, the daughter-in-law or the daughter carries the responsibility for looking after any older relatives, and a working woman is neither available nor can be expected to provide the care and support required by, say, an aged parent. In addition, globalization is contributing to an increase in the pace at which the divide between the attitudes of older and younger generations is widening. Due to the increasing intergenerational differences in expectations, younger persons as well as older persons more and more prefer to live independently. Older persons find it increasingly difficult to adapt to the rapidly changing lifestyles of their offspring.[36]

Means of Income Security

In Southeast Asia, older persons continue to work, mostly in agriculture and the informal sector for as long as they are able. For a large proportion of the older population, earnings from productive employment are the main source of income. In Cambodia and Thailand, for example, surveys showed that 40 percent of older persons cited employment income as their primary source of financial support. However, income-earning capacity declines with age. This may be due to a range of factors, such as deteriorating health, declining strength, regulations setting upper age limits for employment, and discriminatory practices adopted by employers toward older persons. Hence, the risk of falling into poverty increases with age as one drops out of or is disqualified from the formal labor force. Evidence available from Indonesia, Thailand, and Vietnam shows a higher incidence of poverty among the older population (Figure 3).

Older persons need income security to remain above the poverty line as well as to maintain their dignity and independence.[37] In the absence of employment income, other means of support are mainly family transfers, savings and investment income, and contributory pensions. Though intergenerational bonds remain strong and deeply entrenched in the culture of most Southeast Asian countries, it will be difficult to maintain the levels of family support due to the trends in the potential- and parent-support ratios.[38] A vast majority of older persons have been in mostly low-paying, informal jobs during their working life, or involved in farming, and thus have little savings or investment income. For the same reason, only a small fraction of the older population that has been employed in the formal sector and civil service benefits from a pension scheme.

---

[35] For various ways in which out-migration from rural areas affects older persons who remain behind, see John E. Knodel et al., *Migration and Intergenerational Solidarity: Evidence from Rural Thailand* (Bangkok: UNFPA Papers in Population Aging No. 2, 2007).

[36] This is typical in the case of marriages outside the family and even more so of cross-cultural marriages, as the older people may find it particularly difficult to adjust to an offspring's "strange" spouse. For a discussion of increasing internationalization of marriages in Southeast Asia see Chapter Three, "Marriage trends in Southeast Asia."

[37] Ghazy Mujahid, Joseph Pannirselvam, and Brooks Dodge, *The Impact of Social Pensions: Perceptions of Asian Older Persons* (Bangkok: UNFPA Country Technical Services Team for East and South-East Asia, 2008).

[38] John E. Knodel et al., *Thailand's Older Population: Social and Economic Support as Assessed in 2002*, Population Studies Center Research Report 05-471 (Ann Arbor, MI: University of Michigan, 2005).

Figure 3
Higher Incidence of Poverty Among Older Persons

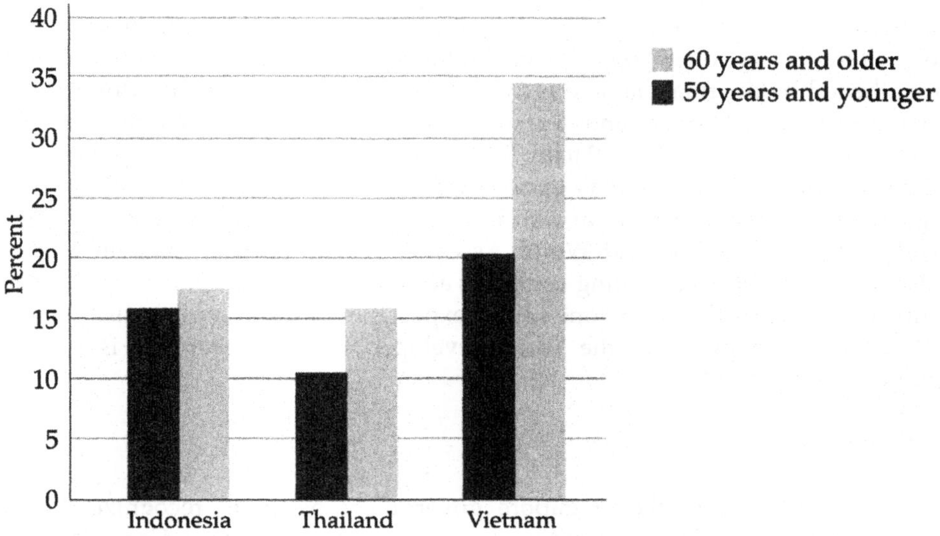

Source: M. Gorman, "Enhancing Social Pensions: A Key Tool in Poverty Reduction," in *Ensuring Social Protection/Social Pensions in Old Age in the Context of Rapid Ageing in Asia* (Bangkok: ESCAP Regional Seminar, UN-ESCAP, 2007).

Demographic trends, incidence of poverty, and the likely means of income support for older persons show that with the population aging, the gap between the financial needs of older persons and resources available to them will continue to widen. Income security for the older population will therefore call for increasing government support in the form of social pensions and welfare benefits.

THE POLICY RESPONSE OF GOVERNMENTS[39]

In each country of Southeast Asia, the government has been quick to recognize the evolving aging situation, and all countries (with the exception of Timor-Leste) have been developing and implementing policies and programs to improve the quality of life of older persons.[40] In every country, the government has identified a mechanism for the coordination of policies and programs aimed at promoting the welfare of the older population. These have included policies to facilitate access to quality health care services, provide appropriate accommodation, and ensure income security during old age. Most countries have also undertaken to improve

---

[39] This section draws heavily on Mujahid, *Population Ageing in East and Southeast Asia,* pp. 42–55, and country statements submitted to the High-Level Meeting on the Regional Review of the Implementation of the Madrid International Plan of Action in Asia and the Pacific organized by the United Nations Economic and Social Commission for Asia and the Pacific in Macao in October 2007. It should be noted that we restrict ourselves to describing official policies, laws, and programs without analyzing the actual or potential demographic importance of these measures. Such an assessment is precluded by lack of information and would also be beyond the scope of this volume.

[40] In Timor-Leste, population aging is not as yet a priority issue.

data collection, promote research, and provide training for needed personnel both in the areas of research and service delivery. Governments have also encouraged nongovernmental organizations (NGOs) to provide assistance, and an increasing number have been initiating and participating in programs and schemes to improve the welfare of the older population. National efforts have in many cases been strengthened by the financial and technical support provided by the United Nations Department of Economic and Social Affairs (UNDESA), Economic and Social Commission for Asia and the Pacific (ESCAP), the United Nations Population Fund (UNFPA), and United Nations specialized agencies, such as the World Health Organization (WHO). Efforts at addressing aging-related issues have accelerated significantly since the Second World Assembly on Aging (convened in Madrid in 2002), at which 159 participating countries adopted the Madrid International Plan of Action on Aging (MIPAA). As one would expect, the longer a country has been faced with an aging population, the more developed and sophisticated is the policy framework it has in place.

Singapore

In the early 1980s, the Singapore government began to recognize the likely impact an aging population would have on society, and set up the Committee on the Problems of the Aged. At present, the lead government agency in charge of issues relating to the elderly is the Elderly Development Division of the Ministry of Community Development, Youth, and Sports (MCDYS). There is also a twenty-one member Inter-Ministerial Committee on Aging Population (set up in 1984), chaired by the Minister for Communications, with the Minister of Community Development, Youth, and Sports and the Minister of Health and Environment as deputy chairs. In 1988, the National Advisory Council on the Aged was formed to undertake a comprehensive review of the status of aging in Singapore. Among the many recommendations implemented was the establishment of a National Council on Family and Aged (NACFA), located in the Ministry of Community Development.

As Singapore's population aging accelerated, the 1990s saw the development of three milestone policies that were implemented to deal with problems relating to social and health care of older persons, namely the Maintenance of Parents Act, 1995, amendments to the Women's Charter, and Advanced Medical Directives Act. In terms of funding policies for services for the elderly, the state applies the "co-payment" principle as far as possible. The individual consumer or his/her family is expected to pay a portion of the charges. This applies to the Medisave Scheme, a compulsory medical savings scheme under Central Provident Fund (CPF), the Singaporean social security system. A sliding scale of charges is imposed, based on household income, for community-based services, such as home nursing, day care, and rehabilitation services. Recipients of public assistance, a financial scheme targeted toward destitute, frail, or disabled elderly people, are entitled to free medical services at the government polyclinics. All Singaporeans older than 60 are entitled to receive a subsidy of 75 percent of fees charged at polyclinics. (That is, in Western terms, the co-pay is 25 percent.) Eldershield, implemented in September 2002, is a special insurance scheme that provides coverage for disability, especially in old age.

In line with its emphasis on family support, an aged-dependent relief is provided under the income tax assessment. Through its Housing and Development

Board (HDB), the government has created strong financial inducements to encourage children to either live with or to live near their elderly parents and/or parents-in-law. The schemes include priority allocation to extended-family applicants for housing grants to buy flats to live close to parents, and housing flats equipped with elderly friendly facilities. The Maintenance of Parents Act, 1995, provides a legal avenue for elderly parents to seek maintenance from their children.

As Southeast Asia's most "aged" country, Singapore provides examples of the importance of ensuring that the elderly remain active. In 2005, it established a Tripartite Committee (government-employers-workers) on the Employability of Older Workers. The committee has recommended enhancing the cost competitiveness of older workers, raising such workers' skills and market value, and shaping positive perceptions toward older workers. It has also recommended legislative changes by the end of 2012 to facilitate opportunities for older workers to work beyond age 62, to 65 and subsequently to 67 years of age. To enhance independent living in old age, all subway stations have been retrofitted to be barrier free since 2006. The first wheelchair-accessible buses were introduced in 2006, and there is a scheme to expand such accessibility to buses on all routes in the near future.

Thailand

Thailand's constitution promulgated in 1997 included a provision that persons aged 60 years and older with insufficient income have the right to receive aid from the state and that the state shall provide aid to older persons and other vulnerable groups. To establish safeguards for the protection of the rights of older persons, the Thai government introduced the Bill on Older Persons in 1998 and established the National Commission on the Elderly in 1999. The government also created the Bureau of Empowerment for Older Persons under the Office of Welfare Promotion, the Protection and Empowerment of Vulnerable Groups, and the Ministry of Social Development and Human Security to coordinate all activities related to the welfare of older persons. In 2002, the government formulated the Second National Plan for Older Persons (2002–2021), which focuses on the preparation for quality aging, the well-being of older persons, social security for older persons, and research to support policy and program formulation. To put safeguards for the rights of persons over 60 into a "legal" instrument, Thailand's parliament passed the Act on Older Persons 2003, which has been in force since January 1, 2004. The National Plan and the Act on Older Persons 2003 have provided the policy framework for welfare promotion, protection, and empowerment of older persons.

The government provides social-welfare assistance to poor and destitute older persons and has also created the Older Persons' Fund. In 2007, the monthly allowance paid to older persons was increased to 500 baht (US$1 = 30 baht) per person. Approximately 2 million older persons, that is, about 23 percent of the entire older population, received this allowance in 2007. Since 2009, the monthly allowances have been made virtually universal for older persons. Free health care is provided for older persons under the national health care scheme. The Ministry of Public Health supports hospitals to run elderly clinics periodically and to provide the elderly with in-home health services. Government initiatives also include support to strengthen income security at old age; provide lifelong education and day centers for health care; promote family assistance, counseling, and social activities for the elderly; promote healthy lifestyles among the young; and create awareness in the community by organizing social activities for older persons. The government seeks to change the society's views on aging, promoting a paradigm shift on aging and ageism, including looking at these not in a negative but in a positive light.

Indonesia

Indonesia's Ministry of Social Affairs is responsible for promoting the status of older persons. Key policy instruments on older persons are (1) Law 13 of 1998 on Older Persons Welfare; (2) National Plan of Action for Older Persons Welfare (2003–2008); and (3) the Presidential Decree on the formation of the National and Regional Commissions on Aging in 2004. The task of the National Commission on Aging is to assist the president in coordinating the implementation of national policies and programs, as well as rendering professional advice and recommendations. The development of older persons' programs is focused on community-based home care in the form of Family Care Centers (PUSAKAS, *Pusat Santunan Keluarga*) and older person empowerment in the rural areas. The main focus of these programs is on the poor and neglected older persons, the majority of whom are females. Specific health programs for older persons have been implemented by, among other actions, establishing integrated geriatric services in hospitals and Community Health Services (PUSKESMAS, *Puskesmas Santun Lansia*). There are many older person health posts in the community as well as special reception counters within health facilities just for older persons, and free medication is provided for persons 80 years and over. The government has also formulated provisions on social assistance and social security, especially for neglected older persons by developing specific Social Security Gotong Royong (literally, joint bearing of burdens), through empowering the potential traditional values of the community in promoting and protecting the status of the elderly. To promote research on aging, UNFPA provided support for developing a multicenter study on Social Cultural Aspects of the Aging Population in Indonesia. This provided the impetus for the Indonesia Research on Aging Population Network (InResAge), which includes participating population and development centers in five regions, namely, North Sumatra, Jogjakarta, East Java, Bali, and South Sulawesi, with Jakarta as the coordinating center. In 2007, UNFPA assisted in undertaking an in-depth situation analysis of population aging in the country.[41]

Vietnam

Vietnam has an elaborate institutional structure to deal with aging issues. The Department of Social Welfare of the Ministry of Labour, Invalids, and Social Affairs (MOLISA) is the coordinating agency, while the Ministry of Health is one of the key ministries implementing special programs for older persons. MOLISA, with provincial departments as well as district and commune divisions, is able to address the issue at various subnational levels. Mass organizations that have a special role include, among others, Vietnam Association of the Elderly (VAE), the VAE's

---

[41] Nugroho Abikusno, *Older Population in Indonesia: Trends, Issues, and Policy Responses* (Bangkok: UNFPA Papers in Population Ageing No. 3, 2007).

network of Elderly People's Clubs, Association of Elderly People for National Salvation, Association of Veneration of Longevity, and Women's Union.

The government has enacted a number of aging-related policies and laws, such as the Law on Health Protection and Care for Vietnamese Citizens (1994) and the Ordinance on the Elderly (2000). MOLISA has coordinated the formulation of the National Program of Action for Aging Care, 2003–2010. The program applies a multidisciplinary approach in order to create an enabling environment for improving care for the elderly that will be implemented by different ministries and concerned agencies in Vietnam. It provides for integration of issues and concerns of the elderly into socioeconomic development plans from central to commune levels.

The government has issued decrees and directives on implementing the Ordinance on the Elderly, specifying the privileges older persons are entitled to and assigning specific tasks to each relevant government agency at both national and local levels to ensure the delivery of necessary services to older persons. Some of the welfare measures initiated include pension schemes for salaried workers working in the state-owned and private organizations; regulations on health insurance for people, including very old people; and social-welfare schemes for disadvantaged people, including older persons. At social-service facilities, including hospitals, clinics, and other public sociocultural facilities, older persons enjoy preferential treatment. Older persons without family are taken care of at Public Social Protection centers established and run by the government. To facilitate the social life and activities of older persons, the Viet Nam Association of the Elderly was founded in 1995, with chapters in all cities and provinces, embracing persons aged 60 and over from communes, wards, and cities, both at the central and local levels. The Association has always enjoyed effective state assistance.

Malaysia

Malaysia's government announced the adoption of a National Policy for the Elderly in 1995 and approved a Plan of Action in 1998. The Department of Social Welfare is responsible for the coordination of the implementation of the action plan. The government also established a high-level National Advisory and Consultative Council of the Elderly. An Elderly Health Care Programme was introduced by the Ministry of Health in 1996, which included the establishment of a National Health Council for the Elderly. Medical care protocols give older persons priority in getting attention and ensuring their comfort while waiting for treatment. Pensioners get free treatment and older persons with little or no income can have their hospital fees waived. An important feature of medical care for older persons is a multidisciplinary approach that includes a thorough geriatric assessment. An increasing percentage of rural health care clinics has provided health care services for older persons and health persons have received training in handling older people. Health centers have formed Senior Citizens Clubs (Kelab Warga Emas) that conduct recreational, social, and health-enhancing activities for members. Physiotherapy and other forms of rehabiliation services are offered at both primary and hospital levels.

The government emphasizes the role of family care for older persons and views institutionalization of older persons as a last resort. As such, it has aimed at encouraging traditional forms of kinship support between generations. For example, public-housing authorities allocate ground-floor flats to families with aged or disabled members. Also, priority in housing allocation is given to adult children whose older parents are residing with them. In 1992, tax deductions for medical expenses incurred with respect to aging parents were introduced. Medical benefits enjoyed by civil servants have been extended to include their parents. To minimize the adverse effect of elderly care on female employment, the government, with the cooperation and support of NGOs, has also established community-based day care centers to provide care for older persons during the day when family members are away. For older persons who are destitute and have no relatives to look after them, the government has established shelter homes and provides financial aid.

Federal schemes have been set up to provide assistance to older persons by means of income supplements. The government also provides various opportunities for ICT (information and communications technology) retraining and lifelong education, as well as job placements to enable older persons to continue to be economically productive and independent, and to enhance their self-worth, attractiveness as workers, and dignity. In 2002, the Institute of Gerontology was established. Affiliated with the University of Putra Malaysia, the institute offers postgraduate studies in the field of old age and aging. Activities implemented by the institute have included a review of existing legal provisions to recommend changes to facilitate the employment of older Malaysians; the undertaking of a profile of older Malaysians; a survey to provide a basis for assessing employers' perspectives on re-entry of older persons into the workforce; and the introduction of U3A (University of the Third Age) on a trial basis.

Philippines

The Philippines Department of Social Welfare and Development (DSWD) is the agency responsible for coordinating aging-related activities. In 2000, the government approved and adopted the Philippine Plan of Action for Older Persons (1999–2004). It addressed the need to institute appropriate policies, strategies, mechanisms, and programs/projects to ensure that senior citizens' rights are upheld. It also promoted the rights and welfare of senior citizens and set priority areas and action points that guide efforts toward the goal of promoting the security and dignity of older persons while maintaining their full participation and human rights. Following a critical appraisal of the achievements of the plan, the government formulated the Philippine Plan of Action for Senior Citizens (2006–2010) in line with the country's commitment to the Madrid International Plan of Action on Aging (MIPAA).

A number of laws have been enacted for the benefit of older persons, including the Senior Citizen's Act (RA 7432), the Senior Citizen's Centre Act (RA 7876), and the Expanded Senior Citizens Act of 2003 (RA 9257). Together, these laws ensure benefits and special privileges for older persons—like a 20 percent discount for older persons on medicines and on a wide range of services such as transportation, hotels, restaurants, and recreation centers—as well as provide assistance in terms of tax exemption to those caring for and living with older persons. A Senior Citizen's Identification Card is issued to each older person and the Office of the Senior Citizens Affairs set up in every local government unit monitors the delivery of the benefits. There are senior citizens centers in all cities and municipalities of the country run by the senior citizens themselves, with support from local government units and NGOs. To promote employment of older persons, private companies are allowed an additional tax deduction from their gross income for wages and salaries paid to older persons.

Myanmar

Issues relating to the welfare of older persons are addressed by Myanmar's Department of Social Welfare in the Ministry of Social Welfare, Relief, and Resettlement. The government provides rice and funds for food, clothes, and the salaries of the administrators of Homes for the Aged that have traditionally been operated by religious and voluntary social organizations for older persons and those in need of care for various reasons. Since its introduction as a component of the National Health Plan (1993–1996), Health Care of the Elderly has aimed to promote the health of older persons and to increase access to geriatric care services. Under this component, the government offers manuals for providing health care to older people and distributes health information pamphlets, and operates clinics, which are open once a week, at various locations. At these clinics, health care providers offer curative care and basic physical exercises are demonstrated to older persons. At the clinics, reading glasses are distributed and intraocular lenses are inserted free of charge to older persons. The Social Security Act provides a Social Security Scheme under which the elderly are entitled to free medical care and cash benefits. However, the provision of cash benefits under this scheme has remained very limited.

Laos

Aging-related issues in Laos are dealt with by the Division of Older Persons in the Department of Social Welfare of the Ministry of Labour and Social Welfare. In 2005, the government approved the First National Policy for the Elderly (NPE). The Sixth National Socio-Economic Development Plan (2006–2010) also touches on aging issues, from the perspective of social security, and proposes an improved pension scheme for retired civil servants. Also, the elderly living alone are identified as one of the vulnerable groups in poverty analyses. The 1999 National Population and Development Policy (NPDP) was revised to include care of older persons as an objective. Implementation measures regarding aging-related issues suggested encouraging families to take the responsibility of care for older persons, enhancing awareness of aging of the general population to prepare them for entry into old age, and creating an enabling environment for increased job opportunities for older persons.

Cambodia

In Cambodia, the Ministry of Social Affairs, Labour, Vocational Training, and Youth Rehabilitation (MoSALVY) coordinates the formulation and implementation of programs relating to older persons. The government's growing concern with population aging was reflected in the adoption of a Policy for the Elderly in 2003. The older population has been identified as a vulnerable group within the development of social safety nets and welfare programs by the National Strategic Development Plan (NSDP) for 2006–2010. To prevent and eradicate the risk of those diseases that threaten older people, the Ministry of Health specifically classifies the management of hypertension and diabetes as one of the priority health service interventions. Emphasis has also been placed on improving data collection and promoting research. The Survey of Elderly in Cambodia, a collaborative effort between the Royal University of Phnom Penh and the University of Michigan, produced an overview of the situation of older persons as well as a special analysis of the impact of the AIDS epidemic on them.

CONCLUSION

Since the turn of the century, population aging has emerged as a crucial issue in almost all countries of Southeast Asia. Even for the three countries—Cambodia, Laos, and Timor-Leste—where older persons (aged 60 and older) account for a low proportion of the total population, the increases projected for the years 2000 to 2025 are far greater than those seen during the last half of the previous century (1950–2000). Moreover, the older population will itself be "aging," that is, the proportion of the oldest old (aged 80 years and over) is projected to increase. Women constitute a majority of the older population and even a bigger majority of the oldest old population. This adds a gender dimension to all aging-related issues, since older women are more vulnerable than older men. Hence, no country in Southeast Asia can be complacent about the inevitable consequences of the demographic projections. The growing size of the older population and its structure will call for increasing efforts to ensure that older persons can lead healthy and active lives, and that their economic and social freedoms are guaranteed. The most pressing issues are the provision of adequate health care services, long-term care services, appropriate living arrangements, and income security.

Governments in Southeast Asia are becoming increasingly aware of the evolving situation, more so since the Second World Assembly on Aging in 2002. Most have put in place an institutional mechanism to address, in a coordinated manner, aging-related problems and have introduced policies, programs, and legislation aimed at enhancing the quality of life of older persons. The primary focus has been on providing health services and long-term care services. The need to address the issue of living arrangements for older persons has been drawing increasing attention. Governments are beginning to realize the importance of providing income security in old age and opportunities for older persons to remain as active as possible. Nevertheless, the governments will need to do much more as population aging continues to accelerate.

In addition to governments, which have taken the lead in dealing with issues arising as a result of population aging, NGOs have also been playing an increasing role mostly in implementing programs and providing welfare services. In a number of Southeast Asian countries, NGOs have substituted for government intervention where public services have been lacking. For example, in the low income countries, NGOs have stepped in to provide basic health services, arrange long-term care for the disabled, establish day care centers, and develop income-generating schemes for older people. NGOs have also been increasingly involved in enhancing awareness of aging and in advocating for larger budgetary allocations for aging-related activities. There are some NGOs, like HelpAge International, the Tsao Foundation, and Help the Aged, that focus on older persons. In addition, some NGOs in other areas of specializations have also given special attention to the problems of older persons within the context of their activities. For example, NGOs working in the area of

HIV/AIDS have paid increasing attention to the impact of the epidemic on older persons.[42]

The government should strengthen the institutional mechanism needed to address aging-related issues, and develop capacity of relevant staff developed to improve their skills in the collection and use of data and conducting research for policy formulation, program and monitoring, and evaluation. For the formulation of effective policies and programs, it is important to collect data on older persons on a regular schedule, and ensure that the data is disaggregated by age, sex, subnational units, and socioeconomic characteristics. With such data, further research can be undertaken to enhance policy makers' understanding of the issues facing the older population. Health programs should be designed specifically to cater to the needs of older persons, with adequate attention being paid to ensuring the availability of medicines and equipment needed for treating diseases of old-age and to providing the required health personnel trained in geriatrics. For older persons in need of long-term care, arrangements should be made for community-based care (health and psychosocial) that has been found to be cost-effective, and also in line with older persons' preference for "aging in place." Where necessary, governments should make provisions for institutional care.

Family ties continue to be strong and families should be encouraged to care for their older relatives through measures such as tax benefits, allowances, and assistance for home improvement assistance. Women constitute the majority of caregivers at the family and community levels. Caregivers should be provided appropriate concessions to facilitate combining their caregiving responsibilities with their employments through measures, such as time off, without affecting seniority or tax credits. Moreover, governments should promote male responsibility in taking care of older persons. In addition, governments should offer avenues for gainful employment for older persons so that they can use their skills and lifelong experience to contribute to development and provide support to the families. In the informal sector, older persons should be encouraged to continue in employment through improved access to credit and to the provision of inputs and means of skills upgrading. In the formal sector, continuation of employment of older persons should be encouraged by increasing the age of mandatory retirement and providing incentives to employers, such as tax rebates, for employing older workers. Governments should also encourage the expansion of contributory pension schemes and increase the scope of social pensions and welfare benefits to ensure income security in old age.

Briefly stated, there are two prerequisites for effectively addressing aging-related issues and problems facing the growing older population:

(a) The negative attitude toward aging and older persons needs to be dispelled. Policy makers, caregivers, service delivery personnel, and

---

[42] The leading NGO in the area of aging has been HelpAge International (HAI). In Southeast Asia, it has been working for almost two decades with network members and partners, as well as international organizations, to implement community projects, conduct research, develop capacity, raise awareness, and ensure the effective implementation of policies to support older people. During emergencies, HelpAge has made a remarkable contribution to ensuring the inclusion of older people in relief operations such as during the tsunami in Indonesia and Thailand and cyclone Nargis in Myanmar.

even older persons themselves view aging as a "problem," and older persons as a "burden." A positive image of aging and older persons should be projected through measures such as media campaigns and highlighting the contributions of older persons at the family, community, and national levels.

(b) As population aging has an impact in every sector, governments should seek to mainstream aging in all development policies, programs, and strategies, including those for poverty alleviation, budgetary policies, infrastructure development, and town planning.

Finally, though governments will have to take the lead and provide an enabling and supportive environment for the implementation of policies and programs needed to address aging-related issues, successful implementation will require the involvement of all sectors of civil society, NGOs, research and academic institutions, faith-based organizations, community-based organizations, media, and the private sector.

CHAPTER 5

CHANGING PATTERNS OF POPULATION MOBILITY IN SOUTHEAST ASIA

Graeme Hugo

Of all the demographic, economic, and social changes that have transformed Southeast Asia since 1950, few have been so dramatic, or as far reaching in their impacts, as the increase in personal mobility. Migration, on a permanent or temporary basis, is now within the calculus of choice of most Southeast Asians as they weigh their life chances. Historically, Southeast Asia has been an important crossroads for migrations from China from the north and India and Europe from the west, while its considerable internal diversity has resulted in high levels of mobility within the region. In the contemporary world, globalization, the internationalization of capital and labor markets, and the revolution in transport and communications has meant that population mobility has assumed an even more important role.

Unfortunately, the exponential increase in population mobility has not been matched by a proportionate improvement in data collection and research relating to such mobility in Southeast Asia.[1] Accordingly, at the outset of this chapter, some comments are made on the limitations of internal and international migration data in Southeast Asia since a recognition of these is essential to understanding the information presented later in the chapter on the patterns, causes, and consequences of changing population mobility in the region. While contemporary internal and international migration patterns are described separately here, it is recognized that there are important linkages between them.[2] This is reflected in subsequent sections that examine the major issues regarding migration in the region, and the causes and consequences of population movement in which internal and international migration are considered together. These discussions are followed by some consideration of

---

[1] Jerrold W. Huguet, "Towards a Migration Information System in Asia: Statistics and the Public Discourse on International Migration," *Asian and Pacific Migration Journal* 17 (2008): 3–4.

[2] Ronald Skeldon, "Interlinkages Between Internal and International Migration and Development in the Asian Region," *Population, Space, and Place* 12,1 (2006): 15–30.

policies in the region relating to migration, and the chapter concludes with an examination of some potential future developments in migration in Southeast Asia.

A significant change has occurred in the global discourse on the complex relationships between population movement, on the one hand, and economic development and social change, on the other.[3] Traditionally, migration, both internal and international, has been viewed as a largely negative influence on development in origin communities. The loss of the "best and brightest" through migration has been seen to result in a concomitant decline in the origin community's ability to develop. Recent thinking, however, has stressed that, in the right context, out-migration can yield positive impacts on origin communities through the effects of remittances, the active participation of the absent diaspora in the origin's economy and society, and through permanent and temporary return and circular migration.[4] (Circular migration refers to temporary and repetitive movements between an origin and destination involving absences of more than one day from the origin to differentiate it from commuting.[5]) Accordingly, economic-development policy is taking increasing cognizance of the potential positive role that migration can play, not only in improving the situation of migrants and the communities they join, but also in improving the areas they leave.

Migration has been depicted as the "stepchild of demography" because, compared with the other two basic demographic processes, fertility and mortality, its measurement remains incomplete and imprecise because the research effort devoted to it is comparatively less.[6] This certainly applies in the Southeast Asian context. International migration data are incomplete, and only a minority of Southeast Asian countries include international migration questions in their population censuses.[7] Even border-control statistics are of limited utility, since there is significant undocumented migration and few countries collect, process, and analyze border-crossing statistics in a way that makes them useful for research and policy.[8] Data on nonpermanent migration are especially sparse, even though these forms of movement are of major and growing significance in the region. Moreover, the international migration data that are collected relate only to immigration. In common with most other countries, Southeast Asian countries do not systematically collect information on people leaving the country, that is, on emigration, although the

---

[3] United Nations, "International Migration and Development" (Report of the Secretary-General, 60th Session, Globalization and Interdependence: International Migration and Development, May 18, 2006); World Bank, *Global Economic Prospects 2006: Economic Implications of Remittances and Migration* (Washington, DC: World Bank, 2006).

[4] Robert E. B. Lucas, "The Economic Well-Being of Movers and Stayers: Assimilation, Impacts, Links, and Proximity" (paper prepared for Conference on African Migration in Comparative Perspective, Johannesburg, South Africa, June 4–7, 2003).

[5] For a discussion of circular migration, see Dovelyn R. Agunias and Kathleen Newland, "Circular Migration and Development: Trends, Policy Routes, and Ways Forward" (Washington, DC, Migration Policy Institute Policy Brief, April 2007).

[6] Sidney Goldstein, "Facets of Redistribution: Research Challenges and Opportunities," *Demography* 13,4 (1976): 423–34.

[7] Graeme J. Hugo, "Challenges in Compiling Stock Statistics on International and Internal Migration in Asia for the 2010 Round of Population Censuses" (paper prepared for the International Association for Official Statistics [IAOS] Conference titled People on the Move: Measuring Environmental, Social, and Economic Impacts within and between Nations, Ottawa, September 6–8, 2006).

[8] Huguet, "Towards a Migration Information System in Asia."

region contains some of the world's major origin countries of international migrants.[9] The major difficulties with international migration data in Southeast Asia are as follows:[10]

- the high incidence of irregular migration, both as a result of clandestine migration and of people entering a country legally, but without permission to work and then seeking to work;
- systematic exclusion of some international labor migration from data-collection systems, as in the case of some highly skilled workers;
- lack of comprehensive and efficient data-collection systems;
- a neglect of temporary migration in data-collection systems that focus on permanent migration;
- a focus on foreigners, with data on nationals not being collected or processed; and
- some destination countries, such as Singapore, do not divulge data on international migration because of its perceived sensitivity.

Accordingly, much of the data we have on international migration in (and out of) Southeast Asia are incomplete and of limited accuracy.

Relative to international migration data, the coverage for internal migration data is better due to population censuses in most nations, including a question on previous place of residence,[11] although different definitions of migration and the varying size and shape of migration-defining spatial units mean that the data are not comparable across countries. There are also real limitations because no countries in the region collect systematic information on circular and other temporary migration, although such patterns have been shown to have substantial social and economic significance.[12] Moreover, although data on more-or-less-permanent migration are collected, they often are only available for movement between very large spatial units, so short-distance movement is often not detected. A particular failing is not collecting in- and out-migration separately for rural and urban sectors to show the significance of rural-urban migration in urbanization processes. A related problem involves the delimitation of urban areas in Southeast Asia. Gavin W. Jones, for example, has shown that "official" statistics of Southeast Asia's megacities severely underbound the functional areas of these cities.[13]

TRENDS IN INTERNATIONAL MIGRATION

For the quarter century following World War II, there was very little international migration in Southeast Asia. Most substantial were the movements associated with decolonization as several of the countries gained their independence

---

[9] World Bank, *Migration and Remittances Factbook 2008* (Washington, DC: World Bank, 2008).

[10] Huguet, "Towards a Migration Information System in Asia"; Graeme J. Hugo, "Improving Statistics on International Migration in Asia," *International Statistical Review* 74,3 (2006): 335–55.

[11] Hugo, "Improving Statistics on International Migration in Asia," 335–55.

[12] Goldstein, "Facets of Redistribution: Research Challenges and Opportunities."

[13] Gavin W. Jones, "Urbanization Trends in Asia: The Conceptual and Definitional Challenges," in *New Forms of Urbanization*, ed. Anthony Champion and Graeme Hugo (Ashgate: Aldershot, 2004).

from European colonial powers. In Indonesia, for example, between 1952 and 1961 there was a net out-migration of more than 100,500 Dutch colonial functionaries, mainly back to the Netherlands (although many also went to Australia), and they were accompanied by loyal groups like the many Ambonese who formed the basis of the contemporary "Moluccan" community in the Netherlands.[14] The outflow from Indonesia between 1952 and 1961 also included more than 142,650 ethnic Chinese who were given a choice of renouncing their Chinese nationality or returning to China.[15] Since the 1970s, however, international migration of Southeast Asians within and out of the region has gathered momentum, increasing not only in scale but also in diversity and economic and social significance.

Table 1
International Labor Migration/Emigration

Mainly emigration	
Philippines	Myanmar
Cambodia	Laos
Indonesia	Vietnam
Mainly immigration	
Singapore	
Brunei	
Both significant immigration and emigration	
Malaysia	
Thailand	

The largest scale international migration in Southeast Asia is temporary-contract-labor migration, which involves both low- and high-skilled workers, although the former predominate.[16] While these movements have their origins in the "contract coolie" programs of colonial times, in the contemporary era they began with the flows of Thai and Filipino workers into Vietnam to work for the Americans during the Indo-China War.[17] Then, following the 1973 increase in oil prices, which fueled a building boom in the Middle East, migrant workers from the Philippines and Thailand, and later Indonesia, flowed to Saudi Arabia and other labor-short, oil-producing, Middle Eastern countries. Since then, the scale of movement and the number of countries involved in migration has increased. With the emergence of labor shortages in Japan and the "Asian Tigers" (i.e., Hong Kong, Singapore, South Korea, and Taiwan) during the 1980s and 1990s, these low-skilled migrant workers increasingly moved to Japan, South Korea, Taiwan, Hong Kong, and Singapore.

Table 1 classifies Southeast Asian nations according to whether they are mainly destinations or origins for labor migrants. Although all nations experience both immigration and emigration, usually one or the other predominates. However, Malaysia and Thailand are interesting in that they record substantial inflows *and*

---

[14] Graeme J. Hugo, "Patterns of Interprovincial Migration," in *United Nations, III, Migration, Urbanization, and Development in Indonesia* (New York, NY: United Nations, 1981), pp. 81–110.

[15] Ibid.

[16] Graeme J. Hugo and Soogil Young, eds., *Labour Mobility in the Asia-Pacific Region* (Singapore: Institute of Southeast Asian Studies, 2008).

[17] Similarly, many Filipinos are currently working in Iraq doing similar types of jobs.

outflows of labor migrants. It is important to point out, however, that all countries have both inflows and outflows. For example, Laos is currently experiencing an influx of Vietnamese workers while sending workers to Thailand. Singapore has significant outflows to Organization for Economic Cooperation and Development (OECD) countries while being a country of net immigration.

Table 2
SEA Migrant Workers in Other SEA Countries

Origin Countries	Number	Main Destinations	Source of Information	Year
Myanmar	3,000,000	Thailand	Karen Human Rights Group, 2010[a]	2010
Thailand	500,000	Saudi Arabia, Taiwan, Myanmar, Singapore, Brunei, Malaysia	Sciortino and Punpuing[b]	2007
Laos	173,000	Thailand	*Migration News*, January 2005	2004
Cambodia	183,541	Thailand	*Migration News*, October 2007	2006
Vietnam	500,000	Korea, Japan, Malaysia, Taiwan	Dang Nhu Loi[c]	2010
Philippines	8,579,378	Middle East, Malaysia, Japan	Philippines Overseas Employment Agency	2009
Malaysia	250,000	Japan, Taiwan	Asian Migrant Center[d]	1995
Indonesia	6,000,000	Malaysia, Saudi Arabia, Taiwan, Singapore, South Korea, United Arab Emirates	Adamrah[e]	2010
Total	19,960,919			

[a]Karen Human Rights Group (KHRG), Abuse between Borders: Vulnerability for Burmese Workers Departed from Thailand, February 22, 2010. [b]Rosalia Sciortino and Sureeporn Punpuing, *International Migration in Thailand 2009* (Bangkok: International Organization for Migration, Thailand Office, 2009). [c]Dang Nhu Loi, presentation to ASEAN Regional Informal Workshop on Bilateral Agreements, Hotel Sofitel Hanoi, Vietnam, September 17–18, 2010. [d]Asian Migrant Center, *Asian Migrant Yearbook 1999* (Hong Kong: Asian Migrant Center Ltd., 1999). [e]M. Adamrah, "RI takes Indian advice on Migrant Workers," *Jakarta Post*, July 20, 2010

Table 2 shows that the Philippines and Indonesia are two of the world's major emigration nations, but Vietnam, and to a lesser extent Cambodia and Myanmar, are of increasing significance. There has been an increase in the scale of out-migration of labor migrants from these origin countries, and this can be demonstrated with the case of Indonesia. Figure 1 shows the number of official labor migrants processed by the Indonesian Ministry of Labor from 1979 to 2008. However, since most workers are on two-year or longer contracts, the actual number of official overseas contract workers (OCWs) actually *working* out of the origin country in any one year is greater than the numbers *deployed* in an individual year. In late 2008, the Minister of Labor announced that there were 5.8 million Indonesians working overseas, including those with official permission and undocumented migrant workers.[18] This represents around five percent of the total national workforce.

Figure 1
Indonesian Overseas Workers Processed by Ministry of Manpower, 1979–2009

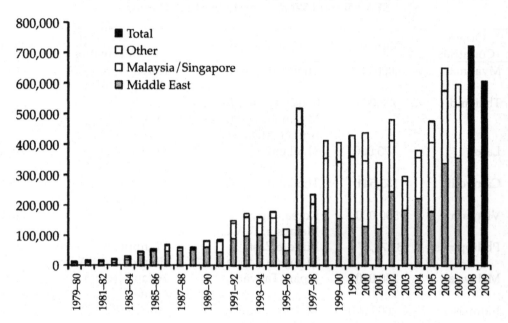

Sources: M. Suyono, "Tenaga Kerja Indonesia di Timur Tengah Makin Mantap," *Suara Karya* (1981): 2–6; Anchalee Singhanetra-Renard, "The Middle East and Beyond: Dynamics of International Labour Circulation among Southeast Asian Workers" (Chiang Mai University, unpublished mimeograph, 1986), p. 52; Pusat Penelitian Kependudukan, *Mobilitas Angkalan Kerja ke Timur Tengah* (Yogyakarta: Gadjah Mada University, 1986); Tri N. Pujiastuti, "The Experience of Female Overseas Contract Workers From Indonesia" (MA dissertation, Department of Geographical and Environmental Studies, University of Adelaide, 2000), p. 2; Tara B. Soeprobo, "Recent Trends of International Migration in Indonesia," paper presented at the Workshop on International Migration and Labour Markets in Asia, Japan Institute of Labour, Tokyo, Japan, February 6–7, 2003; Aris Ananta and Evi Arifin, "Demographic and Population Mobility Transitions in Indonesia," paper presented at PECC-ABAC (APEC [Asia-Pacific Economic Cooperation] Business Advisory Council) Conference on Demographic Change and International Labour Mobility in the Asia-Pacific Region: Implications for Business and Cooperation, organized by Korea National Committee for Pacific Economic Cooperation (KOPEC) and the Korea Labour Institute (KLI), Seoul, Korea, March 25–26, 2008; and Kee B. Kim, "Labour Migration in Asia: Recent Trends and Outlook," paper presented at ADBI-OECD Roundtable on Labor Migration in Asia: Recent Trends and Prospects in the Postcrisis Context, Tokyo, Japan, January 18–20, 2011; and AKAN (Antar Kerja Antar Negara) in Bandung and Jakarta.

---

[18] *Asia Migration News* (AMN), December 2008. AMN is a bi-weekly information service of the Scalabrini Migration Centre. It provides scholars, policy makers, advocates, and students with a summary of news and events related to migration in Asia.

Undocumented labor migration out of Indonesia remains substantial, especially to Malaysia. The Malaysian Home Minister estimated that in late 2006 there were around 600,000 irregular migrant workers in Malaysia (most of them Indonesians) despite periodic sweeps, deportations, and amnesties.[19] The Indonesian Director General of Labor Placement Overseas estimated that in August 2005 there were more than a million Indonesians abroad illegally, including about 400,000 in Malaysia, 400,000 in Saudi Arabia (many illegally overstaying three-month pilgrimage visas), 20,000 in South Korea, and 8,000 in Japan.[20] Accordingly, it is difficult to arrive at an accurate estimate of the numbers of Indonesian labor migrants who are absent at any single point in time. Table 3 presents one set of estimates of contemporary stocks of Indonesian workers in foreign countries around 2006.

Table 3
Indonesia: Estimated Stocks of Overseas Contract Workers, c. 2006

Destination	Estimated Stocks	Source
Saudi Arabia	1,500,000	*Migration News,* October 2010
United Arab Emirates	75,000	Indonesian Embassy, Abu Dhabi
Malaysia	2,600,000	US Dept. of State
Hong Kong	130,000	*Jakarta Post,* June 25, 2009
Singapore	106,000	ASEAN Summit, 2011
Taiwan	120,000	*Jakarta Post,* April 13, 2009
South Korea	30,000	*Jakarta Post,* April 13, 2009
Japan	22,862	Okushima[a]
Philippines	26,000	SCMP, December 10, 1998
Brunei	50,000	ASEAN Summit, 2011
Total	4,659,862	

[a]M. Okushima, "International Trends of Indonesian Migrant Workers and their Employment System in Japan" (introduction to a special issue), *Intercultural Communication Studies* 17 (2005), p. 14.

Turning to a destination perspective, Table 4 provides estimates of the numbers of foreign workers in Southeast Asia. They are relatively most significant in Singapore and Brunei, where they make up more than a third of the workforce (based on World Bank data). Nevertheless, they are also important in Thailand and Malaysia. In Malaysia, government figures put the number of migrant workers at 2,235,200 in 2007, or 20.5 percent of the workforce.[21] Most are employed in manual occupations in the plantation, forestry, construction, manufacturing, and household (domestic service) sectors. At the same time, Malaysia sends significant numbers of relatively low-skilled workers to Singapore, Taiwan, and Japan. Similarly, Thailand has two million workers from neighboring nations, but sends several hundred

---

[19] *Asian Migration News,* October 1–15, 2006.

[20] *Migration News* 12,4 (October 2005), http://migration.ucdavis.edu/mn/more_entireissue. php?idate=2005_10&number=4, accessed February 27, 2012. *Migration News* is produced in the US by the University of California–Davis and summarizes and analyzes the most important immigration and integration developments of the preceding quarter.

[21] Malaysian Government Economic Planning Unit.

thousand workers to the Middle East, Taiwan, Japan, and Malaysia. As in the case of destination stocks, there has been a significant increase in recent times in the stocks of migrant workers in Southeast Asian destination countries.

A distinctive feature of Southeast Asian labor migration has been the increasing significance of women in the movement.[22] In the two major origin countries, Philippines and Indonesia, women have outnumbered men among official labor migrants. Female labor migrants are more clustered in a few occupations than are male labor migrants. Dominant here are household domestic workers, but caregivers ("carers"), nurses, entertainers, and, increasingly, factory workers are also important. Several of the occupations taken up by female labor migrants from Southeast Asia place them at greater risk of exploitation than their male counterparts (for example, many domestic workers do not receive the worker protection available to those employed by businesses and institutions).

Table 4
Estimated Stocks of Foreign Labor in Southeast Asia, c. 2006

Country	Year	Stock	Source
Singapore	2006	699,200	Beng and Chew, 2008
Malaysia	2006	1,869,200	Kanapathy, 2008
Thailand	2005	2,000,000	*Voice of America*, August 23, 2005
Brunei	1999	91,800	*Migration News*, February 2000
Vietnam	2001	30,000	Nguyen, 2003
Indonesia	2004	91,736	Soeprobo, 2005
Philippines	2004	9,408	Skeldon, 2006
Total		4,791,344	

[a]Chew S. Beng and Rosalind Chew, "Coping with International Movement of Personnel: Its Impact on Low Wage Domestic Workers in Singapore" (draft paper presented at the PECC-ABAC Conference on Demographic Change and International Labour Mobility). See also updates supplied in April 2008. [b]Vijayakumari Kanapathy, "Managing Cross-Border Labour Mobility in Malaysia: Two Decades of Policy Experiments" (paper presented at the PECC-ABAC Conference on Demographic Change and International Labour Mobility). [c]Nguyen X. Nguyen, "International Migration of Highly Skilled Workers in Vietnam" (paper presented at the Workshop on International Migration and Labour Markets in Asia, Japan Institute of Labour, Tokyo, February 4–5, 2003). [d]Tara B. Soeprobo, "Recent Trends in International Migration in Indonesia" (paper prepared for Workshop on International Migration and Labour Markets in Asia, Japan Institute for Labour Policy and Training, Japan Institute of Labour, Tokyo, January 20–21, 2005). [e]Ronald Skeldon, "Recent Trends in Migration in East and Southeast Asia," *Asian and Pacific Migration Journal* 15,2 (2006): 277–93.

While the dominant temporary labor migration flow is of low-skilled workers, there are increasing temporary flows of skilled workers within the Asian region. In particular, the large cities of the region have substantial expatriate Asian populations. The ASEAN Economic Agreement planned for introduction in 2015 contains some provisions for free exchange of some skilled workers between

---

[22] Lin L. Lim and Nana Oishi, "International Labor Migration of Asian Women: Distinctive Characteristics and Policy Concerns," *Asian and Pacific Migration Journal* 5,1 (1996).

Southeast Asian countries. As elsewhere in the world, there is a growing divergence in destination countries' policies toward high-skilled migration (which the countries are welcoming) and low-skilled migration (against which nations are erecting more barriers).

Figure 2
Southeast Asian Migrants Residing in OECD Countries, 2000

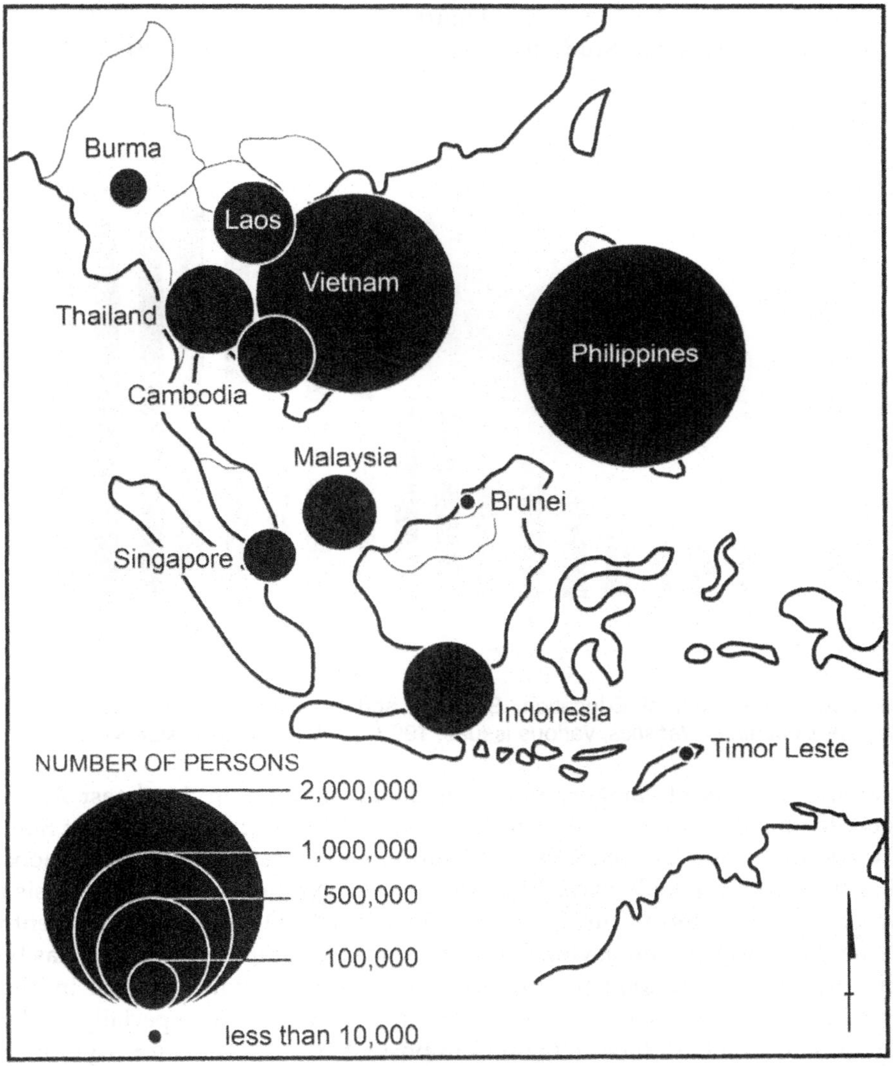

Source: OECD, Database on Immigrants and Expatriates

An increasing trend in recent years has been in temporary and permanent migration to OECD countries.[23] The numbers of people born in Southeast Asia living

---

[23] Andrew Hardy, "From a Floating World: Emigration to Europe From Post-War Vietnam," *Asian and Pacific Migration Journal* 11, 4 (2002); and Hugo and Young, eds., *Labour Mobility in the Asia-Pacific Region*.

in OECD countries at the time of the year 2000 round of population censuses is shown in Figure 2, and this indicates that all countries in the region, especially the Philippines and Vietnam, have significant diasporas in high-income nations. An important characteristic of this migration is that it is increasingly selective of highly skilled workers.[24] OECD nations have become increasingly focused on selecting settlers on the basis of their education and skills, with family reunion becoming less significant.[25]

Figure 3
Southeast Asian Students in Australian Universities, 1991–2007

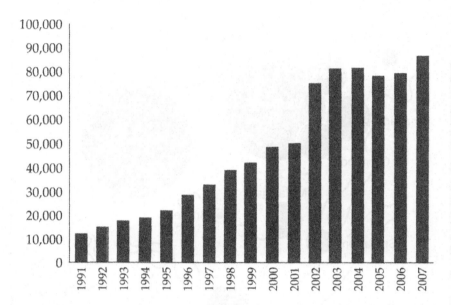

Source: Department of Education, Science, and Training (DEST), *Students: Selected Higher Education Statistics*, various issues, 1992–2008 (Canberra: AGPS Press).

Another important category of international migrants in Southeast Asia is the refugee. In the 1970s and 1980s, the flows out of Indo-China into other Southeast Asian countries and subsequently to third-country settlement destinations saw around two million people leave Vietnam alone. These flows formed the basis of the large contemporary Indo-Chinese communities in OECD nations. More recently, the movement of refugees and asylum seekers from Myanmar into Thailand has been of significance so that the total community of immigrants from Myanmar in Thailand now numbers more than a million. Southeast Asia and especially Indonesia, Malaysia, and Thailand have remained important transit points for asylum seekers

[24] Susan Martin and B. Lindsay Lowell, "International Labour Mobility in the United States" (paper presented at PECC-ABAC Conference on Demographic Change and International Labour Mobility in the Asia-Pacific Region).

[25] Organisation for Economic Co-operation and Development (OECD), *International Migration Outlook: SOPEMI 2010* (Paris: OECD, 2010).

en route to OECD countries. Asylum seekers from Iraq, Afghanistan, and Sri Lanka in recent times have passed through en route to Australia.[26]

An important dimension of south–north migration from Southeast Asia in recent years has been an increasing volume of temporary migration, which involves, overwhelmingly, highly skilled migrants. One important part of this has been the increasing number of students studying in OECD countries. Figure 3, for example, shows a substantial increase in the numbers of Southeast-Asian-origin students studying in Australia. This temporary movement, however, is only one element in a more diverse flow, with OECD countries introducing skilled temporary migration programs, such as the H-1B program in the United States and Australia's 457 initiative, over the last fifteen years. Figure 4 shows the increase in the number of temporary business migrants admitted to Australia from Southeast Asia in recent years. The 457 program gives skilled workers full work rights in Australia for a period of up to four years, and workers can bring their spouses and dependent children with them. Accordingly, in 2008, there were more than 121,000 Southeast Asia-born persons with temporary residence in Australia.

Figure 4
Southeast Asians in Australia with 457 Visas, 1998–2008

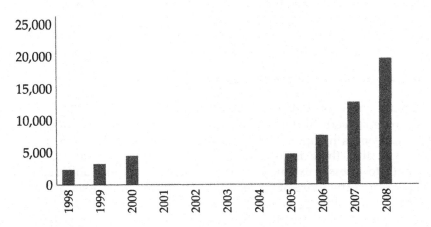

Source: Siew E. Khoo, Graeme J. Hugo, and Peter McDonald, "Skilled Temporary Migration from Asia-Pacific Countries to Australia," *Asian and Pacific Migration Journal* 42,1 (2008): 193–226; DIAC *Immigration Update*, various issues, 2006–08.

An important trend among temporary migrants in OECD countries has been the increasing number who make the transition to permanent residence without returning to their home country.[27] This is especially the case with student migrants. Some nations, in fact, encourage such transitions, and Simmons has coined the term "designer migrants" to describe the phenomenon of countries recruiting migrants

---

[26] United Nations High Commission for Refugees (UNHCR), *UNHCR Global Trends 2010* (Geneva: UNHCR, 2010).

[27] Lesleyanne Hawthorne, "How Valuable is 'Two-Step Migration'? Labor Market Outcomes for International Student Migrants to Australia," *Asian and Pacific Migration Journal* 19,1 (2010).

who obtain local qualifications and then apply for permanent residence.[28] Table 5 shows that, over the 2002–08 period, there were 38,639 "onshore immigrants" (those who stayed beyond their intended term of residence) to Australia from Southeast Asia compared with 107,654 "offshore immigrants" (those who arrived with the intention of staying).

Table 5
Data Collected by Australian Government:
Visa Category of Permanent Additions from Southeast Asia, 2002–03 to 2007–08

Visa Category	Onshore Migrants[a]		Offshore Migrants[b]		Total	
	No.	% of Total	No.	% of Total	No.	% of Total
Skill	9,928	25.7	47,986	44.6	57,914	39.6
Family	27,889	72.2	49,805	46.3	77,694	53.1
Refugee–Humanitarian	439	1.1	6026	5.6	6,465	4.4
Other	403	1.0	3,837	3.6	4,240	2.9
Total	38,639	100.0	107,654	100.0	146,293	100.0

[a] Onshore migrants refers to persons who have successfully transferred from temporary to permanent residence while in Australia.
[b] Offshore migrants refers to persons who immigrated to Australia with the intention of becoming a permanent settler.

Source: DIAC *Immigration Update*, various issues, 2002–08.

The increasing flow of skilled people out of Southeast Asia to OECD countries is an issue of some concern in the region since it represents a brain drain of human capital that is seen as hampering development efforts in the region. It should be noted, however, that there is increasing student migration within the region to Singapore and, to a lesser extent, to Malaysia. Both Singapore and Malaysia have become important destinations of student migrants from within Asia.

One form of international movement that is of growing significance in Southeast Asia, but that is often overlooked, is marriage migration. With the increasing mobility of young adults in the region, it is inevitable that more cross-national marriage is occurring.[29] However, there is also increasing commodification of marriage in the region that is resulting in young people (mainly women) from countries like Vietnam, Cambodia, Thailand, and the Philippines meeting partners in South Korea, Taiwan, Japan, and Singapore via agents.[30]

---

[28] Alan Simmons, "International Migration and Designer Immigrants: Canadian Policy in the 1990s," in *Free Markets, Open Societies, Closed Borders? Trends in International Migration and Immigration Policy in the Americas*, ed. Max Castro (Miami, FL: North-South Center Press, 1999).

[29] Gavin W. Jones and Kamalini Ramdas, *(Un)tying the Knot: Ideal and Reality in Asian Marriage* (Singapore: Asia Research Institute, National University of Singapore, 2004).

[30] Graeme J. Hugo and Hong Xoan Nguyen Thi, "Marriage Migration between Vietnam and Taiwan: A View from Vietnam," in *Female Deficit in Asia*, ed. Isabelle Attané and Christophe Z. Guilmoto (Paris: CICRED, 2007), pp. 365–91.

A feature of international migration in the region is that a significant amount of movement occurs outside of official migration systems.[31] Some officials estimate that the amount of undocumented migration in the region is as large as the documented flows. This is partly in response to many of the destination countries, in which there is a manifest shortage of workers, failing to develop documented avenues for migration. With regard to both documented and undocumented migration in the region, agents of various kinds play an important role. There is concern in some countries, especially in relation to labor migration, that there is excessive rent taking from the migrant workers, not only by migration industry agents, but also by government officials involved in the migration process. As a result, the excessive charges levied on migrant workers can dilute the level of remittances sent to home (origin) communities.[32]

Governments in the region have an increasing interest in international migration as awareness of its potential role in development is appreciated. Moreover, whereas in the past ASEAN eschewed discussions of international migration because of its great sensitivity, there has been increasing multilateral discussion of migration issues. This discussion has been partly in response to the post-9/11 security imperatives, but is increasingly more broad based, that is, concerned with protection of migrant workers, recognition of qualifications, and facilitation of movement of some kinds of migrant workers.[33]

TRENDS IN INTERNAL MIGRATION

While international migration has increased greatly in scale and significance in Southeast Asia, it is the increase in population mobility *within* nations that has had the greatest impact since it has influenced the majority of the population of the region. Not only has past mobility been underestimated, today Southeast Asians travel across a greater area in search for work, engaging in social and economic interaction. Only a minority of these movements are captured in census migration data, but they do give some indications of increasing mobility. For Indonesia, for example, Table 6 shows the increase in the percentage of the population that has moved between provinces over the last thirty years. It has been shown, however, that there is a ratio of around five intraprovincial migrants for every interprovincial migrant.[34] Moreover, these data do not indicate nonpermanent circular migrations and commuting. One indicator of the increased ability of Indonesians to move on a temporary basis is the decreased number of persons per motor vehicle, shown in Table 7. This reflects not only the proliferation of motor vehicles for personal use but the explosion of public and private transport of different sizes, costs, and levels of

---

[31] Graziano Battistella and Maruja B. Asis, eds., *Unauthorized Migration in Southeast Asia* (Quezon City: Scalabrini Migration Center, 2003).

[32] Manolo Abella, "Challenges to Governance of Labour Migration in Asia-Pacific" (paper presented at PECC-ABAC Conference on Demographic Change and International Labour Mobility in the Asia-Pacific Region).

[33] Hugo and Young, *Labour Mobility in the Asia-Pacific Region.*

[34] Graeme J. Hugo, "Population Distribution and Redistribution in Indonesia," *Majalah Demografi Indonesia* 7,13 (1980): 70–100.

comfort.[35] The impact is that labor markets have been dramatically extended and individual levels of mobility increased considerably.

Table 6
Indonesia: Census-Based Measures of Migration, 1971–2000

Year	Migration Measure	Males	Females
1971	Percentage who have ever lived in another province	6.29	5.06
2000	Percentage who have ever lived in another province	10.56	9.57

Source: Biro Pusat Statistik publications on motor vehicles and length of roads (*Statistik Kendaraan Bermotor dan Panjang Jalan*), Jakarta.

Table 7
Indonesia: Number of Persons per Motor Vehicle, 1950–2005

Year	Persons/Motor Vehicle (including motorcycles)	Persons/Motor Vehicle (excluding motorcycles)
1950	1,507	1,691
1961	263	447
1971	129	300
1980	38	123
1990	20	64
2000	11	39
2005	6	23

Source: Indonesia Census of 1971, 1990, and 2000.

Of particular significance has been the increased movement from rural to urban areas that has resulted in a rapid rise in the proportion of the population living in urban areas. There are some difficulties in analyzing this trend because the definition of "urban" varies considerably across the region. Gavin Jones[36] demonstrates this by comparing the situation in the Philippines and Thailand, which in 2000 had 58.6 percent and 31.1 percent of their populations, respectively, living in urban areas. Yet per capita income in the Philippines was only half that of Thailand. In fact, the two countries have quite different definitions of urban areas. In Thailand, "urban" is defined in purely administrative terms, including areas designated as municipalities only, while the Philippines has a more inclusive definition based on population density, administrative functions, percentage of the population in nonagricultural occupations, and whether or not a place has particular facilities, such as a major hospital. Clearly, these issues make it difficult to compare levels of urbanization among countries. Countries vary as to whether they define urban areas purely on

---

[35] A further indicator of rapidly increasing circulation in Indonesia lies in the increase in the number of domestic airline passengers, which tripled between 2000 (from 8.6 million) and 2005 (25.3 million). See Ananta and E. Arifin, "Demographic and Population Mobility Transitions in Indonesia."

[36] Jones, "Urbanization Trends in Asia."

population size (and if so, what that cut-off size is), on administrative status, on the functions and facilities provided by a place, or on a combination of all these.

Figure 5
Growth and Projected Growth of Urban and Rural Population, 1950–2050

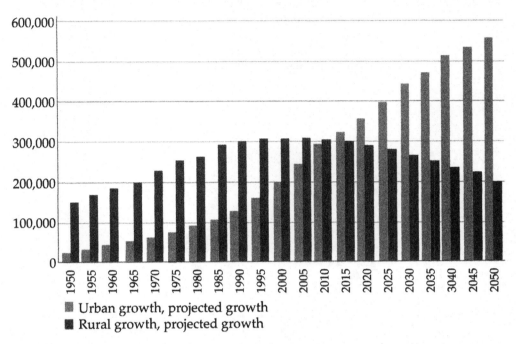

■ Urban growth, projected growth
■ Rural growth, projected growth

Source: United Nations, *World Urbanization Prospects: The 2007 Revision* (New York, NY: United Nations, 2008).

Urban areas do not only grow from rural–urban migration, although this has been a major contributor over recent years in Southeast Asia. Natural increase and reclassification have also been significant. The latter is another complication in making cross-census and cross-country comparisons of urban growth. Nevertheless, it is useful to examine regional trends in official urbanization statistics. In 1950, only 15.4 percent of the region's population lived in urban areas. By 2005, this had increased to 44.1 percent and, according to projections, by 2025 over half the population will live in urban areas.

Figure 5 shows that over the 1950–2005 period the urban population of Southeast Asia grew by a factor of almost nine, from 27.5 million to 245.9 million. Over the same period, the rural population more than doubled, growing from 150.6 million to 311.8 million. However, Figure 5 shows that the region's rural population peaked at 313.3 million in 2000 and since then has been declining. On the other hand, it is projected that the urban population will continue to grow to 326.9 million by 2015, to 439.5 million by 2030, and to 561.6 million by 2050. These figures denote the major transformation that is underway from a way of life and settlement system that was overwhelmingly rural to one that is dominantly urban.

Migration has played a major role in this transformation. Permanent internal resettlement from rural to urban areas has been of fundamental significance, but international migration has also been overwhelmingly directed to large cities and is an increasing element in the growth of the largest cities in the region. Less evident in these data, however, is the large volume of circular migration and commuting from rural to urban areas that is not detected in traditional migration data nor in census counts of urban populations. It predominantly involves individual family members leaving their families behind in the village while they work for a period in the city. Hence, strong networks and linkages between urban and rural areas are being created by these repetitive movements.

Figure 6
Urban Settlements by Population Size, 2000

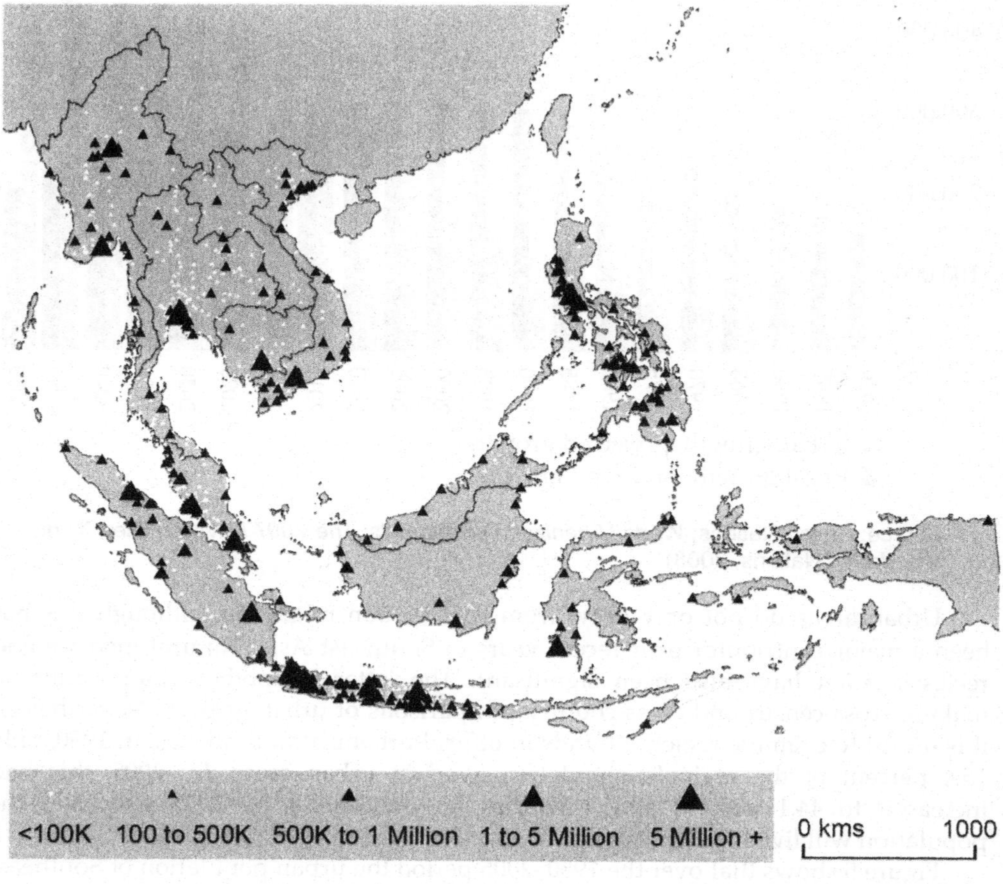

| <100K | 100 to 500K | 500K to 1 Million | 1 to 5 Million | 5 Million + | 0 kms   1000 |

Source: CIESIN, adapted from http://sedac.ciesin.colombia.edu/wdc/downloads/maps/
population/GRUMP/Asia_Settlement_Points_by_Population_Size.pdf

The Southeast Asian settlement system has thus become increasingly urbanized. Figure 6 shows the distribution of urban centers in the region, and a strong coastal orientation is apparent. A particular feature of urbanization in the region has been the emergence of large, complex urban areas with 5 million or more inhabitants. These megacities have taken a particular form. Their origins lay in being entrepôt centers that were the links between the colony and the metropolitan colonial country.[37] Hence, they have a coastal location. They have grown massively and come to dominate the urban hierarchies of Southeast Asian nations, having a disproportionate concentration of education, health, and other services; foreign and local investment; and political and economic power. They also have taken a particular spatial form[38] and have been referred to as extended metropolitan regions (EMRs). As Terence G. McGee[39] describes, they cover extensive areas, envelop surrounding smaller urban centers, and take on a polynuclear form, with urban islands separated by an extensive sea of intensive agriculture mixed with residential development. They have a distinctive, intensive mixture of land use, with agriculture, cottage industry, industrial estates, suburban development, and other uses existing side by side.[40] Their population sizes tend to be severely underestimated in official urban definitions.

Table 8
Growth of Metropolitan Populations in Bangkok, Jakarta, and Manila, 1990–2000

	1990	2000	Average Annual Increase (%)
Bangkok	5,882,000	6,320,000	0.72
BMR*	8,590,000	10,080,000	1.60
Rest of BMR*	2,707,000	3,760,000	3.30
Thailand	54,549,000	60,607,000	1.05
Jakarta	8,259,000	8,385,000	0.16
Botabek	8,876,000	12,749,000	3.70
Jabotabek*	17,135,000	21,134,000	2.10
Indonesia	179,379,000	202,000,000	1.20
Metro Manila	7,945,000	10,491,000	2.90
Manila outer zone	6,481,000	9,458,000	3.90
Manila EMR	14,426,000	19,949,000	3.30
Philippines	60,703,000	72,345,000	1.80

*   BMR is the Bangkok Metropolitan Region;
Jabotabek is the Jakarta extended region.

Source: Gavin W. Jones, "Urbanization Trends in Asia: The Conceptual and Definitional Challenges," in *New Forms of Urbanization*, ed. Anthony Champion and Graeme Hugo (Ashgate: Aldershot, 2004), p. 129.

---

[37] Terence G. McGee, *The Southeast Asian City: A Social Geography of the Primate Cities of Southeast Asia* (London: Bell, 1967).

[38] Gavin W. Jones and Michael Douglass, eds., *Mega-Urban Regions in Pacific Asia: Urban Dynamics in a Global Era* (Singapore: National University of Singapore Press, 2008).

[39] Terence G. McGee, "The Emergence of Desakota Regions in Asia: Expanding a Hypothesis," in *The Extended Metropolis: Settlement Transition in Asia,* ed. Norton Ginsburg, Bruce Koppel, and Terence G. McGee (Honolulu, HI: University of Hawaii Press, 1991).

[40] Jones, "Urbanization Trends in Asia," p. 126.

Table 8 shows Gavin Jones's estimates of the urbanized areas beyond, but contiguous with, the officially defined boundaries of Bangkok, Jakarta, and Manila.[41] The extended boundaries substantially increase the functional populations of these megacities. It should also be noted that population growth rates are much higher in the outer margins of megacities than in their central built-up areas.

Table 9
Selected Cities Vulnerable to Sea-Level Rise: Height above Sea Level and Projected Population Growth, 2005–2025

City	Meters above Sea Level	Population	
		2005	2025
Bangkok, Thailand	2	6,582	8,322
Surabaya, Indonesia	5	2,754	3,962
Jakarta, Indonesia	8	8,543	12,363
Manila, Philippines	16	10,761	14,808
Ho Chi Minh, Vietnam	19	5,072	8,149
Hanoi, Vietnam	6	4,170	6,754
Kuala Lumpur, Malaysia	22	1,405	1,938
Singapore	16	4,327	5,104
Johore Baru, Malaysia	37	797	1,382

Source: United Nations, *World Urbanization Prospects*, 2008.

These megacities have become important foci of rural–urban migrants, circular migrants, and commuters inside the countries in which they are located, and increasingly are attracting significant numbers of international migrants, both low- and high-skilled. As a result, these megacities are becoming ethnically diverse and also have strong concentrations of youth populations.[42] One of the issues that will confront these cities over the coming decades is the fact that, as Table 9 shows, several of the megacities are located in low-lying coastal areas, which makes them vulnerable to the impact of climate-change-induced sea-level rise.[43] This brings into question the future nature of settlement systems in countries like Indonesia, Vietnam, the Philippines, and Thailand.

While rural–urban migration is of particular significance because of its relationship with development, in most countries, migration between rural areas occurs on a higher level. Table 10 shows, for example, that in Vietnam, rural-to-urban migrants made up 27 percent of all internal migrants between 1994 and 1999, while rural-to-rural migrants made up 36 percent. However, much of the rural-to-rural mobility is over short distances and is associated with marriage.

There has been some longer distance rural-to-rural redistribution from more densely settled rural areas to those more lightly settled. However, the frontiers of

---

[41] Ibid., p. 129.

[42] Graeme J. Hugo, "Asian Youth in the Context of Rapid Globalization," in *World Youth Report 2007* (New York, NY: Department of Economic and Social Affairs, United Nations, 2007), pp. 1–45.

[43] Graeme J. Hugo, Douglas Bardsley, Yan Tan, et al., *Climate Change and Migration in the Asia-Pacific Region*, Summary Report to Asian Development Bank, 2009.

agricultural settlement have now largely been extended to include all of the arable lands in the region, and the potential for opening up new agricultural areas in the region is limited.

Table 10
Vietnam: Types of Internal Migration Streams, 1994–1999

Type of Migration	No. of Migrants	Percent
Rural to Rural	1,609,029	36
Rural to Urban	1,182,291	27
Urban to Rural	421,948	9
Urban to Urban	1,137,740	26
Total	4,351,008	100

Source: 1999 Census of Population and Housing, Vietnam

Southeast Asia has seen some of the world's most ambitious attempts to resettle rural populations from densely settled areas to agricultural "colonies" located in less densely settled parts of the country. Indonesia, Vietnam, Thailand, Philippines, and Malaysia have all had government-sponsored resettlement programs, and they remain active in most of these countries, albeit at a lesser scale.[44] The large countries in the region are characterized by substantial interregional differences in population density, although those often reflect similarly large differences in resource endowments. Nevertheless, there does remain some limited potential in some parts of Southeast Asia for agricultural settlement expansion, although it is unlikely to be at the levels that have prevailed in earlier years. Government-sponsored settlement programs, such as the Transmigration Program in Indonesia, have been criticized for their high cost and environmental and social impact in destination areas, but they have resulted in some redistribution of population. In Vietnam, the government has initiated an ambitious program to redistribute people from north to south and to decongest southern cities.[45]

Figure 7 shows the number of families moved under Indonesia's Transmigration Program, which has existed for more than a century and has aimed to resettle agriculturalists from densely settled Java-Bali (842 persons per km in 2000) to the less densely settled outer Indonesian islands, mainly Sumatra, Kalimantan, Sulawesi, and Papua. Over the period 1900–2000, the population of Indonesia living in Java fell from 72 percent to 59 percent. On the face of it this would appear to be a resounding affirmation of the transmigration policy, but it is predominantly due to higher levels of fertility in the Outer Islands and spontaneous migration from Java to the Outer Islands, which is substantially greater than that under official auspices.

---

[44] Thomas R. Leinbach, "The Transmigration Program in Indonesia National Development Strategy: Current Status and Future Requirements," *Habitat International* 13,3 (1989): 81–95.

[45] Jacqueline Desbarats, "Population Redistribution in the Socialist Republic of Vietnam," *Population and Development Review* 13,1 (1987): 43–76.

Figure 7
Number of Families Moved under Indonesia's
Transmigration Program, 1969–2007

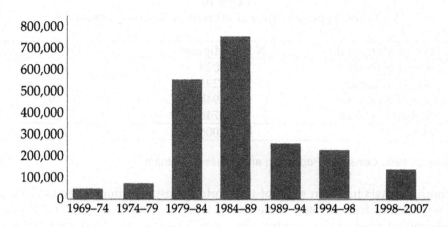

Table 11 shows the migration between Java and the rest of Indonesia over the last three decades. These data indicate that out-migration from Java increased rapidly between 1971 and 1980 and 1990, but more slowly in the last decade; that in-migration to Java increased slowly in the 1970s, but increased in the 1980s and slowed down in the 1990s; and that net migration to the Outer Islands increased rapidly in the 1970s, but more slowly in the 1980s and 1990s. Clearly, Java's significance has grown. Java serves not only as an origin of out-migrants to the Outer Islands, but also as a destination for in-migrants from those islands. The pattern indicates the increased significance of large urban areas, especially Jakarta, in attracting migrants from all over the country.

Table 11
Migration into and out of Java: 1971, 1980, 1990, and 2000

Java	1971	1980	1990	2000	Percentage Change		
					1971–80	1980–90	1990–00
Total Out-migrants	2,062,206	3,572,560	5,149,470	5,380,889	+73	+44.1	+4.5
Total In-migrants	1,067,777	1,225,560	2,434,719	2,231,745	+15	+98.7	-8.3
Net Migration	-994,429	-2,347,000	-2,714,751	-3,149,144	+136	+15.7	+16.0

Source: 1971, 1980, 1990, and 2000 Indonesia census. Based upon the most recent migration data using census question on province of previous residence.

The pattern of interprovincial migration in Indonesia shown by the 2000 census is depicted in Figure 8. A number of patterns are striking. The first is the high degree of reciprocating flows, indicating an important return migration to Indonesia.[46] The crucial significance of Jakarta and West Java as the main destinations of interprovincial migrants in Indonesia, accounting for 33.6 percent of all such in-migrants, reflects the movement to the megacity of Jakarta, which has long overspilled its boundaries into the province of West Java.

Figure 8
Indonesia: Major Interprovincial Migration according to
Province-of-Birth from the 2000 Census

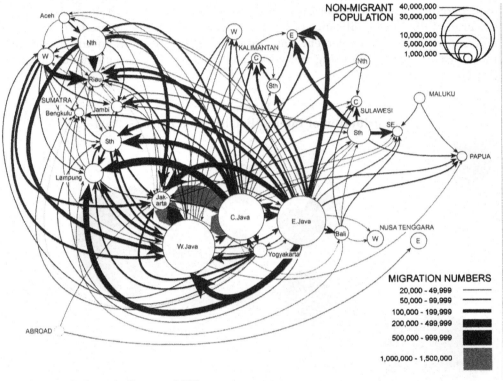

Source: Indonesia Census, 2000

Conflict has been an important cause of population movement within Southeast Asian countries as well as between countries. In Indonesia, for example, this was the case in the early years of independence.[47] More recently, the Tsunami of December 2004 created 500,000 internally displaced persons (IDPs).[48] The ethnic- and economic-

---

[46] Graeme J. Hugo, "Population Mobility in West Java, Indonesia" (PhD thesis, Department of Demography, Australian National University, Canberra, 1975).

[47] Graeme J. Hugo, "Forgotten Refugees: Postwar Forced Migrations within Southeast Asian Countries," in *Refugees: A Third World Dilemma*, ed. John R. Rogge (Totowa, NJ: Rowman and Littlefield, 1987), pp. 282–95.

[48] Mathias Czaika and Krisztina Kis-Katos, "Civil Conflict and Displacement: Village-Level Determinants of Forced Migration in Aceh," *Journal of Peace Research* 46,3 (2009), 399–418; C. Robinson, "Tsunami Displacement and Return in Aceh Province," in *One Year after the Tsunami: Policy and Public Perceptions* (Asia Program Special Report 130), ed. Michael Kugelman (Washington, DC: Woodrow Wilson International Center for Scholars, 2006), pp 18–

based civil conflicts in eastern Indonesia in the late 1990s, however, created well over a million internally displaced persons and Figure 9 shows where they were located around 2000. Almost half of these displaced persons were in camps and the rest, living with relatives or in other private accommodation. Much of the displacement was from areas that in early independence years were areas of in-migration of different ethnoreligious groups either through spontaneous migration or through the Transmigration Program. While these conflicts have been put down as religious or cultural clashes, in fact they are much more complex and associated with stark differences in empowerment, access to services, and wealth. From a migration perspective it is interesting that many of the IDPs returned to the origin areas that their parents, grandparents or even earlier descendents left generations ago. Hugo[49] has argued that the significance of forced migration in Indonesia has been neglected and shows that this movement has been crucially important in urbanization in Indonesia and in establishing networks along which later spontaneous migrants flowed.

Figure 9
Distribution of Internally Displaced Persons, 2000

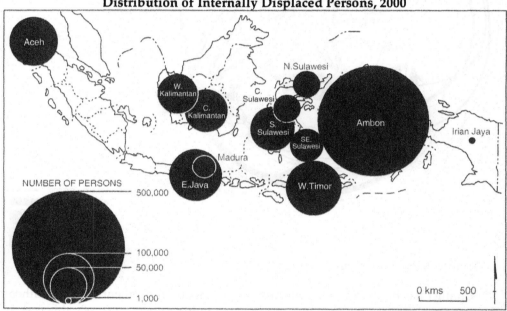

Source: Graeme J. Hugo, "Pengungsi—Indonesia's Internally Displaced Persons," *Asian and Pacific Migration Journal* 11,3 (2002): 297–331.

22; Abdur Rofi, Shannon Doocy, and Courtland Robinson, "Tsunami Mortality and Displacement in Aceh Province, Indonesia," *Disasters* 30,3 (2006): 340–50.

[49] Graeme J. Hugo, "Forced Migration in Indonesia: Historical Perspectives" (paper prepared for International Conference titled Toward New Perspectives on Forced Migration in Southeast Asia, organized by Research Centre for Society and Culture [PMP] at the Indonesian Institute of Sciences [LIPI] and Refugee Studies Centre [RSC] at the University of Oxford, Jakarta, November 25–26, 2004).

MAJOR ISSUES IN POPULATION MOBILITY IN SOUTHEAST ASIA

Migration issues have until recently attracted little attention from Asian policy makers, researchers, and commentators. This has changed not only because of the increased scale of the phenomenon but also because of

- the heightened interest in security following 9/11 and the Bali bombing, and the close relationship between migration and terrorism[50]; and
- the new global discourse on migration and development, which has seen a shift from a focus on brain drain and the negative effects of migration on low-income countries to the potential benefits of emigration for those nations.[51]

In the next section I consider some of the major contemporary and emerging issues relating to migration in the Southeast Asian region.

Opposition to Permanent Settlement of Immigrants

Until recently, all Southeast Asian countries have embraced a model of international migration that opposed permanent settlement of foreigners.[52] The major elements in this model have been as follows:

- Immigration needs to be highly restricted. It is not generally perceived as beneficial for the nation-state. Even in nations where there are good reasons for migration, such as the demand for labor or the arrival of asylum seekers fleeing persecution, immigration is not allowed.
- Emphasis has been on constraint, policing, and exclusion rather than migration management. There is little tradition of the development of a managed migration system.
- Where the need for migrant workers, tourists, and businesspeople has been recognized as essential to the economy, allowances have been strictly on a temporary basis.
- Foreigners should not be allowed to become citizens except in exceptional circumstances.
- The national culture and identity should not be modified in response to external influences.[53]

There are some indications that attitudes toward migration are beginning to change, although the exclusionary ethos remains dominant. Some of these changes are demonstrated by the examples of Singapore, Malaysia, and Thailand.

---

[50] Graeme J. Hugo, "Australian Immigration Policy: The Significance of the Events of September 11," *International Migration Review* 36,1 (2002): 37–40.

[51] United Nations, *International Migration and Development* (Report of the Secretary-General, 60th Session, Globalization and Interdependence: International Migration and Development, United Nations, May 18, 2006).

[52] Stephen Castles, "Migrant Settlement, Transnational Communities and State Region," in *Migration in the Asia Pacific: Population, Settlement, and Citizenship Issues*, ed. Robyn Iredale, Charles Hawksley, and Stephen Castles (Cheltenham: Edward Elgar, 2003), pp. 3–26.

[53] Ibid.

Singapore has a well-developed policy to attract immigrant settlers. However, this is a highly selective policy reserved for skilled migrants. Although Singapore each year admits more than one hundred thousand unskilled workers on a temporary basis, they are not given access to permanent settlement. Nevertheless, a substantial shift and maturing in Singapore migration policy has occurred. Until the 1990s, it saw migration as a "revolving reserve army of labor."[54] While the present policy on settlement is very selective of skilled persons, the attitude toward migrant settlement has relaxed and migration is now seen as a long-term structural component of the nation's economy.

In Malaysia and Thailand, there is the recognition that sectors of their local economies are not going to be able to be supplied with labor from sources within the country and will rely on foreign labor for the foreseeable future.[55] Moreover, despite the fact that there is official opposition to the permanent settlement of immigrants, it is apparent that many Indonesians and Filipinos in Malaysia, and Burmese, Laotians, and Cambodians in Thailand, have been able to settle permanently.

Hence while Stephen Castles, was able a decade ago to state that nothing short of a "conceptual leap" was necessary for Asian destination countries to accept the need for permanent settlement of migrants,[56] there is mounting evidence that, while that leap has not yet been made, some, albeit tentative, short steps have been made in that direction.

Temporary versus Permanent Migration

A crucial question relating to the burgeoning international labor migration occurring in Asia is, to what extent will migration remain temporary? At present the bulk of OCWs return to their homeland. However, the policy makers in destination nations are conscious of the experience with guest workers in Europe in the 1950s and 1960s, whereby temporary labor migration became permanent settlement.[57] There are signs that some Asian labor migrants are settling more or less permanently at their destinations (for example, the Indonesians in Malaysia[58]). However, most of the labor migration is emphatically circular, and nonpermanent migration is built into the structure of economies and societies at both origin and destination. Indeed, it may be that attempts by governments to impose border restrictions may force undocumented migrant workers who would prefer to circulate to settle at the

---

[54] Pang E. Fong and Paul P. L. Cheung, "Regional Labour Flows and Singapore" (paper presented to IUSSP Committee on International Migration, Seminar on International Migration Systems, Processes and Policies, Genting Highlands, Malaysia, September 19–23, 1988); E. F. Pang and L. Lim, "Foreign Labor and Economic Development in Singapore," *International Migration Review* 12 (Fall 1982): pp. 548–76; and Graeme J. Hugo and Anchalee Singhanetra-Renard, "International Migration of Contract Labour in Asia: Major Issues and Implications," in proceedings of International Development Research Centre (IDRC) workshop, Chiangmai University, November 16–20, 1987 (Ottawa: IDRC, May 1991).

[55] Rosalia Sciortino and Sureeporn Punpuing, *International Migration in Thailand 2009* (Bangkok: International Organization for Migration, Thailand Office, 2009).

[56] Stephen Castles, "Migrant Settlement, Transnational Communities and State Region," pp. 3–26.

[57] Stephen Castles, Heather Booth, and Tina P. Wallace, *Here for Good: West Europe's Ethnic Minorities* (London: Pluto Press, 1984).

[58] Graeme J. Hugo, "Labour Export from Indonesia: An Overview," *ASEAN Economic Bulletin* 12,2 (1995): pp. 275–98.

destination because of the danger of being detected during multiple border crossings.

Internationally, the overwhelming body of academic opinion has been opposed to temporary labor migration since it is associated with exploitation of migrant workers and the activities of criminal syndicates. However, an increasing number of commentators is suggesting that it is more the way temporary labor migration has been managed in the past that has been the problem, not circular migration per se.[59] Indeed, there is a longstanding body of evidence indicating that circular migration can be beneficial to migrants and their origin areas and that it is often the preferred strategy of migrants rather than always being a precursor to permanent settlement.[60] The appropriate debate, then, is not so much permanent versus temporary migration, but what is the appropriate mix of migration types to best meet the needs of origin *and* destination countries. Moreover, the question of how best to manage nonpermanent migrations in order that the interests of origin, destination, and migrant workers are protected is one of increasing interest and significance.[61]

How Can the Inflow of Remittances Be Maximized and the Beneficial Effects on Recipients' Low-Income Countries Be Enhanced?

As shown earlier, there is a diaspora of permanent settlers of Southeast Asian origin, most of them living in OECD nations, and Southeast Asia is also the preeminent source of the world's contract labor migrants. Both of these groups are an important source of remittances. However, the measurement of remittances is problematical and this difficulty is exacerbated by the illegality of much movement, the isolation of the home areas, and the long history of remitting money through nonformal, traditional channels. In the past, there has been a tendency to dismiss the developmental impacts of remittances as being peripheral or negative in their impact on Southeast Asian economies. Rigoberto Tiglao, for example, argues in the Philippines case that remittances have insulated the backward agriculture sector from modernization and diverted attention away from the need to attract foreign investment in manufacturing.[62] There is considerable concern[63] that labor migration, in conjunction with remittances, can lead to so-called Dutch disease:

> ... the appreciation of the real exchange rate. The Dutch disease creates a condition of greater vulnerability to external shocks by stimulating imports

---

[59] Global Commission on International Migration (GCIM), "Migration in an Interconnected World: New Directors for Action," Report of the GCIM (Geneva, Switzerland, 2005).

[60] Graeme J. Hugo, "Circular Migration in Indonesia," *Population and Development Review* 8,1 (1982): 59–84; G. J. Hugo, "New Issues Relating to Circular International Migration: Some Observations From Indonesia and Australia" (paper for Migration Policy Institute's Meeting on Migration and Development, San Diego, CA, April 11–12, 2003).

[61] Agunias and Newland, "Circular Migration and Development: Trends, Policy Routes, and Ways Forward."

[62] Rigoberto Tiglao, "The Global View," *Far Eastern Economic Review* (June 19, 1997): 40.

[63] Prema-chandra Athukorala, "International Labor Migration in the Asia-Pacific Region: Patterns, Policies, and Economic Implications," *Asian-Pacific Economic Literature* 7 (1993): 28–57.

and reducing the incentives to develop exports. The Dutch disease also leads to an over-emphasis on capital-intensive methods of production.[64]

However, intensive work by the World Bank is demonstrating that remittances can and do have positive effects on low-income origin communities and states.[65] As awareness of the potential for remittances to enhance development is growing, Southeast Asian origin nation-states are increasingly concerned with maximizing and capturing the inflow of remittances. In terms of maximizing remittances, the World Bank has demonstrated that there is often excessive rent taking by intermediaries and that the flow of remittances can be enhanced by providing safe, cheap mechanisms for remitting funding—having the subsidiary benefit of introducing poor families to the formal financial system.[66] A second set of issues relates to how the remittance inflows can be "captured" to have the maximum developmental impact in origin countries. Great care needs to be exercised here because attempts by Asian governments to tax remittances has resulted in driving them underground. One of the real benefits of remittances is that they—unlike other foreign financial transfers—deliver capital directly into the hands of individuals, families, and communities, and this income must not be disrupted. As Dilip Ratha states, "Migrant remittances are the most tangible and perhaps the most controversial link between migration and development. They can play an effective role in reducing poverty and they provide a convenient angle for approaching the complex migration agenda."[67]

Protection of Migrants, Especially Migrant Workers

Undoubtedly, one of the areas of most concern relating to international labor migration in Southeast Asia relates to the abuse and exploitation of many migrant workers, and improving their protection must be a priority.[68] Origin and destination countries of OCWs vary greatly in the level of their commitment to protecting the rights and well-being of migrant workers. However, there is a need to progress on a number of fronts to guarantee the rights of international labor migrants. OCWs are frequently marginalized in destination countries in a number of ways:

---

[64] M. G. Quibria, "Migration, Remittances, and Trade: With Special Reference to Asian Developing Economies," in *International Trade and Migration in the APEC Region*, ed. Peter J. Lloyd and Lynne S. Williams (Melbourne: Oxford University Press, 1996), p. 97.

[65] World Bank, *Global Economic Prospects 2006: Economic Implications of Remittances and Migration* (Washington, DC: World Bank, 2006); and Donald F. Terry and Steven R. Wilson, eds., *Beyond Small Change: Making Migrant Remittances Count* (Washington, DC: Inter-American Development Bank, 2005).

[66] Terry and Wilson, eds., *Beyond Small Change*.

[67] Dilip Ratha, *Leveraging Remittances for Development* (Washington, DC: Migration Policy Institute, 2007), p. 1.

[68] Nicola Piper, "Rights of Foreign Domestic Workers—Emergence of Transnational and Transregional Solidarity?" *Asian and Pacific Migration Journal* 14 (2005): 1–2; N. Piper and A. Uhlin, "Transnational Advocacy Networks, Female Labor Migration, and Trafficking in East and Southeast Asia: A Gendered Analysis of Opportunities and Obstacles," *Asian and Pacific Migration Journal* 11,2 (2002).

- ethnolinguistic differences,
- noncitizenship that restricts their access to services,
- involvement in vulnerable occupations, like domestic work and the entertainment industry,
- involvement in low-status, low-income occupations, and
- undocumented status.

Destination countries often fail to recognize and protect the rights of OCWs, although there is also a limited commitment of origin nations to providing protection to their nationals working overseas. There is a need to recognize in destination countries that protection of migrant workers is not only important from a human rights perspective, but will result in reduced involvement of organized crime and have beneficial economic outcomes.

The problem of the exploitation of migrants is usually conceptualized as a function of a failure of destination countries to recognize migrants' rights. While this is an important issue, exploitation also results from a lack of awareness on behalf of migrant workers themselves regarding the rights that they do have. Moreover, many do not have strategies and mechanisms available to them to protect themselves at the destination. Research has been clear that migrants adapt and integrate best in situations in which they have strong social networks to assist and support them. It is crucial that migrant workers be linked into such networks where they do not already have such linkages. This involves better preparation for migrant workers before they leave their home country, more and better information about what they can expect upon arrival, and mechanisms for dealing with crises at the destination. Some countries, such as the Philippines, have been quite effective in empowering their overseas workers through appropriate departure training and information provision and also by connecting them with appropriate networks at the destination. Technology, such as mobile phones, can greatly assist this process.

A specific area of concern has been human trafficking, since Southeast Asia figures prominently in the worldwide concern with regard to trafficking. The Sixth East Asia and Pacific Ministerial Conference reported in 2003 that one-third of all trafficking of women and children occurs in Southeast Asia, with 230,000 victims.[69] The United Nations produced the *United Nations Protocol to Prevent, Suppress, and Punish Trafficking in Persons, Especially Women and Children*, which was accepted by the UN General Assembly in November 2000. It defines trafficking in persons:

The recruitment, transportation, transfer, harboring, or receipt of persons by means of threat or use of force or other forms of coercion, of abduction, of fraud, of deception, of the abuse of power or a position of vulnerability, or of the giving or receiving of payments or benefits to achieve the consent of a person having control over another person for the purpose of exploitation. Exploitation shall include, at a minimum, the exploitation or the prostitution of others or other forms of sexual exploitation, forced labor or services, slavery or practices similar to slavery, servitude or the removal of organs.[70]

---

[69] *Asian Migration News*, May 1–15, 2003.

[70] United Nations, *Protocol to Prevent, Suppress, and Punish Trafficking in Persons, Especially Women and Children* (Supplement to the UN Convention against Transnational Organised Crime, Annex II, United Nations Document A/55/383, 2000).

Forced and voluntary migration are a continuum rather than a dichotomy in Asian labor migration. Nevertheless, the trafficking end of that continuum is one that represents a clear abuse of human rights and must be the target of effective policy intervention.

There are no simple solutions to undocumented migration, people smuggling, and trafficking. This is partly because there are mobility strategies embedded in the cultures of some societies that precede the drawing of international boundaries. Moreover, while transnational criminal syndicates are involved, so also are a myriad of small-scale local organizations. Hence, it is not very amenable to policy and program interventions. The full cooperation of all nations involved is absolutely crucial for any intervention to succeed. The whole of the chain of linkages involved in each move needs to be targeted—to affect only part of a trafficking operation means it will continue to operate. People will continue to attempt to move illegally while they feel they have no chance of migration through the legal system. Other people will assist them in this while there is a chance to gain financially from it. However, many of the facilitators are not international criminals but local fishermen and others who are very poor and see involvement in the immigration industry as one of the few options available to them for earning a living. Policies that provide people who otherwise have limited livelihood options with alternative ways of earning a living can potentially deprive the criminal element in the illegal migration system of the means to facilitate the migration. At present, poor people who aid in human trafficking are not very exposed to risk of detection since the bulk of these hands-on operations are very small. Efforts to combat all trafficking movements will need to go beyond improved policing and address the causes of the movement and of the involvement of various groups supporting it. Policies and programs need to be comprehensive and consistent across all nations and groups involved. More information needs to be collected about the operation of undocumented migration in the region to better inform policy making and planning. Full international cooperation will be essential. The legal international migration system must be made to work better so that potential illegal migrants feel they have a fair chance of immigrating through the legal system. Finally, the situation is also complicated by the fact that trafficking is not simply synonymous with undocumented migration, since some trafficking involves documented movement. Moreover, while trafficking across international boundaries attracts a great deal of attention, it is also an issue within national boundaries.

Gender Issues

Migration in Southeast Asia is definitely a gendered process,[71] and it is important to study the movement of women separately from those of men for a number of reasons:
- Patterns differ from those of men,
- The causes and consequences of movement can differ from those of men, and
- The policy implications of movement can differ from those of men.

---

[71] Nicola Piper, "Bridging Gender, Migration, and Governance: Theoretical Possibilities in the Asian Context," *Asian and Pacific Migration Journal* 12 (2003): 1–2.

A key issue relates to protection, since women migrants are often more vulnerable to exploitation than are their male counterparts. This issue arises not only from gender considerations but also because women are disproportionately represented in vulnerable occupations like domestic work,[72] the entertainment industry, and the sex industry.[73] However, from a development perspective, too, there are concerns, since there may be gendered differences in the migration and development relationship not only from the perspective of women migrants but also women left behind by fathers and husbands in origin communities. There are also aspects of migration that especially pertain to men, such as the long separations from families that must be endured in most circular labor migration, the poor living conditions men are often exposed to (such as living on building sites), and unsafe working conditions.

Issues Concerning Brain Drain

A brain drain involving a net loss of skilled persons from less-developed nations in Southeast Asia and a net gain in the more-developed countries of the OECD was documented as long ago as the 1960s.[74] More recent analyses have confirmed that emigration rates in Southeast Asia are higher for skilled groups and that some Southeast Asian countries are experiencing a significant brain drain.[75] Moreover, in recent times, OECD nations have placed greater emphasis on skill in their selection of immigrants,[76] and this, combined with the increasing global competition for talented and skilled workers,[77] has exacerbated the brain drain trend. A comprehensive analysis calculated emigration rates of highly qualified persons (with a university education) for non-OECD nations.[78] The rates are low for large nations such as Indonesia (1.9 percent) and Thailand (1.9 percent) and much higher for small nations. William Carrington and Enrica Detragiache conclude, "These numbers suggest that in several countries the outflow of highly skilled individuals ... is a phenomenon that cannot be ignored by policy makers."[79]

In the early literature, brain drain was seen as having an unequivocally negative impact on development in the origin nations since it deprived them of scarce human resources required for achieving economic and social progress. Even a loss of small

---

[72] Shirlena Huang, Brenda S. A. Yeoh, and Nora A. Rahman, eds., *Asian Women as Transnational Domestic Workers* (Singapore: Marshall Cavendish, 2005).

[73] Lin L. Lim, ed., *The Sex Sector: The Economic and Social Bases of Prostitution in Southeast Asia* (Geneva: International Labour Office, 1998).

[74] Walter Adams, *The Brain Drain* (New York, NY: Macmillan, 1968).

[75] For example, William Carrington and Enrica Detragiache, "How Big Is the Brain Drain?" (IMF Working Paper WP/98/102, Washington, DC, 1998); and Jean-Christophe Dumont and Georges Lemaitre, "Counting Immigrants and Expatriates in OECD Countries: A New Perspective" (paper presented at the Conference on Competing for Global Talent, Singapore Management University, Singapore, January 13–14, 2005).

[76] Graeme J. Hugo, "Migration in the Asia-Pacific Region" (paper prepared for the Policy Analysis and Research Programme of the Global Commission on International Migration, 2005).

[77] Manolo I. Abella, "Global Competition for Skilled Workers and Their Consequences" (paper presented at Conference on Competing for Global Talent, Singapore Management University, Singapore, January 13-14, 2005).

[78] Dumont and Lemaitre, "Counting Immigrants and Expatriates in OECD Countries."

[79] William Carrington and Enrica Detragiache, "How Big Is the Brain Drain?," p. 24.

numbers could therefore be significant. While it is recognized that such effects are still strongly in evidence, there is increasing evidence that the brain drain's effects on development are not necessarily only negative. This partly derives from evidence that, in some contexts, the economies and labor markets in some less-developed countries cannot effectively absorb all of their own skilled people and underemployed skilled workers can make a greater contribution to development by emigrating and remitting earnings to the home country. Hence, an interesting econometric analysis based on Philippines data considered that, in that country at least, training physicians for export would appear to return a net benefit to the nation.[80]

Positive effects on development in origin countries notwithstanding, the issues relating to the loss of human capital remain significant. This is especially the case with respect to the migration of doctors, nurses, and other health professionals.[81] As demand for highly educated workers increases in more developed countries, where fertility rates remain low or continue to fall, the pressures on well-qualified people in low-income countries to move to high-income countries will also increase, thereby contributing to the global talent war.[82]

How Should the Diaspora Be Engaged?

In recent years, some of the world's major development organizations, such as the World Bank,[83] Asian Development Bank,[84] International Labour Organization,[85] USAID,[86] DIFD,[87] and the IOM[88] argued that diasporas can play a role in development, growth, and poverty reduction in low-income origin areas. The increasing emphasis on diasporas in development is especially important in Southeast Asia, since several nations in the region have substantial diasporas. The countries vary in the extent to which they engage with their respective diasporas, with the Philippines being the most active. Diasporas can be mobilized to

---

[80] Robert Goldfarb, Oleh Havrylyshyn, and Stephen Mangum, "Can Remittances Compensate for Manpower Outflows," *Journal of Development Economics* 15 (1984): pp. 1–17.

[81] James Buchan, "Responding to the Health Workforce Crisis, *Id21 Insights* 7 (August 2005): 1–2.

[82] Christine Kuptsch and Pang Eng Fong, eds., *Competing for Global Talent* (Geneva: International Labour Organization and International Institute for Labour Studies, 2006).

[83] D. Ellerman, Policy Research on Migration and Development, 2003, http://econ. worldbank.org/external/default/main?pagePK=64165259&theSitePK=469382&piPK=6416542 1&menuPK=64166093&entityID=000094946_0309160409263, accessed February 17, 2012; Lucas, "The Economic Well-Being of Movers and Stayers."

[84] Asian Development Bank, "Developing the Diaspora" (paper presented at Third Coordination Meeting on International Migration, Population Division, Department of Economic and Social Affairs, United Nations Secretariat, New York, NY, October 27–28, 2004).

[85] Philip Martin, "Migration and Development: Toward Sustainable Solutions" (International Institute for Labour Studies Discussion Paper DP153/2004, Geneva, 2004).

[86] Brett Johnson and Santiago Sedaca, *Diasporas, Emigrés and Development, Economic Linkages and Programmatic Responses* (a Special Study of the US Agency for International Development, Carana Corporation, March 2004).

[87] House of Commons, United Kingdom, *Migration and Development: How to Make Migration Work for Poverty Reduction* (London: The Stationery Office, 2004).

[88] Dina Ionescu, *Engaging Diasporas as Development Partners for Home and Destination Countries: Challenges for Policy Makers* (Geneva: International Organization for Migration, 2007).

- send remittances,
- encourage foreign direct investment,
- act as a bridgehead for export of goods from the home country, and
- act as conduits of knowledge transfer.

Moreover, if emigrants return they bring with them not just their human capital but the experience and network of contacts they have acquired. Hence, there are a number of ways in which the diaspora is having a positive impact on economic development in Southeast Asian countries. An important issue is the extent to which government policy can assist in encouraging such development. There are specific policies and programs that can be utilized to encourage diasporas to link with development-related activities in the home nations. However, part of a diaspora policy has to involve some means to maintain the identification of the diaspora with the home community.

How Should Undocumented Migration Be Tackled?

Graziano Battistella and Maruja Asis estimate that in Southeast Asia there are around 2 million irregular migrants (those without the necessary authorization or documents required under immigration regulations).[89] Undocumented and documented systems are not totally separate, although they are often portrayed as such. Usually, undocumented flows duplicate documented flows, some middlemen and officials are involved in both types of movement, and the networks established by documented migrants are often subsequently utilized by undocumented migrants.

Undocumented labor migration in Asia can be differentiated along a wide spectrum, ranging from totally voluntary movement, in which the mover controls her or his own migration process, through to, at the other extreme, kidnapping and trafficking. While there is a great deal of concern in the region about trafficking of workers, there is an array of other undocumented migration types, and a more meaningful differentiation of undocumented labor migration is depicted in Figure 10.

Figure 10
A Continuum of Undocumented International Labor Migration in Asia

Individually Controlled Movement	Movement under the Auspices of Middlemen	Misleading Promises	Bonded Labor	Kidnapping

Voluntary Movement ────────────────────────► Trafficking

This shows a continuum of types of undocumented movement. At one extreme are labor migrants, who control each aspect of their own movement. The workers arrange all of their own travel and move along familiar, well-established routes.

---

[89] Graziano Battistella and Maruja B. Asis, eds., *Unauthorized Migration in Southeast Asia* (Quezon City: Scalabrini Migration Center, 2003), p. 5.

However, in many undocumented moves, agents ("middlemen") of various types are involved, and their control over the migrant workers varies considerably. In some situations, the chain of middlemen involved reaches back to the home village and they have strong accountability to the home community. In others, the agents are all-powerful in controlling the information that potential workers receive about the migration process and destination and in determining when they move, how much it costs, where they go, and what job they obtain. These movements degrade into trafficking when workers are forced to move and enter indentured situations in destinations. In some cases, potential migrant workers are purposely misled about the type of work at the destination, the conditions, remuneration, and so forth, and are "trapped" at the destination. In other cases, workers (often women and children) are sold into bonded situations often by relatives, while at the extreme, people are kidnapped and trafficked across borders against their will. In all cases, their unauthorized status exposes them to the possibility of exploitation and prevents them from seeking the protection of authorities at the destination. This can add to the marginalization experienced by many migrant groups.

Where countries have attempted to legalize migrations of workers, illegal operators have become so entrenched that it is difficult to persuade undocumented workers to replace their illegal strategies with legal ones. Indeed, in some countries the undocumented approaches have come to be trusted, while governments are not trusted and government avenues for migration are more expensive and more time consuming. There is a tendency to associate all undocumented migration with the insidious practice of trafficking. This is doubly unfortunate because (a) in fact, much undocumented migration is not criminal, as was indicated above, and (b) the bulk of policy and research effort is put into trafficking when there are also highly exploitative corrupt and venal practices that occur in legal migration and need to be the target of policy.

There are clearly no simple solutions to the indisputable significance of undocumented migration and its most insidious subcomponent, trafficking. What does seem clear in Southeast Asia is that so long as no safe, fair, documented avenues for migration exist, where there is a manifest demand for migrant labor, undocumented migration will continue to occur. Policing alone is not the solution. There is also recognition that these issues can rarely be effectively tackled unilaterally. The process occurs across countries and cooperation between counterorigins, destinations, and transit countries will be necessary.

Forced Migration Issues

While most attention here is focused on international refugee flows and there is an international regime through the UNHCR (United Nations High Commission for Refugees) to protect and assist mandated refugees, forced migration in the region also includes much larger displacements of people *within* countries.[90] Although the UNHCR does become involved in such migrations and there are national and bilateral assistance programs for internally displaced persons, IDPs outnumber mandated refugees and are especially vulnerable. The support of displaced persons

---

[90] Eva-Lotta L. E. Hedman, "Forced Migration in Southeast Asia: International Politics and the Reordering of State Power," *Asian and Pacific Migration Journal* 15,1 (2006).

and associated issues of repatriation and/or resettlement are of considerable development concern in countries like Indonesia.

Migration and Health

There is considerable discussion within Southeast Asia about the interrelationships between migration (both internal and international) and health, although the nature of the linkages between them remain little understood.[91] In recent years there has been a particular interest in the connection between mobility and the spread of HIV/AIDS.[92] In some countries, a higher incidence of HIV infection has been identified among mobile groups than in the population that hasn't moved. However, it is crucial that there be a recognition that it is not mobility per se that is a cause of higher rates of infection. It is rather that mobility is associated with many risk factors. Mobility is concentrated among the high-risk populations, such as young adults; mobility places migrants at greater risk than nonmigrants of engaging in high-risk behavior; mobility concentrates people in high-risk occupations, for example, sex work; and mobility has a nexus with the commercial sex industry.[93]

There is a real danger that migrants will be scapegoated as a cause of the spread of the HIV infection and that they become stigmatized and demonized by host societies. Moreover, they can distract the attention of a society from the significance of the disease in the overall population by allowing officials to depict HIV/AIDS as a disease of marginal groups and therefore not of concern to the mainstream population.

Other issues of health and population relate to the greater vulnerability of many migrant groups to health problems. This may result from the living conditions that they often are forced to experience, but can be associated with the difference between the environment and the destination, which exposes them to diseases that may not occur in the origin country.

Should Governments Seek to Influence Internal Migration?

There have been several attempts by Southeast Asian governments to influence their population distributions and the internal migration patterns that shape them. The question of whether such policies are desirable continues to be debated as well. Large-scale land-settlement programs like the Indonesian Transmigration Program are largely a thing of the past in the region and the potential to bring more land into sustainable agricultural production is very limited. Greater concern is being expressed about the rapid rate of urbanization and the high levels of migration of

---

[91] See Mark J. VanLandingham and Hongyun Fu, "Migration and Health in Southeast Asia," chapter 6, in this volume.

[92] Graeme J. Hugo, *Indonesia: Internal and International Population Mobility: Implications for the Spread of HIV/AIDS* (Indonesia: UNDP South East Asia HIV and Development Office, UNAIDS and ILO, 2001); and S. Chantavanich, A. Beesey, and S. Paul, *Mobility and HIV/AIDS in the Greater Mekong Subregion* (Bangkok: Asian Research Center for Migration, 2000). Also see (1) *Mae Saai and Mea Sot*, (2) *Sangkhlaburi and Ranong*, and (3) *Aranyaprathet and Khlong Ya* in Supang Chantavanich, Amornthip Amaraphibal, Aungkana Kamolpech, et al., *Cross-Border Migration and HIV/AIDS: Vulnerability at the Thai-Cambodia Border* (Bangkok: Asian Research Center for Migration [Thai language], March 2000).

[93] Hugo, *Indonesia: Internal and International Population Mobility*.

young people into large cities. There have been attempts to "close" cities or limit migration to them, such as those in Indonesia,[94] but they have not been successful. There has been a shift toward more "accommodationist" policies, which accept that there will continue to be rural–urban migration and initiate policies to provide for growth of cities and the well-being of their inhabitants.

A Negative Attitude toward Migrants

As was indicated earlier, widespread suspicion of migrants persists in Southeast Asian countries, and negative perceptions are often reinforced by governments and media in the region regardless of the lack of evidence available to support the perceptions. As a result of this negative public discourse on migrants, a number of things follow:

1. Those migrants who are allowed to enter a country legally, who are overwhelmingly migrant workers of some kind or another, experience a high degree of *exclusion*. Where there are migrant workers allowed into a country, their rights are considerably restricted. Workers may not be allowed to bring their families; they are limited by the jobs they can hold and are usually restricted to their initial employer; they are not allowed to travel freely; they lack access to basic workers rights; they are subjected to compulsory health tests such as HIV testing; they do not have the capacity to approach agent employers; they cannot marry local people; and they do not have access to citizenship.
2. There is substantial *undocumented migration* in response to the demonstrable need for workers.
3. There is a high degree of *stigmatization* and *stereotyping* of migrants. They are often made scapegoats for a range of ills in the host society. This is facilitated by their "otherness" and often readily observable ethnocultural difference. The stigmatization and stereotyping are exacerbated by media, and national governments are also often at fault, since diverting public anger toward immigrants can deflect criticism from other shortcomings. An example of this is the Indonesian migrant population in Malaysia, which is accused in media of having a high incidence of HIV and, indeed, is blamed for the spread of the disease in the country, as well as being blamed for high rates of crime. This is in spite of the fact that official health and crime data over a long period do not ascribe higher rates to migrants than to natives.[95]

Asian nations, with a few exceptions, have extremely restrictive citizenship policies that make it difficult for immigrants to obtain citizenship, at least legally.[96] In

---

[94] Graeme J. Hugo, "Policies and Programmes Affecting Migration and Urbanization in Indonesia," in *Migration, Urbanization, and Development in Indonesia* (Bangkok: United Nations, Economic and Social Commission for Asia and the Pacific, 1981), p. 147.

[95] Graeme J. Hugo, "Labour Export from Indonesia: An Overview," *ASEAN Economic Bulletin* 12,2 (1995): pp. 275–98.

[96] There is a substantial underground industry in document forgery and, in some countries, significant corruption.

recent years, however, there has been a substantial increase in the numbers of Asian countries recognizing dual citizenship or dual nationality.[97] This has been a function of the growing recognition of the benefits to be derived from maintaining strong linkages with their expatriates. Hence, the Philippine Congress passed the Dual Citizenship law in 2003. The culture of negativity remains an important issue not only in international migration in Asia but also with respect to internal migration where identifiable newcomers are excluded and stigmatized in various ways. There is clearly a need for a greater appreciation of not only the positive effects of migration to balance out the emphasis on negative impacts, but also of the fact that migration is of crucial significance to the prosperity of some sectors in particular countries, cities, and regions.

Migration and the Environment

The relationship between migration and environment is a complex one and is two-way, with environmental change being a factor in initiating migration as well as being a potential consequence of the movement of people.[98] The issue of the environment is becoming of increased interest in Southeast Asia as it is elsewhere. However, development of policies to move toward a sustainable environmental policy in the region needs to consider the implications of, and implications for, the movement of people. As indicated earlier, assessing the potential impact of climate change on future population distribution in Southeast Asian countries is an important priority.[99]

Migration and Poverty Reduction

While most migrants move in order to improve their economic situation, the relationship between population mobility and poverty reduction in Southeast Asia is imperfectly understood. There is a strong view in the region that the poorest groups are the least mobile. This is partly because they do not have the margin to experiment with new locations and new jobs, but also because they often lack information about alternatives and networks at their destinations as well as the formal education and skills to compete effectively there. Hence, mobility is seen by some as exacerbating inequalities. Others, however, point to the poorest people as being forced to move because they can no longer survive in their present location. There is some research that suggests that the influx of remittances in a community can exacerbate inequality, but other work indicates that the second and third rounds of effects of the spending of remittances in origin communities can impact beneficially nonmigrant families.[100] Hence, the poverty-migration relationship in the East Asian region is an issue of considerable significance, but where there is little empirical understanding to guide policy.

---

[97] Steven Vertovec, "Conceiving and Researching Transnationalism," *Ethnic and Racial Studies* 22,2 (March 1999): 445–62.

[98] Graeme J. Hugo, "Labour Export from Indonesia: An Overview," *ASEAN Economic Bulletin* 12, 2 (1995): 275–98; Sara R. Curran and Noah Derman, "Population and Environment in Southeast Asia: Complex Dynamics and Trends," chapter 7, in this volume.

[99] Hugo et al., *Climate Change and Migration in the Asia-Pacific Region*.

[100] J. Edward Taylor, Graeme J. Hugo, Joaquín Arango et al., "International Migration and National Development," *Population Index* 62,2 (1996): 181–212.

The Family and Migration

The social dimensions of migration have been neglected in research on the causes and impacts of internal and international migration in Southeast Asia. The family is changing in Southeast Asia, especially in relation to the changing role of women, moving from extended to nucleated structures. These processes influence, and are influenced by, migration. The family plays an important role in shaping migration, since decisions to migrate are often influenced by, if not dictated by, family considerations.[101] Families often allocate their labor over a wide range of tasks in order to maximize production and minimize risk. Increasingly, this involves deploying different family members in different locations. There is a mix of individual and family considerations in migration decision making.[102]

The role and function of families varies greatly in the region, as does the extent of change that is occurring. But migration has played a role in that change.[103] There has been only limited research on the impact of migration on family structure and functioning. Gonzalez[104] shows how different types of migration differentiated by degrees of permanency have different effects on family structure, and these effects are seen to some extent in Southeast Asia.[105]

There is considerable concern in the region because families are often separated by both internal and international migration when only one family member moves. This has been associated with increased concern for the family members left behind, especially children separated from their mothers.[106] International labor migration often involves the absence of a family member for around two years and can put pressure on the family left behind when there are not extended social structures to support that family.[107] One of the strongest criticisms of circular migration, both internal and international, relate to the family stresses that are created by family members' absences.

Families of migrants at place of origin must adjust, not only to the permanent or temporary absence of family members (a crucial feature of international labor migration), but also to the influences of newly acquired money, goods, ideas,

[101] Douglas S. Massey, Joaquín Arango, Graeme Hugo, Ali Kouaouci, Adela Pellegrino, and J. Edward Taylor, "Theories of International Migration: A Review and Appraisal," *Population and Development Review* 19,3 (1993): 431–66.

[102] Takayoshi Kusago, "Individual Aspiration or Family Survival: Rural-Urban Female Migration in Malaysia," *Asian and Pacific Migration Journal* 7,4 (1998); Graeme J. Hugo, "Labour Export from Indonesia: An Overview," *ASEAN Economic Bulletin* 12,2 (1995): 275–98.

[103] Linda B. Williams, *Development, Demography, and Family Decision-Making: The Status of Women in Rural Java* (Boulder: Westview Press, 2009).

[104] Nancy L. S. Gonzalez, "Family Organization in Five Types of Migratory Wage Labour," *American Anthropologist* 63,6 (1961): 1, 264–80.

[105] Graeme J. Hugo, "Demographic and Welfare Implications of Urbanisation: Direct and Indirect Effects on Sending and Receiving Areas" in *Urbanization and Urban Policies in Pacific Asia*, ed. Roland J. Fuchs, Gavin W. Jones, and Ernesto M. Permia (Boulder, CO: Westview Press, 1987), pp. 147–49.

[106] Graeme J. Hugo and Swarna Ukwatta, "Sri Lankan Female Domestic Workers Overseas— The Impact on Their Children," *Asian and Pacific Migration Journal* 19,2 (2010): 237–64.

[107] Brenda S. A. Yeoh, Elspeth Graham, and Paul J. Boyle, eds., Special Issue: Migrations and Family Relations in the Asia Pacific Region, *Asian and Pacific Migration Journal* 11,1 (2002).

attitudes, behavior, and innovations transmitted by the movers. Adjustment to these "active" impacts depends upon which family members move, the length of absence, and the sociocultural system at the place of origin, especially dominant types of family structure and the degree of flexibility within that structure.

It is clear that an important motivation for a family member's out-migration is to enhance the economic situation of the family. Here, the issue of *remittances* from destination to origin is of major significance. The conventional wisdom about remittances in the 1970s was that they usually had little impact on development since they generally were small in size and were spent on nonproductive investments in the place of origin.[108] However, this popular perception has undergone a substantial revision and the impacts of remittances in sustaining families has become significant.[109]

It is difficult to generalize about the social impact of the departure of migrants from families, given the variety of contexts that migrants leave behind, and it is also difficult to unravel the effects of migration from other forces for change in contemporary Southeast Asian society. Female headship of incomplete nuclear families is common in areas where temporary mobility occurs. In such circumstances, women and children must perform tasks traditionally performed by men.[110]

There has been increasing discussion in the region of transnational families,[111] whereby, family members are spread across two or more countries, but they are strongly linked by regular social and economic transactions. Indeed, a transnational strategy is deliberately undertaken by families in order to sustain themselves.

The splitting of families by migration remains a major issue in the region, yet policies that favor family reunification are limited.[112] Indeed, there is a bifurcation of policy, whereby skilled migrants are permitted (even encouraged) to bring their families with them when they move but most unskilled migrant workers are forbidden to do so.

DETERMINANTS OF MIGRATION

The Global Commission on International Migration concludes,

> In the contemporary world, the principal forces that are driving international migration are due to the "3Ds": differences in development, demography, and democracy ... Because the

---

[108] Michael Lipton, "Migration from Rural Areas of Poor Countries: The Impact on Rural Productivity and Income Distribution," *World Development* 8,1 (1980): 1–24.

[109] Robyn Eversole and Judith Shaw, "Remittance Flows and Their Use in Households: A Comparative Study of Sri Lanka, Indonesia, and the Philippines," *Asian and Pacific Migration Journal* 19,2 (2010).

[110] Carol B. Hetler, "Female-Headed Households in a Circular Migration Village in Central Java, Indonesia" (PhD thesis, Department of Demography, Australian National University, Canberra, 1986); Graeme J. Hugo, "International Labour Migration and the Family: Some Observations from Indonesia," *Asian and Pacific Migration Journal* 4,2-3 (1995): 273–301.

[111] Theodora Lam, Brenda Yeoh, and Lisa Law, "Sustaining Families Transnationally: Chinese-Malaysians in Singapore," *Asian and Pacific Migration Journal* 11,1 (2002): 117–43.

[112] Graziano Battistella, "Family Reunification: Policies and Issues," *Asian and Pacific Migration Journal* 4 (1995): 2–3.

differentials are widening, the number of people seeking to migrate will continue to increase in the future.[113]

Differences between nations and between regions within countries with respect to job opportunities, wages, and security are very important underlying causes of population movement within, out of, and into Southeast Asian countries. Not only have these differentials been widening in recent years, there is every indication that they will continue to diverge.

Table 12
Projected Population Growth, Ages 15 to 34: 2005–2030

2005–2010		2010–2020		2020–2030	
Declining					
Thailand	-0.24	Vietnam	-0.67	Vietnam	-1.26
Myanmar	-0.05	Thailand	-0.45	Thailand	-0.86
		Myanmar	-0.11	Myanmar	-0.65
		Singapore	-0.08	Singapore	-0.48
		Indonesia	-0.06	Laos	-0.23
				Cambodia	-0.17
				Indonesia	-0.17
Growing					
Brunei	0.11	Brunei	0.09	Brunei	0.07
Indonesia	0.28	Cambodia	0.60	Malaysia	0.49
Timor-Leste	0.41	Timor-Leste	0.78	Timor-Leste	0.66
		Laos	0.85	Philippines	0.89
Vietnam	1.08	Malaysia	1.12		
Malaysia	1.22	Philippines	1.59		
Laos	1.55				
Cambodia	1.69				
Philippines	1.76				
Singapore	2.15				

Source: United Nations, World Population Prospects: The 2010 Revision Population Database

For example, the World Bank has identified the widening demographic differentials between high-income populations (marked by low-fertility and aging), wherein workforces face stability or decline, and low-income populations (in which youth populations will continue to grow over the next two decades), as the most powerful force for international migration in the near future:

> A key driver in the demand for international migration over the next twenty years will be slowing growth, then decline, of the labor force in high-income countries. The age group that supplies the bulk of

---

[113] GCIM, "Migration in an Interconnected World: New Directors for Action," p. 12.

the labor force (15–65 years old) is expected to peak near 500 million in 2010 and then fall to around 475 million by 2025.[114]

In Southeast Asia the situation varies from country to country. Table 12 shows that the youth population will grow over the next two decades at quite different rates in different countries. It will continue to grow in Timor-Leste, the Philippines, Malaysia, Cambodia, Brunei Darussalam, and Laos, albeit at reducing rates. However, in Indonesia, Thailand, Myanmar, Vietnam, and Singapore the population aged 15–34 will be declining by the 2020s. This is the age group whose members are most prone to migrate and are also crucial to the vibrancy of the national workforce. The widening differences between countries faced with substantial declines in their working-age population and countries in which this population continues to grow rapidly represents a substantial potential driver of future migration to OECD nations outside the region and between Southeast Asian countries themselves.

Table 13
Southeast Asia Economic Indicators

Country	GNI PPP Per Capita (US$), 2007	Population Living below $1.25 a Day, 2005	Secondary-School-Age Children actually Enrolled, 2006	Population under Age 15, 2006
Brunei Darussalam	49,900	NA	90.1%	28.8%
Cambodia	1,690	40.2%	30.7%	35.8%
Indonesia	3,580	21.4%	60.4%	27.7%
Laos	1,940	NA	34.9%	38.1%
Malaysia	13,570	0.5%	NA	30.5%
Myanmar	NA	NA	45.7%	26.3%
Philippines	3,730	22.6%	60.4%	35.5%
Singapore	48,520	NA	NA	18.0%
Thailand	7,880	0.4%	71.0%	21.2%
Timor-Leste	3,190	NA	NA	44.6%
Vietnam	2,550	21.5%	NA	28.1%
South-East Asia	4,440	18.9%	61.3%	28.5%

Source: United Nations Economic and Social Commission for Asia and the Pacific (UNESCAP), *2008 Statistical Yearbook for Asia and the Pacific* (New York, NY: United Nations, 2009); and Population Reference Bureau, *2008 World Population Data Sheet* (Washington, DC: Population Reference Bureau, 2008).

Economic differences are also widening between countries as is evident in Table 13. These differences tend to coincide with differences in demographic structure and in levels of education to strengthen migration gradients between nations.

---

[114] World Bank, *Global Economic Prospects 2006: Economic Implications of Remittances and Migration* (Washington, DC: World Bank, 2006), p. 29.

Differences between countries with respect to security, freedom, and protection of rights are an important driver of international migration.[115] This is usually interpreted in terms of refugee and humanitarian migrations, whereby people have little or no option but to migrate because of a threat to their lives. Such movement continues to occur and will do so into the future. The less-considered dimension of this driver, however, is where differences in political factors, freedom, and rights are the key factor in nonforced migrations. As Asians become more educated and skilled, many will migrate to places like Australia, not necessarily because they can earn more money. Indeed, many earn less after migration than before. They move because of the freedom, lifestyle, and rights that they and especially their children are able to enjoy.

While the "3Ds" (development, demography, and democracy) have been discussed here in relation to international migration, they are equally applicable *within* Southeast Asian countries. Spatial differences between core and periphery areas within countries are widening and are important drivers of internal migration. In addition to those three forces, however, there are two other elements that are increasingly relevant in increased migration in the Southeast Asian region. The first of these is the increasingly dense pattern of social networks being forged between Southeast Asian countries and destination countries inside and outside of the region. Every time a Southeast Asian person moves to a destination, a substantial number of their immediate family, relatives, friends, and acquaintances gain a piece of social capital at that place that they can cash in to facilitate their own migration to, and settlement in, that destination. The increasing size of Southeast Asian communities in destinations is facilitating the intensification of diasporic linkages. Social networks set up by internal and international migrants with home communities is a major facilitating factor in increasing mobility in the region. The second facilitating factor relates to the burgeoning migration industry within Southeast Asia, which operates to encourage and facilitate migration within and between countries in the region.

All of these factors drive migration, permanent and temporary, not only between Southeast Asian countries and other nations but also within countries from one region to another and from rural to urban areas. Moreover, in addition to these continuing and strengthening forces that are shaping migration in the Southeast Asian region there are a number of emerging factors that need to be considered. Firstly, whereas in the past direct environmentally induced migration has occurred overwhelmingly *within* countries,[116] the specter of climate change and its effects has the potential to change this. There is increasing discussion in the region on the likely impacts of climate change, especially regarding rising sea levels associated with global warming,[117] and, to a lesser extent, changing rainfall patterns, increasing extreme weather events, and so on. Most attention has been focused on the effect of higher sea levels on islands in the Pacific and Indian oceans and on low-lying coastal areas, such as those in Bangladesh. The potential effects in Southeast Asia have not attracted as much attention, although there is a need for an assessment to be made.

---

[115] GCIM, "Migration in an Interconnected World: New Directors for Action."

[116] Graeme J. Hugo, "Environmental Concerns and International Migration," *International Migration Review* 30,1 (1996): 105–31.

[117] John Connell, "Losing Ground? Tuvalu, the Greenhouse Effect and the Garbage Can," *Asia Pacific Viewpoint* 44, 2 (August 2003); Hugo et al., *Climate Change and Migration in the Asia-Pacific Region.*

Catalystic environmental events such as the Indian Ocean tsunami of December 2004, which displaced millions of people across ten nations, have the potential for suddenly displacing large numbers of people in the region. Undoubtedly, discussions regarding environmentally forced migrations both through the gradual impacts of climate change and the sudden onset of extreme events will increase. And while internal migration will continue to be the main outcome, it is possible that international migration will become more pronounced than in the past.

It is also necessary to consider the potential impacts of further globalization on migration in the Asian region. As linkages and relationships among nations are enhanced through increased trade, financial flows, exchange of information, and further penetration of international mass media, it is inevitable that there will be further impacts on the movement of people. It is likely that there will be more internationalization of labor markets, although at the time of writing, discussions at the International Monetary Fund to reduce barriers to the flow of services between countries seem stalled. Indeed, there is already increased discussion within ASEAN along these lines. The onset of economic crises such as the Global Financial Crisis of 2008–2009 also is certain to influence migration patterns.

POLICY

One of the defining recent characteristics of international migration in Southeast Asia has been the increasing involvement of governments in seeking to influence the patterns of immigration or emigration influencing their countries. However, the empirical base to inform policy is limited and it could be argued that one of the most pressing needs in the region is for migration, in general, and international labor migration, in particular, to be considered by national governments in a more objective way. It is clearly an emotional issue, but in many countries, especially in destination nations, there is widespread misunderstanding and misinterpretation of the nature, scale, and effects of contemporary international migration. Indeed, one of the concerns is that the international migration issue is not even on the "radar screen" of both formal and informal discussion. Myths and half-truths abound about migrant workers and their effects. Stereotypes about migrants' involvement in crime, spread of disease, and so forth, need to be exposed as incorrect, and both governments and the public more generally need to see migrants as a continuing, and in some cases an integral, part of the local economy. Indeed, in many cases such workers are necessary for the long-term health of the economy.

Civil society is playing an increasing role with respect to internal and international migration in Southeast Asia, although there is considerable variation from country to country in the nature and level of that activity. Most NGO activity in this area is nationally based, but there are some emerging regional NGOs that are active across several nations. It is particularly important to have NGOs that are active in pairs of origin and destination countries. There are a number of examples of effective NGO activity in improving the protection of migrants, providing support for, and also in advocating for the rights of, migrants, and in lobbying to change policy in both origin and destination countries. In terms of origin countries, the Philippines has the best developed and most comprehensive NGO presence and the NGOs' involvement undoubtedly has improved the lot of Filipino overseas contract workers. With respect to destination countries, NGO activities have been especially important in Taiwan in improving protection for both migrant workers and the foreign brides of Taiwanese men. NGOs have the potential to play an important role in the protection of migrants, especially migrant workers and brides of commodified, arranged international marriages. This is because while governments are constrained in their ability to help nationals in foreign countries by diplomatic convention, NGOs are much more flexible in the types of support they can provide.

Until recently there has been little international cooperation on international migration within Southeast Asia. Indeed, ASEAN, until a decade ago, did not consider migration issues because one of the member countries vetoed any such discussion. However, since then a change has been apparent, albeit a gradual one. Thus far, the cooperation has largely been at the level of discussion, but there are several promising signs. In 2015, ASEAN is scheduled to become a single Free Trade Area, and associated with this have been discussions regarding the free movement of particular highly skilled workers. However, at present, it appears that there is no chance that all of Southeast Asia will be a free labor market for all workers. Other promising developments have included, in 2007, the passing of a resolution regarding the welfare of international labor migrants and the holding of regular meetings on issues of trafficking and people smuggling.[118] There is little doubt that heightened concerns of security have been an important driver of increased discussion within ASEAN regarding international migration, but there are hopeful signs that a more realistic approach to migration is emerging.

A key issue relates to protection of migrant workers, especially women and low-paid workers. Some have argued that such migration is a form of slavery and is inherently exploitative. Others, however, have maintained that it is more the operationalization of labor migration that has led to negative outcomes, and there is a need to establish best practice in the recruitment, training, preparation, movement, working conditions, and return of labor migrants in the region.[119]

There are a number of constraints that are operating to prevent migration from delivering development dividends to migrants, their families, and communities of origin. Governance of migration in the region is weak, there is excessive rent taking and exploitation, and policy remains underdeveloped. There is an urgent need for capacity building to create a cadre of dedicated, well-trained officials and to provide a relevant, timely empirical base to inform decision making. The Global Financial Crisis of 2008-09 notwithstanding, the underlying drivers of international migration in the region remain strong and will strengthen.

With respect to internal migration, policy intervention to influence population movement and distribution within nations has been considerable—as much as in any region of the world. As indicated earlier, several countries have had explicit policies to resettle agriculturalists from more densely settled areas to less densely settled parts of the national space. By and large such policies and programs have now lapsed. Post-unification Vietnam encouraged north to south migration, while Cambodia, under the infamous Pol Pot, sought to move most of the urban population into rural areas, with bloody and tragic results.[120]

Much of the migration policy concern within Southeast Asian countries has focused on urbanization. In the early postwar period, anti-urban policies were pursued in several countries that sought to dampen the rapid growth of urban

---

[118] Hugo and Young, eds., *Labour Mobility in the Asia-Pacific Region.*

[119] Hugo et al., *Climate Change and Migration in the Asia-Pacific Region.*

[120] E. A. Méng-Try, "Kampuchea: A Country Adrift," *Population and Development Review* 7,2 (1981): 209–28.

centers, especially the largest cities. Hence, in Jakarta, a number of anti-urban policies were pursued in the 1970s,[121] and remnants of these have persisted for several decades. In Vietnam, a registration system similar to China's *hukou* prevented people from moving from rural to urban areas for several years after reunification.[122] However, this direction has changed with a recognition that rapid urbanization is an inevitable corollary of development so that cities have become more accommodationist in seeking to provide for their burgeoning populations.

There are new challenges of internal population distribution in the region. Increased dam building in the upper reaches of key rivers in the region, such as the Mekong, are threatening the livelihood of millions of downstream agriculturalists.[123] The spreading growth of megacities presents huge challenges to city governments in providing utilities and services. Fertility declines, increasing education levels, and rural–urban migration is leading to depopulation in some rural areas, so that there are labor shortages in primary industry. Thailand and Malaysia are relying more and more on foreign workers—many of them undocumented—to provide their agricultural, fishing, forestry, and plantation workforces. Moreover, the potential of climate change to influence population distribution is considerable.[124] Indeed, some of the "hot spot" areas likely to be most influenced by climate change are some of the most densely settled parts of the region. In particular, delta areas such as the Mekong and large coastal cities such as Bangkok and Ho Chi Minh City are especially vulnerable. There may well be the need to rethink contemporary settlement systems and population distribution over the next half-century. It is notable that Southeast Asia has been identified as one of the parts of the world most susceptible to the impact of climate change.[125]

CONCLUSION

Increased scale and complexity of population mobility has been both an important consequence, as well as a cause, of rapid social change and economic development in Southeast Asia. While there are many continuities with the past, population movement has produced a markedly different distribution of population in the region from that which prevailed at the end of the period of European colonization. Yet it remains the least well-measured and understood of the demographic processes shaping Southeast Asia's population. Moreover, it is difficult to foresee any future scenario other than one in which enhanced population mobility will play an important role. Hence, there is an urgency to both better measure internal and international migration in the region and to initiate policy-relevant research into its causes and consequences.

---

[121] Graeme J. Hugo, *Population Mobility in West Java* (Yogyakarta: Gadjah Mada University Press, 1978).

[122] Hukou is a system of registration whereby persons wishing to transfer their usual place of residence have to gain official permission.

[123] Michael Douglass, "Cross-border Water Governance in Asia," in G. Shabbir Cheema, Christopher A. McNally, and Vesselin Popovski, eds., *Cross-Border Governance in Asia: Regional Issues and Mechanisms* (New York, NY: United Nations University Press, 2011).

[124] Hugo et al., *Climate Change and Migration in the Asia-Pacific Region.*

[125] Arief A. Yusuf and Herminia Francisco, "Climate Change Vulnerability Mapping for Southeast Asia," Economy and Environment Program for Southeast Asia (Singapore), 2009, number tp200901s1, available at http://ideas.repec.org/p/eep/tpaper/tp200901s1.html, accessed February 28, 2012.

CHAPTER 6

MIGRATION AND HEALTH IN SOUTHEAST ASIA

Mark J. VanLandingham and Hongyun Fu

The ongoing political turmoil in Thailand has complex underpinnings but none more fundamental than the profound divide between urban and rural dwellers. Of course, this divide between city and countryside characterizes not only Thailand but the entire Southeast Asian region; and in addition to the political implications, these divides have far-reaching consequences for the well-being and development of the entire region.

Opportunities to develop human and economic capital are heavily concentrated within cities, and this fact is reflected by the vast numbers of rural citizens who spend increasing amounts of time working in the country's major cities, their industrialized periphery, or abroad. These migration streams have important implications for a wide range of outcomes related to the well-being of both the migrants themselves and the members of the communities left behind. The bulk of the existing literature on this topic focuses on the implications of wide-scale migration upon economic outcomes. In this chapter, we focus on another important key implication of this most recent demographic transformation in the region that has received much less attention: health.[1] We address the health implications of migration by first reviewing historical perspectives on this relationship; by laying out a conceptual framework that examines the potential pathways through which migration might affect health outcomes; by reviewing and summarizing the empirical evidence that evaluates the relationship between migration and health in the context of Southeast Asia; and by proposing a research agenda for moving this emerging field forward.

[1] This research was supported by the Eunice Kennedy Shriver National Institute for Child and Human Development, National Institutes of Health (R03HD042003, R21HD057609, and R01HD46527; VanLandingham, PI). Assistance with the overall project from colleagues at the Institute for Population and Social Research (IPSR), Mahidol University, is gratefully acknowledged. Helpful comments and suggestions by Caitlin Canfield, Kiva Fisher, Lindy Williams, and Phil Guest are also gratefully acknowledged.

A BRIEF HISTORICAL PERSPECTIVE

The potential negative impacts of migration for heath were noted in ancient Greece and Rome.[2] City-states and regional federations were known to quarantine traders and travelers to prevent the spread of infectious disease.[3] A major focus of early twentieth century public health in the United States was on immigrants as potential conduits for the spread of disease, eventually leading to the establishment of the Marine Hospital Service on Staten Island as a screening center for yellow fever, cholera, and tuberculosis.[4]

More recent concerns about the potential implications of migration for disease spread were fueled by outbreaks and the spread of acquired immune deficiency syndrome (AIDS) and severe acute respiratory syndrome (SARS) in Asia, as well as the ongoing threat of a global influenza pandemic.[5] These high-profile examples have in some cases led to formal travel restrictions upon migrants.[6] They serve to illustrate how high and increasing rates of internal and international migration provide fertile conditions for the spread of infectious disease both within and outside the region of the initial outbreak. This issue is particularly salient within Southeast Asia, where several of these new infectious agents initially gained a toehold within the human population.[7]

These potential threats of migration to public health have received massive amounts of coverage in the international media. But migration can have significant

---

[2] Stephen S. Morse, "Factors in the Emergence of Infectious Diseases," *Emerging Infectious Diseases* 1,1 (1995): 7.

[3] Jeffrey Evans, "Introduction: Migration and Health," *International Migration Review* 21,3 (1987): v–xiv.

[4] Ibid.

[5] Caroline A. Ryan et al., "Explosive Spread of HIV-1 and Sexually Transmitted Diseases in Cambodia," *Lancet* 351, 9110 (April 18, 1998): 1175; Ronald Skeldon, "Population Mobility and HIV Vulnerability in South East Asia: An Assessment and Analysis," South East Asia HIV and Development Programme Report (Bangkok: ADP/UNDP, 2000); Suphāng Čhanthawānit, Allan Beesey, and Shakti Paul, "Mobility and HIV/AIDS in the Greater Mekong Subregion," Asian Research Centre for Migration, Chulalongkorn University, South East Asia HIV and Development Programme Report (Bangkok: ADP/UNDP, 2000); Brian D. Gushulak and Douglas A. MacPherson, *Migration, Medicine, and Health: Principles and Practice* (Hamilton, Ontario: BC Decker Inc, 2006); Melissa Curley and Nicholas Thomas, "Human Security and Public Health in Southeast Asia: The SARS Outbreak," *Australian Journal of International Affairs* 58,1 (2004): 17–32; Adrian Sleigh et al., "Population Dynamics and Infectious Diseases in Asia," *World Scientific* (Hackensack, NJ: World Scientific Publishing, 2006), p. 4; Sunal K. Lal and Vincent T. K. Chow, "Avian Influenza H5N1 Virus: An Emerging Global Pandemic," *Issues in Infectious Diseases* 4 (2007): 59–77.

[6] World Health Organization, "Statement on Screening of International Travelers for Infection with Human Immunodeficiency Virus," *Bulletin of the International Union against Tuberculosis and Lung Disease* 63,3 (1988): 38; United Nations Programme on HIV/AIDS, *Report on the Global AIDS Epidemic* (New York, NY: UNAIDS, 2008); John Balzano and Jia Ping, "Coming Out of Denial: An Analysis of AIDS Law and Policy in China (1987–2006)," *Loyola University International Law Review* (2006): 187–212; B. Fielding and Y. Tan, "The Singapore Contribution in the Battle against the Severe Acute Respiratory Syndrome," *Issues in Infectious Diseases* 4 (2007): 1–22.

[7] World Economic Forum, "Global Risks 2006," available at www.weforum.org/pdf/CSI/global_Risk_Report.pdf, accessed on April 16, 2012; Adrian C. Sleigh, Chee Heng Leng, Brenda S. A. Yeoh, Phua Kai Hong, and Rachel Safman, *Population Dynamics and Infectious Diseases in Asia*; Sunil K. Lal, *Emerging Viral Diseases of Southeast Asia*, Vol. 4 (Basel: Krager, 2007).

health impacts—both positive and negative—upon the health of individual migrants as well. This latter topic is attracting significant attention among demographers and other social scientists who are interested in global aspects of migration, including those who focus on the size, structure, location, and well-being of populations in the Southeast Asia region.

A CONCEPTUAL FRAMEWORK

A standard definition of migration is "a permanent change in residence."[8] While motivations underlying such moves vary, common themes include the hope of better employment and educational opportunities, more freedom, the desire to be with friends or loved ones, and escape from difficult circumstances. The degree of choice involved in the move also varies. At one extreme is a decision to move based solely upon one's own or family interest. At the other is forced migration by an unwilling individual. In between these extremes are combinations of choice and the pressure to move. This variation in motives has implications for the potential health consequences of a move.

Keeping in mind this variability, we sketch in Figure 1 a generalized conceptual framework of how migration can affect health. Beginning on the left side of the figure, we highlight features of structure and agency that motivate decisions to move within or outside of the region. Focusing first on structure (the upper left box), we see that modernization and the monetization of world and regional economies will encourage (or necessitate) individual moves from traditional areas (especially rural areas) to more modernized areas (especially urbanized areas), where wage-paying employment is more readily available. Of course, changes in tastes and preferences also occur during this transformation—changes that can be thought of as both structural and individual. These changes in context, associated with modernization, will have important influences on the health outcomes of interest, shown in the far right side of the figure, as indicated by the top arrow.

Individual characteristics and choice also play central roles in migration behavior (the bottom left box). Variability among individuals with regard to their assets (economic, human, and social capital), their personalities (for example, risk-taking propensities), and their health will influence these decisions. Moreover, these predispositions to migrate—often referred to as "selection factors"—can directly influence the health outcomes of interest, shown on the far right of the figure, as indicated by the bottom arrow.

This confounding feature of "selection" in migration and health studies is sometimes referred to as the "healthy / risky migrant hypotheses,"[9] since substantial

---

[8] John Robert Weeks, *Population: An Introduction to Concepts and Issues* (Belmont, CA: Thomson / Wadsworth, 2008).

[9] Ruben G. Rumbaut and John R. Weeks, "Infant Health among Indochinese Refugees: Patterns of Infant Mortality, Birthweight, and Prenatal Care in Comparative Perspective," *Research in the Sociology of Health Care* 8 (1989), pp. 137–96; Ruben G. Rumbaut and John R. Weeks, "Unraveling a Public Health Enigma: Why do Immigrants Experience Superior Perinatal Health Outcomes?" *Research in Sociology in Health Care* 13 (1996): 337–91; Abraído-Lanza, Ana F. Dohrenwend, Bruce P. Ng-Mak, Daisy S. Turner, J. Blake, "The Latino Mortality Paradox: A Test of the 'Salmon Bias' and Healthy Migrant Hypotheses," *American Journal of Public Health* 89,10 (1999): 1543–48; Yao Lu, "Test of the 'Healthy Migrant Hypothesis': A Longitudinal Analysis of Health Selectivity of Internal Migration in Indonesia," *Social Science & Medicine* 67,8 (2008): 1331–39.

evidence suggests that those who choose to migrate enjoy a health status that is superior to those who stay behind. Conversely, individuals suffering from illness or other health challenges are unlikely to be willing to face the challenges that a major move entails.[10] On the other hand, migrants who undergo their journey because compelled to some degree—for example, refugees—are often disadvantaged in a variety of ways, including health status.[11]

Figure 1

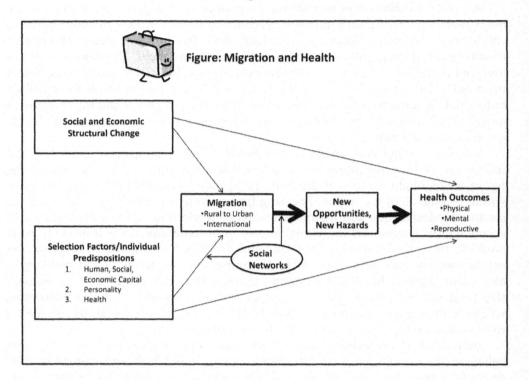

Features of the move itself are also variable (as outlined in the "Migration" box). Changes in residence can be somewhat permanent, while other changes are more temporary or even cyclical. Moves between origin and destination may cross international boundaries (international migration) or may occur within a country's borders (internal migration).

New conditions arising either during or after the move are designated by the "New Opportunities, New Hazards" box. These conditions may be positive or

---

[10] Diana Hull, "Migration, Adaptation, and Illness: A Review," *Social Science & Medicine* 13A (1979): 25–36; Abraído-Lanza et al., *The Latino Mortality Paradox*; K. B. Newbold, "Self-Rated Health within the Canadian Immigrant Population: Risk and the Healthy Immigrant Effect," *Social Science & Medicine* 60,6 (March 2005): 1359–70; Lu, "Test of the 'Healthy Migrant Hypothesis'"; Steven Stillman, David McKenzie, and John Gibson, "Migration and Mental Health: Evidence from a Natural Experiment," *Journal of Health Economics* 28,3 (May, 2009): 677–87.

[11] Judith T. Shuval, "Migration and Stress" in *Handbook of Stress*, ed. S. Bienznite and L. Goldberg (New York, NY: Free Press, 1993), pp. 651–57; Lu, "Test of the 'Healthy Migrant Hypothesis.'"

negative. On the negative side, the disruptions of moving, as well as unfamiliarity and stress associated with the new environment can take a toll on the health of migrants.[12] Traumatic experiences prior to and/or during the move (for example, for refugees), separation from family and community, and language barriers have all been identified as risk factors related to increased risk of physical illness or mental disorder.[13] Health care services in the receiving environments are often more expensive for and less familiar to migrants than the services at origin.[14] Difficulties securing employment and experiences of discrimination may jeopardize migrants' health and well-being.[15] For emigrants from developing regions who move to Western countries, increasing anti-immigration sentiment and discrimination have been found to be associated with chronic health conditions, poorer quality of life, and symptoms of mental disorders.[16]

Much of the attention on the potential health implications of migration has focused on negative impacts, but positive change in health status can result as well. Migrants may benefit from better health care and housing during at least part of their journey. These benefits can have long-lasting positive effects.[17] Those migrants who relocate to more developed societies or to cities may also benefit from a cleaner environment.

Whether the move results in a positive or negative change in health status depends upon other moderating factors (see Figure 1). The significance of social networks and social support for health has been widely reported in the migration

---

[12] John Cassel, "Hypertension and Cardiovascular Disease in Migrants: A Potential Source of Clues?" *International Journal of Epidemiology* 3,3 (September 1974): 204–6; Sally E. Findley, "The Directionality and Age Selectivity of the Health–Migration Relation: Evidence from Sequences of Disability and Mobility in the United States," *The International Migration Review* 22,3 (Fall 1988): 4–29; Shuval, "Migration and Stress"; Wen H. Kuo and Yung M. Tsai, "Social Networking, Hardiness, and Immigrant's Mental Health," *Journal of Health and Social Behavior* 27,2 (June 1986): 133–49; Douglass Massey and Felipe G. España, "The Social Process of International Migration," *Science* 237,4816 (1987): 733–38; William A. Vega, Bohdan Kolody, and Juan R. Valle, "Migration and Mental Health: An Empirical Test of Depression Risk Factors among Immigrant Mexican Women," *The International Migration Review* 21,3 (Fall 1987): 512–30.

[13] Mildred B. Kantor, "Internal Migration and Mental Illness," *Changing Perspectives in Mental Illness* (New York, NY: Holt, Rinehart & Winston, 1969); Elsie Seckyee Ho, "Mental Health of Asian Immigrants in New Zealand: A Review of Key Issues," *Asian and Pacific Migration Journal* 13,1 (2004): 39; Derrick Silove et al., "Anxiety, Depression, and PTSD in Asylum-Seekers: Associations with Pre-Migration Trauma and Post-Migration Stressors," *The British Journal of Psychiatry* 170,4 (1997): 351; Dermot Ryan, Barbara Dooley, and Ciarán Benson, "Theoretical Perspectives on Post-Migration Adaptation and Psychological Well-being among Refugees: Towards a Resource-Based Model," *Journal of Refugee Studies* (2008).

[14] Findley, *The Directionality and Age Selectivity of the Health–Migration Relation.*

[15] Morton Beiser and Feng Hou, "Language Acquisition, Unemployment, and Depressive Disorder among Southeast Asian Refugees: A 10-Year Study," *Social Science & Medicine* 53,10 (2001): 1321–34; Gilbert C. Gee et al., "The Association between Self-Reported Racial Discrimination and 12-Month DSM-IV Mental Disorders among Asian Americans Nationwide," *Social Science & Medicine* 64,10 (May 2007): 1984–96; Gilbert C. Gee et al., "A Nationwide Study of Discrimination and Chronic Health Conditions among Asian Americans," *American Journal of Public Health* 97,7 (July 2007): 1275–82.

[16] Gee et al., "The Association between Self-Reported Racial Discrimination and 12-Month DSM-IV Mental Disorders among Asian Americans Nationwide"; Gee et al., "A Nationwide Study of Discrimination and Chronic Health Conditions among Asian Americans."

[17] Hull, "Migration, Adaptation, and Illness: A Review."

literature.[18] Migrants are not only physically separated from their families, but also separated from their home cultures, including beliefs about mutual rights, obligations, and networks of social interaction. At their destination, migrants may experience strong feeling of loneliness, alienation, and inability to cultivate or sustain social relationships in the new environment.[19] Disruption of existing social networks can weaken exchanges of emotional and financial support, which might otherwise have buffered these individuals against everyday stress and setbacks if these networks had remained intact.[20] On the other hand, maintenance of more traditional cultural beliefs and practices may protect the migrant from some hazards at destination, especially if the migrant is successful at establishing new networks with individuals from his or her place of common origin.[21] For example, Min Zhou and Carl Bankston document a high level of normative integration among Vietnamese immigrant families living within an urban American enclave.[22] These strong social ties appear to play a central role in smoothing the adaptation process.

These new conditions that migrants experience constitute the proximate determinants of the changes in various aspects of health status, which are, in turn, outlined in the far right box in the figure "Health Outcomes." Given that most migrants are quite young and that variations in physical health status within this age group are difficult to discern, reproductive health status—especially involving unwanted pregnancy, HIV, and STIs (socially transmitted infections)—has received a large amount of attention in this literature.

Migrants are typically in the prime age brackets for courtship, sexual experimentation, marriage, and other less formal sexual relationships.[23] In the city, norms and mores regarding sexual behaviors are more tolerant than those in rural areas;[24] much more sexual freedom is reported in the city by both men and women.[25]

[18] Kuo and Tsai, *Social Networking, Hardiness and Immigrant's Mental Health*; D. S. Massey, "The New Immigration and Ethnicity in the United States," *Population and Development Review* (1995): 631–52; Nancy S. Landale and R. Salvador Oropesa, "Migration, Social Support, and Perinatal Health: An Origin-Destination Analysis of Puerto Rican Women," *Journal of Health and Social Behavior* 42,2 (June 2001): 166–83; William Kandel and Douglas S. Massey, "The Culture of Mexican Migration: A Theoretical and Empirical Analysis," *Social Forces* 80,3 (2002): 981–1004.

[19] Wen Kuo, "Theories of Migration and Mental Health: An Empirical Testing on Chinese-Americans," *Social Science & Medicine* 10,6 (June 1976): 297–306.

[20] Carlos E. Sluzki, "Disruption and Reconstruction of Networks Following migration/relocation," *Family Systems Medicine* 10,4 (1992): 359–63.

[21] Kuo and Tsai, *Social Networking, Hardiness, and Immigrant's Mental Health*; Landale and Oropesa, "Migration, Social Support, and Perinatal Health: An Origin–Destination Analysis of Puerto Rican Women."

[22] Min Zhou and Carl L. Bankston, *Growing Up American: How Vietnamese Children Adapt to Life in the United States* (New York, NY: Russell Sage Foundation, 1998).

[23] Tine Gammeltoft, "Being Special for Somebody: Urban Sexualities in Contemporary Vietnam," *Asian Journal of Social Science* 30,3 (2002): 476–92; S. Ghuman et al., "Continuity and Change in Premarital Sex in Vietnam," *International Family Planning Perspectives* 32,4 (December 2006): 166–74.

[24] Jamie Uhrig et al., "HIV Vulnerability Mapping: Highway One, Viet Nam" (report from the UNDP South East Asia HIV and Development Project, 2000); Gammeltoft, "Being Special for Somebody: Urban Sexualities in Contemporary Vietnam"; Michael L. Rekart, "Sex in the City: Sexual Behaviour, Societal Change, and STDs in Saigon," *Sexually Transmitted Infections* 78,1, supplement (2002): i47; Niki Hong-Ngoc Thi Pham, "Vietnam's Urban Sex Culture: Is it Fueling the HIV/AIDS Epidemic?" *Pacific News* 22 (2004): 6–9.

To sum up, the relationship between migration and health is complex. Researchers and policy makers generally express interest in the effects of the former upon the latter, but a person's health can affect the decision to migrate as well. Furthermore, a wide range of other preexisting factors may also influence the decision to migrate, and the association of these factors with health further complicates the relationship between migration and health. It is also important to keep in mind that positive (as well as negative) health outcomes may result from a move and that individuals make migration decisions within the context of the web of social relations in which they are embedded both at origin and at destination.

EVIDENCE FROM SOUTHEAST ASIA

While the empirical literature on migration and health is well-developed for moves between Latin America and North America, much less work has focused on the health consequences of migration from, to, or within Southeast Asia.[26] This is unfortunate, since patterns of migration among Southeast Asians are extensive and complex, including short-term, long-term, and circular forms; volitional, quasi-volitional, and nonvolitional motivations; and internal, intraregional, and extraregional destinations.[27] The literature that does exist tends to focus on the well-being of migrants from the region who have settled in the major receiving countries of the West (especially the United States, Canada, and Australia) and, to a lesser extent, on the well-being of migrants from one country in the region who settled in another. While temporary moves to the Middle East and within country borders are extensive, the empirical literature on the consequences of these types of moves is especially limited. In the second half of the paper, we survey this region-specific literature, highlight major findings, identify gaps, and propose topics for future research.

Migration and Infectious Disease

Major outbreaks of tuberculosis, malaria, and other infectious diseases have been reported among migrants moving internally or intraregionally in Southeast Asia,[28]

---

[25] Nicholas J. Ford and Suporn Saiprasert, "Destinations Unknown: The Gender Construction and Changing Nature of the Sexual Expressions of Thai Youth-Paper Presentation," AIDS Care 6,5 (1994): 517–31; Pham, "Vietnam's Urban Sex Culture: Is it Fueling the HIV/AIDS Epidemic?"; Lynn Morrison, "Traditions in Transition: Young People's Risk for HIV in Chiang Mai, Thailand," *Qualitative Health Research* 14,3 (March 2004): 328–44.

[26] Santosh Jatrana, Elspeth Graham, and Paul Boyle, "Introduction: Understanding Migration and Health in Asia," in *Migration and Health in Asia*, ed. Santosh Jatrana, Mika Toyota, and Brenda S. A. Yeoh (London and New York, NY: Routledge, 2005); Gushulak and MacPherson, *Migration, Medicine, and Health: Principles and Practice.*

[27] Graeme Hugo, "The Future of Migration Policy in the Asia-Pacific Region" (background paper prepared for the IOM World Migration Report 201, University of Adelaide, 2010).

[28] Anchalee Singhanetra-Renard, "Malaria and Mobility in Thailand," *Social Science & Medicine* 37,9 (November 1993): 1147–54; Charles M. Nolan, Gisela Schecter, and Sundari R. Mase, "Evaluation of Tuberculosis Program Services for Burmese Refugees in Thailand Resettling to the United States," available at http://ethnomed.org/clinical/tuberculosis/Eval_TB_Burmese.pdf, accessed on March 20, 2012; Witaya Swaddiwudhipong et al., "An Outbreak of Cholera among Migrants Living in a Thai–Myanmar Border Area," *Journal of the Medical Association of Thailand* 91,9 (2008): 1433–40.

and a study in Thailand has shown that outbreaks of infectious diseases can result in higher death rates among migrants, relative to the general local Thai population.[29]

Among emigrants from the region to the West, a higher burden of infectious disease, for example, hepatitis and tuberculosis, relative to natives, is also reported.[30] For example, an overall tuberculin positivity rate of 38 percent was reported among Southeast Asian refugees in a health-screen program in Colorado between 1981 and 1982.[31] A more recent report showed that immigrants to the United States from the Philippines and Vietnam ranked first and third on the total number of tuberculosis diagnoses during the period 1995 to 2005.[32] Speculation regarding the reasons why migrants suffer a higher burden of infectious disease relative to nonmigrants focuses on greater exposure to disease agents (for example, within crowded living conditions), weakened immune systems due to the stresses associated with migration, and the disruption of regular access to health services.[33]

Migration and HIV/AIDS

Systematic epidemiological data on sexual health among migrants are not available for any country in the region or outside of it. Indeed, data on more general

---

[29] Nucharee Srivirojana and Sureeporn Punpuing, "Ethnic Differential in Health and Mortality among Myanmar, Laos, and Cambodia Migrants in Thailand," presentation at the annual meeting of the Population Association of America, Detroit, MI, April 31–May 2, 2009.

[30] Antonio Catanzaro and Robert J. Moser, "Health Status of Refugees from Vietnam, Laos, and Cambodia," *Journal of the American Medical Association* 247,9 (1982): 1303–8; F. N. Judson et al., "Health Status of Southeast Asian Refugees," *The Western Journal of Medicine* 141,2 (August 1984): 183–88; Jane E. Poss, "Hepatitis B Virus Infection in Southeast Asian Children," *Journal of Pediatric Health Care: Official Publication of National Association of Pediatric Nurse Associates & Practitioners* 3,6 (November–December 1989): 311–15; James W. Carey et al., "Tuberculosis Beliefs among Recent Vietnamese Refugees in New York State," *Public Health Reports* 112,1 (1997): 66; Karen R. Nelson, Hoan Bui, and Jeffrey H. Samet, "Screening in Special Populations: A 'Case Study' of Recent Vietnamese Immigrants," *The American Journal of Medicine* 102,5 (May 1997): 435–40; Kathryn DeRiemer et al., "Tuberculosis among Immigrants and Refugees," *Archives of Internal Medicine* 158,7 (1998): 753; Seiji Yamada et al., "Attitudes Regarding Tuberculosis in Immigrants from the Philippines to the United States," *Family Medicine* 31,7 (1999); Sonia R. Caruana et al., "Knowledge about Hepatitis and Previous Exposure to Hepatitis Viruses in Immigrants and Refugees from the Mekong Region," *Australian and New Zealand Journal of Public Health* 29,1 (February 2005): 64–68; Sonia R. Caruana et al., "Undiagnosed and Potentially Lethal Parasite Infections among Immigrants and Refugees in Australia," *Journal of Travel Medicine* 13,4 (July–August 2006): 233–39; Tara Singh Bam et al., "High Success Rate of TB Treatment among Bhutanese Refugees in Nepal," *International Journal of Tuberculosis and Lung Disease* 11,1 (January 2007): 54–58.

[31] Judson et al., "Health Status of Southeast Asian Refugees."

[32] Kevin P. Cain et al., "Tuberculosis among Foreign-Born Persons in the United States: Achieving Tuberculosis Elimination," *American Journal of Respiratory and Critical Care Medicine* 175,1 (January 1, 2007): 75–79.

[33] Mary E. Wilson, "Travel and the Emergence of Infectious Diseases," *Emerging Infectious Diseases* 1,1 (1995): 39–46; Christy Hanson, "Tuberculosis, Poverty, and Equity: A Review of Literature and Discussion of Issues," *World Bank* (2002); Imelda Bates et al., "Vulnerability to Malaria, Tuberculosis, and HIV/AIDS Infection and Disease, Part 1: Determinants Operating at Individual and Household Level," *The Lancet—Infectious Diseases* 4,5 (2004): 267–77; Imelda Bates et al., "Vulnerability to Malaria, Tuberculosis, and HIV/AIDS Infection and Disease, Part II: Determinants Operating at Environmental and Institutional Level," *The Lancet—Infectious Diseases* 4,6 (2004): 368–75.

measures of well-being for migrants are very limited throughout the region, due, in part, to extensive undocumented migration to, from, and within Southeast Asia.[34] Nevertheless, studies based on convenience samples of highly mobile groups, such as truck drivers, itinerant traders and seafarers, and sex workers, have identified travel and migration as significant risk factors associated with HIV/AIDS in Southeast Asia.[35] For example, migrant fishermen report a high level of risky sexual behaviors and suffer a much higher rate of HIV infection than does the general population.[36] HIV infection rates among sex workers in Thai-Myanmar border areas during the mid-1990s were consistently higher than elsewhere in Thailand, no doubt reflecting, in part, a higher risk among the male migrants who made up a significant portion of the sex workers' clientele.[37] The providers of sex services, many of whom are young female migrants, also constitute a vulnerable risk group for HIV/AIDS in Southeast Asia. Unpublished reports conclude that large numbers of women and underage girls are being trafficked in the region for the commercial sex industry. Many are at high risk for contracting and spreading HIV/AIDS.[38] Southeast Asian women who migrate to other countries for employment as domestic household

---

[34] Hugo, "The Future of Migration Policy in the Asia–Pacific Region."

[35] Chris Lyttleton, "The Good People of Isan: Commercial Sex in Northeast Thailand," *The Australian Journal of Anthropology* 5,1–2 (1994): 257–79; Martina Morris et al., "Bridge Populations in the Spread of HIV/AIDS in Thailand," *AIDS* 10,11 (September 1996): 1265–71; Eleanor Maticka-Tyndale et al., "Contexts and Patterns of Men's Commercial Sexual Partnerships in Northeastern Thailand: Implications for AIDS Prevention," *Social Science & Medicine* 44,2 (1997): 199–213; Allan Beesey, "The Crossroads of Risk and Responsibility: Truck Drivers and HIV/AIDS in Central Vietnam," report from the National Highway One Project—Development Community Response to HIV/AIDS, supported by AUSAID and World Vision, Melbourne, April 1998; Supang Chantavanich et al., "Cross-Border Migration and HIV/AIDS: Vulnerability at the Thai–Cambodia Border, Sangkhlaburi, and Ranong" (report from the UNDP South East Asia HIV and Development Project, Bangkok, 2000), available at www.hivpolicy.org/Library/HPP000872.pdf, accessed on April 2, 2012; Graeme J. Hugo, "Indonesia: Internal and International Population Mobility: Implications for the Spread of HIV/AIDS" (report from the UNDP South East Asia HIV and Development Project, November 2001); Kathleen Ford and Aphichat Chamrathrithirong, "Sexual Partners and Condom Use of Migrant Workers in Thailand," *AIDS and Behavior* 11,6 (November 2007): 905–14.

[36] UNDP and United Nations Regional Task Force on Mobility and HIV Vulnerability Reduction in South-East Asia and Southern Provinces of China, "HIV/AIDS and Mobility in South-East Asia: Rapid Assessment," 2008, available at: http://test.aidsportal.org/atomic Documents/AIDSPortalDocuments/HIVMobilitySouth-EastAsia08.pdf, accessed on April 3, 2012; Achara Entz et al., "STD History, Self Treatment, and Healthcare Behaviours among Fishermen in the Gulf of Thailand and the Andaman Sea," *Sexually Transmitted Infections* 77,6 (2001): 436.

[37] Doug J. Porter, "Wheeling and Dealing: HIV and Development on the Shan State Borders of Myanmar" (volume three of study paper from UNDP HIV and Development Programme, 1995); A. Singhanetra-Renard, *Population Movement and the AIDS Epidemic in Thailand* (Oxford: Clarendon Press, 1997); Huw Jones, "Demographic and Developmental Contexts of AIDS in Northern Thailand," paper presented at workshop on Development, Spatial Mobility, and HIV/AIDS, Paris, September 1–3, 2004), p. 14.

[38] Kritaya Archavanitkul, *Trafficking in Children for Labour Exploitation including Child Prostitution in the Mekong Subregion: A Research Report* (Bangkok: ILO-IPEC,[1998]); Piyasiri Wickramasekara, "Asian Labour Migration: Issues and Challenges in an Era of Globalization" (report and conclusions, ILO Asia-Pacific Regional Symposium for Trade Union Organizations on Migrant Workers, Kuala Lumpur, 2002).

workers[39] report high rates of sexual abuse, exploitation, and HIV/STIs.[40] Early work on the links between rural-to-urban migration and AIDS risk behaviors in Southeast Asia have often focused on rural women who have moved to urban areas to work in the commercial sex industry.[41] Recruiting networks were built up to provide a steady supply of sex workers from rural to urban areas, where most brothels were located.[42] In some poor villages, both the young females who chose to migrate to large cities in order to enter the commercial sex trade, as well as their family members who were left behind, considered this move an opportunity to escape dire poverty.[43]

---

[39] Migration of women from and within Southeast Asia for work in the domestic work and entertainment industries has been steadily increasing since the 1990s, with the Philippines and Indonesia as major sending countries; Hong Kong and Singapore are major destinations. See Piyasiri Wickramasekara, "Female Migrant Workers in Asia: Emerging Issues and National and International Response," resource paper prepared for the International Seminar on International Female Migration and Japan: Networking, Settlement, and Human Rights, International Peace Research Institute, Meiji-Gakuin University, Tokyo, December 12–14, 1995; Brenda S. A. Yeoh, Shirleena Huang, and Joaquin Gonsalez III, "Migrant Domestic Helpers: Debating the Economic, Social, and Political Impacts in Singapore," *International Migration Review* 133,1 (1999): 114–36; and Vivienne Wee and Amy Sim, "Transnational Labour Networks in Female Labour Migration: Mediating between Southeast Asian Women Workers and International Labour Markets," in *International Migration in Southeast Asia: Impacts and Challenges*, ed. Aris Ananta (Singapore: Institute of Southeast Asian Studies, 2004).

[40] Piyasiri Wickramasekara, "Female Migrant Workers in Asia"; Enda Oppenheimer, Matana Bunnag, and Aaron Stern, "HIV/AIDS and Cross-Border Migration: A Rapid Assessment of Migrant Populations along the Thai–Burma (Myanmar) Border Regions" (research report, Institute of Asian Studies, Chulalongkorn University, 1998); Mika Toyota, "Health Consequences of 'invisible' Foreign Domestic Maids in Thailand," *Asian Meta Centre Research Paper Series* (research paper No. 19, Asian Meta Centre for Population and Sustainable Development Analyses, 2000, available at www.populationasia.org/Publications/RP/AMCRP19.pdf, accessed on March 20, 2012); Hugo, "Indonesia: Internal and International Population Mobility: Implications for the Spread of HIV/AIDS."

[41] Nicholas Ford and Suporn Koetsawang, "The Socio-Cultural Context of the Transmission of HIV in Thailand," *Social Science & Medicine* 33,4 (1991): 405–14; Kritaya Archavanitkul and Philip Guest, "Migration and the Commercial Sex Sector in Thailand," in *AIDS Impact and Prevention in the Developing World: Demographic and Social Science Perspectives*, supplement to *Health Transition Review* 4 (1994): pp. 273–95; Archavanitkul, *Trafficking in Children for Labour Exploitation including Child Prostitution in the Mekong Subregion*; Skeldon, *Population Mobility and HIV Vulnerability in South East Asia*; Nguyen Thi Thanh Thuy et al., "HIV Infection and Risk Factors among Female Sex Workers in Southern Vietnam," *AIDS* 12,4 (March 5, 1998): 425–32; Nguyen Thi Thanh Thuy et al., "Sexual Risk Behavior of Women in Entertainment Services, Vietnam," *AIDS and Behavior* 4,1 (2000): 93–101; Joanna Busza and Bettina T. Schunter, "From Competition to Community: Participatory Learning and Action among Young, Debt-Bonded Vietnamese Sex Workers in Cambodia," *Reproductive Health Matters* 9,17 (May 2001): 72–81; Anne Clausen, "Female Labour Migration to Bangkok: Transforming Rural–Urban Interactions and Social Networks through Globalization," *Asia-Pacific Population Journal* 17,3 (2002): 53–78.

[42] Annuska Derks, *Trafficking of Cambodian Women and Children to Thailand* (Phnom Penh: International Organization for Migration and the Center for Advanced Study, 1997); Chris Beyrer and Julie Stachowiak, "Health Consequences of Trafficking of Women and Girls in Southeast Asia," *Brown Journal of World Affairs* (2003): 105–18; Clausen, "Female Labour Migration to Bangkok"; Kate Butcher, "Confusion between Prostitution and Sex Trafficking," *Lancet* 361,9373 (June 7, 2003): 1,983; Jini Roby and Jacob Tanner, "Supply and Demand: Prostitution and Sexual Trafficking in Northern Thailand," *Geography Compass* 3,1 (2009): 89–107.

[43] Terence H. Hull, Endang Sulistyaningsih, and Gavin W. Jones, *Prostitution in Indonesia: Its History and Evolution* (Jakarta: Pustaka Sinar Harapan, 1999); Ford and Koetsawang, *The Socio-*

Waves of rural villagers traveling back and forth between the countryside and major cities to work in a wide range of industries led to a distribution of HIV/AIDS within the region that followed major highway routes.[44] Population displacement and return related to political disruption within the region is also implicated in the spread of these diseases. HIV spread rapidly within Cambodia during the early 1990s with the surge of former refugees returning across the Thai-Cambodia border,[45] particularly within the provinces of Banteay Meanchey, Battambang, Koh Kong, and Siem Riep.[46] According to data from the National AIDS Programme, more than one-third of registered HIV/AIDS cases were found among migrants in the Philippines and Laos.[47] In Thailand, HIV infection rates among migrant fishermen is reported to be as high as 9 percent, while the overall HIV prevalence rate is less than 2 percent within the general adult population (Brahm Press 2008).[48] Antenatal-care

---

Cultural Context of the Transmission of HIV in Thailand, pp. 405–14; Archavanitkul and Guest, "Migration and the Commercial Sex Sector in Thailand"; Skeldon, "Population Mobility and HIV Vulnerability in South East Asia"; Muhadjir Darwin, Anna Marie Wattie, and Susi Eja Yuarsi, *Living on the Edges: Cross-Border Mobility and Sexual Exploitation in the Greater Southeast Asia Sub-Region* (Yogyakarta: Center for Population and Policy Studies, Gadjah Mada University, 2003); Larissa Sandy, "Sex Work in Cambodia: Beyond the Voluntary/Forced Dichotomy," *Asia and Pacific Migration Journal* 15,4 (2006): 449–70.

[44] Lee-Nah Hsu and Jacques Du Guerny, "Population Movement, Development, and HIV/AIDS: Looking towards the Future" (report from the UNDP South East Asia HIV and Development Project, 2000, pp. 1–7), available at www.hivpolicy.org/Library/HPP000872.pdf, accessed on April 2, 2012; Lee-Nah Hsu, "HIV Policy Formation and Strategic Planning for the Communication, Transportation, Post, Construction, and Tourism Sector—Lao People's Democratic Republic" (report from the UNDP South East Asia HIV and Development Project, compiled by Michelle Rodolph, October 2001, p. 28), available at www.hivpolicy.org/Library/HPP000090.pdf, accessed on April 2, 2012.

[45] Ryan et al., "Explosive Spread of HIV-1 and Sexually Transmitted Diseases in Cambodia"; Chantavanich et al., "Cross-Border Migration and HIV/AIDS"; P. M. Gorbach et al., "Changing Behaviors and Patterns among Cambodian Sex Workers: 1997–2003," *Journal of Acquired Immune Deficiency Syndromes* 42,2 (June 2006): 242–47.

[46] Ryan et al., "Explosive Spread of HIV-1 and Sexually Transmitted Diseases in Cambodia"; Lee-Nah Hsu, "Cambodia HIV Vulnerability Mapping: Highways One and Five" (report from National Centre for HIV/AIDS, Dermatology, and STD (Cambodia) and UNDP South East Asia HIV and Development Project, 2000), available at www.hivdevelopment.org/pdf_files/2000-01%20Cambodia%20HIV%20Vulnerability%20Mapping.pdf, accessed on April 2, 2012; J. Du Guerny, "Multisectoral Responses to Mobile Populations' HIV Vulnerability—Examples from People's Republic of China, Thailand, and Viet Nam: A Collection of Papers presented at a Special Session of the 6th Asia Pacific Social Sciences and Medicine Conference (Kunming, Yunnan, People's Republic of China)" (a report from the National Centre for HIV/AIDS, Dermatology, and STD [Cambodia] and UNDP South East Asia HIV and Development Project, 2000), available at www.hivdevelopment.org/pdf_files/2000-01%20Cambodia%20HIV%20Vulnerability%20Mapping.pdf, accessed on April 2, 2012; Tia Phalla, Hor Bun Leng, and Po Samnang, "Mapping HIV Vulnerability along Kampong Thom, Siem Reap, Odor Meanchey, and Preah Vihear, Cambodia," UNDP South East Asia HIV and Development Programme, March 2004, available at http://aidsdatahub.org/dmdocuments/Mapping2004_HIV_Vulnerability_Cambodia.pdf.pdf, accessed on April 2, 2012.

[47] UNDP, "HIV/AIDS and Mobility in South-East Asia: Rapid Assessment."

[48] Brahm Press, "Migrants' Health and Vulnerability to HIV/AIDS in Thailand," Report for the Prevention of HIV/AIDS among Migrant Workers in Thailand (PHAMIT) Project, Raks Thai Foundation, 2008, available at www.phamit.org/download/migrant_health_hiv_vuln_phamit.pdf, accessed on March 20, 2012.

data also reveal significantly higher HIV rates among migrant women relative to nonmigrants (UNDP 2008).[49]

Migration presents major obstacles for protection against the risk of HIV and other STIs among migrants in Southeast Asia, which further facilitates their spread. Migrants typically have considerably less access to STI services, condom supplies and information, education, and communication (IEC) programs targeted at HIV prevention.[50] For example, Burmese migrant factory workers and fishermen working in Thailand reported lower levels of knowledge about HIV and inconsistent condom usage relative to the general Thai population.[51] In addition, Vietnamese migrant women who worked in commercial sex settings in urban areas reported exposure to aggressive behaviors, physical violence, and forced sex, as well as a lack of personal power to negotiate condom use.[52]

Migration and General Health

International migration. Studies focusing on the physical health consequences of migration for international migrants from Asia have demonstrated a wide range of positive outcomes, including lower percentages of infants born with low birth weight, lower infant mortality, better self-reported physical health, and fewer reported health problems (except for tuberculosis and illnesses related to smoking) among Asian immigrants relative to their US-born counterparts.[53] National-level

---

[49] UNDP, "HIV/AIDS and Mobility in South-East Asia: Rapid Assessment."

[50] United Nations Joint Programme on Aids (UNAIDS) and International Organization for Migration, "Migration and AIDS: Abstract," *International Migration: Quarterly Review of the Intergovernmental Committee for European Migration* [Revue Trimestrielle Du Comité Intergouvernemental Pour Les Migrations Européennes: Publicación Trimestral Del Comite Intergubernamental (truncated)] 36,4 (1998): 445–68; S. K. Parida, "Sexually Transmitted Infections and Risk Exposure among HIV-positive Migrant Workers in Brunei Darussalam," in "Population Movement, Development, and HIV/AIDS: Looking towards the Future" (a report from the UNDP South East Asia HIV and Development Project, April 2000, pp. 26–32), available at www.hivdevelopment.org/pdf_files/2000-05%20Population%20Mobility%20in%20Asia%20.pdf, accessed on March 20, 2012; Skeldon, "Population Mobility and HIV Vulnerability in South East Asia"; Entz et al., "STD History, Self Treatment, and Healthcare Behaviours among Fishermen in the Gulf of Thailand and the Andaman Sea"; A. Chamratrithirong et al., "Prevention of HIV/AIDS among Migrant Workers in Thailand (PHAMIT) Project: The Baseline Survey" (Institute for Population and Social Research, Publication No. 297, Nakhon Pathom, Mahidol University, 2004); Thet Aung, Sathirakorn Pongpanich, and Mark G. Robson, "Health Seeking Behaviors among Myanmar Migrants Working in Ranong Province, Thailand," *Journal of Health Resource* 23, supplement (2009): 5–9.

[51] Supang Chantavanich and Shakti Paul, "Reproductive Health for Migrant Burmese Women in Ranong Fishing Community," *Development* 42,1 (1999): 73–74; K. Srithanavboonchai, "HIV Risk among Burmese Migrant Workers in Thailand"; L. C. Mullany, C. Maung, and C. Beyrer, "HIV/AIDS Knowledge, Attitudes, and Practices among Burmese Migrant Factory Workers in Tak Province, Thailand," *AIDS Care* 15,1 (2003): 63–70.

[52] Rosanne Rushing, Charlotte Watts, and Sharon Rushing, "Living the Reality of Forced Sex Work: Perspectives from Young Migrant Women Sex Workers in Northern Vietnam," *Journal of Midwifery & Women's Health* 50,4 (July–August 2005): e41–4.

[53] Nolan W. S. Zane, David Takeuchi, and Kathleen N. J. Young, *Confronting Critical Health Issues of Asian and Pacific Islander Americans* (Thousand Oaks, CA: Sage Publications, 1994); Rumbaut and Weeks, "Infant Mortality among Indochinese Refugees; Rumbaut and Weeks, "Unraveling a Public Health Enigma," pp. 337–91; W. Parker Frisbie, Youngtae Cho, and Robert A. Hummer, "Immigration and the Health of Asian and Pacific Islander Adults in the

analyses based on the 1992–1995 and 2004–2006 National Health Interview Survey (NHIS) have demonstrated further significant health advantages among Asian immigrants, for example, less activity limitation, fewer bed-days owing to illness, and better self-reported health.[54]

Unfortunately, these reported health advantages for Asian immigrants do not generally hold for most of the main immigrant groups coming from Southeast Asia, that is, Cambodian, Laotian, Hmong, and Vietnamese.[55] For example, results from the 2004–2006 NHIS show an overall lower cancer mortality rate among Asian Americans compared with the US general population, but a rate of cervical cancer among Vietnamese American women five times higher than that found among US non-Hispanic White women.[56] The prevalence of liver cancer is especially elevated among immigrants from Southeast Asia.[57] Health knowledge among Southeast Asian immigrants is lower than it is for other Asian American groups,[58] and Cambodian and Vietnamese immigrants were more than three times more likely to report not having visited a doctor because of the cost than were Asian Americans or members of the US general population.[59] Work-related injuries and illness are a major health hazard for migrants from Southeast Asian countries, particularly for undocumented migrant laborers, who often live in unhygienic, substandard living conditions and who often undertake dirty, dangerous, and demanding ("3-D") jobs that are left unfilled by local residents.[60]

United States," *American Journal of Epidemiology* 153,4 (February 15, 2001): 372–80; L. Franzini, J. C. Ribble, and A. M. Keddie, "Understanding the Hispanic Paradox," *Ethnicity & Disease* 11,3 (Autumn 2001): 496–518; David T. Takeuchi et al., "Immigration-Related Factors and Mental Disorders among Asian Americans," *American Journal of Public Health* 97,1 (January 2007): 84–90; Patricia M. Barnes et al., "Health Characteristics of the Asian Adult Population: United States, 2004–2006," CDC Advance Data from Vital and Health Statistics, Hyattsville, MD, National Center for Health Statistics, January 22, 2008, p. 394, available online at www.cdc.gov/nchs/data/ad/ad394.pdf, accessed on March 20, 2012.

[54] Frisbie, Cho, and Hummer, "Immigration and the Health of Asian and Pacific Islander Adults in the United States"; Barnes et al., "Health Characteristics of the Asian Adult Population: United States, 2004–2006."

[55] Steven J. Gold and Nazili Kibria, "Vietnamese Refugees and Mobility: Model Minority or New Underclass?" paper presented to the American Sociological Association, San Francisco, CA, August 1989; Stephen J. McPhee et al., "Behavioral Risk Factor Survey of Vietnamese–California, 1991," *MMWR Morbid Mortal Weekly Report* 41 (1992): 69–72; Frisbie, Cho, and Hummer, "Immigration and the Health of Asian and Pacific Islander Adults in the United States"; Barnes et al., "Health Characteristics of the Asian Adult Population: United States, 2004–2006."

[56] Barnes et al., "Health Characteristics of the Asian Adult Population: United States, 2004–2006."

[57] Ibid.

[58] Carey et al., "Tuberculosis Beliefs among Recent Vietnamese Refugees in New York State."

[59] Achintya N. Dey and Jacqueline Wilson Lucas, "Physical and Mental Health Characteristics of US- and Foreign-Born Adults: United States, 1998–2003," *Advance Data* 369 (March 1, 2006).

[60] M. Carangan, K. Y. Tham, and E. Seow, "Work-Related Injury Sustained by Foreign Workers in Singapore," *Annals of the Academy of Medicine, Singapore* 33,2 (March 2004): 209–13; Jessica R. Sincavage, "Fatal Occupational Injuries among Asian Workers," *Monthly Labor Review* 128 (2005): 49; Jatrana, Graham, and Boyle, "Introduction: Understanding Migration and Health in Asia"; Shigeru Tomita et al., "Prevalence and Risk Factors of Low Back Pain among Thai and Myanmar Migrant Seafood Processing Factory Workers in Samut Sakorn Province, Thailand," *Industrial Health* 48,3 (2010): 283–91.

Much of the research assessing the mental health consequences of international migration from Southeast Asia has focused on refugee populations originating from this region. Researchers have found a wide range of problems, including depression, stress, anxiety, psychiatric symptoms, and posttraumatic stress disorder (PTSD).[61] An analysis by Mina Fazel et al. suggests that refugees from Southeast Asia who have resettled in Western countries are as much as ten times more likely to experience PTSD than were age-matched general populations in their host countries.[62] Much of this refugee literature focuses on premigration trauma and difficult experiences in refugee camps.[63] Less attention has focused on problems related to postmigration adaptation and adjustment to the host environment. An exception is the study by Fran Norris, Mark VanLandingham, and Lung Vu, who report that among

---

[61] Keh-Ming Lin, Minoru Masuda, and Laurie Tazuma, "Problems of Eastern Refugees and Immigrants: Adaptational Problems of Vietnamese Refugees Part IV," *Psychiatric Journal of the University of Ottawa* [Revue De Psychiatrie De l'Universite d'Ottawa] 9,2 (June 1984): 79–84; Elizabeth Hiok-Boon Lin, Loren J. Ihle, and Laurie Tazuma, "Depression among Vietnamese Refugees in a Primary Care Clinic," *American Journal of Medicine* 78,1 (1985): 41–4; J. D. Kinzie et al., "An Indochinese Refugee Psychiatric Clinic: Culturally Accepted Treatment Approaches," *American Journal of Psychiatry* 137,11 (November 1980): 1429–32; David J. Kinzie et al., "The Prevalence of Posttraumatic Stress Disorder and its Clinical Significance among Southeast Asian Refugees," *American Journal of Psychiatry* 147,7 (1990): 913–17; Rumbaut and Weeks, "Infant Health among Indochinese Refugees"; Morton Beiser, "Influences of Time, Ethnicity, and Attachment on Depression in Southeast Asian Refugees," *American Journal of Psychiatry* 145,1 (January 1988): 46–51; Morton Beiser, R. Jay Turner, and Soma Ganesan, "Catastrophic Stress and Factors Affecting its Consequences among Southeast Asian Refugees," *Social Science & Medicine* 28,3 (1989): 183–95; Morton Beiser, Phyllis J. Johnson, and R. Jay Turner, "Unemployment, Underemployment, and Depressive Affect among Southeast Asian Refugees," *Psychological Medicine* 23,3 (August 1993): 731–43; Jerome Kroll et al., "Depression and Posttraumatic Stress Disorder in Southeast Asian Refugees," *American Journal of Psychiatry* 146,12 (December 1989): 1592–97; Dedra Buchwald et al., "Screening for Depression among Newly Arrived Vietnamese Refugees in Primary Care Settings," *The Western Journal of Medicine* 163,4 (October 1995): 341–45; Dedra Buchwald et al., "Prevalence of Depressive Symptoms among Established Vietnamese Refugees in the United States: Detection in a Primary Care Setting," *Journal of General Internal Medicine* 8,2 (February 1993): 76–81; Ladson W. Hinton et al., "DSM-III-R Disorders in Vietnamese Refugees: Prevalence and Correlates," *Journal of Nervous and Mental Disease* 181,2 (February 1993): 113–22; Ladson W. Hinton et al., "Screening for Major Depression in Vietnamese Refugees: A Validation and Comparison of Two Instruments in a Health Screening Population," *Journal of General Internal Medicine* 9,4 (1994): 202–6; W. L. Hinton et al., "Predictors of Depression among Refugees from Vietnam: A Longitudinal Study of New Arrivals," *Journal of Nervous and Mental Disease* 185,1 (1997): 39–45; Nelson, Bui, and Samet, "Screening in Special Populations: A 'Case Study' of Recent Vietnamese Immigrants"; Rita Chi-Ying Chung, Fred Bemak, and Sandra Wong, "Vietnamese Refugees' Levels of Distress, Social Support, and Acculturation: Implications for Mental Health Counseling," *Journal of Mental Health Counseling* 22,2 (2000): 150–61; Y'Lang T. Dong and Timothy Church, "Cross-Cultural Equivalence and Validity of the Vietnamese MMPI-2: Assessing Psychological Adjustment of Vietnamese Refugees," *Psychological Assessment* 15,3 (September 2003): 370–77.

[62] Mina Fazel, Jeremy Wheeler, and John Danesh, "Prevalence of Serious Mental Disorder in 7,000 Refugees Resettled in Western Countries: A Systematic Review," *Lancet* 365 (2005):1309–14.

[63] Rita Chi-Ying Chung and Marjorie Kagawa-Singer, "Predictors of Psychological Distress among Southeast Asian Refugees," *Social Science & Medicine* 36,5 (March 1993): 631–39; Ladson W. Hinton et al., "Predictors of Depression among Refugees from Vietnam"; David J. Kinzie et al., "The Prevalence of Posttraumatic Stress Disorder and its Clinical Significance among Southeast Asian Refugees"; Chung and Kagawa-Singer, "Predictors of Psychological Distress among Southeast Asian Refugees."

Vietnamese immigrants living in post-Katrina New Orleans, those who had experienced extended stays in refugee camps before coming to the United States fared worse on PTSD-related mental health outcomes after Katrina than did those experiencing shorter stays in the camps.[64]

Not all of the results related to mental health are negative. The risk of anxiety and mood disorders among Vietnamese refugees living in Australia is only one-third that of the host population;[65] the overall burden of mental illness among Vietnamese Australians is lower than that found in the general population as well.[66] In North America, immigrants from Vietnam have a generally better mental health status than either immigrant Chinese or mainstream Canadians.[67] Similar findings are reported more recently by David T. Takeuchi et al.: immigrant women from Asia suffer less lifetime depressive, anxiety, substance abuse, and psychiatric disorders than do US-born women, and Vietnamese immigrant women are less likely to suffer any lifetime depression than are Chinese immigrant women.[68] In the study by Norris and coauthors, cited above, Vietnamese Americans had only about one-sixth the prevalence of PTSD compared to the more general population affected by Hurricane Katrina.

Studies comparing emigrants from Southeast Asia to nationals in their respective countries of origin are more rare. Peter Kunstadter, in a comparison of Hmong living in California with Hmong living in Thailand, finds much higher rates of self-reported illness, high blood pressure, fevers of unknown origin, diabetes, and depression among the Hmong Americans.[69]

Steven Stillman et al. attempt to overcome the problem of selection effects by comparing mental health data for winners of a migration lottery who subsequently migrated from Tonga to New Zealand with the comparable data for those who applied for the same lottery but were not selected. Winners were also compared with those who did not apply for the migration lottery.[70] The study identifies important roles for both selection and for migration processes per se. In another attempt to

---

[64] Fran H. Norris, Mark J. Vanlandingham, and Lung Vu, "PTSD in Vietnamese Americans following Hurricane Katrina: Prevalence, Patterns, and Predictors," *Journal of Traumatic Stress* 22,2 (April 2009): 91–101.

[65] Zachary Steel et al., "Long-Term Effect of Psychological Trauma on the Mental Health of Vietnamese Refugees Resettled in Australia: A Population-Based Study," *Lancet* 360,9339 (2002): 1056–62; Zachary Steel et al., "Mental Disorders, Disability, and Health Service use amongst Vietnamese Refugees and the Host Australian Population," *Acta Psychiatrica Scandinavica* 111,4 (April 2005): 300–309.

[66] Derrick Silove et al., "Trauma, PTSD, and the Longer-Term Mental Health Burden amongst Vietnamese Refugees: A Comparison with the Australian-Born Population," *Social Psychiatry and Psychiatric Epidemiology* 42,6 (June 2007): 467–76.

[67] G. M. Devins et al., "Cross-Cultural Measurements of Psychological Well-being: The Psychometric Equivalence of Cantonese, Vietnamese, and Laotian Translations of the Affect Balance Scale," *American Journal of Public Health* 87,5 (May 1997): 794–99.

[68] Takeuchi et al., "Immigration-Related Factors and Mental Disorders among Asian Americans."

[69] Peter Kunstadter, "Health Implications of Globalization at the Village Level—The Good, the Bad, and the Ugly: Some Results of Comparative Research in Thailand and the US" (paper presented at the Woodrow Wilson School of International Studies, Princeton, NJ, Princeton University, March 12, 2001).

[70] Stillman, McKenzie, and Gibson, "Migration and Mental Health: Evidence from a Natural Experiment."

minimize selection-related threats to validity inherent in cross-sectional research designs, Hongyun Fu and Mark VanLandingham[71] also employ a natural experiment approach that involves comparisons among three population-based Vietnamese samples: Vietnamese immigrants living in an urban US setting; Vietnamese nationals who never attempted to emigrate living in an urban Vietnam setting; and Vietnamese nationals who attempted to emigrate to the West but were repatriated (returnees) who live in the same urban wards in Vietnam as those who never attempted to leave. Threats to validity due to selection are minimized since the returnees should possess the same set of a priori characteristics that predispose an individual to emigrate as do those who actually emigrated.

This study finds better outcomes on self-reported general physical heath among immigrants relative to both migration returnees and Vietnamese nationals who never migrated living in Vietnam.[72] However, levels of body mass index (BMI), waist-hip ratio, and risks for being overweight among immigrants were remarkably higher among Vietnamese immigrants relative to the two comparison groups living in Vietnam.[73] This same study also finds mixed consequences of international migration for the mental health of Vietnamese Americans. Immigrants are disadvantaged (worse off) relative to both never-leavers and returnees with respect to vitality, energy and fatigue, and waist-hip ratio. However, they are advantaged (better-off) relative to never-leavers and returnees when one measures whether they have experienced role limitations due to emotional problems.[74] The authors attribute this pattern of mental health results to a "John Henry" effect, that is, incessant exertion required to overcome structural barriers, eventually resulting in negative health consequences.[75] While cultural attributes emphasizing strife, role fulfillment, and self-denial may lead to successful economic outcomes for Vietnamese immigrants in their new home,[76] these attributes may also take a toll on health and well-being,[77] specifically in the dimension of their vitality, energy, and fatigue. Nevertheless, in spite of living in a foreign and stressful environment, Vietnamese Americans meet (and even exceed) the challenge of fulfilling their social obligations, that is, they

[71] Hongyun Fu and Mark VanLandingham, "Disentangling the Effects of Migration, Selection, and Acculturation on Weight and Body Fat Distribution: Results from a Natural Experiment Involving Vietnamese Americans, Returnees, and Never-Leavers," *Journal of Immigrant and Minority Health,* available online on March 17, 2012, DOI 10.1007/s10903-012-9595-5.

[72] Hongyun Fu and Mark VanLandingham, "Mental Health Consequences of International Migration for Vietnamese Americans and the Mediating Effect of Social Networks: Results from a Natural Experiment Approach," *Demography* 49,2 (May 2012): 393–424.

[73] Fu and VanLandingham, "Disentangling the Effects of Migration, Selection, and Acculturation on Weight and Body Fat Distribution."

[74] Fu and VanLandingham, "Mental Health Consequences of International Migration for Vietnamese Americans and the Mediating Effect of Social Networks."

[75] Sherman A. James, Sue A. Hartnett, and William D. Kalsbeek, "John Henryism and Blood Pressure Differences among Black Men," *Journal of Behavioral Medicine* 6,3 (September 1983): 259–78; Harold W. Neighbors, Rashid Njai, and James S. Jackson, "Race, Ethnicity, John Henryism, and Depressive Symptoms: The National Survey of American Life Adult Reinterview," *Research in Human Development* 4,1–2 (2007): 71–87.

[76] Zhou and Bankston, *Growing Up American.*

[77] Jana Haritatos, Ramaswami Mahalingam, and Sherman A. James, "John Henryism, Self-Reported Physical Health Indicators, and the Mediating Role of Perceived Stress among High Socio-Economic Status Asian Immigrants," *Social Science & Medicine* 64,6 (March 2007): 1192–1203.

demonstrate generally better outcomes on the health dimension, "role limitations due to emotional problems." Nonfulfillment of role obligations is simply not an option in this community, albeit perhaps these obligations take a significant toll on health, as manifested in the negative health outcomes described above.

Internal migration. The consequences of internal migration for general health among Southeast Asians is an extremely understudied area. The lack of attention to national, as opposed to international, migration with regard to physical health status is due, in part, to prevailing assumptions emphasizing the benefits of migration for individual migrants and their families rather than the potential negative consequences. It is also commonly assumed that the characteristics of migrant destinations will differ less from characteristics at origin for internal migrants compared with international migrants. Of course, challenges imposed by cross-sectional research designs hamper studies of the effects of national migration in ways that resemble challenges impeding studies of international migrants. Nevertheless, because of the difficulties involved in tracking migrants over time, most studies that examine health differences between those who migrate within a country's borders and those who do not are limited to cross-sectional research designs.

These cross-sectional analyses of internal migration and well-being have yielded inconsistent results. In Thailand, Gordon De Jong et al. found that migration was associated with decreased postmove satisfaction among working-age migrants who had relocated recently.[78] In Vietnam, Mark VanLandingham found significant disadvantages for recent migrants compared to long-term residents in Ho Chi Minh City on the outcomes of physical functioning, bodily pain, general health perceptions, general mental health, role limitations due to emotional problems, and role limitations due to physical health problems.[79] A different study of internal Vietnamese migrants found that temporary migrants were more likely to have reported sick during the three months prior to the survey, relative to both longer-term migrants and nonmigrants in urban areas.[80] However, the short-term migrants reported a lower probability of reporting sick during the year prior to the survey, suggesting a healthy migrant effect. Results from the 2004 Vietnam migration survey also suggest a healthy migrant effect, with migrants reporting better health status even while being disadvantaged with regard to access to health care services.[81]

Analysis of longitudinal data collected recently in both Indonesia and Thailand provides compelling evidence of a substantial "healthy migrant" effect. Employing data from two waves of the Indonesia Family Life Survey, Yao Lu reports a high

---

[78] Gordon F. De Jong, Aphichat Chamratrithirong, and Quynh-Giang Tran, "For Better, for Worse: Life Satisfaction Consequences of Migration," *International Migration Review* 36,3 (2002): 838–63.

[79] Mark VanLandingham, "Impacts of Rural to Urban Migration on the Health of Young Adult Migrants in Ho Chi Minh City, Vietnam," in *Urbanization, Migration, and Poverty in a Vietnamese Metropolis: Ho Chi Minh City in Comparative Perspective*, ed. Hy V. Luong (Honolulu, Hawaii: University of Hawaii Press, 2009).

[80] Liem T. Nguyen and Michael J. White, "Health Status of Temporary Migrants in Urban Areas in Vietnam," *International Migration* 45,4 (2007): 101–34.

[81] Patrick Gubry et al., "Temporary Migration in Big Vietnam Cities: Hanoi and Ho Chi Minh City," in *The Summary Record of the PRUD's International Conference* (Paris: Department of International Cooperation and Development, 2007), pp. 92–97; Tổng cục thống ke, *The 2004 Vietnam Migration Survey: Migration and Health* (Hanoi: General Statistical Office and United Nations Population Fund, 2006), available at http://countryoffice.unfpa.org/vietnam/drive/MigrationandHealth_GSO1206_e.pdf, accessed on March 20, 2012.

likelihood of migration (mainly for employment purposes) among younger people.[82] Those who eventually went on to migrate initially had a lower likelihood of chronic health problems or physical inability than did those who did not migrate. In contrast, older persons who migrate often do so for health-related reasons—for example, to seek treatment of illness or to live with family members. Thus, selection favors the migration of less healthy individuals among the elderly. Elizabeth Nauman et al. analyze data from a long-standing demographic surveillance system in Kanchanaburi, Thailand, and also find that young adults who decide to migrate enjoy better physical health status before they move compared with those who decide to remain.[83] Both those who migrated to urban areas during this period and those who did not experienced slight declines in physical health status between the 2005 and 2007 waves of data collection. These declines were no worse for the migrants than they were for the nonmigrants. For mental health, the picture is very different: individuals who migrated between the 2005 and 2007 waves had worse mental health status before their eventual move than did their rural counterparts who did not move. But among those who moved, the improvement in mental health status was great enough during the two years to erase the initial disadvantage that the eventual movers faced relative to those who stayed behind.[84] A longitudinal framework was essential for discerning the actual effects of a major move, which would have been obscured by selection effects in a cross-sectional analysis of the same data.

SUMMARY AND A PROPOSED RESEARCH AGENDA

As Graeme Hugo describes in his accompanying chapter in this volume, migration throughout the Southeast Asia region is extensive and has a wide range of consequences for places of origin, places of destination, the families of migrants, and the migrants themselves.[85] One set of consequences that has received insufficient empirical investigation concerns the impacts of migration upon the health of those who migrate. In this paper, we have highlighted some significant findings from this literature, along with major substantive and methodological shortcomings. In this final section, we summarize these findings and suggest some strategies for moving the field forward.

The impacts of international migration for Southeast Asians who move to the West are mixed. Surely much of this variation in health outcomes is due to the vast range of circumstances under which migration occurs. Nevertheless, some generalities emerge. Consistent findings of better physical health among immigrants from Southeast Asia—relative to a broad range of reference groups—are evident in many studies. This general finding is consistent with research focusing on immigrants from other developing regions of the world. Advantages in physical health for migrants from Southeast Asia to the West are surely due, in part, to the

---

[82] Lu, "Test of the 'Healthy Migrant Hypothesis.'"

[83] Elizabeth Nauman et al., "Rural-to-Urban Moves and Changes in Health Status among Young Thai Migrants: Distinguishing "True" Migration Effects from Selection Factors and Secular Change" (poster presentation at the annual meeting of the Population Association of America, Dallas, Texas, April 2010).

[84] Ibid.

[85] Hugo, "The Future of Migration Policy in the Asia–Pacific Region."

higher levels of affluence that many migrants experience at destination compared to place of origin. However, alarming indicators for overweight status among Vietnamese immigrants relative to nationals suggest that some of these benefits of migration with regard to physical health may be short-lived. As recent Southeast Asian immigrants spend more time in Western cultures, they may lose some of their health advantages as they acculturate to Western diets and lifestyles, much as Japanese and Samoan immigrants did before them.[86]

Given the vast differences in culture between the sending and destination environments, findings of problematic mental health status among Southeast Asian immigrants living in the West are also understandable. In fact, such problems are anticipated by early qualitative volumes focusing on the adaptation process.[87] Western society, with its emphasis on individuality vis-à-vis the family and social group, is clearly alienating for many Southeast Asian immigrants as they struggle to retain and instill key characteristics of their home culture within their families. That many immigrants from the region—the Vietnamese in particular—are able to do so appears to be a key source of resilience in the face of adversity.[88]

Potentially confounding effects of selection loom large in this literature: migrants do not constitute a random sample of the populations in their countries of origin or destination, but rather consist of those people who either choose to or are compelled to move. Both the positive and negative effects of international migration summarized above are likely due, in part, to premigration differences between those who eventually decide to migrate and those who do not. Specifically, migrants are thought by many to be pre-selected for good physical health (the healthy migrant syndrome), since it is unlikely that those who are frail will choose to undertake the hardships that migration entails. Similarly, those who are dissatisfied with their situation at origin may be the most motivated to move. Convenience samples and even representative cross-sectional samples that employ data collected "after the fact" (post-migration) are particularly susceptible to selection bias, since selection factors co-occur ipso facto with the events of interest, that is, with migration and with health status. This is likely a key reason for the inconsistent findings from research focused on internal migration, for such research is based largely upon cross-sectional analyses that compare the health status of individuals who have recently moved to a destination with that of longer-term residents. Moving this important body of literature forward will require the application of state-of-the-art longitudinal analyses that are able to take into account key pre-migration characteristics that may be associated with both migration and health status along with postmigration measures of health. Where this is implausible because of ethical, monetary, or logistical constraints, innovative use of natural experiment designs should be

---

[86] Abraham Kagan et al., "Epidemiologic Studies of Coronary Heart Disease and Stroke in Japanese Men Living in Japan, Hawaii, and California: Demographic, Physical, Dietary, and Biochemical Characteristics," *Journal of Chronic Diseases* 27,7–8 (September 1974): 345–64; Stephen T. McGarvey, "Cardiovascular Disease (CVD) Risk Factors in Samoa and American Samoa, 1990–1995," *Pacific Health Dialogue* 8,1 (2011): 157–62.

[87] Nazli Kibria, *Family Tightrope: The Changing Lives of Vietnamese Americans* (Princeton, N.J.: Princeton University Press, 1993); Robert Olen Butler, *A Good Scent from a Strange Mountain: Stories* (New York, NY: H. Holt, 1992).

[88] Zhou and Bankston, *Growing Up American*; L. Vu et al., "Evacuation and Return of Vietnamese New Orleanians Affected by Hurricane Katrina," *Organization & Environment* 22,4 (December 1, 2009): 422–36.

employed to overcome at least some of the inherent biases that currently plague studies that attempt to discern the health (and other) consequences of migration. A second methodological step forward involves the incorporation of physical biomarker data into studies of health status. Vast improvements in the affordability, reliability, and logistics of collecting these measures have occurred in recent years, particularly for the large-scale collection of blood-based biomarkers.

From a theoretical point of view, more investment is needed in frameworks that help to predict and explain why migrants enjoy better health status on some outcomes and in some circumstances, but suffer deficiencies on other outcomes and in other settings. Much of the research to date has been more descriptive than explanatory. Substantive topics that require more attention include the health impacts of migration for the large numbers of Southeast Asians migrating to the Middle East for temporary work, as well as for the armies of domestic workers from the region who move to live and work in societies that are very different from home.

CHAPTER 7

POPULATION AND ENVIRONMENT IN SOUTHEAST ASIA: COMPLEX DYNAMICS AND TRENDS

Sara R. Curran and Noah Derman

Southeast Asia encompasses a wide array of natural resource endowments, from abundant fisheries and beautiful coastlines to rivers and floodplains, sustaining agro-ecosystems, as well as tropical and semitropical forests found from low to high elevations. Both mainland and island Southeast Asian communities and nations have benefited from these natural resource endowments. These same communities and nations have also effected significant degradation across all kinds of environments and diminished the amount and quality of environmental services provided from the soils, waters, air, forests, coral reefs, estuaries, and species biodiversity. At the same time, climate change and environmental deterioration also present significant challenges to human populations, especially their health and well-being. The more pessimistic outlook about environmental and population futures in the region is somewhat tempered by the region's remarkable and observable human and ecological resilience.

Although Southeast Asia occupies only 3 percent of the world's total surface, 20 percent of all known species live in its mountains, jungles, rivers, lakes, and seas.[1] In addition, the region is home to three of the world's seventeen "megadiverse" countries—Indonesia, Malaysia, and the Philipines—and has seven of the world's thirty-five recognized biodiversity hotspots.[2] Southeast Asia has one-third, or 284,000 square kilometers, of the globe's coral reefs, which are among the most diverse in the world. In addition, common land and water borders have allowed Southeast Asian countries to support many species that are biologically distinct from species in other regions of the world.

---

[1] ASEAN (Association of Southeast Asian Nations), "ASEAN State of the Environment," in *ASOE Report* (Jakarta: ASEAN Secretariat, 2006), http://ekh.unep.org/files/ASEAN.pdf.

[2] Ibid.

Given the diversity of ecologies and resource endowments, the region's population-environment trends cannot be adequately described in a single chapter. This chapter provides a simple overview of some of the population–environment relationships, suggesting that these relationships are dynamic, reciprocal, and highly variable. The review begins with those studies that have shown how resource-rich environmental conditions influenced human adaptation, particularly population growth and expansion of settlements. The second part of the review shows how subsequent population dynamics and human drivers have affected environmental change, primarily environmental deterioration. The third part of the review shows how more recent environmental deterioration and global warming related climate and weather events do and will influence population morbidity and mobility.

Figure 1
Population and Environment Dynamics
(and showing how this chapter is organized)

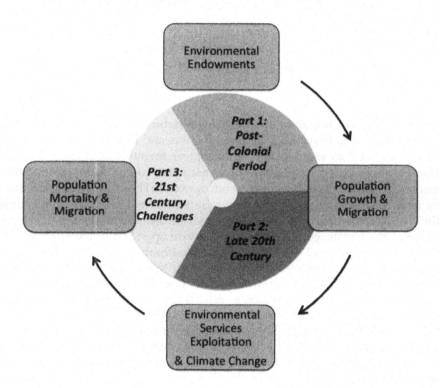

The review relies on existing empirical literature, which has shifted focus over time. Research about population trends during the late colonial and post-colonial period focuses primarily upon how natural resource endowments influenced population growth. Later research focuses upon how population growth, population density, and migration have had an impact on the quality and quantity of environmental endowments and services. And much of this scientific effort corresponds to evidence collected during the late 1980s through early 2000s. Finally, the most recent research focuses on how deteriorating environmental conditions can influence human health and on how climate change may influence human population mobility, settlements, and morbidity. The patterning of scientific investigation mirrors the historical progression of human–environment interactions in the region. Figure 1 offers a schematic overview of the theorized dynamic relationship between population and environment as described and organized in this chapter.

As with most scientific work on population–environment dynamics, intervening institutions such as markets, governments, and social and cultural organizations that regulate particular forms of consumption or production are frequently identified as critical and necessary to explain outcomes on either side of the dynamic. These are identified throughout the chapter.

A preponderance of research about the region focuses upon the human impacts on environmental endowments. Much less work focuses upon how environmental conditions influence the components of population growth and structure. Generally, research in the region and field is cross-national, descriptively comparative, case-based, or evaluates evidence from clinical samples. Where there have been quantitative assessments of generalizable or population-based samples, this chapter highlights those results.

The evidence presented is limited by the countries or cases that have been examined and the subquestions that have been explored within the field. Insofar as demographic factors have been included in studies of environmental conditions comparing countries throughout the region, the assessed relationship is rarely evaluated statistically or even causally. Furthermore, the factors included in any case study are context dependent and generally not consistent across place. This makes it difficult to generalize about patterns and trends. Finally, the countries that have received the most empirical attention are those that have large populations, rich natural resource endowments, a capacity to provide national and regional data on both population and environment variables, or a policy environment and institutional capacity to invest in collaborative, interdisciplinary research country-wide. These countries are Indonesia, the Philippines, Thailand, and, to a lesser extent, Vietnam and Malaysia.

PART 1: POST-COLONIAL PERIOD—ENVIRONMENTAL ENDOWMENTS INFLUENCE POPULATION GROWTH AND MIGRATION

In this section, the review focuses on how environmental conditions had an impact on population trends in Southeast Asia historically through the early post-colonial period. For the most part, the wealth of resource endowments encouraged population growth via fertility, migration, and lower mortality. These associated patterns were facilitated, or mediated, by political interests related to post-colonial initiatives to establish national boundaries and intensive investments in agricultural technology in order to improve yields for both food security and export markets.

For the centuries preceding the post-colonial period, the geography of Southeast Asia, on the one hand, encouraged populations to migrate and mix with other communities and cultures and, on the other hand, allowed isolated populations to flourish in remote mountain valleys. Historically, land- and marine-based ecologies in Southeast Asia have always had a large carrying capacity and were conducive to population growth, given the abundance of natural resources. A large variety of natural resources exists in Southeast Asia, with substantial variation across countries.[3] Early Southeast Asian settlements had vast and productive land available to them. For example, as most historians and archeologists agree, the transition from upland, shifting cultivation to settled, lowland rice cultivation is most likely due to agricultural innovations and the supporting physical environment, not to population pressure.[4]

The plethora of waterways and ocean ports allowed for migration of populations and trade of goods and resources among populations in coastal areas and river basins. The unifying influence of the sea was reflected in the emergence of extensive maritime kingdoms (throughout present-day Indonesia), while on mainland Southeast Asia, kingdoms were each confined largely to a single major river basin.[5] As in other regions of the world, the accessibility to ports and trade helped create the large urban centers and major megacities in Southeast Asia: Manila, Jakarta, Singapore, Bangkok, Ho Chi Minh City, and Kuala Lumpur.

In the steep, mountainous areas of Southeast Asia, isolated populations were able to flourish, as evident in the large diversity of cultures and languages in the highlands. The spectacular, scenic mountain regions are home to a multitude of linguistically diverse peoples who were able to establish complex cultivation systems to produce a variety of food crops.[6] Currently, ethnic minorities still mainly inhabit these mountainous areas. For example, in the highlands of Vietnam, there are fifty-three ethnic groups, about 1.2 million people claiming to be nonpermanent residents, who depend directly on the use of forest resources and subsistence farming.[7] Similar statistics can also be claimed for Thailand, Indonesia, and the Philippines. The wealth of the natural environment allowed these communities to flourish and persist, despite significant political, social, and health-related incursions that challenged their existence.

Population growth since the post-colonial period in Southeast Asia was unique and of specific demographic interest because of how quickly multiple small populations became demographic giants (see Hirschman and Bonaparte, this volume). Southeast Asian growth rates were significantly higher than the growth rates of countries at comparable stages of development.[8] The reasons stipulated for the rapid population increase include reduced warfare among competing indigenous elites, preventative measures against disease and curative medicine, and an overall increase in improved living conditions, mostly from permanent settlements afforded by the varied landscapes' ecological capacity to support that growth. Whereas in 1950 the region included 7.2 percent of the world's population, by 2008 Southeast

---

[3] R. Hill, *Southeast Asia: People, Land and Economy* (New York, NY: Allen and Unwin, 2002).

[4] N. Tarling, *The Cambridge History of Southeast Asia: From Early Times to circa 1800* (Cambridge: Cambridge University Press, 1992).

[5] Hill, *Southeast Asia: People, Land and Economy.*

[6] R. A. Cramb, "Farmers' Strategies for Managing Acid Upland Soils in Southeast Asia: An Evolutionary Perspective," *Agriculture, Ecosystems and Environment* 106 (2005): 69–87.

[7] T. Gomeiro, D. Peitinella, G. P. Trieu, et al., "Vietnamese Uplands: Environmental and Socio-economic Perspective of Forest Land Allocation and Deforestation Process," *Environment, Development and Sustainability* 2 (2000): 119–42.

[8] C. Hirschman, "Population and Society in Twentieth-Century Southeast Asia," *Journal of Southeast Asian Studies* 25 (1994): 381–416.

Asia included 11.4 percent of the world's population, with much of the growth in the population occurring between 1950 and 1990.[9]

From the post-colonial period onward, governmental policy decisions have notably influenced both the environment and population. During this time, nation building was paramount, and each nation's natural resource endowments and population growth were seen as assets for extending, asserting, and defining national boundaries. Many of the Southeast Asian nations articulated explicit needs to secure their autonomy and establish their boundaries and settlements. While there are very complex geo-political issues involved,[10] the most relevant for environment–population patterns is the encouragement of frontier settlement. The combination of population growth, national leaders' willingness to respond to citizens' needs, and the availability of land for cultivation provided a unique mix of imperatives that converged and supported policy initiatives that encouraged frontier development.[11] From 1950 through the 1970s, various national governments in Indonesia, Malaysia, the Philippines, and Thailand variously implemented programs to strongly influence (sometimes forcibly) the settlement of frontier regions.[12]

In many ways, the Philippines was in the vanguard in this endeavor, with the National Land Settlement Act of 1939 (NLSA). However, the NLSA was not a significant program in the government budget until after 1950, when the act was used, at first, to justify significant land pioneering as part of a counter-insurgency effort and, then, as an essential element of an agrarian reform movement.[13] In Indonesia, after the war of independence (1945–1949), government officials created the Transmigration Program to relieve population pressures and establish a national presence on remote, resource-endowed islands. The Transmigration Program became increasingly important in the context of a country trying to unify a nation after years of turmoil. For example, in the early 1950s many of the demobilized soldiers of the republican army were given land to cultivate in the province of Lampung, which was at that time still the major pioneering area of Indonesia.[14] The Transmigration Program continued through the 1960s and 1970s, reemerging as a response to rapid rates of population growth and uneven population distribution in Indonesia.[15] During the height of the government's efforts to direct transmigration,

---

[9] Population Reference Bureau, *World Population Data Sheet* (Washington, DC: Population Reference Bureau, http://www.prb.org/Publications/Datasheets/2008/2008wpds.aspx (accessed February 10, 2009).

[10] V. L. Forbes, "Geopolitical Change: Direction and Continuing Issues," in *Southeast Asia Transformed*, ed. L. S. Chia (Singapore: Institute of Southeast Asia, 2003).

[11] T. R. Leinbach, "The Transmigration Program in Indonesia National Development Strategy: Current Status and Future Requirements," *Habitat International* 13,3 (1999): 81-95.

[12] R. DeKoninck, "Southeast Asian Agriculture Post-1960: Economic and territorial expansion," in *Southeast Asia Transformed*, ed. L. S. Chia (Singapore: Institute of Southeast Asian Studies, 2003); G. Hart, A. Turton, and B. White. *Agrarian Transformations: Local Processes and the State in Southeast Asia* (Berkeley: University of California Press, 1989); Leinbach, "The Transmigration Program in Indonesia National Development Strategy."

[13] DeKoninck, "Southeast Asian Agriculture Post-1960."

[14] R. DeKoninck and S. Dery, "Agricultural Expansion as a Tool of Population Redistribution in Southeast Asia," *Journal of Southeast Asian Studies* 28 (1987): 1–26; DeKoninck, "Southeast Asian Agriculture Post-1960."

[15] P.M. Fearnside, "Transmigration in Indonesia: Lessons From Its Environmental and Social Impacts," *Environmental Management* 21 (1997): 553–70.

by some estimates, the program moved approximately half a million people per year from the densely settled islands of Java and Bali, in particular, to sparsely settled areas in Sumatra, Kalimantan, and Irian Jaya.[16]

Similar approaches were taken by Thailand in the late 1960s.[17] And in Malaysia, the Federal Land Development Authority (FELDA) served as a policy tool to create a safety valve against agrarian problems linked to inadequate and inequitable land distribution.[18] Although much of this land development was also driven by efforts to develop export markets in rubber and palm oil, it resulted in significant redistribution of population and contributed to overall national population growth.[19]

Finally, by the end of the 1970s, extensive investments in agricultural intensification throughout Southeast Asia led to improved yields of rice, especially, but also of many other lowland and upland crops, including maize, root crops, and fruits. Intensification efforts included the development of new seeds, as well as the application of synthetic fertilizers and pesticides. The resulting increased yields improved nutrition and food security, supporting growing populations. Table 1 summarizes some of these trends in agricultural intensification, especially during the 1970s. For example, from 1970 through the 1980s, Indonesia was able to double its average yields, and Malaysia was able to achieve self-sufficiency in rice production.[20] While increased production served to improve food security in most nations, the yields were far greater than necessary to feed the population, and, subsequently, much was exported to satisfy a growing world market demand.[21] The growth in surplus revenues via export markets served to increase national incomes and underwrite subsequent investments in industrialization initiatives during the 1980s.

The combination of stabilized political conditions, increased investment in agricultural land development, and improved health care led to population growth. Annual population growth for most countries in the region during this period are 2 percent or more, with more remote regions in Indonesia and Malaysia approaching 3 percent or more.[22] Table 1 provides some evidence for how natural resource

---

[16] N. Sastry, "Forest Fires, Air Pollution, and Mortality in Southeast Asia," *Demography* 39 (2002): 1–24.

[17] K. Bowie, *Rituals of National Loyalty: An Anthropology of the State and the Village Scout Movement in Thailand* (New York, NY: Columbia University Press, 1997); P. Hirsch, *The Politics of Environment in Southeast Asia: Resources and Resistance* (London: Routledge, 2002); H. Uhlig, *Spontaneous and Planned Settlement in Southeast Asia: Forest Clearing and Recent Pioneer Colonization in the ASEAN Countries and Two Case Studies on Thailand* (Hamburg: Institute of Asian Affairs, 1983).

[18] C. MacAndrews, *Mobility and Modernization: The Federal Land Development Authority and Its Role in Modernizing Rural Malay* (Master's thesis, Massachusetts Institute of Technology, 1976); J. McMorrow and M. A. Talip, "Decline of Forest Area in Sabah, Malaysia: Relationship to State Policies, Land Code, and Land Capability," *Global Environmental Change* 11,3 (2001): 217–30; B. Shamsul and B. Lee, *FELDA: Three Decades of Evolution* (Kuala Lumpur: Federal Land Development Authority, 1998); R. Wikkramatileke, "Federal Land Development Authority in West Malaysia 1957–1971," *Pacific Viewpoint* (1972): 62–86.

[19] T. K. Bahren, *Land Settlement in Malaysia: A Case Study of the Federal Land Development Authority Projects* (Rome: AGRIS, Food and Agriculture Organization, 1988); MacAndrews, *Mobility and Modernization*.

[20] DeKoninck, "Southeast Asian Agriculture Post-1960."

[21] C. L. Sien, *Southeast Asia Transformed: A Geography of Change.* (Singapore: Institute of Southeast Asian Studies, 2003).

[22] Hirschman, "Population and Society in Twentieth-Century Southeast Asia."

abundance and capacity through the expansion of land use for agricultural purposes—intensification through improved yields per unit farmed—are associated with subsequent increases in population size over similar time periods for selected countries in Southeast Asia. The role of natural resources endowments in accelerating population growth also follows an indirect pathway, as it is the natural resource endowments that facilitated growing state capacity to harness technology, extend boundaries, and provide for citizens.

Table 1

Patterns of Rice Paddy Growth and Productivity and Population Size

	Time Period	Paddy Area Harvested (ha)	Paddy Yields (kg/ha)	Population Size	
				Date	Census (millions)
Myanmar	1959–61	4,083,000	1,657	1963	22.5
	1974–76	5,044,000	1,791	1973	28.5
				1983	35.0
Cambodia	1959–61	1,328,000	1,047	1963	5.8
	1974–76	1,002,000	1,286	1975	7.6
				NA	NA
Indonesia	1959–61	7,144,000	1,737	1960	97.0
	1974–76	8,465,000	2,687	1971	119.2
				1980	147.5
Malaysia	1959–61	516,000	1,984	1970	10.4
	1974–76	741,000	2,737	1980	13.7
Philippines	1959–61	3,278,000	1,133	1960	27.1
	1974–76	3,572,000	1,713	1970	36.7
				1980	48.1
Thailand	1959–61	5,333,000	1,380	1960	26.3
	1974–76	8,012,000	1,820	1970	34.4
				1980	44.8

Note: Data for Laos and Vietnam are not available for the periods shown here.

Adapted from R. DeKoninck, "Southeast Asian Agriculture Post-1960: Economic and territorial expansion," Table 5.1; and C. Hirschman, "Population and Society in Twentieth-Century Southeast Asia," Table 1.

PART 2: LATE TWENTIETH CENTURY—POPULATION-DRIVEN EXPLOITATION OF ENVIRONMENTAL ENDOWMENTS AND SERVICES

The intense and extensive establishment of nations, national economies, and dramatic population growth throughout the postwar, post-colonial period also laid the foundation for the rapid deterioration of environmental resource endowments and quality of environmental services in the last few decades of the twentieth century. From the 1980s onward, populations in the region continued to grow, even though population growth rates began to slow (see Hirschman and Bonaparte, this volume). The combination of population growth and economic growth began to take its toll on the natural resource stocks and the quality of environmental services throughout the region.

Overview of Late-Twentieth-Century Trends

The effort to collect and evaluate scientific evidence about the human–environment dynamics affecting Southeast Asia began to build momentum during this period of time. As a consequence of the scientific effort to account for human-driven impacts on environment, the United Nations Environment Programme (UNEP) established a fairly extensive monitoring system in the late 1980s and documented environmental trends from 1990 to 2000.

Table 2a
Population, Income, and Environmental Outcomes

	Year	Population (millions)	GNI (US$/capita)	Arable land (ha/capita)	Forestland (% of total land area)
Brunei Darussalam	1990	0.257	21,670	NA	85.8
	1995	0.297	24,020	NA	NA
	2000	0.338	24,100	NA	83.9
Cambodia	1990	9.1	140	0.38	56.1
	1995	10.7	250	0.32	NA
	2000	12.0	260	0.28	52.9
Indonesia	1990	178.2	620	0.12	65.2
	1995	194	1,000	0.15	NA
	2000	210.4	570	NA	58.0
Laos	1990	4.14	200	0.19	56.7
	1995	4.6	370	0.18	NA
	2000	5.22	290	0.17	54.4
Malaysia	1990	18.2	2,380	0.093	65.9
	1995	20.6	4,030	0.088	NA
	2000	23.3	3,370	0.080	58.7
Myanmar	1990	40.78	NA	0.24	60.2
	1995	44.74	NA	0.22	NA
	2000	50.13	NA	0.21	52.3
Philippines	1990	61	740	0.089	22.4
	1995	68.3	1,040	0.08	NA
	2000	75.6	1,040	0.074	19.4
Singapore	1990	3	11,470	NA	NA
	1995	3.5	23,010	NA	NA
	2000	4	24,190	NA	NA
Thailand	1990	55.84	1,520	0.32	31.1
	1995	59.4	2,770	0.29	NA
	2000	62.41	2,010	0.23	28.9
Vietnam	1990	66.2	120	0.08	28.6
	1995	73	240	0.07	NA
	2000	78.3	390	0.07	30.2

Table 2b
Environmental Outcomes

	Year	Potable Water (cu. meters/ capita)	CO_2 Emission (metric tons/capita)	SO_2 Emission (metric tons/capita)	Number of Threatened Species
Brunei Darussalam	1990	NA	22.6	2.66	n.a.
	1995	NA	17.5	8.76	n.a.
	2000	NA	17.1	n.a.	n.a.
Cambodia	1990	10.68	0	16.51	n.a.
	1995	10.04	0.1	18.21	40
	2000	10.79	0.1	n.a.	46
Indonesia	1990	14.02	0.9	711.96	n.a.
	1995	12.81	1.2	796.59	467
	2000	13.38	1.1	n.a.	416
Laos	1990	NA	0.1	11.76	n.a.
	1995	NA	0.1	12.88	54
	2000	NA	0.1	n.a.	58
Malaysia	1990	26.3	3.0	369.58	n.a.
	1995	22.64	5.8	429.95	513
	2000	26.07	5.4	n.a.	405
Myanmar	1990	25.96	0.1	56.91	n.a.
	1995	23.25	0.2	56.22	71
	2000	19.31	0.2	n.a.	50
Philippines	1990	5.18	0.7	618.99	n.a.
	1995	4.76	0.9	418.44	249
	2000	6.33	1.0	n.a.	506
Singapore	1990	0.22	14.2	334.8	n.a.
	1995	0.21	19.1	418.4	24
	2000	0.17	21.0	n.a.	17
Thailand	1990	1.97	1.7	760.89	n.a.
	1995	3.05	3.1	1233.38	442
	2000	3.42	3.2	n.a.	434
Vietnam	1990	5.6	0.3	165.62	n.a.
	1995	5.04	0.5	193.61	416
	2000	4.59	0.5	n.a.	416

Source, Tables 2a and 2b: Adapted from United Nations Environment Programme, *Environmental Indicators Southeast Asia* (Bangkok: UNEP Regional Resource Center for Asia and the Pacific, 2004).

A summary of these selected trends in environmental outcomes can be found in Tables 2a and 2b, which show changes in land cover, water availability, air pollution, and biodiversity as reported by the United Nations Environment Programme (UNEP). The UNEP report is one of the few that offers a full comparison of both population growth and environmental outcomes, although the evidence of a relationship is merely descriptive; it does not assess a statistical association, and does not allow for an evaluation that controls for initial environmental resource endowments, human capital, wealth, population density, or institutional influences.

Table 2a shows that arable land per capita has declined slightly in most countries, although in Indonesia, notably, arable land per capita grew slightly in the early 1990s, even while population continued to grow. This trend is due in large part to Indonesia's continued transmigration program, which is also associated with conversion of forested areas into agricultural land. Laos, Myanmar, and Vietnam increased their populations fairly substantially between 1990 and 2000, while maintaining similar levels of arable land per capita over the same period, possibly suggesting that expansion into hinterlands accommodated population growth. The largest declines in arable land per capita occurred in Cambodia, Malaysia, the Philippines, and Thailand. In these countries, some explanations for these trends include the lack of available land for expansion and to serve as a safety valve for population growth (Cambodia and the Philippines), significant deterioration of land quality (the Philippines), or significant efforts to set aside previously arable land for conservation or forests (Thailand).

Equivalent measures of deforestation rates are not collected throughout the region, and the only relatively consistent measure is percentage of forested land. Problems with this measure are numerous, as it does not allow distinct assessment of forest quality, plantation forests for harvest, and natural or wild forest. For the most part, all countries in the region experienced declining forest cover between 1990 and 2000, but these declines are relatively small, ranging from a 2 percent decrease to an 8 percent decrease in forested lands. Only Vietnam shows an increase in percentage of forested land (28.6 percent to 30.2 percent).

Throughout the region, water availability per capita has either held steady or increased in most countries. This is due to significant investments in dams and catchment.[23] Only in Myanmar has water availability declined significantly over the decade, most likely due to very limited financial and institutional capacity.

CO_2 and SO_2 per capita emissions in Malaysia, Singapore, and Thailand more than doubled as these countries grew economically over the decade. In all other countries, per capita emissions remained relatively flat. The countries with the largest numbers of threatened species or the greatest declines in biodiversity were those with the largest land areas and coastlines, including Indonesia, Malaysia, Philippines, Thailand, and Vietnam. Pattanavibool notes that much of the explanation for biodiversity threats in Thailand is due to fragmentation of ecosystems supporting diverse wildlife.[24] Brooks notes that catastrophic extinctions have followed deforestation in Singapore.[25]

While the UNEP report offers a broad, cross-national comparison across a number of environmental outcomes, it does not fully capture the extent to which human-driven impacts dramatically changed environmental endowments in the region, nor does it examine the decade of the 1980s, a time period seen by many scholars as the most critical period of human-driven environmental change in the

---

[23] S. Postel, *Water for Agriculture: Facing the Limits* (Washington, DC: Worldwatch Institute, 1989).

[24] A. Pattanavibool, "Fragmentation and Wildlife in Montane Evergreen Forests, Northern Thailand," *Biology Conservation* 107 (2002): 155–64.

[25] B. W. Brooks, "Catastrophic Extinctions Follow Deforestation in Singapore," *Nature* 424 (2003): 420–23.

region. To fill this gap and for the remainder of this section, this review summarizes the significant bodies of research about (a) deforestation and soil erosion; (b) marine and coastal resources deterioration, primarily associated with over-exploitation and migration; and (c) urbanization and its impacts on land-use conversion, air quality, and water quality.

Deforestation, Diminishing Arable Land, and Deteriorating Coastal Resources

As population and economic growth caught up with national boundaries and their frontiers, the most glaring consequence throughout Southeast Asia was dramatic deforestation and soil erosion. Some estimate that in Thailand between 1975 and 1985, forestland was reduced by 75 percent in frontier regions.[26] In the Philippines, forest loss in some parts of the Sierra Madre Mountains was as high as 90 percent during this period.[27] Others estimate that forested land in the Philippines shrunk to less than one million hectares by 1988, down from 10 million hectares in 1950.[28] Similar environmental transformations occurred in Indonesia's frontiers.[29] The World Bank estimates that between 1985 and 2000, in both the Malaysian and Indonesian portions of Borneo, 850,000 hectares of forest were lost annually.[30] In Kalimantan during the same period, 56 percent of forest was lost.[31] Overall, Sodhi notes that less than half of the original forests throughout Southeast Asia are currently standing and that the rate of deforestation has accelerated since the 1990s.[32] From 1990 to 2000, approximately 23,000 square kilometers of forest in Southeast Asia were cleared annually.[33]

For the most part, to the extent that population growth is associated with deforestation, the causal influence operates indirectly through, and is primarily a result of, economic growth and global market integration. From the late 1970s onward, timber and logging companies in many countries were granted special concessions[34] and were supplying both local and global market demand for fine woods, pulp, and paper. In addition, much deforestation is attributed to these

---

[26] S. R. Curran and A. Cooke, "Unexpected Outcomes of Thai Cassava Trade: A Case of Global Complexity and Local Unsustainability," *Globalizations* 5,3 (2008): 111–27.

[27] V. T. King, *Environmental Challenges in South-East Asia* (Oslo: Curzon Press, 1998); D. M. Kummer, *Deforestation in the Postwar Philippines* (Chicago, IL: University of Chicago Geography Research Papers, 1992).

[28] T. Moya and B. Malayang, "Climate Variability and Deforestation-Reforestation Dynamics in the Philippines," *Environment, Development, and Sustainability* 6 (2004): 261–77.

[29] Sien, *Southeast Asia Transformed*; Forest Watch Indonesia and Global Forest Watch, *The State of the Forest: Indonesia* (Bogor and Washington, DC: Forest Watch Indonesia and Global Forest Watch, 2002).

[30] The World Bank, *World Development Report* (Washington, DC: The World Bank, 2000).

[31] World Wildlife Fund, "Forests of Borneo." (Washington, DC: World Wildlife Fund, 2007), http://www.panda.org.assets.panda.org/downloads/borneo_forest_cc_final_12nov07_lr.pdf (accessed February 20, 2009).

[32] N. S. Sodhi, "Southeast Asian Biodiversity: An Impending Disaster," *Trends in Ecology and Evolution* 19 (2004): 654–60.

[33] N. S. Sodhi and B. W. Brook, *Southeast Asian Biodiversity in Crisis* (Cambridge: Cambridge University Press, 2006); S. Zhao, C. Peng, H. Jiang, et al., "Land Use Change in Asia and the Ecological Consequences," *Ecological Research* 21 (2006): 890–96.

[34] Sien, *Southeast Asia Transformed*; Kummer, *Deforestation in the Postwar Philippines*.

concessions' capacities, as well as poor governance of common property resources and loose land tenure regulations.[35] In fact, the equation is somewhat more complicated. First, on average, most of the dramatic deforestation occurred independent of, or prior to, population settlement. Oftentimes, early logging preceded migration to agrarian settlements, and these settlements then precipitated more logging. In addition, the growing agrarian economies intensified land use for agriculture, limiting opportunities for reforestation.[36] In addition, besides the early deforestation patterns in Thailand and Philippines, in most parts of Southeast Asia the highest rates of deforestation have occurred since the 1990s, once population growth rates had slowed and migration patterns had already started to switch from rural settlement destinations to urban destinations. Thus, patterns of natural resource extraction appear to be more closely related to economic growth and global market integration rather than population growth per se.[37] Recently, these conclusions about the proximate drivers of deforestation have been further supported by research that demonstrates how swidden farming (sometimes called slash-and-burn agriculture), the predominant farming practice of many farmers in upland communities throughout the highlands of mainland and island Southeast Asia, is not the primary cause of deforestation-related soil erosion and watershed depletion.[38]

Similar patterns of resource degradation can also be charted for coastal and marine estuaries. Coral reef degradation and mangrove forest loss are among the most commonly cited patterns, especially in association with migrant settlements along coasts; agricultural runoff that includes pesticides, salts, and nitrates; and overfishing and poor fishing practices.[39] Throughout the region, estimates of mangrove forest loss for the period 1975–2000 were 20 percent.[40] In fact, much of the

---

[35] H. Brookfield and Y. Bryon, *Southeast Asia's Environmental Future: The Search for Sustainability* (London: Oxford University Press, 1993).

[36] Ibid.

[37] G. Amacher, W. Cruz, D. Grebner, et al., "Environmental Motivations for Migration: Population Pressure, Poverty, and Deforestation in the Philippines," *Land Economics* 74,1 (1998): 92–101; I. Douglas, "The Local Drivers of Land Degradation in South-East Asia," *Geographical Research* 44,2 (2006): 123–34; Hirsch, *The Politics of Environment in Southeast Asia*; King, *Environmental Challenges in Southeast Asia*; Sastry, "Forest Fires, Air Pollution, and Mortality in Southeast Asia."

[38] O. Mertz, C. Padoch, J. Fox, et al., "Swidden Change in Southeast Asia: Understanding Causes and Consequences," *Human Ecology* 37 (2009): 259–64; C. Valentin, F. Agus, R. Alamban, et al., "Runoff and Sediment Losses From 27 Upland Catchments in Southeast Asia: Impact of Rapid Land Use Changes and Conservation Practices," *Agriculture, Ecosystems, and Environment* 128 (2008): 225–38.

[39] S. Cassels, S. R. Curran, and R. Kramer, "Do Migrants Degrade Coastal Environments? Migration, Natural Resource Extraction, and Poverty in North Sulawesi, Indonesia," *Human Ecology* 33,3 (2005): 329–63; S. R. Curran and T. Agardy, "Common Property Systems, Migration, and Coastal Ecosystems," *Ambio*, Special Issue: Population, Consumption, and Environment, 31,4 (2002): 303–5; C. Z. Giri, Z. Zhu, et al., *Mangrove Forest Distributions and Dynamics (1975-2005) in the Tsunami-Impacted Region of Asia* (Washington, DC: US Geological Survey, 2007); World Resources Institute, *Reefs at Risk in Southeast Asia* (Washington, DC: World Resources Institute, 2002).

[40] Giri, *Mangrove Forest Distributions and Dynamics*.

region's population lives within the coastal zone, placing heavy pressure on marine resources.[41]

For the most part, the primary human drivers for deteriorating coastal ecosystems in the region are rapid urbanization and agricultural development that yields sedimentation, fertilization, and pesticide run-off, as well as other non–point-source pollution into freshwater river systems, estuaries, and coastal waters.[42] Sometimes resource extraction and economic-development activities associated with environmental degradation along the coasts have been associated with the remittances from out-migrants. Origin communities and households will use migrant remittances to extend resource extraction with destructive technologies, as has been shown in Vietnam.[43] For example, fishers who have received funds from out-migrants will invest in bigger boats, sea floor trawling methods, or large-scale dynamiting. On the other hand, remittances can provide a secondary income that can reduce dependence on local natural resources and enhance their quality or support investments in new economies, such as eco-tourism, that seek to enhance and conserve environmental endowments.[44] Conclusive evidence demonstrating either a negative or positive relationship between migration, remittances, and environmental conditions remains indeterminate. Results are mixed because most studies are small-scale cases and not broadly systematic analyses that evaluate competing hypotheses with a large enough sample size.

Urbanization, Land Loss, and Pollution

Rapid urbanization fueled by significant rural-to-urban migration during the 1990s, along with remarkable industrialization from the 1980s onward, marks the most recent and significant impact of human-driven influences upon the environment.[45] Table 3 displays trends and projections of urbanization and shows

---

[41] D. L. Bryant, L. Burke, J. McManus, et al., *Reefs at Risk: Map-Based Indicator of Threats to the World's Coral Reefs* (Washington DC: World Resources Institute, 1998); L. Burke, L. Selig, and M. Spalding, *Reefs at Risk in Southeast Asia* (Cambridge: World Resources Institute, 2002); C. King and Z. Adeel, "Strategies for Sustainable Coastal Management in Asia and the Pacific—Perspectives from a Regional Initiative," *Global Environmental Change* 12 (2002): 139–42; P. Marcotullio, "Urban Water-Related Environmental Transitions in Southeast Asia," *Sustainability Science* 2 (2007): 27–54; J. W. McManus, "Tropical Marine Fisheries and the Future of Coral Reefs: A Special Emphasis on Southeast Asia," *Earth and Environmental Science: Coral Reefs* 1(1997): S121–27.

[42] D. Hidayati, *Coastal Management in ASEAN Countries: The Struggle to Achieve Sustainable Coastal Development* (Tokyo: UNU, 2000); Y. Jiang, K. Hugh, A. Hua, "Megacity Development: Managing Impacts on Marine Environments," *Ocean and Coastal Management*. 44,5–6 (2001): 293–318; Marcotullio, "Urban Water-Related Environmental Transitions in Southeast Asia."

[43] N. Adger, P. M. Kelly, A. Winkels, et al., "Migration Remittances, Livelihood Trajectories, and Social Resilience in Coastal Vietnam," *Ambio: A Journal of the Human Environment* 31,4 (2002): 358–66; S. R. Curran, "Migration, Social Capital, and the Environment: Considering Migrant Selectivity and Networks in Relation to Coastal Ecosystems," in *Population and Development Review*, ed. W. Lutz, A. Prskawetz, W. Sanderson, Supplement to vol. 28 (2002).

[44] Curran, "Migration, Social Capital, and the Environment"; N. Kontogeorgopoulos, "Ecotourism and Mass Tourism in Southern Thailand: Spatial Interdependence, Structural Connections, and Staged Authenticity," *Geography Journal* 61 (2004): 1–11.

[45] F. Costa, A. K. Dutt, L. J. C. Ma, et al., eds., *Urbanization in Asia: Spatial Dimensions and Policy Issues* (Honolulu, HI: University of Hawaii Press, 1989).

that 50 percent of the population may be settled in urban regions by 2010.[46] Countries that are providing much of the region's momentum toward urbanization include Indonesia, Malaysia, the Philippines, and Thailand. But, some of the smaller countries in the region are quickly catching up. Cambodia, Laos, and Myanmar will soon have more than 30 percent of their respective populations classified as settled in urban areas.

Table 3
Urbanization: Trends and Projections, 1970–2010

	Urbanization (percentage)				
	1970	1980	1990	2000	2010
Cambodia	11.7	12.4	17.6	24.1	31.6
Indonesia	17.1	22.2	30.6	40.3	49.7
Laos	9.6	13.4	18.6	25.1	32.6
Malaysia	33.5	42.0	49.8	57.5	64.4
Myanmar	22.8	24.0	24.8	28.4	35.4
Philippines	33.0	37.5	48.8	59.0	66.6
Thailand	20.8	24.5	32.0	40.0	NA
Vietnam	18.3	19.2	19.9	22.3	27.4
Total	20.4	24.3	30.2	37.3	44.8

Adapted from G. Jones, "The Thoroughgoing Urbanisation of East and Southeast Asia," *Asia Pacific Viewpoint* 38,3 (1997): Table 1.

There are two pathways by which urbanization exerts an impact on environmental outcomes. Urban settlements tend to sprawl, for the most part, rather than grow upward, affecting significant land use changes in neighboring rural areas. Throughout the region, urban corridors connecting urban centers have extended in many places, converting agricultural land to urban land and roads (see selections in Sien[47]). These changes in land use are far more permanent than those associated with the conversion of forest to agricultural land; the latter can often be converted back to forest in a relatively short period of time. Some estimates identify rural and agricultural land loss to urban settlements in the region as the most recent and significant environmental change.[48]

A second way in which urbanization influences environmental outcomes is through negative externalities such as waste production in the form of water runoff, sewage, solid waste, and air pollution. A newly recognized form of waste is radiant heat reflection, which can raise the temperatures of local microclimates.[49] Again, although population growth per se is not directly responsible for this increase in waste, or the most proximate cause, the rapidity of population growth has not been matched by concomitant institutional infrastructures to manage the externalities

---

[46] G. Jones, "The Thoroughgoing Urbanisation of East and Southeast Asia," *Asia Pacific Viewpoint* 38, 3 (1997): 237–49.

[47] Sien, *Southeast Asia Transformed.*

[48] Ibid.

[49] Zhao, "Land Use Change in Asia and Ecological Transformation."

associated with population density and associated waste.[50] In fact, some scholars suggest that the patterns of urbanization in Southeast Asian countries combine to generate a unique set of environmental challenges, unlike urban environmental problems found in cities in the United States and western Europe.[51] These scholars argue that because Southeast Asian cities grew so fast, include places of both extreme poverty and extreme wealth, and were very loosely zoned for industry, services, and residences, that therefore the mix of environmental problems ranges across the entire continuum from brown (visible particulate pollution that is easier to see and somewhat technically easier to address) to gray (invisible particulate, toxic pollution that is much harder to address technically, persists without breaking down quickly, and is resistant to remediation), and green (permanent loss of environmental resource endowments or increase in climate change vulnerabilities).

The intensity and full range of problems present significant challenges for local and national governments. For Southeast Asia, the brown issues include significantly high and heavy air particulate counts, limited access to adequate water supplies, sanitation, and drainage. The grey issues include air and water pollution, overdrawn groundwater, ground subsidence, coastal area degradation, and flooding due to poor surface water management and limited infrastructure. The green issues include water scarcity, increasing water consumption per capita, increasing surface radiant temperatures, and increasing vulnerability due to climate change.[52]

For example, in Thailand emissions of organic water pollutants have grown to 356 tons/day, of which more than 40 percent is caused by the food and beverage industry. The generation of household solid waste and industrial hazardous waste has increased significantly and currently poses a major threat to the quality of surface and groundwater, as only a handful of environmentally safe disposal facilities are available.[53] Consequently, the water quality in most Asian rivers, lakes, streams, and wetlands has been heavily degraded, mainly due to (a) agricultural runoff of pesticides and fertilizers and (b) industrial and municipal wastewater discharges, all of which cause widespread eutrophication.[54] By the end of the 1990s, the bacterial level resulting from human waste found in Asian rivers was three times higher than the world average and fifty times higher than World Health Organization guidelines.[55]

Taken as a whole, while population growth appears to be associated with dramatic environmental deterioration throughout the region, the evidence points to more proximate causes, such as how markets and government policies have influenced population movement and settlement, as well as population wealth and the organization of consumption and production. In particular, economic growth and the combination of both global and local markets with government policies

---

[50] Marcotullio, "Urban Water-Related Environmental Transformations in Southeast Asia."

[51] Ibid.

[52] Ibid.

[53] The World Bank, *World Development Report.*

[54] S. K. Karn and H. Harada, "Surface Water Pollution in Three Urban Territories of Nepal, India and Bangladesh," *Environmental Management* 28,4 (2001): 483–96; J. Liu and J. Diamond, "China's Environment in a Globalizing World," *Nature* 435 (2005): 1179–86; Marcotullio, "Urban Water-Related Environmental Transitions in Southeast Asia."

[55] UNEP, *Environmental Indicators Southeast Asia;* Marcotullio, "Urban Water-Related Environmental Transitions in Southeast Asia."

conducive to economic development led to significant demand for environmental resource exploitation. In the most recent decades, growing population density in urban areas that lack institutional infrastructures to manage the subsequent negative externalities associated with large numbers of people producing waste also suggests what appears to be a strong association between population growth and environmental deterioration.

PART 3: TWENTY-FIRST CENTURY CHALLENGES—POPULATION VULNERABILITIES TO ENVIRONMENTAL POLLUTION AND CLIMATE CHANGE

Even as population growth rates have slowed, economic growth rates have held steady or increased, and as the overall health of populations in Southeast Asia has improved, the health of the environment and its services has deteriorated. In some parts of the region, pollution has begun to have an impact on human health and has increased the vulnerability of humans to the effects of climate change, especially severe weather (droughts and cyclones), sea level rise, and overall temperature increases.

Research in Asia on human adaptation to environmental conditions has examined the full array of population variables, including fertility responses, mortality, and migration. Demographers have frequently studied how land availability influences fertility. Particular forms of morbidity and disease burdens are also known to result from pollution. And, finally, research about climate change predicts that human populations will be more vulnerable in the future because disease-vector distributions will grow spatially; urban and rural areas with poor infrastructure will suffer with a greater intensity of cyclones and droughts; coastal populations will be flooded and experience declining water quality; and agricultural crops will suffer with the loss of land (due to a rise in sea level), temperature increases, and water salinization. Livelihood adaptations, socioeconomic and political responses to mitigate or facilitate adaptation, and resettlement of populations are possible responses and will directly and indirectly influence population dynamics. Although research and science have not yet fully elaborated the impact of environmental deterioration on population health and mobility, what follows is a summary description of some of the research that has emerged from the region in the last decade. The bulk of the research findings in these fields has emerged only since the turn of the century.

Natural Resource Endowments and Fertility

Although the role of land availability and its influence upon fertility was theorized several decades ago, the most recent research findings suggest that land tenure and land quality are far more specific and important factors. Larger landholdings are associated with higher fertility in the Philippines,[56] and greater potential access to land in frontier areas is associated with higher fertility in Thailand.[57] Furthermore, greater land security or land ownership is frequently

---

[56] V. A. Hiday, "Migration, Urbanization, and Fertility in the Philippines," *International Migration Review* 12,3 (1978): 370–85.

[57] M. Vanlandingham and C. Hirschman, "Population Pressure and Fertility in Pre-Transition Thailand," *Population Studies* 55,3 (2001): 233–48.

associated with lower fertility rates.[58] More recently, scholars have focused less on landholding size and tenure and more on land quality. With regard to the impact of land quality on human fertility, results are mixed in Southeast Asia and around the world.[59] In other parts of Asia (e.g., Nepal and Pakistan), deterioration of nearby water and fuelwood resources tends to increase the marginal value of having one more child in the family to help with harvesting natural resources from ever-more-distant locales.[60] Unfortunately, no similar studies have been carried out in Southeast Asia to evaluate the specific relationship between environmental resource deterioration or resource quality and fertility. One explanation for the lack of studies is that all of the countries in Southeast Asia have undergone dramatic fertility decline in the last thirty years (see chapters by Hirschman and Bonaparte and by Hull, this volume) and, for the most part, environmental resource deterioration followed fertility decline or coincided with it.

Environmental Deterioration, Morbidity, and Mortality

A number of studies examine pollution for its impact on population processes in Southeast Asia, particularly morbidity and mortality. Air, water, and land-based pollution are all associated with higher rates of morbidity throughout Southeast Asia. The impacts of pollution on morbidity have been primarily identified in urban places, river systems, or coastal and marine fisheries.[61] Recently, specific case studies have found statistically significant impacts of air pollution on increasing morbidity and mortality. These impacts range from the predominant and large effects of indoor and outdoor smoke on pulmonary and cardiovascular impairments to the economically driven exposures to chemical hazards that fall disproportionately upon the poor. For example, 37 percent of the global burden of disease (GBD) attributed to indoor smoke occurs in Southeast Asia. Air pollution and both indoor and outdoor smoke have been linked specifically to cardiovascular and pulmonary stress.[62]

---

[58] Hiday, "Migration, Urbanization, and Fertility in the Philippines."

[59] A. De Sherbinin, D. Carr, S. Cassels, et al., "Population and Environment," *Annual Review of Environment and Resources* 32 (2007): 345–73; W. Lutz and S. Scherbov, "Quantifying Vicious Circle Dynamics: The PEDA Model for Population, Environment, Development, and Agriculture in African Countries," *IIASA Interim Report IR-99-049* (Laxenburg: International Institute for Applied Systems Analysis, 1999); A. Marcoux, "Population and Environmental Change: From Linkages to Policy Issues," *SDdimensions* (Rome: Sustainable Development Department, Food and Agriculture Organization, 1999), http://www.fao.org/sd/wpdirect/WPre0089.htm; B. O'Neill, F. L. MacKellar, and W. Lutz, *Population and Climate Change* (Cambridge: Cambridge University Press, 2001).

[60] A. Biddlecom, W. Axinn, J. S. Barber, "Environmental Effects on Family Size Preferences and Subsequent Reproductive Behavior in Nepal," *Population and Environment* 26,3 (2005): 583–621; D. Filmer and L. H. Pritchett, "Environmental Degradation and the Demand for Children: Searching for the Vicious Circle in Pakistan," *Environment and Development Economics* 7 (2002): 123–46.

[61] Karn and Harada, "Surface Water Pollution"; Liu and Diamond, "China's Environment in a Globalizing World"; Marcotullio, "Urban Water-Related Environmental Transitions in Southeast Asia"; United Nations Environment Programme, *Environmental Indicators Southeast Asia* (Bangkok: UNEP Regional Resource Center for Asia and the Pacific, 2004).

[62] H. N. Saiyed, "Environmental Health Problems of Children Living in Rural Areas of Developing Countries," in *Conference Booklet of the International Conference on Environmental Threats to the Health of Children: Hazards and Vulnerability*, Supplemental Abstracts 36 (Geneva: World Health Organization); Sastry, "Forest Fires, Air Pollution, and Mortality in Southeast

Heavy metal and chemical hazards produce morbidity risks such as lead poisoning from air pollution in the region's megacities, such as Bangkok.[63] Water-born pollution, manifested either as bacterial or chemical toxins, has also shown significant effects on morbidity in other studies around the region, specifically through higher rates of infectious diarrhea as well as poisonings.[64] Others indicate strong associations between cause of death due to toxic or chemical exposure with cancers and congenital disorders in the region.[65] The growing export of post-consumer electronic waste from Europe and North America to many countries in Southeast Asia with limited institutional infrastructure to control recycling and disposal has resulted in a growing number of dump sites at which the burning of plastics, acid baths, and disposal of electric wiring or components has led to concentrated amounts of lead, mercury, cadmium, and other heavy metals in the soil, surface water, and groundwater that are associated with birth defects and cancers.[66] In sum, much of the exposure to these risks is concentrated in urban and periurban, poverty-prone communities where institutions that protect against polluters or pollution are minimal. When considering any of the preceding studies, it is important to keep in mind two human dimensions: (a) the individual- and the household-based selective processes influencing human settlement and (b) the private and public sector regulations or policies influencing settlement processes. Both sets of institutions, private and public, mediate the impact of human exposure to risks associated with deterioration of environmental conditions and services. Unfortunately, many of the studies about the effects of pollution on human health are based on small samples or are clinic-based studies that cannot estimate dose responses, be used to generalize to larger populations, or account for possible unobserved family, socioeconomic, and other institutional factors that might protect or exacerbate exposures and morbidity or mortality risks.

Climate Change Impacts on Population Processes

A growing number of scholars are calling for research on how climate change will influence morbidity, mortality, and migration. Climate-induced environmental change is linked to declines in water tables, droughts, heat waves, air pollution, sea

---

Asia"; K. R. Smith, C. F. Corvalán, and T. Kjellström, "How Much Global Ill Health is Attributable to Environmental Factors?" *Epidemiology* 10 (1999): 573–84; W. C. Tan, Diwen Qiu, B. L. Liam, et al., "Human Bone Marrow Response to Acute Air Pollution Caused by Forest Fires," *American Journal of Respiratory Critical Care Medicine* 161,4 (2000): 1213–17; N. Vichit-Vadakan, N. Vajanapoon, and B. Ostro, "The Public Health and Air Pollution in Asia (PAPA) Project: Estimating the Mortality Effects of Particulate Matter in Bangkok, Thailand," *Environmental Health Perspective* 116,9 (2008): 1179–82.

[63] W. A. Suk, K. M. Ruchirawat, K. Balakrishnan, et al., "Environmental Threats to Children's Health in Southeast Asia and the Western Pacific," *Environmental Health Perspectives* 111,10 (2003): 1340–47.

[64] W. J. M. Martens, *Modeling the Effect of Global Warming on the Prevalence of Schistosomiasis* (Amsterdam: National Institute of Public Health and Environmental Protection Report No. 461502010, 1995); G. L. S. Su, "Impact on Drinking Water Sources in Close Proximity to the Payatas Dumpsite, Philippines," *Journal of Public Health* 15,1 (2007): 51–55.

[65] Suk et al., "The Public Health and Air Pollution in Asia."

[66] L. Yáñez, D. Ortiz, J. Calderón, et al., "Overview of Human Health and Chemical Mixtures: Problems Facing Developing Countries," *Environmental Health Perspectives* 110, suppl. 6 (2002): 901–9.

level rise, and greater intensity of weather-related events such as floods and cyclones.[67] Global studies of climate change, health, or population often mention the region as a vulnerable one.[68]

For example, studies in the region have documented how global-warming-induced drought leads to higher forest-fire threats and significant cardio-pulmonary and cancer risks.[69] Because of relatively high-quality demographic (vital statistics) and environmental (particulate matter and visibility indices) data from some countries (Malaysia[70]) or ongoing demographic surveillance studies (Indonesia[71]) that measure pre- and post-dose and event exposure, cause and effect could be demonstrated between drought, forest fires, and morbidity. These results, combined with studies of climate-change-related temperature rise definitively linked to the droughts and forest fires in Southeast Asia in 1997, 1998, and 2000, have identified one link between climate change and mortality.[72]

Others have begun to document how the combination of climate change and population distribution in the region will increase human exposure to diseases, such as vector-borne diseases (schistosomiasis, malaria, or dengue fever) or cross-animal infectious diseases (SARS or H1N1), as well as other diseases.[73] For example, in

---

[67] J. A. Patz and R. S. Kovats, "Hotspots in Climate Change and Human Health," *British Medical Journal* 325,7372 (2002): 1094–1100; M. S. Suh, "Impacts of Land Use/Cover Changes on Surface Climate Over East Asia for Extreme Climate Cases using RegCM2," *Journal of Geophysical Resolution* 109 (2004): 1–14; D. Werth and R. Avissar, "The Local and Global Effects of Southeast Asian Deforestation," *Geophysical Resources Letters* 32,20 (2005); Zhao et al., "Land Use Change in Asia and Ecological Consequences."

[68] International Organization for Migration, *Climate Change, Environmental Degradation, and Migration* (Geneva: Expert Seminar, International Organization for Migration, 2009); G. J. Hugo, D. Bardsley, Y. Tan, et al., *Climate Change and Migration in the Asia-Pacific Region: Summary Report to Asian Development Bank* (Manila: Asian Development, 2009); Patz and Kovats, "Hotspots in Climate Change and Human Health"; C. Small and R. J. Nicholls, "A Global Analysis of Human Settlement in Coastal Zones," *Journal of Coastal Research* 19,3 (2003): 584–99.

[69] M. Brauer and J. Hisham-Hashim, "Fires In Indonesia: Crisis And Reaction," *Environmental Science and Technology* 32,17 (1998): 404–7; E. Frankenberg, D. McKee, and D. Thomas, "Health Consequences of Forest Fires in Indonesia," *Demography* 42,1 (2005): 109–29; D. Glover and T. Jessup, *Indonesia's Fires and Haze: The Cost of a Catastrophe* (Singapore: Institute of Southeast Asia, 1999); D. Glover and L. P. Onn, "The Environment, Climate Change, and Natural Resources in Southeast Asia: Issues and Challenges," *ASEAN Economic Bulletin* 25 (2008): 1–6; J. Goldammer, "History of Equatorial Vegetation Fires and Fire Research in Southeast Asia Before the 1997–98 Episode: A Reconstruction of Creeping Environmental Changes," *Mitigation and Adaptation Strategies for Global Change* 12 (2008): 13–32; A. Heil and J. Goldammer, "Smoke-Haze Pollution: A Review of the 1997 Episode in Southeast Asia," *Regional Environmental Change* 2,1 (2001): 24–37; D. Murdiyarso and L. Lebel, "Local to Global Perspectives on Forest and Land Fires in Southeast Asia," *Mitigation and Adaptation Strategies for Global Change* 12 (2007): 3–11; Sastry, "Forest Fires, Air Pollution, and Mortality in Southeast Asia"; Tan et al., "Human Bone Marrow Response to Acute Air Pollution."

[70] For example, Sastry, "Forest Fires, Air Pollution, and Mortality in Southeast Asia."

[71] For example, Frankenburg et al., "Health Consequences of Forest Fires in Indonesia."

[72] Glover and Jessop, *Indonesia's Fire and Haze*; Glover and Onne, "The Environment, Climate Change, and Natural Resources in Southeast Asia"; Goldammer, "History of Equatorial Forest Fires."

[73] Martens, *Modeling the Effect of Global Warming on the Prevalence of Schistosomiasis*; D. Pimental et al., "Ecology of Increasing Diseases: Population Growth and Environmental Degradation," *Human Ecology* 35,6 (2007): 653–68; R. W. Snow, C. A. Guerra, A. M. Noor, et al., "The Global

studies of dengue fever—a vector-borne infection reliant on mosquito species possessing salinity-tolerant larvae and pupae—findings show that, with rising sea levels, saline- and brackish-water area will increase throughout Southeast Asia and thereby increase the spread of the disease.[74] Besides expanding the geographic distribution of mosquitoes, rising temperatures in endemic regions, including all of Southeast Asia, are likely to decrease the incubation period for mosquito larvae and increase the number of mosquito offspring. This, in turn, may result in a longer dengue fever season and an increase overall in per capita exposure to the mosquitoes.[75]

Throughout Southeast Asia, a bulk of the population is settled in coastal regions or near-coastal regions, which are considered particularly vulnerable to sea level rise and climate-induced environmental change. This situation has given rise to new scholarship regarding those settlements' vulnerability and resilience.[76] While potentially threatened by rising disease burdens, as noted above, settlements along the coast will also be vulnerable to slow-onset sea level rise and gradual land loss. These same settlements will also face increased vulnerability to flooding with expected increases in the number of episodic, extreme weather events such as cyclones.[77]

The Southeast Asian region, since 1990, has born the modal share of the world's hydrological and meteorological disasters and suffered the highest proportion of deaths due to these types of disasters. (Hydrological disasters include floods, storm surges, landslides or mud slides, and subsidence; meteorological disasters include cyclones and typhoons.[78] Since 2000, Southeast Asian hydrological and meteorological disasters have had the greatest human impact when compared to similar disasters in every other part of the world. Some have argued that the intensity of damage and suffering is partially due to the devastation of coastal zone resources—such as mangrove forests—that buffer inland areas, and are also partially a result of high levels of settlement concentration in coastal zones along the entire continuum of settlement sizes, from villages and small towns to megacities.[79] The massive growth of megacities in the region has dramatically increased the number of

---

Distribution of Clinical Episodes of *Plasmodiium falciparum* Malaria," *Nature* 434,7030 (2005): 214–17.

[74] R. Ramasamy and S. N. Surendran, "Possible Impact of Rising Sea Levels on Vector-Borne Infectious Diseases," *BMC Infectious Diseases* 11,1 (2011): 18–23.

[75] S. Banu, W. Hu, C. Hurst, et al., "Dengue Transmission in the Asia-Pacific Region: Impact of Climate Change and Socio-Environmental Factors," *Tropical Medicine and International Health* 16 (2011): 598–607.

[76] N. Adger, T. P. Hughes, C. Folke, et al., "Social-Ecological Resilience to Coastal Disasters," *Science* 309, 5737 (2005): 1036–39; R. J. Nicholls, "Coastal Flooding and Wetland Loss in the Twenty-First Century: Changes Under the SRES Climate Change and Socio-Economic Scenarios," *Global Environmental Change* 14,1 (2004): 69–86; Small and Nichols, "A Global Analysis of Human Settlement in Coastal Zones."

[77] Intergovernmental Panel on Climate Change (IPCC), "Climate Change 2007: Impacts, Adaptation, and Vulnerability," *Contribution of Working Group II to the Fourth Assessment Report of the IPCC* (Geneva: IPCC, 2007).

[78] EM-DAT, *The OFDA/CRED International Disaster Database* (Brussels: Université Catholique de Louvain, 2009), www.emdat.be (accessed September 15, 2011); International Organization of Migration, *Climate Change, Environmental Degradation, and Migration.*

[79] Small and Nichols, "A Global Analysis of Human Settlement in Coastal Zones."

people who could be affected by both severe weather and slow-onset sea level rise.[80] Cities in the region facing significant threats, according to climate forecasts, include Ho Chi Minh City, Metro Manila, Jakarta, and Bangkok. It is possible that the combination of sea level rise, storm surges, and riverine-flood risks will combine to significantly displace residents in these metropolitan areas and that these displacements will increase in frequency either to change each city's landscape or to diminish its importance as a destination for rural migrants.[81]

The possibility of environmental refugees fleeing the slow-onset sea level rise or climate change has not been thoroughly examined for the region. And, most research on climate change and migration, more generally, finds that climate has little impact on migration because most people are temporarily displaced and soon return or derive off-site coping mechanisms, primarily through remittances from household members who had migrated prior to extreme weather events or any significant slow-onset environmental change.[82] Some researchers have suggested that there will be short-term demographic changes resulting from shifts in agro-ecosystems due to climate change. Recent climate-modeling forecasts overlain upon different agro-ecosystems in the region predict significant stressors on rice production, especially in the Mekong River basin.[83] Increasing heat stress in Myanmar, Thailand, Laos, and Cambodia from March to June; Vietnam from April to August; the Philippines from April to June; and Indonesia in August will cause 20 percent to 30 percent reduction in yields among the current region-specific rice varieties.[84] In addition, some countries in the region that are highly dependent upon rain-fed irrigation will be particularly vulnerable to expected precipitation anomalies resulting from climate change.[85] Finally, the megadeltas in Vietnam and Myanmar are the backbone of the rice economies in their respective countries, and these will be affected by rising sea levels that will increase flooding and salinity. In all cases, development, distribution, and adoption of new rice varieties that are tolerant of higher temperatures, greater flooding, or higher salinity will be necessary. It could be that successful adaptation assisted by facilitating institutions is more likely than significant out-migration over the long run. Even so, short-term perturbations in population distribution may still result, as short-term migration to supplement household incomes then compensates for greater annual and seasonal climate variability and financial uncertainties associated with farming. In sum, "climate change impacts are unlikely to fundamentally alter existing patterns of migration in the short-term, except to increase the scale of movement."[86]

---

[80] Hugo et al., *Climate Change and Migration in the Asia-Pacific Region*.

[81] Ibid., p. 21.

[82] See recent reviews by S. L. Perch-Nielsen, M. B. Bättig, D. Imboden, "Exploring the Link between Climate Change and Migration," *Climatic Change* 91 (2008): 375–93; and C. Raleigh and L. Jordan, "Climate Change and Migration: Emerging Patterns in the Developing World," in *Social Dimensions of Climate Change: Equality and Vulnerability in a Warming World*, ed. R. Mearns and A. Norton (Washington, DC: The World Bank, 2010), pp. 103–32.

[83] R. Wassmann, S. V. K. Jagadish, K. Sumfleth, et al., "Regional Vulnerability of Climate Change Impacts on Asian Rice Production and Scope for Adaptation," *Advances in Agronomy* 102 (2009): 91–133.

[84] Ibid.

[85] Ibid.

[86] Hugo et al., *Climate Change and Migration in the Asia-Pacific Region*, p. 9.

As environmental deterioration has been identified as an influence on health outcomes, a growing number of primarily clinically based studies or very small-scale case studies of such influences have been conducted. Of these, few have assessed dose responses, and most are cross-sectional studies. The only population-based studies of the health impacts of environmental deterioration occurred when researchers analyzed the impact of the 1997 forest fires; in this case, there were coincidental and ongoing demographic surveillance studies that facilitated pre- and post-assessments of impacts. Given the extent of environmental deterioration across the region and the wide range of populations exposed to deteriorating conditions, the region could benefit from a concerted and systematic effort to assess population health risks and vulnerabilities in relation to environmental deterioration and the threats of climate-change-induced environmental deterioration. Most countries in the region have fairly high quality collection systems for vital statistics data and the capacity to overlay spatial data of environmental quality in order to begin preliminary assessments of statistical association with morbidity and mortality.

The possible effects of climate change upon the region's populations have received some speculative attention.[87] Forecasts focus on several possible results. Climate-change-related meteorological and hydrological disasters are increasingly likely and will mostly have an impact on the region's populations living in megacities.[88] Furthermore, the region's agrarian-based populations, particularly those growing rice will be especially vulnerable to rising temperatures that result in heat stress, as well as to the meteorological and hydrological system changes that will result in precipitation anomalies throughout the region—greater flooding and higher salinity in the river deltas.[89] These changes will demand shifts in agricultural production and may result in greater numbers of temporary migrants out of rural areas.[90]

CONCLUSION

The preceding review provides a general picture of what is known about the interaction of population processes with environmental conditions and natural resource endowments in Southeast Asia. In order to simplify an otherwise complex set of interactions, the chapter is organized to evaluate how environmental conditions facilitated particular demographic dynamics during the early to mid-twentieth century. This is followed by a review of evidence about how population drivers influenced environmental outcomes during the late twentieth century. Finally, the chapter reviews evidence of how environmental deterioration influences human health and well-being and predictions about how climate change is expected to influence population dynamics. In this way, the chapter offers a description of the cyclical nature of the dynamic relationship.

In Part 1, the evidence shows that natural resource endowments in the region allowed the flourishing of populations and societies. This growth was particularly robust in the post-colonial period, with the decline in war and the decrease in food

---

[87] Hugo et al., *Climate Change and Migration in the Asia-Pacific Region.*

[88] Ibid.

[89] Wassmann et al., "Regional Vulnerability of Climate Change Impacts on Asian Rice Production and Scope for Adaptation."

[90] Hugo et al., *Climate Change and Migration in the Asia-Pacific Region.*

insecurity and mortality. Growing populations and extensive resource endowments coincided with nation-building projects that encouraged migration to hinterlands and border settlements. The availability of land resources served as a critical safety valve for population pressures on nation-states.

In Part 2, the evidence shows how the processes of population settlement and growing population densities have coincided with deteriorating forestlands, soil quality, and coastal or marine environments. The empirical evidence is mixed in causally relating population growth specifically to declines in environmental resource quality and quantity. Growing consumption, global and local market demands, and government policies that encouraged resource exploitation to enhance economic growth are more proximate and consistent explanations than population growth or settlement. While population growth and density are more directly linked to negative externalities in urban settlements, government policies are also critical mediating factors. The lack of zoning, minimal waste-management facilities, and limited policies regulating industrial pollution coincided with extremely rapid population growth to place large numbers of people at risk of exposure to severely polluted air and water.

In Part 3, the analysis demonstrated that environmental degradation appears to have increased exposure to all types of pollution, from brown to grey and green, with apparent impacts on population morbidity and mortality. A growing number of studies forecasting the impact of climate change note how the region may be particularly vulnerable to increased pollution. Vulnerabilities are related to particular "hot spots" in the region, especially those megacities along the coastlines and rice-based agro-ecosystems that are dependent on rain-fed irrigation or found in the two major mega-deltas of Myanmar and Vietnam.

Wherever possible, tabular data in this chapter show a wide range of evidence across countries, while the discussion in the text emphasizes some countries more than others. The countries over-represented are the larger ones, including Indonesia, Malaysia, Thailand, and the Philippines, where geography, population, openness to investigation, environmental threats, and significant scientific capacity have converged to facilitate the gathering and evaluation of evidence. In sum, while at first the evidence about population–environment dynamics in the region appears haphazard, a second assessment suggests otherwise. As a theoretically derived organization of the evidence that focuses on how environmental conditions facilitated population growth and settlement, how population drivers are associated with (but not the most proximate explanation for) environmental deterioration, and how environmental deterioration and climate change pose morbidity risks and may increase migration, this review offers the opportunity to view a uniquely comprehensive body of evidence that may be quite unusual for any part of the world. As such, it offers the region's scholars ample justification for large-scale, multidisciplinary analyses of how population, environment, and sustainable development have evolved and might proceed.

Further justification for focusing on the region as a critical site for investigation in this field is the importance of mediating institutions. The evidence summarized in parts 1 through 3 consistently identifies critical and necessary mediating factors influencing how population–environment processes and outcomes relate to each other. First, institutions, particularly in the form of policies (broadly defined), are critical for shaping both population processes and environmental conditions. Second, markets and large economic actors can reshape environmental capital quite independently from population processes. Finally, the selectivity of human behavior as a result of a multitude of social relations can generate a wide range of outcomes that variously influence population outcomes and environmental resource quality. These three dimensions yield a complex empirical reality and a challenging policy environment.

Since the 1990s, alongside documentation of declining environmental resource endowments, policy scholars began to take note of rapidly emerging national and regional regulatory efforts and cooperation to meet environmental challenges.[91] Within a decade, Tomich and colleagues noted how environmental regulation appeared to be yielding health, economic, and environmental benefits throughout the region.[92] Oosterveer et al.[93] and Sodhi et al.[94] also note how greening policies toward industry and biodiversity are yielding co-benefits or positive externalities for economies. And, the forest fires in 1997 proved a valuable lesson in both the short and long term for policy makers. In the short term, the forest fires revealed both the remarkable interdependency of the region's nations upon neighboring countries' environmental policies and regulation and the weaknesses of their regional institutions for yielding adequate cooperation and prevention.[95] The institutional reorganization and building undertaken in response to the Indonesian forest fires now serves as an exemplary model for responses to other regional challenges from SARS to tsunamis.[96] The emergence of institutions across localities holds promise for the region and offers many important opportunities for understanding population, environment, and sustainable-development dynamics.

One of the striking finds from this review is the breadth of evidence that can be marshaled to complete a theoretically driven comprehensive review of the literature about population-environment dynamics. The region is home to great biodiversity and environmental amenities, significantly deteriorated environmental sites, and noted vulnerability to climate change, as well as tremendous variability in human settlements, human capital, innovative institutions, and livelihoods. In addition, the scientific investigative capacity of the region is growing. From an empirical standpoint, Southeast Asia may provide an ideal opportunity for scholars and policy makers to truly understand how best to bring into balance population and environmental dynamics for a sustainable future.

---

[91] T. Panayatou, "The Environment in Southeast Asia: Problems and Policies," *Environmental Science and Technology* 27,12 (1993): 2269; M. Seda, *Environmental Management in ASEAN: Perspectives on Critical Regional Issues* (Singapore: Institute of Southeast Asian Studies, 1993).

[92] T. Tomich, "Policy Analysis and Environmental Problems at Different Scales: Asking the Right Questions," *Agriculture, Ecosystems, and Environment* 104 (2004): 5–18; T. Tomich, D. Thomas, and M. Van Noodrwijk, "Environmental Services and Land Use Change in Southeast Asia: From Recognition to Regulation or Reward?" *Agriculture, Ecosystems and Environment* 104 (2004): 229–44.

[93] P. Oosterveer, S. Kamolsiripichaiporn, R. Rasiah, "The 'Greening' of Industry and Development in Southeast Asia: Perspectives on Industrial Transformation and Environmental Regulation; Introduction," *Environment, Development, and Sustainability* 8 (2006): 217–27.

[94] N. S. Sodhi, L. P. Koh, R. Clemens, et al., "Conserving Southeast Asian Forest Biodiversity in Human-Modified Landscapes," *Biological Conservation* 143 (2010): 2375–84.

[95] Ibid.; Y. T. Kassim, "The Haze: Why Is Jakarta so Slow?" *Business Times*, October 2, 1997.

[96] L. Tacconi, F. Jotzo, and R. Q. Grafton, "Local Causes, Regional Co-operation and Global Financing for Environmental Problems: The Case of Southeast Asian Haze Pollution," *International Environmental Agreements* 8 (2008): 1–16.

CONCLUSION

Michael Philip Guest and Lindy Williams

To what extent is a volume on population issues in Southeast Asia salient or instructive? As documented by all chapters in this volume, there is immense diversity in population and social indicators among the eleven countries represented. The recent economic trajectories of these societies have been very different and have interacted with their demographic profiles to produce vastly contrasting changes in population parameters. For example, variations in age structure that have emerged across the region are related to historical patterns of marriage and fertility, as well as to declining mortality. And migration, both internal and international, has been responding to economic and other opportunities and constraints, which are in turn influenced by demographic change.

Many of the common attributes, such as religion, language, and socio-economic conditions, that bind together countries in other geographic areas to form coherent regional identities is missing in Southeast Asia. For example, the region is linguistically diverse, hosting a multitude of languages from a number of different language families, possibly representing several paths of immigration. The populations of the eleven countries that make up Southeast Asia also represent most of the major religions and belief systems of the world. Majority Buddhist populations in Cambodia, Laos, Myanmar, and Thailand live in proximity to majority Muslim populations in Brunei, Malaysia, and Indonesia, predominantly Christian populations in the Philippines and Timor-Leste, and alongside the Confucian populations in Singapore and a large part of Vietnam. Religion is very much a part of the histories of Southeast Asian states, as is their experience with foreign rule. All but one of the countries that make up contemporary Southeast Asia today[1] were ruled by colonial powers. Brunei, Malaysia (including Singapore), and Myanmar were colonized by the British; Cambodia, Laos, and Vietnam by the French; Indonesia by the Dutch; the Philippines by Spain and then the United States; and Timor-Leste by the Portuguese. The colonial administrations attempted to alter local social structures in a number of ways during the process of wealth extraction, with varying degrees of success.

---

[1] Thailand

Although all of the authors who have contributed to this volume draw comparisons among countries in Southeast Asia, they also point out that there are common features that make Southeast Asia a viable unit of analysis. These include the regional emphasis on wet-rice cultivation, the relatively high social position of women, and self-identification by the states as members of a coherent regional entity. The creation of the political, and increasingly economic, organization of ASEAN (Association of Southeast Asian Nations) in 1967 has strengthened this regional identity. Ten of the eleven countries normally classified as belonging to Southeast Asia are members of ASEAN, while Timor-Leste has observer status. ASEAN has gained increasing global influence in recent years and is providing economic coherence to a region with vastly different economic capacities and political structures.

To a large extent, the level of economic and social development of each country has been shaped by their linkages to the global market, linkages that were influenced by earlier colonial relations. Cambodia, Laos, and Myanmar have exhibited the slowest economic growth and social transformation. The Philippines, which had one of the strongest economies in the 1960s, has stagnated. Vietnam has achieved rapid economic expansion during the last thirty years. And Indonesia, Malaysia, and Thailand, although developing at different speeds, have all progressed economically and in terms of their social indicators. Brunei and Singapore, both small states, have informally attained "developed-world status," both being categorized as "high-income" by the World Bank[2] and being on target to achieve most of the Millennium Development Goals by 2015.[3] Timor-Leste has only recently emerged from decades of conflict and has experienced relatively stunted economic growth as a result. As noted in several of the chapters, the ASEAN Economic Agreement is expected to be introduced in 2015. This agreement will move Southeast Asia one step closer to being a unified economic power. All of these changes are occurring against a backdrop of increasing demographic size and complexity. As Hirschman and Bonaparte demonstrate in Chapter 1, the region, which was once sparsely populated, is now home to many more people than live in Europe.

Although demographic change may occur relatively slowly by some standards, it can have profound consequences. For example, declining fertility or mortality taking place over a generation or more will eventually produce substantial changes in the age structure of the population. Such changes have been occurring to varying degrees throughout Southeast Asia. Transformation of demographic parameters can also influence rates of economic growth. For instance, lower fertility can, in part through changes in the age structure, lead to conditions conducive to economic expansion. This "demographic dividend" occurs when a comparatively large percentage of the population is in the ages most likely to be in the labor force, and a comparatively small percentage of the population is either very young or very old and, so, unlikely to be working. If birth rates drop past a certain point, however, fertility may be considered too low and governments may devise measures to encourage higher fertility. High rates of internal and international mobility also both respond to, and contribute to, economic opportunities. It is becoming increasing clear that demographic dynamics can have a direct influence on environmental conditions

---

[2] World Bank, *World Bank Annual Report, 2010* (Washington, DC: World Bank, 2010)

[3] United Nations Statistics Division, "Millennium Development Goals Indicators," http://mdgs.un.org/unsd/mdg/Data.aspx, accessed February, 22, 2011.

as well, which, in turn, can affect demographic behavior. These are all important reasons to document the demographic developments that have been taking place in Southeast Asia.

In the lead chapter by Hirschman and Bonaparte, the authors describe regional historical demographic challenges within the context of colonial relations. They note that these relations tended to slow socioeconomic development and contribute to rapid population increase. They explain why population growth would have decelerated during the Great Depression and World War II and then highlight the importance of declining mortality throughout the region in the years following World War II. Indeed, they argue that improvements in mortality control constitute "the greatest human achievement of the twentieth century." These advances have led to substantial increases in life expectancy throughout Southeast Asia, although they have occurred unevenly, with poorer countries faring less well than richer countries to date.

Despite the widespread downturn in fertility throughout the region in recent decades, the fertility declines within countries have also been very uneven. Hirschman and Bonaparte discuss the most widely accepted, albeit still contested, reasons for fertility transitions, concluding that the answer is not likely to be straightforward but to lie somewhere amidst "the complex interplay of rapid socioeconomic change (including access to modern healthcare), organized family planning programs, and spatial and social diffusion processes that vary in significance and intensity over time."

In Chapter 2, Hull focuses more explicitly on fertility change in the region. He adds that while the trend toward lower fertility has been universal throughout Southeast Asia, leading to below-replacement-level fertility in Singapore and Thailand and near-replacement-level fertility in Indonesia, Malaysia, and Vietnam, there have been substantial differences in how low birth rates have been attained. He discusses a number of the institutional structures that have affected the level of access of individuals to contraception and abortion. He concludes by speculating about what lies ahead. Whether or not there will be convergence regionally is uncertain, given the variety of economic and cultural contexts involved. The (uneven) expansion of women's education throughout the region is one institutional change that is likely to continue to influence fertility, however.

Hull identifies increasing levels of "singlehood" as one of the factors that has contributed to the fertility declines. This point is taken up by Jones and Gubaju (see Chapter 3), who analyze changing marriage patterns in Southeast Asia. One of the most fundamental change they document has been the shift away from the norm of partners marrying at young ages and entering arranged unions to one of marriages increasingly occurring at later ages with the choice of spouse being left to the persons themselves. Divorce rates have been climbing in many countries, although unevenly. The increases that are occurring may be due, in part, to rising individualism and to a growing disinclination on the part of one or both spouses to maintain a strained marriage for the sake of family reputation. Finally, the authors note that, while those who eventually do get married can now seek partners in wider marriage markets, increasingly, people, particularly women, are choosing not to marry at all.

Mujahid (see Chapter 4) explains how changes in fertility and mortality have transformed age structures in the region. He describes how the rapidity of the demographic transition in some countries, particularly Singapore and Thailand, has resulted in the relatively fast pace of population aging in those nations. Other countries, including Indonesia and Vietnam, appear to be following a similar path.

Mujahid notes that structural changes that have occurred have created numerous economic and social challenges that will have to be addressed in the years ahead. In addition, his data illustrate the extent to which aging populations will be predominantly female and rural. Mujahid discusses many of the potential socioeconomic and cultural consequences of projected changes in age structures and examines their likely impacts on health care services and long-term care facilities, the living arrangements of older persons, factors affecting their income security, and the potential incidence of poverty. Finally, he discusses some pertinent policies that have been implemented to date, and he concludes with recommendations for the future.

Hugo (see Chapter 5) documents how the increasing levels of population movement within and among countries of the region are related to differences in the demand for labor. In large part, this is thought to be a response to economic opportunities and constraints, but it is also related to the age structures of local and regional populations. For example, Singapore and Thailand are both faced with declining populations at young adult ages, and international migration has become one of the ways in which these countries are able to meet the labor demands of their economies. Overseas labor migration is of growing importance, and Hugo's chapter highlights recent trends. Hugo outlines a number of the critical debates and controversies surrounding current migration patterns. These include rising local opposition to immigrant settlement in many receiving communities, the pros and cons of temporary versus permanent labor migration, the role of remittances in low-income sending nations, the exploitation of and attempts to protect both documented and undocumented migrant workers, issues particular to the movement of women, the potential for the migration of skilled workers to create a brain drain, and an array of other topics.

In Chapter 6, VanLandingham and Fu analyze how population movements are related to health. Like Hugo, they consider both international and internal migration. They attempt to assess how each has been found to affect both physical and mental-health outcomes. The authors design a conceptual framework based on their extensive review of the literature. The framework illustrates how a combination of macro and micro factors influences whether or not migration occurs. Then, the complex of opportunities and hazards faced by the individual, along with some potentially mediating effects of social networks, exert more immediate and direct effects on health outcomes. The effects of migration on individuals are likely to vary by the type of move undertaken, but any form of migration can produce both favorable and unfavorable outcomes. For example, the authors demonstrate that mental-health consequences are quite mixed among refugee populations. Indeed, they find mixed results for a number of their health assessments.

Unfortunately, the literature on health consequences for migration to, from, and within Southeast Asia remains exceedingly limited. One exception may be the research that focuses on migration and HIV/AIDS. Although the data collected on this topic are often derived from convenience samples, the compilation of information from these studies provides compelling evidence that migration facilitates the spread of HIV/AIDS, particularly among vulnerable populations. VanLandingham and Fu suggest a plan for more effective data-collection strategies that would enable researchers to understand more fully the complex of health effects that result from internal and international migration.

Finally, Curran and Derman (see Chapter 7) discuss the dynamic relationship between environmental factors and population processes in Southeast Asia. Their conceptual scheme has three components: (1) the impact of environmental factors on population from the 1950s to the 1970s, (2) the effects of population processes on the environment, and (3) more recent effects of the environment on population. Although the chapter attempts to cover, historically, a substantial amount of ground, the authors show that many of the relationships they consider to be important have not been studied, or have not been studied in adequate depth. They highlight the effect of population dynamics—specifically population growth between the 1950s and 1970s—on the environment, in particular deforestation and the loss of mangrove habitats. As Curran and Derman point out, however, available evidence does not suggest that population growth per se bears primary responsibility for the substantial environmental destruction that has occurred to date. Perhaps the most controversial aspect of their discussion is the review of fragmentary evidence on the impacts of varying environmental conditions, primarily urbanization-induced change, on population processes. These environmental effects, while undoubtedly occurring, have resulted in predictions about future demographic shifts, particularly those involving migration, that will require substantial attention and analysis.

The chapters in this volume combine to provide an accounting of recent trends and current levels of a wide range of demographic parameters. Collectively, they offer some understanding of what the future of Southeast Asia may look like. How will economic and social change over the next twenty or thirty years affect human populations and how will population changes affect society and the economy? We now attempt to address some of these issues through the lessons learned in this book's chapters.

The populations of Southeast Asia are undergoing rapid change. Over the last four decades, the most striking of these changes has been the recent decline in fertility levels. From an average, forty years ago, of more than five children per woman, average total fertility is now approximately 2.3 children per woman. Yet there remains a great deal of diversity represented in this average. Hull argues that "what we should be identifying and attempting to predict are some of the key social institutional changes that, once taken, will carry individuals into an entirely new decision framework." However, even without a thorough understanding of the institutional changes most relevant to fertility decline, fertility has fallen in all countries of the region.

It appears almost certain that if current trends in social and economic development and fertility continue, almost all countries of Southeast Asia will experience fertility below the replacement level within the next thirty years. This does not mean that the transition to low fertility will be the same for all Southeast Asian countries. The reasons for declines in fertility will vary, with couples in some countries (most notably the Philippines) facing a more difficult reproductive health environment than others. Nonetheless, replacement levels of fertility will be reached across Southeast Asia, with the majority of the population experiencing levels of fertility of fewer than two children per women.

What is more difficult to foresee is what will happen to fertility levels after they have reached the replacement level. At present, there is virtually no theory to help predict what will transpire, and this is where the advice of Hull is especially relevant. He argues that fertility decline is unlikely to stop once levels of around two children per women are reached. The two Southeast Asian countries with fertility levels that have already fallen below the replacement level are instructive on this point. Singapore reached replacement-level fertility in the middle to late 1970s, but fertility has continued to fall and the total fertility rate (TFR) is now estimated to be approximately 1.2, a level that has been sustained for some time with some minor fluctuations. Thailand attained replacement-level fertility by around 1990, but the country's fertility has also continued to decline, and the Thai TFR is now approximately 1.6. In the large urban center of Bangkok, the fertility rate is much lower still.

Countries in Europe have had a longer history of below-replacement levels of fertility than have those in Southeast Asia. After several decades of attempts to boost birth rates, several nations have recently begun to see fertility increases. While some of this rise has been the result of a change in the tempo of childbearing,[4] there is also some evidence of what Hull calls a "new decision framework." Family-friendly policies, particularly in northern Europe, have promoted increasing levels of fertility.[5] Considered critically important to the success of these policies has been the acceptance by men of a more equitable role in domestic work.[6] It is now thought that where men agree to do a higher proportion of housework and take paternal leave from their employment at levels comparable to women's participation in maternal leave, fertility may increase again. Even where these adaptations have been most readily accepted, however, fertility has typically not returned to the replacement level of just over two children per woman.

In Southeast Asia, some institutional changes have been benefiting women, while others have not. This mix is important for understanding current levels of and trends in childbearing. For example, women are clearly gaining in education and labor-force opportunities. These are among the factors that have been repeatedly shown to be correlated with lower levels of fertility, both through reductions in levels of desired fertility, and, as Jones and Gubhaju point out, through changing expectations about marriage. They note that the three factors playing the greatest role in reducing fertility are also the ones that make marriage less attractive. These are (a) increasing costs of childbearing, (b) increasing pressure to engage in "intensive parenting," and (c) the sluggish pace of change in role expectations within the domestic sphere, notably those expectations regarding the relative burdens placed on men and women concerning domestic work and child care. There is still considerable scope for greater involvement of men in domestic work. The relatively high social position of Southeast Asian women, mentioned in several chapters, has not been translated into an equitable household division of labor. While women are successfully navigating the institutions that deal with people as individuals (for example, through gains in education and employment), such gains have not been matched by improvements in those institutions that deal most directly with people as members of a family.[7] Both are considered crucial for creating a family-friendly environment that would allow fertility to rise.

[4] Thomas Sobotka, "Is Lowest-Low Fertility Explained by the Postponement of Childbearing?" *Population and Development Review* 30,2 (2004): 195–220.

[5] Gerda Neyer and Gunnar Andersson, "Consequences of Family Policies on Childbearing Behavior: Effects or Artifacts?" *Population and Development Review* 34,4 (2008): 699–724.

[6] Peter McDonald, "Very Low Fertility: Consequences, Causes, and Policy Approaches," *The Japanese Journal of Population* 6,1 (2008): 19–23.

[7] Peter McDonald, "Gender Equity, Social Institutions, and the Future of Fertility," *Journal of Population Research* 17,1 (2000): 1–16.

It appears likely that, without fairly profound changes in the relative contributions of men to family life, particularly in the realm of childrearing, we will see little of the upward change in fertility that is now being experienced in parts of Europe. If only modest change occurs in the household division of labor, we should expect to see fertility continue to decrease in much of Southeast Asia. It will presumably reach a floor at some point, possibly at around 1.3 children per woman, and will likely remain at that level unless there is both a reformulation of policies surrounding the family and widespread change in behavior within the family.

Rapid declines in fertility have altered, and will continue to alter, the age structure of the population for the foreseeable future. These changes are being reinforced by ongoing decreases in mortality in much of the Southeast Asian region. As Mujahid states, the combined effects of the decline in fertility and the region's increasing life expectancy have reduced the proportion of the population at younger ages and increased the proportion of the population 60 years old and older; at present, both the number and the proportion of older persons in the population are increasing.

The differing pace of the demographic transitions that have been observed within Southeast Asia's nations also means that countries are at very different stages in the transitions of their age structures. For Singapore, the country with the earliest declines in fertility, it is predicted that by 2025 approximately 27.1 percent of the population will be 60 years old and older, while projections are lower for Timor Leste (5.2 percent), Laos (8.4 percent), the Philippines (8.9 percent), and Cambodia (9.5 percent). Growing interest in the older population, even among those countries that have not yet experienced a major increase in the proportion of older persons in their populations, is evident. As Mujahid points out, "population aging" is associated with a number of challenges in the health and social arenas, and all countries within Southeast Asia should consider strategies to address this issue now.

The aging of a population provides both opportunities and challenges at each stage of the process. The countries that have experienced more recent fertility declines are currently experiencing growth in the relative size of their populations at working ages; in other words, they are benefiting from the demographic dividend described above. For example, in Thailand the proportion of the population of working age is now at its peak, and the country will soon enter a period in which that proportion will decline. Meanwhile, the proportion of the population of working age in Vietnam will continue to grow for another decade. Laos is still in the first stages of the demographic transition, and there the population remains relatively young.

One of the primary reasons to monitor the proportion of the population at working age is to understand its potential impact on economic growth.[8] The rapid economic growth that has been experienced by some Southeast Asian countries has been partly attributed to the investments in education that these countries have been able to make,[9] in combination with changes in their age structures.[10]

---

[8] Kua Wongboonsin and Philip Guest, *The Demographic Dividend: Policy Options for Asia* (Bangkok: Chulalongkorn University, College of Population Studies, 2005).

[9] Wolfgang Lutz, K. C. Samir, Hafiz Khan, et al., *Future Aging in Southeast Asia: Demographic Trends, Human Capital, and Health Status,* Interim Report, IR-07-026, (Vienna: International Institute for Applied Statistical Analysis, 2007).

[10] Ronald Lee and Andrew Mason, "What Is the Demographic Dividend?" *Finance and Development* 43,3 (2006).

It has been shown that changing age structure will potentially influence short- and long-term social and economic development throughout Southeast Asia, and, in addition, will require nations to identify policy priorities for their aging populations. It is now also recognized that the number and proportion of the population of young adults tend to be associated with rates of residential mobility. For example, a recent analysis of international migration in Asia noted that those countries with rapid growth among working-age populations tend to be countries with disproportionate out-migration, while those with low or negative rates of growth among the working-age population tend to record net in-migration.[11] Hugo also highlights the role of changing age structures as a potential driving force in international migration, stating that in half of the countries of Southeast Asia, the number of people between the ages of 15 and 34 will be declining, and that it is this age group that not only has the highest rates of migration but also provides much of the vibrancy of the workforce. In the other countries of the region, the number of people in this age group will continue to increase. Differences in the rate of change in the age structure, combined with cross-national differences in economic conditions, have contributed to new patterns of international migration. This can be expected to continue for the next two decades.

Internal migration will also be directly affected by the relative proportions of young adults in the population. The economic boom that has been experienced in much of Southeast Asia over the last thirty years has contributed to large-scale urbanization, much of which was fueled by the movement of young people from rural to urban environs. In many respects, the dynamics of internal migration are similar to those of international migration. Indeed, the demographic impetus for internal migration is expected to fall over the next several decades in those sending contexts in which the number of persons ages 15 to 34 is declining and rise where the young population is growing. Of course, uneven opportunities in urban and rural areas and across national borders complicate both forms of migration and will continue to offset in profound ways simple age-structure effects.

The shifts in population mobility that are likely to occur over the next several decades have a number of important implications. One question that has been considerably underresearched to date concerns the relationship between population mobility and health. There is increasing interest in research on internal movement and health elsewhere in Asia,[12] and some research has begun.[13] Although the research that has been done to date has generally found evidence of a "healthy migrant" effect, there is also concern that the institutional framework of health care is often biased against migrants. Furthermore, the negative impact on heath resulting from the types of work that migrants are often channeled into requires further study. The projected increases in internal and international migration make analysis of the impacts of migration on the health of individuals, both migrants and nonmigrants, a priority.

---

[11] Regional Thematic Working Group on International Migration Including Human Trafficking, *Situation Report on International Migration in East and South-East Asia* (Bangkok: International Organization for Migration, Southeast Asian Regional Office, 2008).

[12] Xiaojiang Hu, Sarah Cook, and Miguel A. Salazar, "Internal Migration and Health in China," *The Lancet* 372, 9651 (2008): 1717–19.

[13] Yao Lu, *Test of the "Healthy Migrant Hypothesis": A Longitudinal Analysis of Health Selectivity of Internal Migration in Indonesia*, On-Line Working Paper Series (Los Angeles, CA: California Center for Population Research, UCLA, 2007), http://escholarship.org/uc/item/8ff262rn.

The last point that we wish to highlight is the interaction between environmental change and demographic processes. Curran and Derman provide a review of issues in the literature that focus on the significant interrelationships between the two that exist in the context of Southeast Asia. We wish to take up one of these issues—the impact of climate change on population distribution—in order to stress the uncertainty of demographic projections and to demonstrate the potential consequences of such changes.

Curran and Derman argue that environmental change has the potential to result in large-scale migration over the coming decades. These authors also note that while insufficient research has been undertaken on this topic within Southeast Asia, climate-induced migration is predicted to be particularly severe there because of high population density in low-lying coastal areas.[14] Findings from a conference undertaken on behalf of the National Intelligence Council of the US Government concluded that other environmental factors resulting from such activities as the building of dams on the Mekong River will potentially result in greater migration pressures, but climate-induced changes are also likely to have a significant impact on population movements in the years ahead.

A recent study conducted on behalf of the Asian Development Bank[15] agrees with this assessment, and, although it cautions against undertaking projections to quantify the impact of climate change, it concludes that the major impetus for future environmentally-induced migration is most likely to come from coastal flooding. The authors argue that about one-third of the population of Southeast Asia resides in low-lying coastal areas where the impact of climate change could be severe. Most of the ensuing migration will likely be internal migration, with a high proportion being rural to urban, but international migration patterns will no doubt also be affected.

Although the studies that have been undertaken in Southeast Asia generally stress that the magnitude of *environmentally induced* migration cannot be predicted, it seems likely that much of the movement may be temporary movement out of an affected area until the danger has passed. The longer-term threat of *climate change* will likely result in longer-term population responses, including the gradual movement of people away from areas that are threatened, perhaps with those who are generally the most likely to migrate under other circumstances, such as young adults and those with sufficient human capital, moving first.

We have highlighted several of the most important demographic trends that are taking place in Southeast Asia today and attempted to draw out some of the implications of these trends. Changes in other demographic processes, including mortality, are occurring and will continue to affect the social and economic structure of the societies of Southeast Asia. While our list is not exhaustive, we believe that it does provide a rationale for the importance of further study of the population processes occurring in Southeast Asia and beyond. It is this belief that has motivated the creation of the current volume.

---

[14] National Intelligence Council, *Southeast Asia: The Impact of Climate Change to 2030: Geopolitical Implications*, Washington, DC, Conference Report, CR-2010-02 (2010).

[15] University of Adelaide, Flinders University, the University of Waikato, *Climate Change and Migration in Asia and the Pacific* (Mandaluyong City: Asian Development Bank, 2009).

CONTRIBUTORS

EDITORS

Michael Philip Guest has recently retired as Chief of the Demographic Analysis Branch in the Department of Economic and Social Affairs Population Division at the United Nations. Guest is a demographer whose research interests include migration and fertility. He has taught as a professor at the Institute for Population and Social Research of Mahidol University in Bangkok and acted as program associate and country representative in the Population Council's Bangkok office. In addition, he has coordinated a range of program activities dealing with reproductive health, interventions research, expansion of contraceptive choice, gender, and development research.

Lindy Williams is a professor and director of graduate studies in the Department of Development Sociology at Cornell University, where she is a member of the graduate fields of Asian Studies; Feminist, Gender, and Sexuality Studies; and International Development. Her research interests include family sociology and demography, and the majority of her work is focused geographically in Southeast Asia. Her most recent research examines the impact of overseas labor migration of adults from the Philippines on the children they leave behind.

CONTRIBUTORS

Sabrina Bonaparte is a PhD candidate in the Department of Sociology at the University of Washington–Seattle, where she received an MA in Ethnomusicology and an MA in Sociology. Her work in Ethnomusicology on Balinese musical performance led to her research on the demography of Southeast Asia.

Sara R. Curran joined the faculty of the Henry M. Jackson School of International Studies and the Daniel J. Evans School of Public Affairs in 2005. She holds degrees from the University of Michigan (BS, natural resource management), North Carolina State University (MS, sociology and economics), and the University of North Carolina at Chapel Hill (PhD, sociology). Curran researches internal migration in developing countries, globalization, family demography, environment and population, and gender.

Noah Derman is currently the Deputy Director of Development in Gardening (DIG), an organization that uses sustainable agriculture as a tool for income generation and promoting health and nutrition for vulnerable populations. Noah holds a master's degree in Public Health from the Global Health Department at the

University of Washington's School of Public Health and an International Development Certificate from the Evans School of Public Affairs. He has lived and worked in Southeast Asia for five years.

Hongyun Fu currently serves as the Director of Programs at Population Services International in China (based in Kunming). She received her doctoral degree in the Department of International Health and Development at Tulane University. Prior to her doctoral program, she completed a master's degree in sociology, with a concentration in demography. She has extensive training and experience in quantitative and qualitative methodology, program design, monitoring, and evaluation. Over the past eleven years, she has worked in a range of programs focusing on a variety of public health issues, including migration and HIV/AIDS risk-taking behaviors, sexual/reproductive health, youth transition to adulthood, and the behavioral treatment of substance use, studies which were conducted in China, Vietnam, Thailand, and the United States.

Bina Gubhaju is a Postdoctoral Fellow (Changing Family Cluster) at the Asia Research Institute at the National University of Singapore. She recently completed her PhD in Sociology and Demography at the Pennsylvania State University. Her dissertation examines specific socio-economic, demographic, empowerment, and programmatic factors that intersect in determining women's contraceptive choices, as well as sustainability of the use of family planning.

Charles Hirschman is the Boeing International Professor in the Department of Sociology and the Daniel J. Evans School of Public Affairs at the University of Washington–Seattle. He received his BA from Miami University in 1965 and his PhD from the University of Wisconsin in 1972. He has written widely on the social demography of Southeast Asia, and also on immigration and race and ethnic inequality in the United States. He is a former president of the Population Association of America.

Graeme Hugo is University Professorial Research Fellow, Professor of the Department of Geographical and Environmental Studies, and Director of the National Centre for Social Applications of Geographic Information Systems at the University of Adelaide. His research interests are in population issues in Australia and South East Asia, especially migration.

Terence H. Hull is the John C. Caldwell Professor of Population, Health, and Development at the Australian National University. Since 1970, he has carried out research on fertility, family planning, and infant and maternal mortality across Asia, with a special focus on Indonesia.

Gavin Jones earned his PhD at the Australian National University in 1966, after which he joined the Population Council, where he worked first in New York, then in Thailand and Indonesia, before returning to Australia. He was with the Demography and Sociology Program at Australian National University for twenty-eight years, serving as head of the program for six years. In 2003, he joined the Asia Research Institute at the National University of Singapore.

Ghazy Mujahid has a Masters in Economics from the University of Karachi (Pakistan) and a Doctorate in Economics from the University of Cambridge (UK). He has more than thirty years of experience working in the area of population and development in Europe, the Middle East, Africa, and Asia.

Mark J. VanLandingham is the Thomas C. Keller Professor at Tulane University's School of Public Health and Tropical Medicine. His major research areas of interest include the HIV epidemic in Southeast Asia; the health consequences of migration (for both rural-to-urban and international migrants); and the social, demographic, and public health consequences of Hurricane Katrina for New Orleans.

SOUTHEAST ASIA PROGRAM PUBLICATIONS

Cornell University

Studies on Southeast Asia

Number 57 *Demographic Change in Southeast Asia: Recent Histories and Future Directions*, ed. Lindy Williams and Michael Philip Guest. 2012. ISBN 978-0-87727-757-6 (pb.)

Number 56 *Modern and Contemporary Southeast Asian Art: An Anthology*, ed. Nora A. Taylor and Boreth Ly. 2012. ISBN 978-0-87727-756-9 (pb.)

Number 55 *Glimpses of Freedom: Independent Cinema in Southeast Asia*, ed. May Adadol Ingawanij and Benjamin McKay. 2012. ISBN 978-0-87727-755-2 (pb.)

Number 54 *Student Activism in Malaysia: Crucible, Mirror, Sideshow*, Meredith L. Weiss. 2011. ISBN 978-0-87727-754-5 (pb.)

Number 53 *Political Authority and Provincial Identity in Thailand: The Making of Banharn-buri*, Yoshinori Nishizaki. 2011. ISBN 978-0-87727-753-8 (pb.)

Number 52 *Vietnam and the West: New Approaches*, ed. Wynn Wilcox. 2010. ISBN 978-0-87727-752-1 (pb.)

Number 51 *Cultures at War: The Cold War and Cultural Expression in Southeast Asia*, ed. Tony Day and Maya H. T. Liem. 2010. ISBN 978-0-87727-751-4 (pb.)

Number 50 *State of Authority: The State in Society in Indonesia*, ed. Gerry van Klinken and Joshua Barker. 2009. ISBN 978-0-87727-750-7 (pb.)

Number 49 *Phan Châu Trinh and His Political Writings*, Phan Châu Trinh, ed. and trans. Vinh Sinh. 2009. ISBN 978-0-87727-749-1 (pb.)

Number 48 *Dependent Communities: Aid and Politics in Cambodia and East Timor*, Caroline Hughes. 2009. ISBN 978-0-87727-748-4 (pb.)

Number 47 *A Man Like Him: Portrait of the Burmese Journalist, Journal Kyaw U Chit Maung*, Journal Kyaw Ma Ma Lay, trans. Ma Thanegi, 2008. ISBN 978-0-87727-747-7 (pb.)

Number 46 *At the Edge of the Forest: Essays on Cambodia, History, and Narrative in Honor of David Chandler*, ed. Anne Ruth Hansen and Judy Ledgerwood. 2008. ISBN 978-0-87727-746-0 (pb.)

Number 45 *Conflict, Violence, and Displacement in Indonesia*, ed. Eva-Lotta E. Hedman. 2008. ISBN 978-0-87727-745-3 (pb.)

Number 44 *Friends and Exiles: A Memoir of the Nutmeg Isles and the Indonesian Nationalist Movement*, Des Alwi, ed. Barbara S. Harvey. 2008. ISBN 978-0-877277-44-6 (pb.)

Number 43 *Early Southeast Asia: Selected Essays*, O. W. Wolters, ed. Craig J. Reynolds. 2008. 255 pp. ISBN 978-0-877277-43-9 (pb.)

Number 42 *Thailand: The Politics of Despotic Paternalism* (revised edition), Thak Chaloemtiarana. 2007. 284 pp. ISBN 0-8772-7742-7 (pb.)

Number 41 *Views of Seventeenth-Century Vietnam: Christoforo Borri on Cochinchina and Samuel Baron on Tonkin*, ed. Olga Dror and K. W. Taylor. 2006. 290 pp. ISBN 0-8772-7741-9 (pb.)

Number 40 *Laskar Jihad: Islam, Militancy, and the Quest for Identity in Post-New Order Indonesia*, Noorhaidi Hasan. 2006. 266 pp. ISBN 0-877277-40-0 (pb.)

Number 39 *The Indonesian Supreme Court: A Study of Institutional Collapse,* Sebastiaan Pompe. 2005. 494 pp. ISBN 0-877277-38-9 (pb).

Number 38 *Spirited Politics: Religion and Public Life in Contemporary Southeast Asia,* ed. Andrew C. Willford and Kenneth M. George. 2005. 210 pp. ISBN 0-87727-737-0.

Number 37 *Sumatran Sultanate and Colonial State: Jambi and the Rise of Dutch Imperialism, 1830-1907,* Elsbeth Locher-Scholten, trans. Beverley Jackson. 2004. 332 pp. ISBN 0-87727-736-2.

Number 36 *Southeast Asia over Three Generations: Essays Presented to Benedict R. O'G. Anderson,* ed. James T. Siegel and Audrey R. Kahin. 2003. 398 pp. ISBN 0-87727-735-4.

Number 35 *Nationalism and Revolution in Indonesia,* George McTurnan Kahin, intro. Benedict R. O'G. Anderson (reprinted from 1952 edition, Cornell University Press, with permission). 2003. 530 pp. ISBN 0-87727-734-6.

Number 34 *Golddiggers, Farmers, and Traders in the "Chinese Districts" of West Kalimantan, Indonesia,* Mary Somers Heidhues. 2003. 316 pp. ISBN 0-87727-733-8.

Number 33 *Opusculum de Sectis apud Sinenses et Tunkinenses (A Small Treatise on the Sects among the Chinese and Tonkinese): A Study of Religion in China and North Vietnam in the Eighteenth Century,* Father Adriano de St. Thecla, trans. Olga Dror, with Mariya Berezovska. 2002. 363 pp. ISBN 0-87727-732-X.

Number 32 *Fear and Sanctuary: Burmese Refugees in Thailand,* Hazel J. Lang. 2002. 204 pp. ISBN 0-87727-731-1.

Number 31 *Modern Dreams: An Inquiry into Power, Cultural Production, and the Cityscape in Contemporary Urban Penang, Malaysia,* Beng-Lan Goh. 2002. 225 pp. ISBN 0-87727-730-3.

Number 30 *Violence and the State in Suharto's Indonesia,* ed. Benedict R. O'G. Anderson. 2001. Second printing, 2002. 247 pp. ISBN 0-87727-729-X.

Number 29 *Studies in Southeast Asian Art: Essays in Honor of Stanley J. O'Connor,* ed. Nora A. Taylor. 2000. 243 pp. Illustrations. ISBN 0-87727-728-1.

Number 28 *The Hadrami Awakening: Community and Identity in the Netherlands East Indies, 1900-1942,* Natalie Mobini-Kesheh. 1999. 174 pp. ISBN 0-87727-727-3.

Number 27 *Tales from Djakarta: Caricatures of Circumstances and their Human Beings,* Pramoedya Ananta Toer. 1999. 145 pp. ISBN 0-87727-726-5.

Number 26 *History, Culture, and Region in Southeast Asian Perspectives,* rev. ed., O. W. Wolters. 1999. Second printing, 2004. 275 pp. ISBN 0-87727-725-7.

Number 25 *Figures of Criminality in Indonesia, the Philippines, and Colonial Vietnam,* ed. Vicente L. Rafael. 1999. 259 pp. ISBN 0-87727-724-9.

Number 24 *Paths to Conflagration: Fifty Years of Diplomacy and Warfare in Laos, Thailand, and Vietnam, 1778-1828,* Mayoury Ngaosyvathn and Pheuiphanh Ngaosyvathn. 1998. 268 pp. ISBN 0-87727-723-0.

Number 23 *Nguyễn Cochinchina: Southern Vietnam in the Seventeenth and Eighteenth Centuries,* Li Tana. 1998. Second printing, 2002. 194 pp. ISBN 0-87727-722-2.

SEAP Series

Number 23   *Possessed by the Spirits: Mediumship in Contemporary Vietnamese Communities.* 2006. 186 pp. ISBN 0-877271-41-0 (pb).

Number 22   *The Industry of Marrying Europeans,* Vũ Trọng Phụng, trans. Thúy Tranviet. 2006. 66 pp. ISBN 0-877271-40-2 (pb).

Number 21   *Securing a Place: Small-Scale Artisans in Modern Indonesia,* Elizabeth Morrell. 2005. 220 pp. ISBN 0-877271-39-9.

Number 20   *Southern Vietnam under the Reign of Minh Mạng (1820-1841): Central Policies and Local Response,* Choi Byung Wook. 2004. 226pp. ISBN 0-0-877271-40-2.

Number 19   *Gender, Household, State: Đổi Mới in Việt Nam,* ed. Jayne Werner and Danièle Bélanger. 2002. 151 pp. ISBN 0-87727-137-2.

Number 18   *Culture and Power in Traditional Siamese Government,* Neil A. Englehart. 2001. 130 pp. ISBN 0-87727-135-6.

Number 17   *Gangsters, Democracy, and the State,* ed. Carl A. Trocki. 1998. Second printing, 2002. 94 pp. ISBN 0-87727-134-8.

Number 16   *Cutting across the Lands: An Annotated Bibliography on Natural Resource Management and Community Development in Indonesia, the Philippines, and Malaysia,* ed. Eveline Ferretti. 1997. 329 pp. ISBN 0-87727-133-X.

Number 15   *The Revolution Falters: The Left in Philippine Politics after 1986,* ed. Patricio N. Abinales. 1996. Second printing, 2002. 182 pp. ISBN 0-87727-132-1.

Number 14   *Being Kammu: My Village, My Life,* Damrong Tayanin. 1994. 138 pp., 22 tables, illus., maps. ISBN 0-87727-130-5.

Number 13   *The American War in Vietnam,* ed. Jayne Werner, David Hunt. 1993. 132 pp. ISBN 0-87727-131-3.

Number 12   *The Voice of Young Burma,* Aye Kyaw. 1993. 92 pp. ISBN 0-87727-129-1.

Number 11   *The Political Legacy of Aung San,* ed. Josef Silverstein. Revised edition 1993. 169 pp. ISBN 0-87727-128-3.

Number 10   *Studies on Vietnamese Language and Literature: A Preliminary Bibliography,* Nguyen Dinh Tham. 1992. 227 pp. ISBN 0-87727-127-5.

Number 8   *From PKI to the Comintern, 1924–1941: The Apprenticeship of the Malayan Communist Party,* Cheah Boon Kheng. 1992. 147 pp. ISBN 0-87727-125-9.

Number 7   *Intellectual Property and US Relations with Indonesia, Malaysia, Singapore, and Thailand,* Elisabeth Uphoff. 1991. 67 pp. ISBN 0-87727-124-0.

Number 6   *The Rise and Fall of the Communist Party of Burma (CPB),* Bertil Lintner. 1990. 124 pp. 26 illus., 14 maps. ISBN 0-87727-123-2.

Number 5   *Japanese Relations with Vietnam: 1951–1987,* Masaya Shiraishi. 1990. 174 pp. ISBN 0-87727-122-4.

Number 3   *Postwar Vietnam: Dilemmas in Socialist Development,* ed. Christine White, David Marr. 1988. 2nd printing 1993. 260 pp. ISBN 0-87727-120-8.

Number 2   *The Dobama Movement in Burma (1930–1938),* Khin Yi. 1988. 160 pp. ISBN 0-87727-118-6.

Cornell Modern Indonesia Project Publications

All CMIP titles available at http://cmip.library.cornell.edu

Number 75   *A Tour of Duty: Changing Patterns of Military Politics in Indonesia in the 1990s.* Douglas Kammen and Siddharth Chandra. 1999. 99 pp. ISBN 0-87763-049-6.

Number 74   *The Roots of Acehnese Rebellion 1989–1992*, Tim Kell. 1995. 103 pp. ISBN 0-87763-040-2.

Number 72   *Popular Indonesian Literature of the Qur'an*, Howard M. Federspiel. 1994. 170 pp. ISBN 0-87763-038-0.

Number 71   *A Javanese Memoir of Sumatra, 1945–1946: Love and Hatred in the Liberation War*, Takao Fusayama. 1993. 150 pp. ISBN 0-87763-037-2.

Number 69   *The Road to Madiun: The Indonesian Communist Uprising of 1948*, Elizabeth Ann Swift. 1989. 120 pp. ISBN 0-87763-035-6.

Number 68   *Intellectuals and Nationalism in Indonesia: A Study of the Following Recruited by Sutan Sjahrir in Occupation Jakarta*, J. D. Legge. 1988. 159 pp. ISBN 0-87763-034-8.

Number 67   *Indonesia Free: A Biography of Mohammad Hatta*, Mavis Rose. 1987. 252 pp. ISBN 0-87763-033-X.

Number 66   *Prisoners at Kota Cane*, Leon Salim, trans. Audrey Kahin. 1986. 112 pp. ISBN 0-87763-032-1.

Number 64   *Suharto and His Generals: Indonesia's Military Politics, 1975–1983*, David Jenkins. 1984. 4th printing 1997. 300 pp. ISBN 0-87763-030-5.

Number 62   *Interpreting Indonesian Politics: Thirteen Contributions to the Debate, 1964–1981*, ed. Benedict Anderson, Audrey Kahin, intro. Daniel S. Lev. 1982. 3rd printing 1991. 172 pp. ISBN 0-87763-028-3.

Number 60   *The Minangkabau Response to Dutch Colonial Rule in the Nineteenth Century*, Elizabeth E. Graves. 1981. 157 pp. ISBN 0-87763-000-3.

Number 57   *Permesta: Half a Rebellion*, Barbara S. Harvey. 1977. 174 pp. ISBN 0-87763-003-8.

Number 52   *A Preliminary Analysis of the October 1 1965, Coup in Indonesia (Prepared in January 1966)*, Benedict R. Anderson, Ruth T. McVey, assist. Frederick P. Bunnell. 1971. 3rd printing 1990. 174 pp. ISBN 0-87763-008-9.

Number 48   *Nationalism, Islam and Marxism*, Soekarno, intro. Ruth T. McVey. 1970.

Number 37   *Mythology and the Tolerance of the Javanese*, Benedict R. O'G. Anderson. 2nd edition, 1996. Reprinted 2004. 104 pp., 65 illus. ISBN 0-87763-041-0.

Copublished Titles

The Ambiguous Allure of the West: Traces of the Colonial in Thailand, ed. Rachel V. Harrison and Peter A. Jackson. Copublished with Hong Kong University Press. 2010. ISBN 978-0-87727-608-1 (pb.)

The Many Ways of Being Muslim: Fiction by Muslim Filipinos, ed. Coeli Barry. Copublished with Anvil Publishing, Inc., the Philippines. 2008. ISBN 978-0-87727-605-0 (pb.)

Language Texts

INDONESIAN

Beginning Indonesian through Self-Instruction, John U. Wolff, Dédé Oetomo, Daniel Fietkiewicz. 3rd revised edition 1992. Vol. 1. 115 pp. ISBN 0-87727-529-7. Vol. 2. 434 pp. ISBN 0-87727-530-0. Vol. 3. 473 pp. ISBN 0-87727-531-9.

Indonesian Readings, John U. Wolff. 1978. 4th printing 1992. 480 pp. ISBN 0-87727-517-3

Indonesian Conversations, John U. Wolff. 1978. 3rd printing 1991. 297 pp. ISBN 0-87727-516-5

Formal Indonesian, John U. Wolff. 2nd revised edition 1986. 446 pp. ISBN 0-87727-515-7

TAGALOG

Pilipino through Self-Instruction, John U. Wolff, Maria Theresa C. Centeno, Der-Hwa V. Rau. 1991. Vol. 1. 342 pp. ISBN 0-87727—525-4. Vol. 2., revised 2005, 378 pp. ISBN 0-87727-526-2. Vol 3., revised 2005, 431 pp. ISBN 0-87727-527-0. Vol. 4. 306 pp. ISBN 0-87727-528-9.

THAI

A. U. A. Language Center Thai Course, J. Marvin Brown. Originally published by the American University Alumni Association Language Center, 1974. Reissued by Cornell Southeast Asia Program, 1991, 1992. Book 1. 267 pp. ISBN 0-87727-506-8. Book 2. 288 pp. ISBN 0-87727-507-6. Book 3. 247 pp. ISBN 0-87727-508-4.

A. U. A. Language Center Thai Course, Reading and Writing Text (mostly reading), 1979. Reissued 1997. 164 pp. ISBN 0-87727-511-4.

A. U. A. Language Center Thai Course, Reading and Writing Workbook (mostly writing), 1979. Reissued 1997. 99 pp. ISBN 0-87727-512-2.

KHMER

Cambodian System of Writing and Beginning Reader, Franklin E. Huffman. Originally published by Yale University Press, 1970. Reissued by Cornell Southeast Asia Program, 4th printing 2002. 365 pp. ISBN 0-300-01314-0.

Modern Spoken Cambodian, Franklin E. Huffman, assist. Charan Promchan, Chhom-Rak Thong Lambert. Originally published by Yale University Press, 1970. Reissued by Cornell Southeast Asia Program, 3rd printing 1991. 451 pp. ISBN 0-300-01316-7.

Intermediate Cambodian Reader, ed. Franklin E. Huffman, assist. Im Proum. Originally published by Yale University Press, 1972. Reissued by Cornell Southeast Asia Program, 1988. 499 pp. ISBN 0-300-01552-6.

Cambodian Literary Reader and Glossary, Franklin E. Huffman, Im Proum. Originally published by Yale University Press, 1977. Reissued by Cornell Southeast Asia Program, 1988. 494 pp. ISBN 0-300-02069-4.

HMONG

White Hmong-English Dictionary, Ernest E. Heimbach. 1969. 8th printing, 2002. 523 pp. ISBN 0-87727-075-9.

VIETNAMESE

Intermediate Spoken Vietnamese, Franklin E. Huffman, Tran Trong Hai. 1980. 3rd printing 1994. ISBN 0-87727-500-9.

Proto-Austronesian Phonology with Glossary, John U. Wolff, 2 volumes, 2011.
ISBN vol. I, 978-0-87727-532-9. ISBN vol. II, 978-0-87727-533-6.

To order, please contact:
Mail:
Cornell University Press Services
750 Cascadilla Street
PO Box 6525
Ithaca, NY 14851 USA

E-mail: orderbook@cupserv.org

Phone/Fax, Monday–Friday, 8 am – 5 pm (Eastern US):
Phone: 607 277 2211 or 800 666 2211 (US, Canada)
Fax: 607 277 6292 or 800 688 2877 (US, Canada)

Order through our online bookstore at:
www.einaudi.cornell.edu / southeastasia / publications /

9 780877 27757